D0930232

# MARKETING
# IN THE
# INTERNATIONAL
# ENVIRONMENT

# MARKETING IN THE INTERNATIONAL ENVIRONMENT

**EDWARD W. CUNDIFF**

*Emory University*

**MARYE THARP HILGER**

*The University of Texas*
*San Antonio*

PRENTICE-HALL, INC., Englewood Cliffs, N. J. 07632

Editorial/production supervision and interior design: Linda C. Mason
Cover design: Ben Santora
Manufacturing buyer: Ed O'Dougherty

©1984 by Prentice-Hall, Inc., Englewood Cliffs, New Jersey 07632

All rights reserved. No part of this book may be
reproduced, in any form or by any means,
without permission in writing from the publisher.

Printed in the United States of America
10  9  8  7  6  5  4  3  2  1


ISBN 0-13-557372-6


Prentice-Hall International, Inc., *London*
Prentice-Hall of Australia Pty. Limited, *Sydney*
Editora Prentice-Hall do Brasil, Ltda., *Rio de Janeiro*
Prentice-Hall Canada Inc., *Toronto*
Prentice-Hall of India Private Limited, *New Delhi*
Prentice-Hall of Japan, Inc., *Tokyo*
Prentice-Hall of Southeast Asia Pte. Ltd., *Singapore*
Whitehall Books Limited, *Wellington, New Zealand*

# CONTENTS

## 5  The Cultural Context  109

## 6  The International Economic
Environment  139

# PART III  MANAGEMENT TOOLS IN INTERNATIONAL MARKETING  193

## 12   Pricing Decisions   299

## 13   Promotional Policy   322

# 14   Distribution Decisions   348

## PART V   PLANNING AND CONTROL   373

# 15   Coordination and Controlling International Marketing Strategy   375

# 16   Planning for the Future   395

# Appendixes

# Index

# PREFACE

This book is designed to provide an understanding of marketing strategy from a multinational or international point of view. It is designed to meet the needs of students in an international marketing course, to teach them to focus on the world as the potential marketplace rather than the local or domestic economy. Foreign nations are viewed both as sources of new potential sales but as sources of potential competition in the domestic market. It shows that the same basic marketing inputs and strategies can be used successfully in widely different markets as long as they are adjusted in terms of environmental differences. The marketing expert does not need new and different marketing expertise to compete in foreign market; instead, he or she needs to become familiar with the environmental differences that require adaptation of strategy from nation to nation, and even from market to market within nations.

The plan of presentation starts with a definition of international marketing and its context and moves to a section on the environment for international marketing decisions. This section starts with the macroeconomic environment and the theoretical underpinning of international economic transactions. It then compares differences in business environment, the cultural environment, the economic setting in different nations, and the political and legal structure that determines how a firm can operate in each nation. The third section in the book deals with the tools necessary for effective management in new and complex multinational environments. It includes marketing research and the sources of research information in different economies, and it addresses the problems of establishing organizational structures and relationships to manage subunits that are widely separated geographically and that must adjust to widely varying environments. Part four of the book is concerned with the standard marketing strategy inputs as they must be adjusted to foreign markets. It includes product decisions for both industrial and consumer goods, pricing decisions, promotion decisions, and distribution decisions, both channels and physical distribution. Finally, it covers some of the problems of developing and coordinating marketing strategy among varying foreign markets. The last section looks at the future and directions of change in foreign markets and foreign marketing.

Each chapter has been planned as an independent teaching unit, starting with coverage of the relevant subject material and followed by questions for classroom discussion and a teaching case. The cases have been drawn from real life situations.

We are indebted to a great many people for the successful completion of this book. Perhaps most important are our present and former students who have helped us to define and evolve our ideas about international marketing, both in their classroom reaction and feedback and in their outside work and independent study. We are also grateful to our faculty associates, both at Emory University and at The University of Texas at San Antonio for their informal feedback and intellectual support while we were writing the book. Invaluable research assistance was provided by several conscientious and able research assistants, including Jeffrey T. Larson, Brian Peabody, and Eric Jaillet. Several colleagues at other universities provided excellent feedback and guidance throughout the development of this book. We are indebted to Sandra Huszagh, University of Georgia—Athens; Irene Lange, California State University—Fullerton; and Henry Vanderleest, Ball State University, for their insightful suggestions. Finally, we are particularly grateful to Mrs. Judy Pate for her patience and dependability in typing and reproducing and handling all related correspondence. For the errors or inadequacies in the manuscript we will take full personal responsibility.

Edward W. Cundiff
Marye Tharp Hilger

# PART I

# INTRODUCTION

# chapter 1

# THE WORLDWIDE MARKET

The young model in the ad has evidently just stepped out of the bath, and has draped herself modestly—but not too modestly—in a lush red bath towel. The text of the ad, in German, heralds the virtues of the Aristocrat line of towels. The manufacturer? Fieldcrest Mills, an American textile manufacturer that increased its export business 58 percent in a single year by applying new selling techniques in the European market.

Fieldcrest's strategy was simple enough: it duplicated what it had learned in the United States, namely that consumers would pay a premium for high-fashion "designer" towels and sheets. So it persuaded European and Japanese department stores to install "boutiques" featuring similar items—even offering one store a written guarantee that the boutique would double the store's profits on the floor space it occupied. One result of all this selling, according to *Fortune* magazine, is that "Foreign consumers are now developing a taste for those fashionable U.S. bed and bath products." Another result is that Fieldcrest—and the textile industry as a whole, which increased its exports from $2.2 billion in 1978 to $3.2 billion in 1979—is making considerably more money than it otherwise would.

Ten years ago, about one-tenth of all the goods produced in the United States were sold abroad. Last year the figure was up to nearly one-fifth. Agricultural exports alone rose from $300 million worth in 1970 to $27 billion in 1980; manufactured goods went from $4.1 billion to $26 billion. From the viewpoint of the economy as a whole, these exports had an importance well beyond the revenue they provided to individual companies and industries—namely, they allowed the United States to pay its ever-growing bill for foreign oil and other key imports. "We no longer export to buy luxuries," wrote MIT economist Lester C. Thurow not long ago, "we export to buy necessities."*

---

## INTRODUCTION

Marketing is a universal economic activity that is present in every human society. It is the mechanism that provides individuals and organizations with the products and services they want or need. As such, marketing activity transcends geographic and political divisions and serves markets wherever they exist. Some marketers never sell outside their own communities, but others, when conditions are right, may sell their products many miles from home, even in other countries around the world. A farmer in the Rio Grande Valley area of Texas may raise truck garden crops and never sell anything farther than three-hundred-miles away in San Antonio. A farmer next door may raise grapefruit and sell them in New York City, or even in London or Tokyo. Exchange is a dynamic and boundless human activity.

International trade takes place when an entrepreneur sees an opportunity to make a profit by serving the needs of users, or potential users, of a product in some other part of the world. Such trade has been carried on for as long as there have been people whose wants could not be served by local suppliers. Archeologists tell us that in prehistoric Europe, as early as the Stone Age, enterprising peddlers carried amber and flint from the Baltic coast to the Mediterranean to exchange for cowrie shells from the Red Sea or the Indian Ocean. Throughout human history, goods have moved from one place to another as marketers have perceived the opportunity to enhance their resources and standard of living through exchange.

Political or legal boundaries can pose "psychological" or perceptual constraints on exchange processes. It is often more difficult for a marketer to recognize foreign opportunities for exchange or to understand what resources are needed in order to execute exchanges. While marketing opportunities are not determined by the limits of a country's borders, exchanges across boundaries require the desire and ability to interpret an unfamiliar environment for those opportunities. As history shows, this is a natural process, one of matching resources, skills, goods, services, and/or money. Therefore, when opportunities are recognized and the environment is meaningfully interpreted, there is nothing fundamentally different about executing exchanges in any part of the world. The principles which guide the successful retailer of running shoes in Atlanta, and the one in Athens, are the same. Those same principles also guide the decisions of the grape-

---

*"A Guide to Enterprise," © 1981, WGBH Educational Foundation, published in Association with "Enterprise," a television series on American Business, produced for PBS by WGBH, Boston, Mass., p. 7.

fruit farmer in south Texas and those of multinational corporations like IBM.

The process and principles of marketing strategy are universal; the goal is to execute exchanges with the market. The process includes identification of profitable opportunities, and interpretation of the organization's internal and external environments. This analysis provides the basis for designing products and services, prices, distribution, and communication strategies that will facilitate and hopefully consummate the desired exchanges. Figure 1–1 illustrates this process.

The key element in international marketing or exchange is the ability to recognize foreign opportunities; to interpret the external, uncontrollable environment; and to understand how the firm's resources match requirements for a profitable marketing exchange. The objective of this book is to provide you with the analytical tools necessary to identify and respond to market opportunities in foreign environments.

Many successful marketers suffer from myopia regarding foreign mar-

**FIGURE 1–1**   The universal process of marketing strategy development.

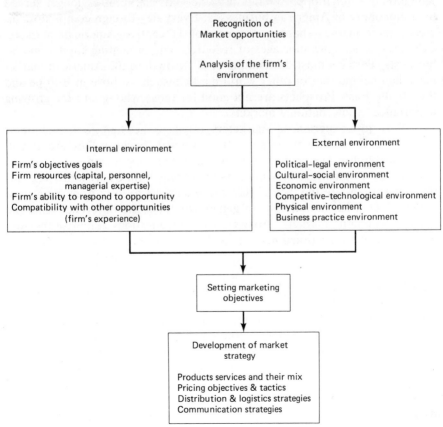

kets. They seek out every unsatisfied market within their own country, but never think to look afield for rich new opportunities. Or if they recognize such foreign opportunities, they may be unwilling or afraid to assume the additional risks. But ultimately for all marketers there comes a time when the local market is saturated and they must either settle for a stable market with no further growth, or broaden their horizons. There are only two real alternatives for achieving continuing growth: expansion into new markets in other countries, or development of additional products to serve local markets. Expansion into new markets will often offer the most promising long-term alternative, but many businesses, particularly American firms, turn to the "new product" growth alternative without seriously considering marketing abroad.

Until very recently, American business was blessed with virtually limitless resources and opportunities. It was insulated from competition by geographic and informational isolation. The U.S. market is still the largest single consumer and industrial market in the world. These factors have combined to create psychological barriers to recognition and aggressive exploitation of foreign opportunities. But the U.S. market is no longer served by a monopoly of American businesses. Every day foreign competitors increase their market share in the previously captive American markets. U.S. firms are facing shortages of resources and escalating capital and labor costs. Perhaps most devastating of all, growth in the American market has fallen behind that of other world markets such as those in Europe and the Middle East. Prospects are not good for those who ignore the growing importance of international markets.

Why are experienced marketers often so hesitant to launch their products in international markets? It is primarily because they are unwilling or unable to transfer their proven expertise in opportunity analysis and strategy development to new markets about which they may know very little. What, then, are the factors that cause markets to vary from country to country? To what extent can we generalize about the differences and the similarities among markets? Answers to these questions comprise the subject matter of international marketing.

## COMPARATIVE MARKETING

International marketers need to know how much of their expertise in one market is transferable to new markets in different countries. They know that they may not be able to market their product successfully in a foreign country without making some changes in overall strategy. But what they need to know is how much of their strategy can be transferred unchanged across national borders and how much must be adapted to the new market. And will these same generalizations apply in a third country? The dimensions of marketing strategy are the same in any environment. Marketing management must decide what products to offer, how to price them, how to distribute them, and how to communicate information about them to the market. However, since the environment for the decision maker varies from country to country, it is necessary to understand how a change in environment will affect the decisions to be made.

Comparative marketing is the framework for comparing relationships between marketing and its environment in two or more countries. This comparison makes it possible to identify similarities and differences in relationships, in patterns, or in causes and effects; it helps the marketer know how and when to extend or adapt a strategy designed for one market to another market. It is as useful a tool for the Akron firm considering opportunities in San Diego as it is for the same firm considering market potential in Brazil. Comparative marketing study focuses on the firm's external environment and how that determines effective strategy, as compared to the same relationship between environment and strategy in another situation. Therefore, it is especially important to understand environmental similarities and differences in such areas as cultural and social factors, political and legal factors, economic and physical-demographic factors, and competitive and technological factors.

## Differences in Cultures and Societies

A culture determines its members' needs and expectations. Norwegian citizens may place a high priority on job and social-security guarantees (cradle-to-grave protection), while South Africans may expect their society to provide only the opportunity to make their own future. At the same time, a black South African may have the same ambitions but will have fewer opportunities than the white. Values and attitudes also vary widely from culture to culture. A citizen of China places high value on contribution to the State and on honesty and the rights of others. The typical Mexican places relatively more value on personal rights and has a laissez-faire attitude about the rights of others. Residents of a society that operates under a Judeo-Christian influence are likely to be much more strongly oriented toward improvement of personal economic conditions than are residents of a Hindu society—who tend to accept their lot as it is.

As important as broad cultural values in a society are social roles. The place of social classes and the level of social mobility affect many patterns of consumption; and in a society such as India, the lingering presence of a caste structure has an important effect on social roles and consumption patterns. Ethnic groups within a society, such as are found in Canada, Belgium, and Switzerland, create submarkets within the total market. Racial diversity, such as is found in most of Latin America, the United States, and the USSR, has the same effect. There are variations from one society to another in the relative influence of different reference groups (such as families, peers, members of professional groups) on the consumption behavior of their members. Analysis of how cultural factors affect marketing is a critical step in international and comparative marketing.

### Political and Legal Differences

The concept of sovereignty is of little or no interest to the domestic marketer, but it may strongly influence the actions of an international marketer. Governments are protective of their sovereign rights, and they are likely to restrict the actions of businesses, particularly foreign-owned businesses, that are perceived as a threat to national sovereignty. One aspect of sovereignty is concerned with national security. In the name of national security, a government may protect local industries having the potential to contribute to national defense, at the expense of foreign competitors. Sovereign nations feel the need to establish separate monetary systems, even though it might be more efficient to join a larger monetary system. The existence of these separate systems makes it necessary for the international marketer to cope with the many problems involved in foreign exchange. Sovereign nations are usually anxious to protect local languages and customs, and so they may oppose certain products or marketing techniques that constitute a threat to their individuality.

Any country's legal framework strongly determines marketing opportunities and affects the business and marketing activities that can be conducted within its borders. For example, a tradition of consumer protection may provide controls over product safety and liability, truth in advertising, labeling, and pricing that are not present in another country. The existing political structure is equally important. The government's attitude toward competition from foreign products and their effects on the balance of trade may determine degrees of competition and whether or not a market can be entered profitably. An assessment of short- and long-term political trends is a very necessary factor in determining the profit potential of a foreign market.

### Economic and Physical Differences

The wealth of a market is a determining factor in its market potential. But total wealth is perhaps less important than its distribution among the population—Saudi Arabia is a much poorer market for many products than other nations having less total wealth but a broader distribution of that wealth. Trends in gross national product and standard of living per capita are equally important in estimating the growth potential of a market. The availability of capital, credit, and borrowing power have varying degrees of importance, depending on the products to be sold. Inflation has not affected all countries equally in recent years and for this reason, some markets that were very attractive to international marketers in the early 1970s (Scandinavia, Italy, and Argentina, for example) have not been as profitable as those with less-severe inflation (Germany, Brazil, and South Africa).

Important physical characteristics include the absolute and relative numbers in the population, and their location and density. An urban population is much easier to reach than a rural one. Other physical characteristics, such as climate, accessibility, and ease of communication, affect the style of marketing and the ability of a marketer to operate profitably in a foreign market.

The balance of international payments is another economic factor in international marketing. Most nations want to keep the total value of their exports and imports essentially in balance. And if they are not in balance, the preference is for an excess of exports over imports—a "favorable" balance of payments. While economists do not agree that export trade balances should be always favorable, politicians are often strongly attracted by the idea of the "favorable" balance. Thus the international firm may find that the only way it is allowed to enter the market in a country with an "unfavorable" trade balance is by the costly and sometimes inappropriate route of investing in local production facilities.

### Variations in Business Practice

The concept of "competition" varies as much as any other aspect of the marketing environment. In Israel, competitors sit down together to decide what prices to charge for agricultural products; international oil producers decide production and price levels in collusion. Business firms in Japan check out their objectives with the government to make sure their goals are compatible with those of the government. In the U.S., most of these practices would be unthinkable, perhaps even illegal.

Not only are competitive relations variable, but the typical international marketer will face different levels of technology in world markets. In very underdeveloped areas there may be little demand for industrial and capital goods. In Latin America, Asia, and Africa, the marketer faces economic dualism where sophisticated and primitive markets exist side by side. Domestic products may either be too advanced or considered obsolete in foreign markets. The differences depend to a great extent on the relative costs of labor and capital in an economy, but they are also related to legal and cultural constraints placed on competition and innovation.

Marketers who introduce products into a new country must adjust "normal" business practices to the new environment. If they hope to compete successfully, they cannot expect other businesspersons, or even their own employees in a host country, to adjust to their ideas. Methods of doing business vary markedly in different countries. Normal working hours, for example, may vary according to weather, hours of daylight, and local customs. Social relationships between business people may be controlled by culture and tradition. Consequently, the responsibility for, and participation in, business entertaining may be very different from the way it is in the home country. Use of credit, mixing of business and pleasure, responsibility for the environment, labor relations, and relations with government regulators—each of these things must be handled in a way that is compatible with local practice.

## Comparative Marketing as a Managerial Tool

The environment for the marketing decision maker varies from one society to another, and the variations may be very broad. In order to be successful, marketing strategy should be designed to fit each different environment. Only then will it achieve optimum results. But if a marketer must design an entirely new strategy for each new market entered, there are little or no opportunities for economies of scale, and marketing costs will be high. By providing for comparison between markets on any number of factors, comparative marketing gives us a basis for potential groupings of nations with respect to common characteristics. Essentially, the costs of "standardizing" marketing strategy across environments can be estimated, and the directions for how and when to "adapt" can be identified. Figure 1–2 provides an illustration of a comparative analysis.

The preliminary basis for grouping the nations of the world in Figure 1–2, is by type of economic system: capitalist, socialist, and communist. Most countries' economic systems are actually a mixture of these broad categories. The capitalist nations are further subdivided by level of economic development. In any such division, it is difficult to draw a line between nations at the top of one stage and those at the bottom of the next stage, but a large majority would pretty clearly fall into one of the four categories. The number of socialist countries is small and they are all pretty similar. Probably only the Scandinavian countries fit in this category, so no further subdivision is necessary. Comparison of the communist countries would also benefit from further subdivision, but such subdivision has not been carried out in this exhibit.

A small number of environmental factors are presented in Figure 1–2 to illustrate the potential usefulness of comparative analysis. When the capitalist nations are arranged in ascending order of economic development and are followed by socialist and then communist countries, we find, for example, that the level of government involvement in, and control over, economic activities typically increases in each subgroup. Levels of social stratification within the societies seem to follow somewhat the same continuous pattern, except that the highest levels of social stratification are in the underdeveloped capitalist countries, and the lowest levels are in the socialist countries. Although communist countries theoretically have no social stratification and should, therefore, fit at the end of this continuum, their level of social stratification (based on political and occupational factors rather than economic ones) may be higher in some instances than in socialist or affluent capitalist nations. Per-capita income and disposable in-

FIGURE 1–2 Variations in environmental factors in different types of economies.

| LEVEL OR TYPE OF ECONOMIC DEVELOPMENT | LEVEL OF GOVERNMENT CONTROL & INVOLVEMENT | PER-CAPITA INCOME & DISPOSABLE INCOME | MARKETING INSTITUTIONS | EFFECT OF CULTURE ON BUYING MOTIVES | LEVEL OF SOCIAL STRATIFICATION |
|---|---|---|---|---|---|
| *Capitalist* | | | | | |
| Underdeveloped (Burma or Uganda) | Very low | Low income; little disposable | Unspecialized; few services | Possessions not a measure of status | High |
| Developing (Indonesia or Egypt) | | | | | |
| Mature (Great Britain or Brazil) | | High income; high disposable | Specialized; diverse services | Possessions are important measure of status | |
| Affluent (Germany or the U.S.) | | | | Possessions less important | Low |
| *Socialist* (Scandinavia) | | Moderately high | Well-developed | Possessions less important | |
| *Communist* (Bulgaria, USSR) | Very high | Low to moderate | Varying degrees of specialization | Possessions of some importance | Based on noneconomic factors |

come appear to be useful ways of differentiating among capitalist nations, showing higher levels with higher stages of development. The level of specialization and services provided by marketing institutions such as retailers, advertising agencies, and marketing research organizations, also rises with the level of economic development. Finally, the importance of possessions as measures of status varies among categories of nations.

This example of comparative analysis is an unsophisticated one, designed purely for illustration of the concept. A more detailed and carefully designed comparison between groups of nations can provide the marketing planner with valuable information when designing a strategy for entering a new market or for improving performance in existing markets. There are no rules about what elements of the environment should be compared or which ones will generate the best groupings. The marketer may find that groups of nations with economic characteristics in common can be successfully penetrated with similar marketing strategies. Of course, it would still be necessary to adjust these strategies for differences in cultural or geographic factors, but the elements of commonality should increase the prognostication of success and reduce the necessary managerial input. The important points to remember are: 1) there is a need to understand environmental differences and similarities because they determine the appropriate marketing strategies in any context; and 2) comparative analysis is not a cookbook solution for isolating important environmental variations among countries, but it does provide a framework for emphasis on *similarities* rather than differences.

## SIMILARITIES AND DIFFERENCES IN INTERNATIONAL MARKETS

In a market as large and sophisticated as the United States, diversity is more expected than homogeneity. The domestic marketer is accustomed to dealing with differences in climate, regional customs, distribution of income, and even differences in language used in certain areas. The effective marketer adjusts for these differences, but doesn't lose sight of the fact that there are often more important similarities than differences. Thus, the U.S. market is viewed in total as a market for washing machines, for detergents, for cigarettes, and so on. It is important for the marketer to recognize that the same thinking applies to international marketing. There is a world market for automobiles, for soft drinks, for computers; and concern with the differences between national markets must not be allowed to interfere with recognition of the similarities. Thus, as a market for many consumer products, Palermo, located in an underdeveloped part of Italy, is more nearly like Akron, Ohio or Salem, Oregon than it is like the villages and rural areas surrounding it. Marketers who focus only on the differences can become so discouraged with the problem of coping that they refuse to try to compete in foreign markets. They are unable to recognize the profitable marketing opportunities that exist. Therefore, it is also important for the international marketer to recognize market differences that affect but do not preclude profitable opportunities.

## Stages of Economic Development

All nations represent markets for some products, but the wealthier, more highly developed nations provide markets for an enormously wide range of products and services. Figure 1–2 illustrated the potential value of classifying nations according to levels of economic development. A number of economists have developed schemes for defining stages of economic development, and a fair amount of research has been carried out to support some of these hypotheses. More detail on how levels of development affect demand for consumer and industrial products is provided in Chapters 10 and 11. At this point it is only necessary to recognize that stages of economic development represent one of the important differences between international markets.

## The Concept of Multinational Markets

The giant multinational corporations have developed a holistic approach to world markets. They minimize the importance of national boundaries whenever it is legally and culturally possible, and develop their strategies in economic rather than political terms. Such companies are largely apolitical in that their loyalties tend to be to their shareholders wherever they are located rather than to any one country. If a firm is selling pharmaceuticals, it can most profitably plan its strategy in terms of world markets rather than national ones, and it will identify markets which can potentially be served by company products, or for which company products can be adapted. The richest markets in terms of market potential and level of competition are selected first, and a strategy to penetrate these markets is then designed. Market penetration may only require an investment in marketing inputs, such as promotion and packaging, or it may require capital investment in production facilities. If the market potential merits the investment, then it is likely to be made. Political and social factors are considered only as they affect potential profitability. Occasionally this primary profit orientation causes problems for the multinational—for example, interested groups brought pressure on American multinational corporations to get out of South Africa because of its apartheid policy—but it has kept management's attention focused on the richest, most promising markets around the world.

Another dimension of multinational markets occurs in the various regional economic groups such as the European Community—a common market. Various countries in different parts of the world have grouped together to form economic unions, thus creating large potential markets and sharing their economic resources. Multinational economic cooperation works to reduce tariffs and other legal barriers to trade between the member countries. More important differences, such as culture and market size variations, may still remain. The net result is that international marketers inside or outside such a regional market must not be deceived by the apparent size of the total market. The marketer must instead realize the potential differences between the member countries and decide if the union is a natural and profitable grouping for his or her own objectives and marketing strategies.

### The Mechanics of International Marketing

The mechanics of international marketing are different from domestic marketing. They require dealing with such issues as international balance-of-payments problems, with foreign exchange, with import duties and tariffs, with widely varying approaches to the handling of credit, with different methods of transferring title to goods, and with different modes of transportation. These are new areas of expertise which the international marketer must acquire. He or she must be willing to invest both the time and money necessary to acquire or buy needed knowledge and information. This mass of new information and the continuing red tape necessary to carry out marketing transactions in foreign countries frightens away many domestic marketers, who let this extra trouble and expense blind them to potential long-term growth and profit.

### The Scarcity of Market Information

The marketer in the most affluent economies is accustomed to having good access to marketing information when making decisions. The availability of large amounts of reliable secondary data, and the presence of marketing research experts to provide primary data, make it possible to buttress marketing decisions with facts. In many countries, secondary data about the market is unavailable or inaccurate, and primary data is difficult and expensive to collect even where the expertise is available. In these situations the marketer must learn to make decisions based on inadequate data, while at the same time trying to improve the quality and quantity of the data that are available.

## THE INTERNATIONAL MARKETER

Until recently, most international marketing has been conducted by marketing middlemen—export or import agents who have recognized the opportunity to serve an untapped or unsatisfied foreign market at a profit. Today, however, there are many different types of businesses engaged in international marketing. As international markets increase in importance to growth objectives of all types of organizations, the diversification of organizations will continue.

### Import Agents

Import agents are usually oriented solely toward a single market—their home base of operation. They scour the world for products to import into the home market for resale at a profit. In many instances agents will focus on only one or on a limited number of source countries, in which they become a specialist. They assume the responsibility for development and implementation of a marketing strategy for the products they import, although many times they will pass on to retailers, or other middlemen, the responsibility for product promotion. In developing countries, import agents often have the most channel power due to their access to world supplies.

### Export Agents

Export agents frequently confine their sources of supply to the countries from which they operate. They may actually sell these products in a number of foreign markets, since their objective is to find promising new markets for products available in their home country. Export agents must find import agents or other middlemen in the markets where they seek to sell their products to distribute and promote these goods. Export management companies act as "export departments" for many small manufacturers, at times even commissioning production for a foreign buyer.

### Retailers

Large retailers often serve as international marketing entrepreneurs. Sears, McDonalds, Avis, and Hilton are significant international marketers today. Large department stores and retail chains send buyers into foreign markets to locate distinctive products that will broaden their lines and make them more interesting. Neiman-Marcus, for example, recently featured products acquired in the People's Republic of China. An important element in the consumer image of such retailers lies in their ability to be the first on the market with different or exciting new products. These merchants take the initiative in seeking out their own sources for foreign products, essentially taking over all marketing responsibilities from the producers. Franchisers like Kentucky Fried Chicken and McDonald's are finding foreign markets to be their strongest growth markets. Even firms in service industries such as banking, accounting, and rentals are becoming important international marketers.

### Producers

An ever-increasing number of producers have come to think of marketing in multinational rather than domestic terms. The largest volume of international marketing is conducted by these manufacturers, who realize that new markets in foreign countries often provide more potential for increased sales than nearly saturated domestic markets. Products may be subcontracted for production in less-costly labor markets (designer blue jeans made in Taiwan) or producers may sell in markets with less-rigorous competition. The growth-oriented producer identifies unserved or inadequately served markets throughout the world and adjusts marketing and production strategies so as to make penetration of specific markets feasible and profitable. Producers can, of course, use any of the other international marketers just mentioned, or they can develop their own networks in foreign markets.

### Involvements of U.S. Firms in International Markets

In general, American industry has been less interested in international marketing than industry in some of the other highly developed nations. Although there have been notable exceptions, both in terms of individual firms and specific industries, American businesspersons have been inward looking. Neither do they seek foreign markets, nor do they want to face foreign competition in their own market. Throughout much of its history, the United States has followed a policy of protecting its industry from foreign competitors through tariffs. American manufacturers have had less motivation to look outward; the American market is so large and rich that it provides the American manufacturer with enormous growth potential without ever looking abroad. The entire Dutch market, for example, is smaller than each of several American states, so Dutch firms seeking continuing growth must turn to foreign markets earlier in their growth than most similar American firms. The Phillips Company, a Dutch electronics manufacturer, gets a major share of its sales volume from outside the Netherlands. Yet the General Electric Company, an equally large American firm, sells a large portion of its products within the American market.

Although American business has not been very interested in international marketing, there is now a growing interest because American markets are becoming saturated in many industries, and because reduced trade barriers have increased the competition from foreign manufacturers. A few American industries and a few individual firms have had a long-term commitment to international marketing, either as importers or exporters of goods or of technologies. A fair portion of the giant multinational corporations are American. The international oil industry, for example, is dominated by American companies, but with respect to the American market, this industry is a net importing industry. With the exception of the profits received from foreign subsidiaries, the industry's effect on the American economy is negative. These companies must make large international payments abroad and they provide comparatively little employment for American nationals.

If our economy is to remain healthy, imports must be balanced by exports. The U.S. aircraft industry is one such exporting industry; it is heavily involved in foreign markets, which account for a large share of its total sales volume. Boeing Aircraft, for example, exported almost $1.5 billion worth of aircraft as long ago as 1977. Most of its production takes place within the United States, producing a sizeable contribution to gross national product, and its receipts from foreign sales help the U.S. balance-of-payments position.

A third type of international firm is neither an importer nor an exporter of goods in the domestic economy; instead, it imports or exports technology. Such a firm may build production facilities within the foreign market it seeks to serve. IBM, instead of exporting American-made computers to Europe, has built production facilities in several European locations, and it does the same thing in other parts of the world. The American automobile industry has done most of its international marketing in this manner; General Motors, Ford, and Chrysler have all had production plants in Europe, building cars to sell in European markets. Foreign firms do the same thing in the American market. Lever Brothers, a subsidiary of British Unilever, has manufactured and marketed detergents in the American market for many years. Other ways of importing or exporting technology are through licensing the use of technologies and through franchising in the service industries.

Major U.S. exporters are concentrated in just a few industries. Figure 1–3 lists the twenty-five biggest American industrial exporters in 1981. The largest single export industry is the aircraft industry with four of the top twenty-five firms, accounting for over $12 billion in exports. Transportation and related equipment producers are also major exporters with exports of almost $20 billion by seven firms. And, Boeing is the largest single American exporter. The chemical and farm equipment industries also rank in the top twenty-five, with $5.6 and $3.7 billion in exports respectively. The lower ranking for computer exports does not reflect the true importance of the American computer industry in world markets because IBM, the real world leader in computer sales, gets almost all of its foreign sales volume from products manufactured abroad. Another major source of export sales for the United States is the agricultural industry. American farm goods are highly competitive in world markets. There are a number of other industries that have had a strong involvement in world markets, but whose total industry sales are not large enough to include individual firms in the top twenty-five. For example, the medical products and pharmaceutical industries, the sewing machine industry, the oil-field machinery and equipment industry all bring in a quarter or more of their volume from export sales.

**FIGURE 1–3**  The twenty-five largest U.S. exporters, 1981.

| FIRM | EXPORTS (MILLIONS OF DOLLARS) | SALES (MILLIONS OF DOLLARS) | EXPORTS AS % OF SALES |
|---|---|---|---|
| 1. Boeing | $6,106 | $ 9,788 | $62% |
| 2. General Motors | 5,731 | 62,699 | 9 |
| 3. General Electric | 4,348 | 27,240 | 16 |
| 4. Ford Motor | 3,743 | 36,247 | 10 |
| 5. Caterpillar Tractor | 3,513 | 9,155 | 38 |
| 6. McDonnell Douglas | 2,769 | 7,385 | 38 |
| 7. E.I. duPont de Nemours | 2,646 | 22,810 | 12 |
| 8. United Technologies | 2,636 | 13,668 | 19 |
| 9. International Business Machines | 1,857 | 29,070 | 6 |
| 10. Eastman Kodak | 1,803 | 10,337 | 17 |
| 11. Westinghouse Electric | 1,312 | 9,368 | 14 |
| 12. Signal Companies | 1,219 | 5,343 | 23 |
| 13. Raytheon | 1,148 | 5,636 | 20 |
| 14. Union Carbide | 1,090 | 10,168 | 11 |
| 15. Monsanto | 1,042 | 6,948 | 15 |
| 16. International Harvester | 1,008 | 7,327 | 14 |
| 17. Hewlett-Packard | 971 | 3,578 | 27 |
| 18. Weyerhauser | 946 | 4,502 | 21 |
| 19. Dow Chemical | 924 | 11,873 | 8 |
| 20. Archer-Daniels-Midland | 900 | 3,648 | 25 |
| 21. Exxon | 896 | 108,107 | 1 |
| 22. Philip Morris | 834 | 8,307 | 10 |
| 23. Occidental Petroleum | 765 | 14,708 | 5 |
| 24. Ingersoll-Rand | 759 | 3,378 | 22 |
| 25. Northrup | 716 | 1,991 | 36 |

*Source:* "The 50 Leading Exporters," *FORTUNE,* August 9, 1982, pp. 68–69. © 1982 Time Inc. All rights reserved.

## INTERNATIONAL MARKETING ORIENTATION

In all countries, some firms become havily involved in international marketing, while other ones in the same industries show little interest or motivation to sell outside their domestic borders. The railroad locomotive manufacturers in the United States have long been committed to foreign markets, and exports have accounted for over half their sales volume for a number of years. Yet, the other major manufacturer of transportation vehicles in the United States, the automobile industry, has given scant attention to foreign markets. It has never seriously attempted to export automobiles, and even in those markets where it has established assembly plants it has never been a major competitor. When Chrysler Motor Company got into serious financial difficulties in 1979, one of its first ways of raising cash was to sell its foreign plants. The world market for automobiles is enormous and apparently profitable. It is hard to understand how the American automobile industry, one of the financially strongest and historically most innovative of American industries, has had so little interest in the potential of world markets. It seemingly had no interest in the development of small cars with less profit per unit, so it not only missed opportunities for growth into new markets, but it ultimately suffered a sizeable loss of its American market to foreign manufacturers. The lesson to be learned here is that myopia with respect to foreign markets—a lack of interest in the potential for new growth and profit in foreign markets—not only restricts an industry's profitability, but ultimately it may weaken its ability to compete with imports in domestic markets. Industry must seek to be competitive in world markets.

Individual firms often have different attitudes about their own foreign marketing activities. These attitudes might be called their international marketing orientation.[1] The "ethnocentric" firm, for example, sees foreign market opportunities and environments as essentially no different than those of domestic markets. The firm uses the same marketing strategies abroad that it uses at home. Subsidiaries outside the home country have very low status in an ethnocentric organization. Because this type of firm does not value comparative analysis, there are limits on the long-term success of its approach to international marketing.

A "polycentric" firm recognizes *only* the differences in national markets and their environments. It treats every market where it operates as if it were unique; each subsidiary develops individual marketing strategies based on its knowledge of local needs and resources. While international marketing strategies developed in this organizational context may be quite effective, the approach is not likely to be a profitable one in the long term. Lessons learned from mistakes made in the Sudan might be applicable to operations in Quebec. So, duplication of effort can result from seeing all national markets as unique.

The ideal orientation for an organization interested in international markets is a "geocentric" approach. The geocentric firm effectively uses comparative analysis to spot both similarities and differences in various markets. It pursues market opportunities that it has the resources to exploit, regardless of national boundaries. There is no such thing as a "foreign" market—only markets that have more or less similar environments. This is truly worldwide marketing and is the future for all of us!

In today's interdependent world, tariffs and other impediments to trade are lower than at any other time in recent history. The exchange of ideas and goods has increased enormously. In such an environment, the

---

[1]These international orientations are described in more detail in Howard V. Perlmutter, "The Tortuous Evolution of the Multinational Corporation," *Columbia Journal of World Business*, Jan.–Feb. 1969, pp. 9–18.

firm that seeks to remain competitive and dynamic no longer has the option of ignoring international marketing. It is a matter of survival to be competitive not just in local markets, but in the world.

## SUMMARY

Marketing is a universal activity that centers on facilitating exchanges. The principles of marketing strategy development are the same whether applied to domestic or foreign markets. Nevertheless, opportunities in international marketing are often more difficult to access because of the many differences in the environment of the market. Differences in any of the external environments—political-legal, social-cultural, economic, competitive-technological, physical-demographic, or business practice— may render a firm's domestic marketing strategy unsuccessful when extended to a foreign market.

An essential tool in interpreting differences and similarities in the environments of different markets is comparative analysis. This framework makes it possible to identify similarities and differences in how markets relate to their environments in different settings. Comparative analysis is often useful in international marketing because the marketer can use it to spot patterns that allow countries to be grouped together so that a common marketing strategy may be extended to several countries in a group. Any variety of environmental factors may be used in comparative analysis, depending on the marketer's judgment.

An aspect of the environment that is particularly important in international marketing is the country's level of economic development. Other dimensions that are frequently important are multinational markets, and unique market institutions that can facilitate the international marketing task. In recent years, more and more firms have gotten involved in foreign marketing. The extent of a firm's interest in foreign markets is often determined by its domestic opportunities. Its style of foreign marketing depends on its international orientation—whether it is ethnocentric, polycentric, or geocentric. The ideal orientation is geocentric because the firm uses comparative analysis to determine its approach to foreign market opportunities.

## DISCUSSION QUESTIONS

1. What is international trade?
2. Explain how "psychological" constraints affect foreign market opportunity analysis.
3. What is meant by the statement: "The process and principles of marketing strategy are universal"?

4. Describe the process of marketing strategy development.
5. Why have American businesses been less interested in foreign markets than firms in other countries? What factors are causing them to rethink their situation?
6. Explain comparative marketing.
7. Use comparative analysis to study the foreign market opportunities for an industrial chemicals firm.
8. Describe the environmental factors you feel would be important in a comparative analysis of world markets for a toy manufacturer.
9. How can variations in business practices affect international marketing strategy?
10. Why is economic development important in interpreting foreign market opportunities?
11. What is unique about developing international marketing?
12. Describe the types of businesses involved in international marketing.
13. Find the most recent listing of leading U.S. exporters and summarize the differences you find from the firms listed in Figure 1–3.
14. Differentiate between ethnocentric, polycentric, and geocentric approaches to international marketing.

# CASE 1    THE BIG STATE SPRING COMPANY

In the spring of 1981, Bill Willett, Sr. quit his job as an assembly line foreman for a manufacturing firm in Corpus Christi, Texas. He had grown tired of being an employee and wanted to open a business of his own. For a number of years he had been a compulsive basement tinkerer and self-taught engineer. Many friends and business associates began bringing him their engineering problems to solve. Based on this incentive, he opened a small machine shop/fabrication service. Within a few months, he found that one of the products that seemed to be in significant demand among the oil-field suppliers that were his customers, were small quantities of high quality compression and expansion springs. These springs were available in larger quantity from any number of large manufacturers nationwide. The problem was that the large firms were unwilling to deal with anybody on orders of less than 10,000 units. Especially in the oilfield service industry but later in other industries, Bill found there was a significant need for his very high quality, handmade compression and expansion springs in smaller quan-tities. He was therefore able to carve out for himself a marketplace niche consisting of firms that needed a few hundred very high quality products, meaning very little tolerance or production differences from spring to spring. By mid-1975, his springs were in many industries nationwide, information about them having been passed by word-of-mouth from customer to customer.

In early 1974, another fortuitous event took place. The manager of a local bakery brought him a worn-out mixing whip from an industrial mixing machine, a machine that was used to mix dough. He asked Bill if he could repair it and Bill, always a compulsive thinker, said "Well, leave it here and I'll give it a whirl." Three days later the baker came back to pick up his work and was astounded to find that Bill had remanufactured it to specifications that were significantly better than new at a price that was 25% of the cost of a replacement from Hobart, the major supplier of industrial mixing equip-ment. Within the next two to three years, again word-of-mouth took over and Big State Spring Company got heavily into the business of manufac-turing industrial whips for Hobart mixing machines. By 1979 two things had happened: The whip manufacturing had increased to the point where it was more than half of the yearly sales of Big State Spring Company and Bill Willet, Sr. was in the process of retiring to his basement and fulltime tink-ering. His son, Bill, Jr., had worked in the firm in all capacities from book-

This case was prepared by Dr. Robert J. Hoover, Associate Professor, Corpus Christi State University.

keeping through the manufacturing process. He was to take over the company. Bill, Jr. had not inherited his father's facility for basement engineering but had acquired formal training in business as well as an understanding of how the operation that had grown up around him worked. He began to wonder if possibly there were foreign markets for the springs and/or the whips, but he did not know how to go about assessing the viability of these markets. Realizing that he could not handle the production as well as the business end of the firm by himself, Bill, Jr. hired John Barne to assist him.

## QUESTIONS

1. What sources of information should Bill and John try to access in establishing the existence of and viability of markets for their two products?
2. What are this firm's motives for international marketing?
3. What foreign market entry strategies would be most appropriate for Big State?
4. Develop a comparative market analysis framework to help Big State assess foreign market opportunities.

# PART II

# THE ENVIRONMENT FOR INTERNATIONAL MARKETING

This section of your text follows the process that a firm might use in analyzing foreign market opportunities. This was shown in Figure 1–1. The firm must first assess its own strengths, weaknesses, and objectives in pursuing opportunities in foreign markets. Chapter 2 details the firm's internal environment for international marketing, including the process for analyzing opportunities, options for entering foreign markets, and financing international marketing.

Chapters 3 through 7 concern elements of the firm's external environment that affect international marketing strategy. Chapter 3 describes the historical and theoretical rationale for world trading patterns that continue to influence international business. In Chapter 4 we orient you to possible ways in which business relationships, organizational structure, and competition may differ in world markets. Chapter 5 focuses on how the elements of culture affect buyers and their purchase motivations in different environments. In Chapter 6 we introduce you to the firm's political and legal environments. These are especially important in international marketing because they affect the firm's organizational structure as well as its marketing strategy in foreign markets. The last chapter in this section, Chapter 7, describes the important institutions of the international economic environment which affect marketing strategy.

# chapter 2

# THE ORGANIZATIONAL AND FINANCIAL ENVIRONMENTS OF INTERNATIONAL MARKETING

Back in 1921, a young physician-cum-businessman from America had an idea for helping out famine-plagued Russia. With the Soviet treasury bare and dead bodies piling up along railroad sidings, Armand Hammer cabled V.I. Lenin in Moscow, offering to arrange the immediate shipment of $1 million in U.S. grain in exchange for Russian furs and hides. Lenin quickly agreed, later sweetening the pot with a full ton of prime caviar. With that, what was likely the first barter deal in Soviet-American trade was struck. Hammer himself, now the 80-year-old chairman of Occidental Petroleum Corp., is still bartering with the Russians—and these days, he has plenty of company.

By most accounts, bartering between East and West is bigger than ever. Last year, barter deals accounted for roughly 30 percent of all Western exports to members of the Council for Mutual Economic Assistance—the so-called Comecon countries—compared to 10 or 15 percent in 1976. Fewer and fewer of these transactions are the kind of simple swap Hammer engineered 57 years ago; under such names as buy-backs, compensation contracts and counter-purchase agreements, bartering has become increasingly sophisticated, with a new industry of middlemen assisting in many of the deals.*

*"The Barter Boom", *Newsweek*, June 26, 1978, p. 63. Copyright 1978 by Newsweek, Inc. All rights reserved. Reprinted by permission.

## INTRODUCTION

Throughout the world, firms are responding to the potential for growth found in foreign markets. Exports have been the fastest-growing sector of the U.S. economy for the past decade. Foreign production by U.S. firms has dramatically increased, especially in industries such as electronics. At the same time, foreign firms are investing in American business, buying American banks, manufacturing firms, and real estate; they have also increased penetration of American markets, having captured over 25 percent of the American automobile market.

The manner in which firms exploit foreign market opportunities depends on each business firm's internal and external environments. The firm's internal environment includes its personnel and financial resources, as well as the importance it places on international markets in meeting its overall profit and growth objectives. Even within an individual firm, different managers see foreign markets differently—some focus on similarities with the domestic market and its market environment while other managers see only the unique aspects of foreign demand. This view of foreign markets affects the firm's international marketing style.

The firm's external environment is composed of financial, economic, political, legal, technological, and cultural factors. These will also affect how the firm responds to foreign marketing opportunities. What is unique about international marketing is that the firm faces multiple environments; the resources it uses effectively within one national market may not be useful at all in another. Likewise, the manner in which it organizes to exploit opportunities may also vary from market to market. The firm's external environments are considered in the next four chapters, while this chapter is devoted to the firm's internal, financial, and organizational climates for international marketing decisions.

This chapter focuses first on the process through which firms decide to get involved in foreign markets. Next, alternative strategies for entering foreign markets are considered, along with the impact of each strategy on the firm's overall foreign marketing strategy. Special attention is given to the multinational corporation, a growing phenomenon in world marketing. Financial influences in the international marketing decision are then discussed. Last, we review some of the sources of financial support for firms desiring to exploit opportunities in foreign markets.

## FOREIGN MARKET OPPORTUNITY ANALYSIS

How do firms go about deciding to get involved in international marketing? In some cases, the decision may be unconscious—the firm simply decides to fill an unsolicited foreign order. In other situations, a firm may respond to increased competition in the domestic market by increasing its exports to foreign markets. A baby-food manufacturer might strengthen its international marketing activities in response to declining birth rates in the U.S., or in order to take advantage of high per-capita birth rates abroad. These different situations describe different motivations and stimuli for international marketing decisions.

## Operational versus Strategic Decisions

Two different types of international marketing decisions are *operational* and *strategic* ones. A firm might see international sales as meeting either its operational or strategic goals. Strategic objectives are tied to broad goals such as growth, diversification, and/or return on investment. Operational decisions concern the tactics or actions a firm uses to implement strategy. However, if a firm does not have effective planning or information systems, operational decisions may be made without strategic guidance. For example, excess inventories may be easily disposed of in export markets, but that does not mean a firm has decided to "produce for export," a strategic decision. A further distinction is that operational problems usually have shorter time horizons and are therefore easier to solve than strategic ones.

The difference between operational and strategic foreign marketing is significant because it influences the firm's commitment of resources to international markets, and as a result, its style of international marketing. A firm which has limited operational purposes for international marketing is unlikely to invest heavily in either personnel or capital for foreign opportunities. It is more likely to be an exporter, using outside intermediaries for the special skills needed to get its products to foreign buyers. In contrast, a firm that views international marketing as a strategy for meeting long-term corporate goals is more likely to acquire internal expertise for use in exploiting and identifying foreign opportunities.

Another aspect of foreign opportunity analysis is related to whether the firm is motivated to solve problems or is seeking opportunities through investment in international markets. Problem solving can be either operational or strategic, as can opportunity seeking. A firm might look to foreign markets as a way to unload temporary excess inventories, or it may look to foreign markets for long-term survival that is threatened by declining demand in domestic markets. A firm may respond to a one-time foreign opportunity (unsolicited orders) or it may seek long-term growth through foreign market penetration. Therefore, another way of classifying international decisions is the overall purpose that motivates a firm to enter foreign markets—to solve problems or respond to opportunities.

The commitment of a firm's resources will of course be contingent on the firm's objectives (strategic or operational) and its motivation (problem solving or opportunity seeking) for international marketing. These factors influence the extent of company analysis of foreign opportunities. Some firms are content to export to assured foreign buyers without investigating that country's political or cultural environments, or any other national markets for that matter. Other firms are concerned with having a thorough knowledge of the foreign market and its conditions, even if they have limited operational objectives in a foreign market.

### Internal versus External Stimuli

Any firm's process for decision making is tailored to its decision objectives. The international marketing decision conforms to this rule. The decision process can be set in motion by internal or external factors. Some examples of internal factors are reduced working capital, excess production capacity, reduced market share, increased costs of production inputs, or decreasing profitability within product lines or market segments. While these performance indicators result from the firm's interaction with its external environment, such information emanates from internal sources. Various external sources of information not within the control of the firm might also set an international marketing decision in motion. Examples of external sources are government incentives for exporting or foreign investment, unsolicited foreign orders, competitor success in foreign markets, or government programs of support for international activities.

Figure 2–1 summarizes the different styles that firms use when deciding to get involved in international marketing. In Situation I a firm might face a nonrecurring problem such as excess inventories. The international marketing decision will likely be stimulated by this internal performance information rather than knowledge of the attractiveness of the foreign market. Situation II describes the case of a firm that anticipates environmental threats in the domestic market by deciding to invest in international ones. The decision may be prompted by indicators showing performance trends (such as decline in market share) or by anticipation of the effects of exter-

**FIGURE 2–1**  A typology of international marketing decisions.

| | | Motivation to Export | |
|---|---|---|---|
| | | Problem solving | Opportunity seeking |
| Export Decision Objectives | Operational | Internally stimulated  I | Externally stimulated  IV |
| | Strategic | Internally or externally stimulated  II | Internally or externally stimulated  III |

nal environmental trends (such as new competitors, government regulations, or changing demographics of the domestic market). In both problem-solving cases, strategic or operational, the firm is "pushed" into international marketing. Situation III describes the firm that identifies its long-term survival with foreign market opportunities. Its international entry decision can be stimulated by internal factors (such as management belief that foreign markets are the key to meeting corporate goals), or by external factors (such as increasing disposable incomes abroad). Last, Situation IV describes the case when an environmental opportunity presents itself to the firm (such as unsolicited orders) and the firm responds without a commitment to international marketing per se.

This typology sheds light on why so many firms have different styles of international marketing. It also explains why there is no one "best" style. The option that a firm uses in deciding how to enter foreign markets or what resources to commit to that effort, depend on whether the decision is operational or strategic, problem solving or opportunity seeking, or internally or externally stimulated.

### The Process of Analyzing Foreign Opportunities

What factors should a firm consider when it is debating whether or not to enter foreign markets? The answer to this question would vary, of course, depending on which situation in Figure 2–1 applies to the firm. It follows that the *intensity* of information seeking will always be conditioned by the firm's objectives for international sales. Nevertheless, it is useful to know what questions to ask in evaluating a foreign opportunity or in deciding how to implement a decision to enter foreign markets. A model of the international marketing decision presents us with a framework to describe this process.

Figure 2–2 describes a model for the decision process that is a systematic tool for evaluating foreign market opportunities. As indicated, the ideal place to begin is to evaluate the firm's objectives and resources for exploiting foreign markets. The answers to questions such as "What is our dominant reason for going abroad?" help the firm develop criteria for the selection of a foreign market. For example, if a firm's dominant reason for going abroad is to have access to sources of supply, that would sharply limit its foreign market alternatives. If the firm is seeking growth, that would affect the selection of an appropriate market. Likewise, if marketing objectives center on market penetration, then those markets where there are already a number of competitors would be eliminated. If a firm wants to enter several foreign markets, it might select those that have geographic, cultural, or other similarities, and it will analyze each potential market according to these criteria. The level of needed control over marketing strategy would have to be matched to a country's legal-political climate and distribution infrastructure. Profit goals may be impeded by a country's political or economic environment and thus these factors set limits on via-

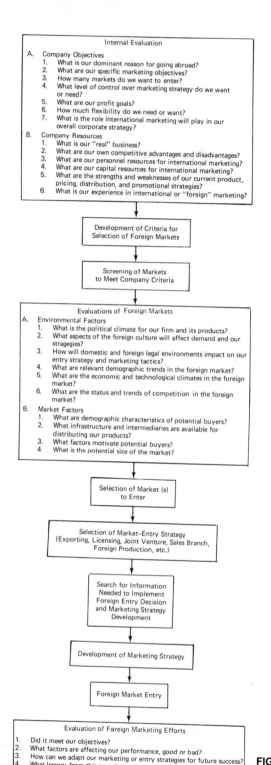

**FIGURE 2–2** The international marketing decision process.

ble country alternatives. Last, the firm's desired level of flexibility in its marketing programs is affected by country environmental factors. Thus, by beginning the foreign marketing decision with an evaluation of company objectives, the firm is able to make all the following steps easier.

Not all firms have suitable resources for exploiting foreign markets. It takes commitment of personnel, capital, and managerial skills to successfully develop foreign opportunities into foreign sales. The firm needs to have a clear idea of its competences before it diversifies its resource use. For example, a firm whose competitive strengths are in mass production, mass distribution, and mass communication needs to select markets where these skills are effective; otherwise, it must have the capacity to "acquire" alternative skills. It follows too that domestic marketing strengths, such as discount prices and low-cost distribution will not work in all foreign markets.

These questions help establish a match between the firm's resources and the characteristics of foreign markets. Once criteria have been established, many countries can be screened out. The mass-production firm mentioned before, would not be likely to consider underdeveloped countries unless, of course, they fit into an objective to diversify the firm's competences.

After eliminating countries that do not match the firm's criteria for selection, specific foreign markets can be assessed. The political-legal climate of a market might cause the firm to eliminate some markets. Iran, for example, is a large market for consumer and industrial products in the Middle East, but its recent hostility toward Americans, its general instability, and its business regulations make it unattractive to most U.S. firms. Likewise, an investigation of cultural, demographic, economic, and technological factors will facilitate selection of only those markets that meet company goals. Another part of this process is the study of factors that directly affect the market: how often people buy, who the decision makers are, product use patterns, and so on. If a firm is unable to meet its control or flexibility objectives because intermediaries or distribution infrastructure (because of lack of roads, for example) are not available, such markets would not be good alternatives.

Once a firm has selected potential foreign markets, it can then decide how best to enter each market. (These options are discussed in the following section.) At this point there may be need for more specific information to help the firm implement its decisions to enter a foreign market. And, of course, the firm will evaluate its foreign marketing efforts as part of the ongoing planning process and the need to continually improve its performance.

This model of the international marketing decision process is an ideal one. Some firms decide to enter foreign markets because management wants to travel there or because an executive's wife speaks the language. While these may be extreme cases, the point needs to be made that the need for information depends on the company's objectives. Thus, this description of the decision process may be too elaborate for the firm that invests in foreign markets to fulfill managers' travel dreams, but it ties selection of foreign markets into company objectives and resources. The more limited are the company's objectives, the less intense will be the need for information on foreign markets; and the decision will be simpler than the model implies.

## FOREIGN MARKET ENTRY STRATEGIES

One of the most important decisions in international marketing is how to enter foreign markets. The entry decision affects the firm's ability to control its foreign market strategy, as well as its profit potential. Furthermore, different entry strategies are associated with different levels of risk to the firm.

### Exporting

The least-risky way of entering foreign markets is exporting. Export selling requires a minimal commitment of resources or adjustments to the firm's domestic planning. One form of exporting involves sales directly to foreign buyers or intermediaries, and the shipping of products from domestic production facilities to the foreign market. Direct exporting also includes establishing foreign distributors, who are exclusive agents for a firm in a particular national or regional market. The firm may have to invest in extra production capacity in order to serve the foreign market, or it may adapt products for foreign tastes. Most direct exporters, however, do not make even these minimal investments for foreign markets. The absence of a compelling need to adjust the firm's organization or marketing strategies is what makes exporting attractive to the novice international marketer and to firms with limited capital or personnel resources. The short-term profitability of this entry strategy should be apparent.

An alternative form of exporting is called indirect exporting because the firm actually sells to domestic intermediaries who in turn locate foreign markets for the firm's products. Indirect exporting increases geographic separation between buyers and sellers and thus decreases the firm's access to foreign market information. On the other hand, rarely does an indirect exporter need to invest internally in acquisition of foreign marketing skills or the specialized knowledge required to document foreign shipments. Most indirect exporters use special intermediaries such as an export trading company or an export management company (they handle products for about one-third of U.S. exporters) to find foreign buyers, to document product shipments, and to facilitate payment for the goods. When individual markets for a firm's products are limited in size, indirect marketing may be the only profitable way to enter the market. For an example of exporting using a domestic intermediary see Appendix C, which is a diary of an actual export sale, including all documentation.

Both types of exporting place severe constraints on marketing strategy and its control. The exporter may not have information about product-use patterns, buyer behavior, or even foreign buyer characteristics. Pricing within the foreign market may be determined by intermediaries irregardless of competing product prices, product image, or demand elasticity. Even in the case where a firm sells direct to foreign buyers, most firms use a version of F.O.B. pricing. As such, the foreign buyer's final price, which must include the costs of transportation and documentation, can be prohibitive.

The loss of control that the firm faces when exporting may be compensated for through lower risk when export sales are insignificant. However, if foreign markets are important to the firm's strategic goals, exporting provides inadequate profit potential over the long term. Some firms use exporting to "test the waters" in foreign markets and if successful, they later choose an entry strategy that allows more control. Unfortunately, export sales are not always a good indicator of potential foreign demand because there may have been few attempts to meet specific needs of foreign buyers. Since market strategy is not often tailored to the needs of the foreign market, long-term profits, and even potential sales, are limited. Furthermore, exporting is a vulnerable competitive position since local firms are closer to the market and often have the advantages of better market knowledge.

### Foreign Licensing

Licensing provides a way of exploiting "saleable know-how" in foreign countries.[1] Know-how can be in the form of physical products, production processes, management techniques, marketing strategies, or any combination of these. Two fast-growing areas of international licensing arrangements are management contracts and franchising.

Management contracts are popular as a means of acquiring special technology and management expertise without the seeming permanence of foreign investment. Many developing countries have opted to nationalize ownership of strategic industries (petroleum or communication, for example) for political and economic purposes. Then, they hire back the original foreign owners to manage the firms and to transfer technical and managerial know-how to their own citizens. In other situations foreign firms may be invited to set up a "turnkey" operation in the foreign market. Investment capital is provided by the local government or investors, and management will eventually be turned over to local citizens. Firms such as PepsiCo and Fiat have used turnkey arrangements to penetrate markets in the USSR. As in the case of many other licensing contracts, the companies continue to receive royalties for the use of their brand names and production processes. An extra advantage is that they are the preferred suppliers for components to the Soviet firms.

[1]Michael Z. Brooke and H. Lee Remmers, *International Management and Business Policy* (Boston: Houghton-Mifflin Company, 1978).

International franchising is another type of licensing that has experienced rapid growth in the last two decades. In 1980 there were over 15,000 franchises of U.S. firms in other countries; Kentucky Fried Chicken, for example, had over 1,300 stores outside the U.S. in 1981, and 27.5 percent of its total sales were from non-U.S. markets. One of the largest international franchisers is Coca-Cola International, Inc., which has granted bottler franchises in over one hundred thirty-five countries, even in the People's Republic of China. World franchising is most apparent in soft drinks, hotels, fast foods, and car rentals. One of the reasons for the growth of franchising is the ability to control and even standardize far-flung operations with virtually no investment other than what was required to establish a strong domestic market position. Control is exercised through a contractual relationship between franchiser and franchise holder, and it often covers such details as employee interviewing, bookkeeping, and specific promotions. Another advantage of franchising is the ability to expand quickly with local expertise in each market.

For all its advantages of control, low risk, minimal investment, and local market knowledge, licensing provides only limited profit potential. Some firms only receive a one-time royalty fee for the use of their patents. Others, such as franchisers, may receive royalties tied to sales volume of their franchisee or license holders, but this is their only return. If the operation is profitable, they only share in the contracted royalties, not in profits. There are two other problems in licensing that also bear noting. One concerns selection of licensees. It is a difficult process for the firm to evaluate foreign candidates' ability to use the license effectively. There needs to be information on potential candidates' capital resources, managerial experience and expertise, local market knowledge, and marketing skills. All too often selections of licensees are based only on capital-related criteria. The lack of marketing abilities is the most often-mentioned reason for licensee failures.[2] Another potential problem in licensing is the possibility that the licensee may become a competitor in the future, using expertise gained through the contractual arrangement and local market knowledge and contacts, to "beat" the foreign company out of the market. This situation happens frequently when relations with the licensee are not good, and it cannot totally be avoided through contracts because they are difficult to enforce in foreign legal systems. In 1977, Coca-Cola abandoned the huge market in India and revoked licenses for use of its products rather than divulge the contents of its secret concentrate, as ordered by the government.[3] Perhaps the most troublesome aspect of licensing is that poor use of licenses can result in shoddy products, lack of quality control, bad customer relations, or other defects that may hurt the overall image of the firm granting a license.

[2]Richard N. Farmer and Barry M. Richman, *International Business: An Operational Theory*, Homewood, Ill. Richard D. Irwin, 1976, p. 40.

[3]*Time*, November 28, 1977, p. 92.

### Joint Ventures

Joint ventures involve shared ownership between local and foreign partners. Countries like Mexico restrict almost all foreign investment ventures to some form of shared ownership between Mexican and foreign partners. Thus, it is sometimes the only way of owning production and marketing of products in a foreign market. It is particularly attractive to countries which have policies designed to keep national wealth at home. Joint ventures offer the promise of foreign management, marketing, and production expertise that will be "transferred" to local partners. From the international firm's point of view, a joint venture provides access to local market knowledge, a local identity, and shared risk.

A joint venture exists when ownership is anything less than 100 percent by the foreign company. Profits are, of course, limited to percentage of ownership. Shared management is the major problem with using joint ventures as a way of entering foreign markets. Local partners must be found who have the necessary capital and compatible management philosophies. Capital is not always a problem, but when management is shared by partners from different cultures with different business traditions, there is potential for conflict. The closer the arrangement is to a fifty-fifty partnership, the higher the potential is for conflict about marketing approaches, budgeting, dividends, and so forth. One of many examples, Genesco had to abandon its joint venture with Interstyle of Switzerland in the late 1960s due to conflicting management philosophies.[4]

This case is not unique; the casualty rate of joint ventures has been high. Nevertheless, it is a politically appealing alternative to foreign ownership, and success stories are more frequent than well-publicized failures. The sharing of financial and political risks is often not as important as the market access and expertise acquired in a joint venture. Distribution in Japan is notoriously complex and sometimes inaccessible to foreign firms. The key to success there for foreign firms has long been joint ventures with established Japanese firms already tied into the labyrinthine distribution system.

### Foreign Production

Choosing to establish production facilities in a foreign country requires the greatest commitment of a firm's resources for foreign market entry. Such direct investments demand use of the firm's personnel, capital, and managerial talents. In return, the firm is able to devise and execute what it feels is the best marketing strategy for penetrating the foreign market. This entry strategy offers the largest potential profits and control. Due to tariff barriers and high transportation costs, it may be the only feasible way to compete effectively in the foreign market.

---

[4]*Business Europe,* October 4, 1968, pp. 317–18.

Foreign direct investment is justified when the market is large and potential sales substantial. However, it does expose the firm to more risks than the other alternatives. The firm faces the possibility of political risks—from minor regulatory changes that discriminate against the foreign firm to confiscation of its assets. Financial risks are higher too because the firm may not be able repatriate the profits it makes, or because devaluation may have a negative effect on the value of its fixed assets in the foreign market. Most important of all, successful foreign direct investment necessitates managerial expertise that many domestic firms do not have. Production must be adapted to the foreign labor force's abilities; supervision has to be effective; and variable operating conditions necessitate new forms of organization, communication, and control. Furthermore, foreign production does not assure that the firm will understand the market or achieve competitive success.

We began this section by noting that there is no one superior market-entry strategy. The best one is the one that matches the firm's objectives, resources, and foreign market conditions. Figure 2–3 shows how the entry options just discussed vary in terms of risk and control. Not all foreign direct investments are high risk or offer total control for all firms but, in general, the entry strategies fit into the continuum as shown. Other factors that need to be considered are market size and legal and political environments within the foreign market.

**FIGURE 2–3**  Comparison of foreign market entry strategies.

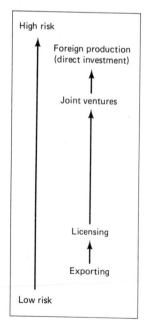
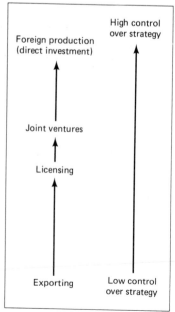

## THE MULTINATIONAL CORPORATION ─────────────────

Just as the new corporate form of business organization reshaped the nineteenth century, the multinational corporation (MNC) is shaping our twentieth century. In the 1800s the public-stock corporation gave business access to large amounts of capital by diluting ownership. The result substantially increased the scale at which businesses could operate, and also increased their power as social-political institutions. Today's multinational corporation gives firms access to unparalleled growth through worldwide market penetration and even broader political and social influence. The largest twenty multinational corporations each have gross sales that are greater in value than the gross national product of seventy-three of the World Bank's 101 member countries. General Motors alone, with over $66 billion in sales, supercedes the GNP of about 130 world nations. (See Figure 2–4 for some of the largest world corporations.) Such size implies

**FIGURE 2–4**   The world's largest economic entities—nations and businesses.

*ALL COUNTRIES & COMPANIES WITH GNP OR GROSS SALES IN EXCESS OF $10 BILLION*

|  | *GNP 1979 ($ Million)* | *Gross Sales 1979 ($ Million)* |
|---|---|---|
| 1. United States | $2,369,400 | |
| 2. USSR | 1,155,593 | |
| 3. Japan | 839,427 | |
| 4. West Germany | 582,776 | |
| 5. France | 460,953 | |
| 6. Peoples' Republic of China | 375,000 | |
| 7. UK | 277,933 | |
| 8. Italy | 238,390 | |
| 9. Canada | 219,450 | |
| 10. Brazil | 214,850 | |
| 11. India | 121,180 | |
| 12. Poland | 119,100 | |
| 13. Mexico | 117,446 | |
| 14. Spain | 104,910 | |
| 15. Netherlands | 99,003 | |
| 16. East Germany | 89,100 | |
| 17. Sweden | 83,548 | |
| 18. Exxon | | 79,106[a] |
| 19. Romania | 78,900 | |
| 20. Belgium | 78,545 | |
| 21. Czechoslovakia | 76,600 | |
| 22. Saudi Arabia | 71,230 | |
| 23. General Motors | | 66,311 |
| 24. Yugoslavia | 64,400 | |
| 25. Switzerland | 59,873 | |
| 26. Royal Dutch Shell Group | | 59,416 |
| 27. Indonesia | 56,650 | |

**FIGURE 2–4**  *Continued*

*ALL COUNTRIES & COMPANIES WITH GNP OR GROSS SALES IN EXCESS OF $10*
*BILLION*

| | GNP 1979<br>($ Million) | Gross Sales 1979<br>($ Million) |
|---|---|---|
| 28. Iran | 56,070 | |
| 29. Argentina | 52,000 | |
| 30. Austria | 47,374 | |
| 31. American Telephone & Tel. | | 45,408 |
| 32. Venezuela | 45,180 | |
| 33. Mobil | | 44,721 |
| 34. Ford Motor Company | | 43,514 |
| 35. Denmark | 43,347 | |
| 36. South Africa | 41,900 | |
| 37. South Korea | 40,950 | |
| 38. British Petroleum | | 38,713 |
| 39. Nigeria | 38,412 | |
| 40. Texaco | | 38,350 |
| 41. Turkey | 36,910 | |
| 42. Norway | 35,723 | |
| 43. Hungary | 35,700 | |
| 44. Iraq | 32,020 | |
| 45. Standard Oil of California | | 29,948 |
| 46. Finland | 27,738 | |
| 47. Republic of China (Taiwan) | 27,690 | |
| 48. Greece | 27,206 | |
| 49. Algeria | 27,100 | |
| 50. Bulgaria | 26,700 | |
| 51. Philippines | 25,190 | |
| 52. Thailand | 24,670 | |
| 53. Gulf Oil | | 23,910[a] |
| 54. IBM | | 22,863 |
| 55. Colombia | 22,760 | |
| 56. General Electric | | 22,460 |
| 57. Unilever | | 21,748 |
| 58. Libya | 20,200 | |
| 59. ENI | | 18,985 |
| 60. Standard Oil (Indiana) | | 18,610 |
| 61. Peru | 18,436 | |
| 62. Fiat | | 18,300 |
| 63. Pakistan | 17,960 | |
| 64. Chile | 17,836 | |
| 65. Sears Roebuck & Company | | 17,514 |
| 66. New Zealand | 17,427 | |
| 67. Francaise des Petroles | | 17,305 |
| 68. Peugeot-Citroen | | 17,270 |
| 69. Portugal | 17,258 | |
| 70. International Tel. & Tel. | | 17,198 |
| 71. Israel | 16,926 | |
| 72. Volkswagenwerk | | 16,766 |
| 73. Phillips Gloeilampenfabrieken | | 16,576 |

**FIGURE 2–4**   *Continued*

*ALL COUNTRIES & COMPANIES WITH GNP OR GROSS SALES IN EXCESS OF $10 BILLION*

|  | GNP 1979<br>($ Million) | Gross Sales 1979<br>($ Million) |
|---|---|---|
| 74. Malaysia | 16,380 | |
| 75. Atlantic Richfield | | 16,234 |
| 76. Renault | | 16,117 |
| 77. Kuwait | 15,990 | |
| 78. Hong Kong | 15,771 | |
| 79. Siemens | | 15,070 |
| 80. Daimler-Benz | | 14,942 |
| 81. Hoechst | | 14,785 |
| 82. Shell Oil | | 14,431ᵃ |
| 83. Egypt | 14,270 | |
| 84. Bayer | | 14,196 |
| 85. BASF | | 14,138 |
| 86. Petróleos de Venezuela | | 14,116 |
| 87. North Korea | 14,100 | |
| 88. Toyota Motor | | 14,012 |
| 89. Safeway Stores | | 13,717 |
| 90. Thyssen | | 13,637 |
| 91. Elf-Aquitaine | | 13,386 |
| 92. Nestlé | | 13,017 |
| 93. U.S. Steel | | 12,929 |
| 94. K-Mart | | 12,858 |
| 95. Cuba | 12,700 | |
| 96. Nissan Motor Company | | 12,652 |
| 97. Conoco | | 12,647 |
| 98. Hitachi | | 12,632 |
| 99. Nippon Steel | | 12,595 |
| 100. United Arab Emirates | 12,548 | |
| 101. E.I. duPont de Nemours | | 12,572 |
| 102. Chrysler | | 12,002 |
| 103. Mitsubishi Heavy Industries | | 11,960 |
| 104. Ireland | 11,543 | |
| 105. Aetna Life & Casualty | | 11,447ᵇ |
| 106. Morocco | 11,415 | |
| 107. Imperial Chemical Industries | | 11,391 |
| 108. J. C. Penney | | 11,274 |
| 109. Tenneco | | 11,209 |
| 110. Matsushita Electric Industrial | | 11,127 |
| 111. Western Electric | | 10,964 |
| 112. Sun | | 10,666 |
| 113. Petróbras (Petróleo Brasileiro) | | 10,279 |

ᵃSales not including excise taxes.

ᵇTotal (not sales) revenues for 1979.

*Source:* "The Largest Industrial Companies in the World," *Fortune,* May 4, 1981; and *World Statistics in Brief* (New York: United Nations, 1979), Series V, #4.

power, and nation-states have not yet come to grips with the power (actual or potential) of the MNC. Small countries probably feel more threatened by this potential power than they should feel, and developed countries systematically underestimate the impact of their large multinationals on the rest of the world. The problem remains that political systems are national but the multinational corporation is supranational.

### Different Types of Multinational Corporations[5]

What is the multinational corporation? That is not an easy question to answer because they come in all sizes and use various organizational strategies and operations. This difficulty in defining the MNC poses many problems in designing coherent policies to regulate or support international activities of business firms. It also leads to more controversy about the effects of the multinational company on world economics, politics, and culture.

One method of classifying firms with international operations is based on the firm's structure. It might be very easy, for example, to differentiate firms with ownership of operations in several countries, from those firms with operations in only one nation. The former are multinational corporations because they do business in several countries. This definition is quite broad and includes firms that issue foreign licenses, joint ventures, and/or have foreign production. Alitalia, as well as Krupp Steel and Hilton International, would be included—quite a heterogeneous group of international businesses.

Alternatively, we could define multinational corporations as those with either multinational ownership or multinational decision makers. These are also structural criteria, but quite restrictive ones. There are few firms that truly have multinational ownership, perhaps as few as three (Unilever, Royal Dutch Shell, and Agfa-Gevaert). While many companies like Ford or Kodak sell their shares in various countries, the majority of their shares are held by citizens of their home country. Unilever, Royal Dutch Shell, and Agfa-Gevaert are headquartered in small countries (England, Holland, and Sweden) and foreign expansion had to be financed externally. Likewise, even when top decision makers are multinational, the firm may still operate in the interests of its home country. Furthermore, nationalistic labor policies in most countries of the world create a barrier to real multinational decision making.

One more way to analyze international firms based on a structural criterion is to investigate the firm's organizational structure. A truly multinational corporation would assign worldwide responsibilities for decision making. International operations would not be considered separate and

---

[5]This section draws from Yair Aharoni's, "On the Definition of a Multinational Corporation," *Quarterly Review of Economics and Business,* August 1971, pp. 27–37.

apart from domestic ones in a firm that has organized in an optimum way to conduct worldwide business. While this definition has intuitive appeal, dozens of international firms would not qualify. Many businesses continue to feel their best method of running international operations is to set them apart, to be run by specialists in a separate division. Chapter 9 discusses the merits of different ways of organizing international marketing activities.

If we look only at a multinational corporation's structure, we find much heterogeneity. We might include exporters if we use the criterion of multinational decision makers; we might include joint ventures if we use multinationality of ownership; and we might include a diverse group of firms if we use multinationality of operations or integrated organizational structure. This seeming contradiction actually reinforces a basic point about multinational companies—they are in fact quite heterogeneous.[6]

An alternative criterion for classifying multinational companies is based on performance factors. This simply means looking at measures of the firm's performance in world business—its sales, its assets, its earnings, or its employees. If a firm sells in multiple countries then it might be a multinational corporation. A problem with this definition is that it is too broad. It includes the small Denver exporter that sells medical products in over eighty countries, but that owns no foreign assets nor has any foreign registration. Earnings and assets are equally problematic criteria since they do not give stability to a classification scheme. If IBM had no foreign earnings during one financial reporting period, it would not be included in such a listing, yet, clearly most of us would agree that it is a multinational corporation. If only those companies with at least 20 percent of their total assets as foreign assets are classified as MNCs, even General Motors wouldn't qualify!

The major problem in using performance as a basis for defining multinational corporations is that arbitrary decisions must be made about cutoff points. For example, should we say that only those firms with 50 percent foreign assets, earning, sales, or employees are MNCs? Using this criterion only eleven U.S. firms would have qualified in 1965. If the cutoff point was 25 percent, eighty-two U.S. companies would have qualified. Clearly, it is a problem to decide the "proper" amount of foreign performance for defining a multinational corporation. And, of course, different firms would be included if different criteria were used—earnings, sales, or assets. Foreign employees present yet another problem because a firm may have a 90 percent foreign labor force, but all managers may be nationals.

If you are frustrated by this discussion of different "types" of multinational corporations, perhaps you can sympathize with the governments that want to regulate the activities of multinationals. And this leads to what

---

[6]Nicholas K. Bruck and Francis A. Lees, *Foreign Investment, Capital Controls, and the Balance of Payments* (New York: NYC Institute of Finance), April 1968, Appendix Table 1.

we believe is the "best" definition of a multinational corporation: A multinational corporation is one that acts and thinks internationally. It seeks opportunities in world markets, it commits resources to exploit those opportunities, and its survival is not contingent on performance in one national market. World operations alone do not necessarily reflect international "thinking" in this definition. Likewise, the absence of foreign operations does not mean a company doesn't "think internationally." A firm must have a strategic commitment to world markets, but its current strategy may not include foreign marketing. To conclude, let us quote Yair Aharoni on the subject of multinational corporations:

> . . . the phenomenon under discussion is a very complicated one and cannot be captured by one name . . . There are distinct differences between a company such as Unilever with manufacturing subsidiaries in dozens of countries; a company such as Trans World Airlines which also operates in dozens of countries but with distinctly different operations; a company such as Bethlehem Steel with mining operations in several countries all supporting the company's manufacturing activities in the United States; a company such as Gulf Oil which owns and operates oil fields in several countries, transports oil, and markets oil; and a company such as Omega Watches, with manufacturing operations in one country, but an export network and sales and service outlets all over the world. Whether or not we wish to call all these companies multinational, there are notable differences in the problems faced by these companies and in their solutions.[7]

### Areas of Conflict between MNCs and Nations

However it is defined, the multinational corporation is an important political and social institution of the twentieth century. The introduction of similar products throughout the world is making our cultures more like each other. South Africans, Japanese, Swedes, Americans, and Thais drink Coca Colas, take pictures with Kodak cameras, buy Sony TVs on VISA credit cards, talk on ITT-developed telephones, feed their babies Gerber foods, and pay bills sent out on IBM computer cards. The multinational corporation is a change agent, and it is making us all more interdependent, if not alike. While cultural homogenization ultimately helps us to relate to each other in spite of cultural differences, it has a negative effect on our distinctiveness. And the more we are interdependent, the more potential there is for conflict. The potential of MNCs to influence lifestyles and politics of countries may dilute the actual power of governments and cultural traditions to influence lifestyles and national politics. Whether or not MNCs exercise this power, they are perceived to have it.

Almost every nation of the world recognizes as its sovereign right the

[7]Yair Aharoni, "On the Definition of a Multinational Corporation," *Quarterly Review of Economics and Business,* August 1971, p. 34.

power to set rules for business transactions within and across its national borders. These rules are guided by the government's view of what will most benefit its citizens. In contrast, the multinational corporation makes decisions with the purpose of ensuring its long-term survival, irregardless of the interests of any particular national group. The domestic firm only has to concern itself with the interests of one national group, while the multinational may find itself subject to rules guided by conflicting national interests. Restricting Israelis' abilities to buy foreign exchange may be good for the Israeli economy, but it may hurt an Israeli company that is trying to invest in new foreign markets. Yet in the long term, expansion and growth of the Israeli firm will also benefit the Israeli economy. Therefore, the MNC may find its corporate interests are in conflict with short- or long-term national policies, and political, social, or economic goals.

It is the multinational corporation's ability to act "transnationally" that can circumvent, even subvert, national policies. This aspect poses the greatest threat to countries. By shifting capital, labor, or other resources within the multinational system, the MNC can counterbalance the effects of national policies on itself. Profits can be moved to low-tax nations through intracompany pricing of components, royalties, and consultant fees. Intracompany loans can supply capital to subsidiaries that face capital shortages created by inflation-fighting economic policies. Profits and dividends can be smuggled out of a country in the form of intracompany payments for goods and services when national policies forbid their flow out of the country. Capital from other subsidiaries can be provided to political parties or candidates who support a foreign company's interests. Operations can be closed and moved elsewhere if national labor policies are too restrictive for profitable operations of the multinational company.

All of these are actions that real companies have taken in response to national policies. Their significance is in illustrating the potential power of the multinational corporation from a host country's point of view. Analysis of the climate for international marketing would not be complete without understanding the external expectations, and sometimes hostility, faced by multinational corporations. It is indeed ironic that a strategic commitment to world markets subjects a firm to the strongest suspicions of its motives and international marketing style.

On the positive side, most multinational companies provide resources that many countries would not otherwise have. Along with technological dependence on multinational companies, countries receive the benefits of technology transfers to local citizens and an ability to compete in world markets. Exports of components assembled in one subsidiary to another in a foreign country help to build a positive trade balance for a country. In a broad sense, many multinationals contribute to industrialization of developing countries, create employment, build the country's capital base, diversify the economy, and strengthen labor skills and experience—all of which are usually important to a country's national development goals.

The benefits of multinational corporations to individual nations are as variable as the companies themselves. The same is true for conflicts between multinational companies and nation-states. At this point it is sufficient to note that this new twentieth-century institution is changing the balance of power between governments and business. As an international marketer, you may be a decision maker within a multinational corporation. Such commitment to world markets will affect how your firm's marketing decisions are viewed, as well as your impact on the markets you choose to pursue.

Multinationality is best described as a managerial attitude, but each firm still operates today in a "national" environment. Therefore, whether a firm operates in one or twenty markets, it must appraise its objectives, opportunities, and resources with respect to each individual one. The climate within each national market will impinge upon the firm's organization and entry strategies within it.

## FINANCING INTERNATIONAL MARKETING

Every firm's financial resources set limits for its marketing objectives and strategies. This is especially true of international marketing decisions. The decisions as to which national markets to pursue and how to enter those markets must take into consideration their financial requirements and resulting effects on the firm's financial position. What is unique in the case of international marketing is the variety of types of financial risks to which the firm will be exposed and, on the positive side, the unique sources of funding for international marketing efforts.

### Financial Risks in International Markets

As in any investment decision, measurement of financial risk in international marketing is a key problem. The firm must decide how much risk it is exposed to and whether the risks are justified in light of market opportunities. Measurement is particularly difficult for international ventures because a firm needs to be able to forecast future exchange rates, political conditions, and rates of inflation in foreign markets, among other factors. Next it must estimate what the impact of these conditions will be on its own profits. While this may sound like an impossible task, it is a necessary requirement before a firm can decide on its best foreign market entry strategy, or on which nations offer the best opportunities.

*Foreign exchange risk.* As long as most countries of the world believe it is in their interest to have their own currency, there will be foreign exchange risk for international marketers. This risk is created by the possibility of one or both of two conditions: nonconvertibility and changing currency values.

A currency is convertible into another currency when it can be changed directly. A U.S. dollar, for example, can be exchanged for .87 Canadian dollars, 150 Mexican pesos, or 1 Panamanian balboa. It cannot be exchanged directly for Russian rubles. The ruble is not convertible because the USSR is not a member of the International Monetary Fund (IMF)—a group of member countries who have agreed to place reserves with the IMF to support the value of their currency relative to that of other members. A currency may become suddenly nonconvertible when a government places restrictions on its citizens' abilities to buy foreign currencies. Such policies, of course, change frequently and thus create hazards for firms making payments to persons in other countries or for foreigners who receive payments in that currency.

While it is difficult to forecast the convertibility of a currency, a good indicator is the level of a country's reserves with the IMF. When a country is using up its reserves (perhaps because its imports exceed exports over a long period of time), it is likely that some restrictions will be imposed on purchases of foreign currencies. If this is not sufficient, devaluation is likely. Devaluation or revaluation refer to changes in the value of one currency in relation to another. Devaluation makes it more "expensive" to buy foreign currencies and can result from poor monetary or fiscal controls within the country. High rates of inflation, the printing of currency for which there are insufficient reserves, and trade imbalances are examples of conditions that might precipitate a currency devaluation. There are, of course, other factors that might cause devaluation. The drop in world oil prices and high external debts caused two major devaluations of the Mexican peso in 1982. Revaluation occurs when a currency is "strong," or undervalued in comparison to others. When the U.S. dollar was declining in value during the 1970s due to high rates of inflation, trade deficits, and other economic conditions, the West German mark was "revalued" upward several times. In 1974 one U.S. dollar would buy 2.58 German deutsche marks, in 1976 it would only buy 2.51; and by 1978 it would buy only 2.07 marks. These numbers reflect a revaluation of more than 24 percent in deutsche marks relative to the U.S. dollar. In 1981, the situation reversed and the U.S. dollar increased about 33 percent in terms of most European currencies.

A U.S. firm expanding operations in Germany would have found it 24 percent more expensive in 1978 than in 1974 to finance the expansion. Furthermore, a profit of one million deutsche marks would have been worth 24 percent more dollars in 1978 if it was returned at that time to the U.S. However, in 1981 it would have cost one-third more to buy dollars. This simple example illustrates only a few of the effects of variable foreign exchange rates on the international marketer. If a firm was exporting to Germany, it could have forced foreign buyers to pay in U.S. dollars and it would have avoided foreign exchange risk. The buyers would have had to assume the risk. However, since all transactions involving multiple currencies carry foreign exchange risk, the risk can be managed by an individual firm, but it cannot be avoided in international transactions as long as there are floating exchange rates and the risks of devaluation or revaluation.

Foreign market opportunities must ultimately be translated into profits. Profits made in a nonconvertible currency may not be permitted to be repatriated to headquarters or to subsidiaries in another country. Exchange rates of currencies often change in response to differences in short-term interest rates in two countries and their relative balance-of-payments positions (discussed in Chapter 6). A large investment in a foreign plant may be a good organizational response to market potential in a country, but if the country's currency declines in value, it may be difficult to recoup the investment through profits in that currency. Therefore, marketing opportunities must be considered simultaneously with analysis of potential foreign exchange risks.

*Other risks in international marketing.* Foreign exchange risk is only one of the unique aspects of financial risk in international marketing. Other significant uncertainties are associated with assets and investments made in unstable political, labor, and capital environments. Unstable political conditions may lead to confiscation of the inventories or fixed assets of a "foreign" company, with or without compensating payments. Labor unrest is often focused on visible foreign firms. Regulation changes can impact on a firm's product designs, sources of materials, media for promotion, distribution margins, pricing strategies, and so on. Controls on a foreign company's ability to borrow, or otherwise finance these operations, are sometimes instituted to protect local firms from foreign competitors. Most of these issues are discussed in detail in later chapters.

The firm must assess such risks and estimate a capital cost for them when it is evaluating a foreign market's potential. For this reason, most firms use expanded financial analysis and special techniques to estimate the financial aspects of such risks. In the simplest case, a firm might attach a premium to its usual definition of a desirable return on investment (ROI). For example, while a 20 percent ROI may be sufficient for a decision to invest in a domestic market, a 25 percent projected ROI may be required for foreign ventures. Other references can provide you with details on foreign investment decision models.[8] The point here is that the financial and profit requirements of foreign marketing must include compensation for the

---

[8]See, for example, Robert B. Stobaugh, "How to Analyze Foreign Investment Climates," *Harvard Business Review,* Sept.–Oct. 1969, pp. 100–108; P.T. Haner, "Determining the Feasibility of Foreign Ventures," *Business Horizons,* Fall 1966, pp. 35–44; Jack Zwick, "Models for Multi-Country Investments," *Business Horizons,* Winter 1967, pp. 69–74; or Stefan H. Robock, Kenneth Simmonds, and Jack Zwick, *International Business and Multinational Enterprises,* 3rd ed. (Homewood, Ill.: Richard D. Irwin, 1983), chaps. 2, 3, 18.

additional risks. Estimating such risks is an integral part of foreign market opportunity analysis.

*Risk management in international operations.* There are many opportunities to "manage" risk for the knowledgeable international marketer. The foreign market entry strategy is a good example of how a firm can choose to pursue a foreign opportunity and at the same time decide how much risk it wishes to be exposed to. If a market is attractive, but its currency is declining in value, or political conditions are unstable, the firm can choose to serve the market through exports. This will only expose the firm to payment and shipment risks, while direct foreign investment exposes the firm to fixed asset risks, personnel-related risks, long-term profit and opportunity-cost risks, and others. Exporting has other limitations, but it is a strategy that can be used to minimize the firm's exposure to financial risks.

Foreign exchange risk can be managed in two ways. One is to pass the risk to other parties in an international transaction. Many firms simply do not accept payment in any currency except their own; the buyer must assume responsibility for converting his or her currency into that of the seller. The problem with this strategy of risk management is that it may severely limit the market and it makes the firm vulnerable to competitors more willing to assume these risks. Therefore, it is simply not a good rule to assume that international markets can be pursued without facing foreign exchange risk.

A second method of managing foreign exchange risk is hedging. In hedging, the firm buys or sells a contract for a specific amount of a currency to be delivered at a future date at an exchange rate guaranteed in the contract. So, if an American exporter knew that he or she was to receive 100,000 British pounds ninety days later, that firm would be able to buy a contract for 100,000 pounds-worth of U.S. dollars, to be delivered in ninety days. Hedging contracts are sold on what is called the "forward" market. Currency prices are quoted at "spot rates" (the rate of exchange for a transaction today) or "forward rates" (the rate of exchange for a transaction at a specific time in the future). The difference in the two rates is determined by speculation about what the spot rate will be at the time the contract comes due, and by short-term interest rates in the two countries. If interest rates are higher in Country A than they are in Country B, the forward rate for Country A's currency will be at a premium above the spot rate.

To illustrate hedging on a small scale, let's assume there are three American exporters each with $1,000. The "Superpatriot" keeps all money in dollars and invests it in ninety-day U.S. Treasury Certificates paying 3.32 percent per year. At the end of ninety days, the Superpatriot will have $1,008.30 (see Figure 2–5 for the full example). The "Risk Taker" notes that British Treasury Bills are paying 6.67 percent interest per year for ninety-day notes. This firm buys British pounds, invests this money in

**FIGURE 2–5**  Playing the foreign exchange game.

*Superpatriot*

| | |
|---|---|
| September 1 | $1,000 |
| | buys U.S. Treasury Certificate paying 3.32% annual interest |
| December 1 | receives principal plus interest |
| | net proceeds: $1,000 + [$1,000 × (.0332 ÷ 4)] = $1,008.30 |

*Risk Taker*

| | |
|---|---|
| September 1 | $1,000 |
| | buys British pounds at spot rate of $1 = .413£ or $2.4213 = 1£ |
| | takes the 413£ and buys British Treasury Bill paying 6.67% annual interest |
| December 1 | cashes the Treasury Bill and receives principal plus interest: 412£ + [413£ × (.0667 ÷ 4)] = 419.8971£ |

Case A (minor dollar increase relative to the pound)
December 1    buys 419.8971£ worth of U.S. dollars at spot rate of $1 = .4133£ or $2.4194 = 1£
net proceeds: $1,015.90

Case B (large dollar increase relative to the pound)
December 1    buys 419.8971£ worth of U.S. dollars at spot rate of $1 = .419£ or $2.3867 = 1£
net proceeds: $1,002.17

*Risk Averter*

| | |
|---|---|
| September 1 | $1,000 |
| | buys British pounds at spot rate of $1 = .413£ or $2.4213 = 1£ |
| | takes the 413£ and buys British Treasury Bill paying 6.67% annual interest |
| | buys a forward contract to sell British pounds (principal plus interest) for U.S. dollars in 90 days at the forward rate of $1 = .415£ or $2.4096 = 1£ |
| December 1 | executes forward contract for 419.8971£ and receives dollars |
| | net proceeds: $1,011.78 |

Treasury Bills and then buys dollars back at the spot rate ninety days from now. The net proceeds of this transaction are $1,015.90. Although the dollar increased in value by $.0003 relative to the pound and this cost the Risk Taker a small amount, the higher British interest rate made the risk taking worthwhile. If, on the other hand, the dollar had increased significantly in value relative to the pound, it would have taken more pounds to get the equivalent amount of dollars, and the Risk Taker would have been worse off than the Superpatriot. Both cases are illustrated in the example. The third American firm used hedging to avert foreign exchange risk. This firm took $1,000, bought British pounds at the spot rate, then bought a contract to sell the principal plus interest (in pounds) in exchange for U.S. dollars at the forward rate. This firm nets $1,011.78 at the end of ninety days.

This example used a small amount of principal and unrealistically low interest rates. For firms with millions of dollars of transactions with subsidiaries and foreign buyers, the benefits of hedging are more significant. Forward contracts for foreign exchange can be purchased through large international banks or through foreign exchange brokers. The larger the value of a firm's international transactions, the more important it is to use hedging to avert exchange risk.

Yet another technique used to manage risk in international marketing transactions is the use of asset and liability management. Borrowing in a currency with potential for devaluation means the firm will pay back less than the value of the original loan plus interest. Therefore, a firm should maximize its liabilities in a weak-currency nation and try to minimize its assets there. For example, an exporter might borrow to finance production for exports in that country and realize a higher profit on the transaction. Likewise, if a currency is strong, that encourages foreign production and direct investment. If a currency is likely to be revalued upward, a firm would want to maximize its assets there but minimize its liabilities.

Credit has become an aggressive competitive tool in international marketing, and it can also be used to reduce risk. The use of credit swaps in the form of goods, services, or interest payments is an effective way to reduce exposure of assets to foreign exchange risk. Many firms doing business in the USSR or the People's Republic of China find barter arrangements of "goods for other goods" an effective way of entering the market with a minimum exposure to risk. Other currently popular versions of barter are described in more detail in Chapter 11. Such arrangements, of course, limit the markets for products, as well as the levels of market penetration. Furthermore, many firms are not well equipped to find markets for the foreign products they receive in the swap. This has been especially true in dealing with China, whose trading companies want industrial and high-technology products in exchange for Chinese handicrafts.

In addition to the individual steps a firm might take to minimize the risks incurred in international marketing, there are agencies that provide insurance against specific risks. For American firms, one agency is the Foreign Credit Insurance Association (FCIA). This group of private insurance companies provides commercial credit risk insurance in conjunction with the political risk insurance offered through the Export-Import Bank— an independent government agency. Another important agency is the Overseas Private Investment Corporation that offers protection against political risks such as confiscation of property. At the international level most industrialized countries provide political risk insurance and many underdeveloped countries are beginning to protect their exporters too. The Agency for International Development (AID) underwrites many international ventures from less-developed countries.

### Financial Sources for International Marketing

International marketers are able to draw from many sources in financing their operations. Shares can be sold in home markets, in subsidiary countries, or in third-party nations. Most export and import operations can be financed by local commercial banks, the Small Business Administration, or other short-term lenders. Since government guarantees often protect these private financial institutions from losses, they have become the principal source of funds for short- and medium-term loans. In addition to the traditional sources of debt and equity financing, there are unique sources that support the activities of the international marketer.

*Private sources.*    The international firm with ownership of operations in several countries is able to borrow in any of its host environments. When funds are not available in one country, subsidiaries in other areas are often able to secure funds for intracompany transfers. There are also unique banking institutions that help the international marketer. Foreign correspondent banks speed transfers of payments and funds. Major correspondent banking systems are now international in scope. The Bank of London, for example, has correspondent banks in most countries that have significant trade with Great Britain. The BankAmerica Corporation and Citicorp are other examples of large systems with international correspondents. Such banks are preferred by multinational companies because funds can be transferred more easily among subsidiaries, and headquarters is able to guarantee loans through the correspondent relationship.

In addition to commercial banks, there are overseas development banks and, in the U.S. there are Edge Act banks. Overseas development banks, and even nonbanking institutions (such as trade associations or regional development consortia), are important sources of investment capital for longer-term international projects. Edge Act banks are allowed to have offices in multiple states in the U.S. and to have diversified loan portfolios that are not permitted for other commercial banks. An Edge Act bank is thus able to offer international marketers a broader array of services and financing.

*Public sources.*    The most important function of public agencies in financing international business efforts has been the provision of loan guarantees to private institutions. In the United States, the Export-Import Bank (Eximbank) plays a major role in encouraging U.S. exports through direct loans, financial guarantees, and credit insurance. In 1977, about 30 percent of Eximbank funds went for direct loans and financial guarantees to private lenders and U.S. exporters.[9] Interest rates on Eximbank loans, or loans with Eximbank guarantees, are usually at lower rates than those available through commercial banks. Most Eximbank loans are for short- or medium-term projects of U.S. businesses, but they have also financed large projects for foreign competitors.

There are two other U.S. public agencies that have been important sources of funds for international marketers. The Agency for International

[9]Ann Crittenden, "The Imbroglio over the Export-Import Bank," *New York Times,* February 12, 1978, sec. 3, p. 1.

Development (AID) administers U.S. government economic and defense aid programs with foreign countries. Most of the aid programs it supervises have provisos that require those countries to buy from U.S. suppliers. As such, AID is indirectly loaning money to the U.S. suppliers by providing their buyers with low-cost capital. AID also makes loans for development purposes, most of them direct to governments but sometimes to private firms involved in a development project. The Overseas Private Investment Corporation (OPIC), in addition to its insurance programs for political risk, also guarantees loans made by private lenders to U.S. firms with investments in high-risk countries. In agricultural goods, the Commodity Credit Corporation (CCC) finances a majority of U.S. commodity exports through purchases of the exporter's accounts receivable.

Many other countries have public agencies similar to the Eximbank, OPIC, AID, and CCC. Direct subsidies of exports have, in fact, been more common in Japan, Canada, and other industrialized nations than in the United States, until recently. An American firm with a subsidiary in any one of these countries can benefit from their programs of export promotion, as well as from U.S. programs.

International agencies complement the national sources of funds just discussed. The World Bank, an agency associated with the United Nations, provides financing to governments for development projects. The loans allow governments to then spend the monies in the purchase of goods and services needed for a project. The World Bank and its affiliate, the International Development Association, do not lend directly to private firms, but these firms benefit from such loans in any case. The International Finance Corporation (IFC), also a World Bank affiliate, makes loans directly to private firms that are participating in development projects. Similarly, other sources of direct financing are the various development banks, such as the Inter-American Development Bank (IDB) which finances projects in the Western Hemisphere. The Organization of Petroleum Exporting Countries (OPEC) has established a development bank to fund oil exploration and related energy development projects. There are many regional development banks (the Asian Development Bank, African Development Bank, European Investment Bank) that provide financing for development projects in their particular regions. In summary, national and international public agencies can be both direct and indirect sources of funds for international marketing activities.

## SUMMARY

This chapter has covered a variety of topics related to a firm's internal organizational and financial environments for international marketing. A firm's resources and objectives for international marketing activities are determinants of, and constraints on, its choices of foreign market entry strategies as well as what markets offer profitable opportunities. Therefore, a first step in developing international marketing strategy is a review of resources and objectives.

There are a variety of roles that foreign markets can play in relation to a firm's overall objectives. International markets can be effective in meeting short-term sales goals or in solving nonrecurrent problems—these indicate an operational focus in which the firm may have no real commitment to international marketing per se. Alternatively, international markets may be an important part of the firm's long-term strategic goals. From another point of view, firms can use international markets to meet problem-solving or opportunity-seeking goals. Also, the firm's decision to get involved in international marketing may begin internally, or it may be in response to external stimuli.

The nature of a firm's objectives for international marketing will affect its needs for information and its extent of decision analysis. Ideally, the firm begins a foreign marketing decision with an introspective analysis of its objectives and resources. Next, it can screen out markets that do not fit its resulting criteria. It can then review environmental and market factors for eligible countries and again reduce the number of viable market options. At this point it selects an entry strategy based on more intensive review of environmental and market factors in candidate countries. After choosing an entry strategy, it then develops an appropriate marketing strategy and later evaluates these efforts. Many firms with limited objectives for international marketing use a simpler process for decision making than this model implies.

The foreign market entry decision is contingent on environmental factors as well as on the firm's desires for control and exposure to risk. Exporting, either direct or indirect, to foreign buyers offers the least risk and the least control. Licensing of foreign firms via licenses, management contracts, or franchising, offers more control over marketing strategy, but also more risk. Joint ventures offer the advantages of shared risk and access to local expertise, but can generate management conflicts. Foreign production offers the highest long-term profit potential and control, but it is the most expensive and risky. The best entry strategy depends again on the firm's resources and objectives.

An important participant in international business today is the multinational corporation. MNCs include many different types of corporations, some with operations in multiple countries and others with only sales in world markets. MNCs can be classified by structural or performance characteristics, but the true multinational is one that "thinks" worldwide. The growing dominance of MNCs in world business is a threat to many countries because the MNC is supranational in its scope and interests.

The last section of this chapter focused on the financial environment for international marketing. There are unique risks that affect the profitability of foreign market opportunities. The most significant of these is foreign exchange risk associated with nonconvertibility and fluctuating currency values. Other risks affect assets and liabilities, as well as specific marketing decisions. Risks can be reduced by hedging, by the use of credit, and by risk insurance. Unique sources of financing for international marketing come from private sources such as large correspondent banking systems, and public sources such as the World Bank.

## DISCUSSION QUESTIONS

1. What is the difference between operational objectives and strategic objectives for international marketing? Give examples of each.
2. How can foreign markets meet "problem solving" goals of firms?
3. Describe some external stimuli that might prompt a firm to get involved in international marketing.
4. Referring to Figure 2–1, why is Situation I an internally stimulated international decision, and Situation IV an externally stimulated one?
5. What is the ideal first step in an international marketing decision? Why?
6. Why don't all firms use the international marketing decision process described in Figure 2–1?
7. Describe the advantages and disadvantages to a firm of each foreign market entry strategy.
8. Differentiate between direct and indirect exporting.
9. Why are joint ventures preferred by host countries as an entry strategy for foreign firms?
10. Describe three different ways of defining a multinational corporation.
11. What are the sources of conflict between MNCs and nation-states?
12. What are the sources of foreign exchange risk? How can such risks be averted?
13. Explain how financial risks affect international marketing strategy.
14. Using outside sources, develop a list of sources of financing for an American exporter of farm equipment.

# JHB IMPORTS

In the fall of 1968, JHB Imports was formed in Denver, Colorado. The primary thrust of JHB was to import high quality, handmade buttons from the Far East for sale in the United States. The partners in JHB, June, Harriet, and Betty, had long had a mutual interest in clothing and had become disenchanted with the availability of high quality non-mass produced buttons in the United States. On vacation trips, they had noted that the type product they were looking for seemed to be readily available in foreign markets. Starting with relatively little capital and operating out of Betty's home, they began to import buttons and repackage them on cards for local distribution to sewing shops and notion counters of department stores and related retailers. Much to their amazement, they initially found a very significant demand for their product, and by the late 1960's had established both regional and national distribution for their buttons. In spite of being much more expensive than domestically produced buttons, their product had significant appeal because of its uniqueness. However, growth began to slow by the mid-1970's. They were by then relatively well established in sewing specialty shops nationwide but found attempts to increase sales further met with little success. They had long since moved out of Betty's house, leased an industrial park location and seen their workforce, made up almost exclusively of women, increase to about thirty-five. All of these employees were involved strictly in repackaging from bulk to smaller quantities of imported buttons. JHB felt that the reason for the slackening sales had to do with the overall slow down of sewing on the part of American women. With more and more women holding fulltime jobs, the time that could be allocated to the creative activity of sewing seemed to be on the decrease. JHB felt this might not be the case in Western Europe and wondered what might be involved in importing buttons in bulk from the Far East, repackaging them onto cards and then exporting them to the Western European market where sewing was still a much more common occurrence than in the United States. They had heard about foreign trade zones in the United States where products could be imported, processed, and then shipped on to a foreign market without paying U.S. customs duties. They thought this might be appropriate for their operation, but they didn't know anything about how to get involved in a foreign trade zone or the European market.

This case was prepared by Dr. Robert J. Hoover, Associate Professor, Corpus Christi State University.

## QUESTIONS

1. What sort of data would help JHB make the decision on whether or not to export to the Western European market?
2. Discuss the advantages and disadvantages of a foreign trade zone for this firm's operations. (See Chapter 6 for discussion of FTZ's.)

# chapter 3

# THE HISTORY AND THEORY OF INTERNATIONAL MARKETING

The *Important Thing* to do in approaching a foreign market is to find out if there really is a market for your product or service.

When you consider doing business abroad, do not hesitate to visit and talk with local foreign competitors. Find out where and how they market their products. Examine and evaluate their products and compare them with your own.

As of 15 years ago, one of the things to do when evaluating entry into a foreign market was to visit the U.S. embassy in the capital of each foreign country, and meet with the commercial attaché to discuss the prospects for your business in that country.

I will never forget our marketing manager making such a visit to the U.S. embassy in Paris. He explained that we were considering the importation of a water softener into France and noted that it sold for approximately $350 in the United States. In France it would probably have to sell for about $500, considering transportation, duty and taxes.

The commercial attaché responded rather pessimistically by stating that the current per capita income was then something like $462 annually in France and that he sincerely doubted if the French people would consider spending more than their annual per capita income for a device that they didn't know they needed.

Our marketing manager agreed that not every man, woman, and child in France was a prospect for our $500 device, but he said he did believe that 0.5% of all of the people in Western Europe could be prospects. When he applied this formula to the 400 million people in Western Europe, the result was 2 million prospects who could afford our product.

Today our French marketing company has one of the largest sales volumes of any of our subsidiary or independent companies outside the United States. This only goes to prove that per capita income or standard of living indices may not be valid indicators of the market potential of a given product or service.*

## INTRODUCTION

The world of international marketing is shaped to a great extent by world economic conditions, patterns of trade, and economic institutions. No decision to pursue foreign market opportunities can ignore the powerful impact these factors have on marketing and market-entry strategies. An international marketer can learn a lot about foreign opportunities simply by understanding the predominant trends in world trade today and why they have developed. Every country has developed policies and institutions to promote or regulate international business based on its historical experiences with trade and current economic needs. In international marketing we must contend with both the domestic and the foreign economic conditions of the moment, and with the effects of past trading patterns.

The theoretical explanations of world trading patterns and international business are also useful to the international marketer. The law of comparative advantage provides a theoretical framework for identifying foreign market opportunities. Its principles also address the topics of international pricing and currency adjustments. The product life-cycle theory of trade suggests a timed, strategic approach to world markets that is contingent on a product's stage in worldwide diffusion.

This chapter is designed to build your understanding of the historical environment and theoretical rationale for international marketing. The first section focuses on historical views of world trade. This should give you an appreciation for the experiences and perceptions that may influence individual transactions today. The next section describes several theoretical explanations for international business. These theories focus on the basic motivations for transacting business in different countries. They should help you predict patterns of international business and trade. They are the basis on which the institutional environment that affects international business has been developed. These economic institutions and policies are described in Chapter 6.

---

*Donald M. Hintz, "Overseas, Culligan Found Water Hard, Marketing Easier," *Marketing News*, November 4, 1977, p. 3.

## HISTORICAL VIEWS
## OF INTERNATIONAL TRADE

International trade is a predominant aspect of world history, and it is as old as humanity. The Chinese traded with Mongols, Aztecs with Mayas, Phoenicians with Minoans, Romans with Egyptians, American Indians with colonists, and on and on. Active trade between two alien groups has often been the precursor of cultural integration and assimilation, as was the case with American Indians. The Romans used trade to expand their empires without war. Cuauhtemoc, the head of the Aztecs, tried to dissuade Cortés from coming to Tenochitlán (Mexico City) by sending him gold from the Aztec Empire, pottery from Cholula, quetzal feathers from Guatemala, wool from Tlaxcala, and fresh flowers from Xochimilco. Trade has therefore been used to meet various goals throughout world history. The New World was discovered by accident while European explorers were seeking shorter trade routes to the Far East and its silks and spices.

International trade continues to be motivated by economic as well as other objectives. It is important for the international businessperson to recognize that the economic role of trade is even today linked to political, social, and defense motives. The U.S. uses foreign aid to fight Communism and Britain uses its old colonies to supply resources that it does not have domestically. Even when an individual transaction, such as sales of John Deere tractors to farmers in Argentina, is not motivated to meet the kinds of noneconomic goals just outlined, the transaction has implications for international relations. Increased agricultural productivity in Argentina may make more grain available in world export markets. That may help less-developed countries who cannot feed themselves, but it lowers prices, and that in turn may hurt American farmers. The essence then of international trade is that it is inexorably linked to relationships between countries. Furthermore, trade today is seen within the context of countries' past relationships with each other.

### Economic Imperialism

The United States would not exist today if the British had not been economic imperialists. Their attempts to tax the American colonists prompted the Boston Tea Party and unified forces in the decision to revolt against British rule. However, this case was not a unique one in the seventeenth and eighteenth centuries. The prevailing philosophy of world powers at that time was that political strength was dependent on access to world economic resources. Empire building was the quickest way to dominate a foreign land's resources and to add to the inventory of resources of the mother country.

England, France, Spain, and Portugal are notable examples of countries that pursued and benefited from the philosophy of economic imperialism. They became the major powers of the sixteenth through eighteenth centuries. Trade with their colonies was important to maintaining wealth and defense at home. Trade led to pursuit of more resources, more trade, and the need to protect their spans of influence. As areas of the world began to fall into one colonial sphere or another, the impetus to exploit the respective colonies for even more resources became critical. By the beginning of the nineteenth century, almost all of Africa, the Americas, the Caribbean, and the Pacific islands were colonized and settled by Europeans to further ensure access to resources by their mother countries. Unfortunately for the Europeans, the colonists began to identify more and more with their new countries and their own economic interests. Colonists throughout the world resented the exploitation of their wealth for the benefit of distant European powers.

The point of this historical review is that countries as disparate today as India, the United States, Peru, the Philippines, India, and South Africa all share a history of having been exploited by a foreign power. To greater or lesser degrees, their peoples remain sensitive to the use of their economic resources by foreigners. Japan limits foreign access to its markets through protective tariffs. The American government makes it impossible for foreigners to own companies in industries critical to defense. Mexico expropriated assets of foreign companies in petroleum and telephones, even though it was unable to staff those industries with competent nationals at the time. International businesses must be aware of the history of foreign exploitation in many countries, and alert to the unfortunate possibility that their current investments may be viewed as exploitive—in spite of contributions made to local development. Mining, farming, and other industries that physically remove natural resources from one country for use in another, have been particularly susceptible to these suspicions in the twentieth century.

## Patterns of Trade: Developed versus Underdeveloped Countries

During the nineteenth and twentieth centuries a new pattern of division among world countries emerged. It did not mirror the classification of "colonies" and "mother countries" that existed earlier; it was based on the extent of industrial development that occurred in individual countries after the decline of economical imperialism. Countries such as the United States, Germany, Australia, and the USSR have, for various reasons, been able to diversify and develop their economies.

There are many definitions of economic development and even more ideas about how to stimulate it.[1] Nevertheless, there is agreement that de-

[1]See, for example, Pan A. Yotopoulos and Jefferey B. Nugent, *Economics of Development* (New York: Harper & Row, 1976); Theodore Morgan, *Economic Development: Concept and Strategy* (New York: Harper & Row, 1975); W. W. Rostow, *The Stages of Economic Growth* (London: Cambridge University Press, 1973); Albert O. Hirschman, *The Strategy of Economic Development* (New Haven; Yale University Press, 1967).

veloped economies tend to have more industrial capacity than underdeveloped ones. They are also more likely to have higher agricultural productivity, more capital-intensive investments in manufacturing, and overall higher standards of living. Underdeveloped countries have more of their gross national product tied to agriculture, and agriculture is more likely to be labor-intensive. A further distinction could be income distribution: Underdeveloped countries typically have a majority of very poor people, a small minority of wealthy persons, and virtually no one in between. Income tends to be more equitably distributed in developed countries, although there are patterns in individual countries that do not fit either of these stereotypes.

Since underdeveloped economies are labor-intensive and dependent on agriculture and natural resources, they have almost naturally become the resource suppliers for the developed world. In order to acquire manufactured goods unavailable in their local economies, they have traded agricultural production and natural resources for industrial and manufactured products that come from the developed world. Figure 3–1 illustrates the traditional patterns of trade between developed and less-developed countries, and it substantiates the pattern just described. For example, the Central American "Banana Republics" have exported fruits and coffee and imported capital goods and manufactured products. African and Middle Eastern countries have exported minerals and petroleum in exchange for products made with these resources.

**FIGURE 3–1**    Principal imports and exports of selected countries in 1979.

| COUNTRY | PRINCIPAL EXPORT PRODUCTS | PRINCIPAL IMPORT PRODUCTS |
|---------|---------------------------|---------------------------|
| **Developed Countries** | | |
| United States | Machinery, nonelectric transportation equipment, crude materials, excluding fuels (agriculture) Chemicals | Minerals, fuels, etc. Machinery, transportation equipment Basic manufactures Food and live animals Crude materials, excluding fuels (agriculture) |
| Japan | Machinery, transportation equipment Basic manufactures Iron & steel | Minerals, fuels, etc. Crude materials, excluding fuels (agriculture) Food and live animals Basic manufactures Machinery, transportation equipment |
| United Kingdom | Machinery, transportation equipment Basic manufactures Chemicals | Machinery, transportation equipment Basic manufactures Minerals, fuels, etc. Food and live animals |

**FIGURE 3–1**    *Continued*

| COUNTRY | PRINCIPAL EXPORT PRODUCTS | PRINCIPAL IMPORT PRODUCTS |
|---|---|---|
| West Germany | Machinery, transportation equipment<br>Basic manufactures<br>Chemicals | Minerals, fuels, etc.<br>Machinery, transportation equipment<br>Basic manufactures<br>Food and live animals<br>Crude materials, excluding fuels<br>  (agriculture) |

*Developing Countries*

| COUNTRY | PRINCIPAL EXPORT PRODUCTS | PRINCIPAL IMPORT PRODUCTS |
|---|---|---|
| Brazil | Coffee<br>Animal feed<br>Iron ore concentrates | Minerals, fuels, etc.<br>Machinery, transportation equipment<br>Chemicals<br>Food and live animals<br>Basic manufactures |
| Mexico | Petroleum, crude & partly refined<br>Coffee<br>Fish, fresh & simply preserved | Machinery, transportation equipment<br>Chemicals<br>Basic manufactures<br>Crude materials, excluding fuels<br>  (agriculture)<br>Food and live animals |
| Nicaragua | Coffee<br>Cotton<br>Meat, fresh, chilled or frozen | Machinery, transportation equipment<br>Chemicals<br>Basic manufactures<br>Minerals, fuels, etc. |
| Zaire | Copper<br>Coffee<br>Ores, concentrates of nonferrous<br>  metals | Machinery, transportation equipment<br>Basic manufactures<br>Food and live animals<br>Chemicals<br>Mineral, fuels, etc. |
| Egypt | Cotton<br>Petroleum, crude & partly refined<br>Textile yarn & thread | Machinery, transportation equipment<br>Basic manufactures<br>Food and live animals<br>Chemicals<br>Crude materials excluding fuels<br>  (agriculture) |
| Saudi Arabia | Petroleum, crude & partly refined<br>Petroleum products | Machinery, transportation equipment<br>Basic manufactures<br>Food and live animals |
| Thailand | Rice<br>Vegetables, fresh, frozen or simply<br>  preserved<br>Sugar and honey | Machinery, transportation equipment<br>Minerals, fuels, etc.<br>Basic manufactures<br>Chemicals<br>Crude materials, excluding fuels<br>  (agriculture)<br>Food and live animals |

*Source:* United Nations, *1979 Yearbook of International Trade Statistics,* Vol. 1 (New York: UN Publishing Service, 1980), tables and Special Table K.

While the pattern of trade for developed and underdeveloped countries has in some respects taken advantage of their relative *abilities* to trade, it has not resulted in a better distribution of world wealth. In fact, rich countries are comparatively richer today than in 1850. A major reason for the growing discrepancy has been the higher productivity of manufacturing as compared to agriculture during the last 130 years. In addition, underdeveloped countries have become more dependent on the capital-intensive technologies that they must import from the developed world in order to increase their agricultural productivity. It is in essence a "Catch-22": If they are more productive, they can acquire more of the world's wealth, but they must pay for it at lower levels of productivity. In the meantime, the developed world has further increased its productive capacity, and so on.

In recent years resentment has built in developing countries over their roles as poorly paid resource suppliers to rich, consuming nations. Countries such as Saudi Arabia and Venezuela are using income from petroleum exports to finance industrial development. World coffee growers (especially Brazil and Colombia) are trying to get coffee buyers to peg coffee prices to indexes of the costs of manufactured goods. Producer cartels sprang up in the 1970s for several other minerals and commodities.

The efforts to change traditional patterns of trade between developed and underdeveloped countries have influenced policies in both groups of countries. These policies are having a strong impact on international businesses. The less-developed countries look favorably on firms that will produce in their countries and export manufactured goods to other markets. They have instituted "import substitution" laws which affect imports adversely and favor local industry. They also discriminate against investments that are unlikely to transfer technology to nationals. The result of such decisions is that international firms face restrictions in entering underdeveloped markets and pressure to transfer ownership or control to local citizens. Simultaneously, these countries remain important as resource and labor suppliers for operations of international firms in various parts of the world.

### Recent Patterns of World Trade: Diversification

Since 1960, world trade patterns have been changing. The changes have resulted from diversification of products traded by individual countries and diversification of the countries that are major world traders. The United States has had a dominant role in the trading patterns that have evolved in recent times. For that reason, special attention is focused on the United States.

In the previous sections, traditional patterns of trade have been characterized as trade from colonies to mother countries; trade of raw materials from less-developed countries to developed economies; and trade of manufactured goods from developed countries to less-developed ones. The mother countries did very little exchange of products among themselves. Likewise, underdevelopeed countries were relatively isolated from each other in regard to trade. In recent times, however, developed countries have begun to trade more and more with each other. The major market for Japanese products is the United States. And U.S. products have their largest foreign markets in Western Europe and Canada. Figure 3–2 shows the destination of exports and source of imports for several developed countries, and it substantiates the importance of trading partners within the developed world. Developed countries continue to trade mostly with each other today because they are the major world markets for the kinds of high-technology products produced and consumed in developed economies. While these countries still export a great deal of manufactured products to developing countries in exchange for their raw materials, this type of trade is less significant in terms of relative volume and value. Today, trade in manufactured goods is the major component of world trade. Figure 3–3 and Figure 3–4 illustrate how these patterns have developed in the last thirty years.

While developed countries have begun to trade more and more with each other, there have also been changes in the world trade activities of less-developed countries. They have become exporters of manufactured goods to the developed world. Areas such as Mexico, Taiwan, the Philippines, and Hong Kong have recently produced clothes, televisions, electronic components, and many other products whose market destinations are the U.S., Canada, Western Europe, and other developed and developing countries. The less-developed countries are now supplying each other with manufactured goods, and in many cases they compete effectively against higher-cost goods from developed countries. Firms in developed countries are even competing against their own subsidiaries from developing countries for the home market. The overall result of these changing trade patterns in manufactured goods has been a broader world base of supply and more intense competition among suppliers.

Diversification of world trade in manufactured goods has been both a cause and a result of significant changes in how businesses *enter* foreign markets. Many years ago the term *international trade,* as measured by exports and imports, was synonomous with international business and international marketing. Today, more and more firms are choosing foreign market investment through licensing, joint ventures, and wholly owned foreign production facilities.

Figure 3–5 shows the book value of foreign direct investments for firms headquartered in several countries. It underlines the growth of foreign direct investment as an alternative to exporting. This phenomenon also explains some of the diversification of world trade patterns in recent

**FIGURE 3–2**    Trading partners of selected developed countries, 1978.

| COUNTRY | DESTINATION OF EXPORTS (% OF TOTAL EXPORTS) | | SOURCE OF IMPORTS (% OF TOTAL IMPORTS) | |
| --- | --- | --- | --- | --- |
| United States | Canada | 19.6 | Canada | 18.8 |
| | Japan | 9.0 | Japan | 14.5 |
| | W. Germany | 4.6 | W. Germany | 5.7 |
| | Mexico | 4.6 | United Kingdom | 3.3 |
| | United Kingdom | 4.6 | Mexico | 3.7 |
| | | 42.4% | | 46.0% |
| Japan | United States | 25.7 | United States | 18.8 |
| | S. Korea | 6.1 | Saudi Arabia | 10.7 |
| | W. Germany | 3.7 | Australia | 6.7 |
| | Saudi Arabia | 3.3 | Indonesia | 6.6 |
| | Hong Kong | 3.1 | Iran | 5.3 |
| | | 41.9% | | 48.1% |
| West Germany | France | 12.2 | Netherlands | 12.6 |
| | Netherlands | 9.9 | France | 11.6 |
| | Belgium-Luxemburg | 8.3 | Italy | 9.6 |
| | | 30.4% | | 33.8% |
| United Kingdom | United States | 9.5 | W. Germany | 11.0 |
| | W. Germany | 8.3 | United States | 10.3 |
| | Netherlands | 6.0 | France | 7.8 |
| | | 23.8% | | 29.1% |
| Ireland | United Kingdom | 47.1 | United Kingdom | 49.4 |
| | France | 8.9 | United States | 8.4 |
| | W. Germany | 8.3 | W. Germany | 7.1 |
| | | 64.3% | | 64.9% |
| France | W. Germany | 17.4 | W. Germany | 19.0 |
| | Italy | 10.9 | Italy | 10.1 |
| | Belgium-Luxembourg | 10.3 | Belgium-Luxembourg | 9.2 |
| | | 38.6% | | 38.3% |
| Denmark | W. Germany | 16.7 | W. Germany | 20.0 |
| | United Kingdom | 14.3 | Sweden | 13.0 |
| | Sweden | 12.8 | United Kingdom | 11.4 |
| | | 43.8% | | 44.4% |
| Greece | W. Germany | 20.8 | W. Germany | 15.6 |
| | Italy | 10.8 | Japan | 12.7 |
| | France | 6.6 | Italy | 9.7 |
| | | 38.2% | | 38.0% |

*Source:* United Nations Statistical Office, *1978 World Trade Annual,* Vol. 1 (New York: Walker & Company, 1980).

years. More business firms have the option today of producing in one of several national environments, depending upon such factors as labor costs and access to raw materials. They can choose to serve markets in a variety of nations from many different points across the globe.

Special comment must be made about the U.S. role in world trade and recent changes in its status as the largest single world trader. Foreign

**FIGURE 3–3**  Changing nature of world trade.

| EXPORTS | | 1948 % of World Trade | 1958 % of World Trade | 1967 % of World Trade | 1977 % of World Trade | 1980 % of World Trade |
|---|---|---|---|---|---|---|
| *From* | *To* | | | | | |
| Developed Countries | Developed Countries | 45.9% | 44.3% | 52.1% | 45.9% | 45.1% |
| Developed Countries | Developing Countries | 22.5 | 18.9 | 13.8 | 15.3 | 14.8 |
| Developed Countries | Centrally Planned Countries | ND | 2.0 | 2.8 | 3.0 | 3.1 |
| Developing Countries | Developed Countries | 22.0 | 16.4 | 13.6 | 18.2 | 19.3 |
| Developing Countries | Developing Countries | 9.7 | 5.2 | 3.7 | 5.9 | 7.0 |
| Developing Countries | Centrally Planned Countries | ND | .7 | 1.0 | 1.0 | 1.0 |
| Centrally Planned Countries | Developed Countries | ND | 1.9 | 2.7 | 2.6 | 2.9 |
| Centrally Planned Countries | Developing Countries | ND | 1.1 | 1.7 | 1.6 | 1.6 |
| Centrally Planned Countries | Centrally Planned Countries | ND | ND | ND | ND | 4.3 |
| Unidentified | | ND | 9.1 | 8.1 | 6.0 | 12.4 |
| | | 100% | 99.6% | 99.5% | 99.5% | 99.2% |

*Source:* United Nations 1973 and 1978 Yearbooks of International Trade Statistics, New York: U.N. Publishing Services, 1973 and 1978.

trade (exports and imports) has never been critical to the state of economic health in the United States. We have the largest single market in the world, substantial amounts of natural resources, and physical isolation from all but two other countries of the world. It is not surprising, then, that our economy has not been dependent on access to foreign products or technology or on our ability to sell our wares in other countries.

Figure 3–6 shows the percentage of U.S. exports and imports in relation to gross national product as compared to several other countries, from 1950 to 1977. It is obvious from these figures that many other countries are more dependent on foreign trade for domestic economic health than is the United States. However, it has become more difficult in recent years to continue our high standard of living without buying resources and products from other countries. In fact, we have always relied to some extent on resource inputs from other countries and on sales of manufactured

**FIGURE 3–4**  Changing national shares of world trade.

| | 1950<br>% OF TOTAL | | 1960<br>% OF TOTAL | | 1970<br>% OF TOTAL | | 1979<br>% OF TOTAL | |
|---|---|---|---|---|---|---|---|---|
| | Imports | Exports | Imports | Exports | Imports | Exports | Imports | Exports |
| Developed Market Economies | 66% | 61% | 66% | 67% | 72% | 71.6% | 70% | 66% |
| Developing Market Economies | 26.3 | 31.5 | 22 | 21 | 17 | 17.7 | 20 | 24.5 |
| Centrally Planned Economies | 7.6 | 7.5 | 12 | 12 | 10.6 | 10.6 | 9.5 | 9.3 |
| Total | 99.9% | 100.0% | 100% | 100% | 99.6% | 99.9% | 99.5% | 99.8% |
| *Shares of Selected Countries:* | | | | | | | | |
| U.S. | 14.1% | 16.7% | 11.1% | 16.0% | 12.1% | 13.5% | 12.9% | 10.9% |
| Japan | 1.5 | 1.3 | 3.3 | 3.1 | 5.7 | 6.1 | 6.6 | 6.3 |
| W. Germany | 4.3 | 3.2 | 7.4 | 8.8 | 9.0 | 10.9 | 9.3 | 10.5 |
| United Kingdom | 11.6 | 10.4 | 9.6 | 8.2 | 6.6 | 6.1 | 6.1 | 5.6 |
| OPEC | 3.6 | 6.6 | 4.0 | 6.0 | 3.0 | 5.7 | 6.0 | 12.7 |

*Source:* United Nations, *1979 Yearbook of International Trade Statistics* (New York: UN Publishing Service, 1980).

goods abroad. We drink tea and coffee, wear diamond rings, use copper plumbing fixtures, drive cars made from bauxite—all products that are almost 100 percent imported. In the 1960s and 1970s, however, we became even more dependent on imports to meet domestic demand. By 1982 about one out of four automobiles sold in the U.S. was foreign-made and over 40 percent of our electronic products were assembled or produced in foreign countries. Exacerbating these trends, we are importing a substantial portion of our fossil-fuel needs, even after admirable conservation efforts during the 1970s. The deficit in the U.S. trade balance (the value of imports over exports) has been widening since 1971. The point is that the health of the U.S. economy is becoming dependent on world trade.

While exports have never been a large part of our GNP, the United States is still the largest single world exporter. Our large domestic market has made it possible for domestic producers to concentrate on sales at home. Many American businesses have viewed foreign markets simply as "cream." Therefore, our businesses have not been as anxious to solicit foreign buyers as have firms in export-dependent countries such as Japan, Belgium, and other European countries. For many years, neglect of foreign

**FIGURE 3–5** Value of foreign direct investments of firms headquartered in selected countries.

| Country | 1967[a] $ (billions) | 1967[a] % of Total | 1971[a] $ (billions) | 1971[a] % of Total | 1974[a] $ (billions) | 1974[a] % of Total | 1978[a] $ (billions) | 1978[a] % of Total |
|---|---|---|---|---|---|---|---|---|
| United States | $ 59.4 | 55.0% | $ 86.0 | 52.0% | $118.6 | 47.8% | $168.1 | 45.2% |
| United Kingdom | 17.5 | 16.2 | 24.0 | 14.5 | 34.0 | 13.7 | 41.1 | 11.0 |
| Switzerland | 4.2 | 3.9 | 6.7 | 5.1 | 17.0 | 6.8 | 27.8 | 7.5 |
| West Germany | 3.0 | 2.8 | 7.2 | 4.4 | 15.3 | 6.2 | 31.8 | 8.5 |
| Japan | 1.4 | 1.3 | 4.4 | 2.7 | 12.7 | 5.1 | 26.8 | 7.2 |
| France | 6.0 | 5.5 | 9.5 | 5.8 | 12.6 | 5.1 | 14.9 | 4.0 |
| Netherlands | 2.2 | 2.1 | 3.5 | 2.2 | 11.3 | 4.6 | 23.7 | 6.5 |
| Canada | 3.7 | 3.4 | 5.9 | 3.6 | 8.2 | 3.3 | 13.6 | 3.7 |
| Sweden | 1.5 | 1.4 | 3.4 | 2.1 | 4.5 | 1.8 | 6.0 | 1.6 |
| Italy | 2.1 | 1.9 | 3.3 | 2.0 | 4.0 | 1.6 | 3.3 | 0.9 |
| Belgium/Luxemberg | 2.0 | 0.4 | 3.2 | 2.0 | 4.0 | 1.6 | 4.7 | 1.3 |
| Australia | 0.3 | 1.9 | 0.6 | 0.4 | 4.0 | 0.4 | 1.1 | 0.3 |
| Other Noncommunist Countries | 4.9 | 4.2 | 7.3 | 4.2 | 5.0 | 2.0 | 8.9 | 2.4 |
| Total Noncommunist | $108.2 | 100.2% | $165.0 | 100.0% | $248.1 | 100.0% | $371.8 | 100.0% |

[a]United Nations, *Multinational Corporations in World Development* (New York: Praeger Publishers, 1974).

[b]United Nations, Centre on Transitional Corporations, March, 1982.

**FIGURE 3–6** Exports and imports as percentage of GNP in selected countries.

| | 1950 | | 1960 | | 1970 | | 1977/1979 | |
|---|---|---|---|---|---|---|---|---|
| | *Imports* | *Exports* | *Imports* | *Exports* | *Imports* | *Exports* | *Imports* | *Exports* |
| **United States** | 4.0% | 4.2% | 4.3% | 5.0% | 5.5% | 5.7% | 9.4% | 7.9% |
| **Canada** | 19.9 | 22.1 | 19.0 | 17.7 | 20.9 | 23.7 | 24.5 | 24.5 |
| **United Kingdom** | N.D.[a] | N.D. | 22.4 | 21.1 | 22.2 | 23.1 | 30.3 | 31.3 |
| **West Germany** | 10.6 | 13.5 | 16.4 | 19.0 | 18.9 | 21.0 | 23.4 | 25.8 |
| **Belgium** | 27.9 | 23.5 | 33.4 | 32.4 | 41.2 | 43.4 | 47.2 | 46.4 |
| **Japan** | 7.0 | 7.1 | 10.4 | 10.9 | 9.5 | 10.7 | 10.5 | 17.7 |
| **Mexico** | 14.0 | 14.2 | 12.6 | 10.3 | 10.3 | 8.3 | 10.5 | 10.2 |
| **South Africa** | 27.8 | 30.9 | 25.7 | 31.4 | 25.6 | 22.3 | 25.4 | 31.7 |
| **India** | 7.4 | 7.7 | 8.2 | 5.2 | 4.7 | 4.0 | 7.1 | 6.1 |

[a]N.D. = no data available

*Source:* World Bank, *World Tables*, 2nd ed. (Baltimore: Johns Hopkins Press, 1980).

markets did not hurt American firms. We were more technologically advanced than other producer countries, and our economy was not as disrupted by World War II as European and Japanese economies. We had the edge even if we were sometimes indifferent to foreign buyers.

With diversification in sources of supply for manufactured goods, the United States' share of world trade has been declining (see Figure 3–4). Unfortunately, slow economic growth and double-digit inflation in the domestic economy during the 1970s made the domestic market less attractive to growth-seeking U.S. firms. In the 1980s, U.S. firms must develop foreign buyers in order to meet growth objectives. Slow economic growth is predicted worldwide for the latter part of the twentieth century. Foreign markets will be harder to capture due to increased competition and more aggressive and sophisticated competitors. Nevertheless, we must continue to seek diversified markets as a means of meeting business growth objectives.

There are two major ways the United States can regain its share of world exports. One is to diversify the type of products that our firms sell in foreign markets. Figure 3–7 shows a breakdown of U.S. exports and imports by commodity. It should be apparent that a few American industries account for the lion's share of exports. Even within each category (for example, "machinery and equipment") very few products (automobiles, trucks, tractors) dominate export sales. By getting other products, other industries, and even smaller firms involved in foreign markets, we could change the shrinking status of the U.S. in world exports.

**FIGURE 3–7**   U.S. exports and imports by commodity.

|  | *1960* | *1965* | *1970* | *1977* |
|---|---|---|---|---|
| *Exports* | | | | |
| Food & beverages | 20.7% | 21.1% | 16.0% | 18.9% |
| Non-food agriculture | 6.2 | 5.5 | 4.9 | 5.0 |
| Fuels, minerals & metals | 7.7 | 8.2 | 9.2 | 6.3 |
| Machinery & equipment | 37.5 | 36.8 | 41.7 | 43.0 |
| Other manufactures | 27.8 | 28.4 | 28.3 | 26.9 |
|  | 99.9% | 98.0% | 99.1% | 99.8% |
| *Imports* | | | | |
| Food & beverages | 23.6% | 19.6% | 16.1% | 9.9% |
| Non-food agriculture | 10.3 | 8.5 | 4.6 | 3.3 |
| Fuel and lubricants | 11.3 | 10.4 | 7.7 | 29.9 |
| Non-fuel minerals & metals | 11.6 | 11.3 | 7.7 | 4.5 |
| Machinery & equipment | 10.2 | 13.8 | 25.0 | 24.7 |
| Other manufactures | 32.1 | 36.4 | 35.9 | 27.6 |
|  | 100.1% | 100.0% | 97.0% | 99.9% |

*Source:* World Bank, *World Tables,* 2nd ed. (Baltimore: John Hopkins Press, 1980).

Another way to increase U.S. exports is to build trade with countries with which we now have limited exchange. Figure 3–8 shows where American exports go and where our imports are from. You should note that most of our exports go to Canada and Western Europe. Latin America is already a large market for American exports but perhaps offers an even higher potential. Likewise, we could build more trade with the Middle East, South Asia, and Africa. Most important, American businesses must become more aware of the potential in foreign markets.

## THEORETICAL BASES
## FOR INTERNATIONAL BUSINESS

Why do countries trade with each other? Why do businesses produce in different nations? What are the benefits of international exchanges of products and services? These questions are addressed by various theories of international trade which are important to understand because they help predict actual patterns of trade. On a broad level, these theories can help the decision maker choose among foreign opportunities, but on a more practical level, they are useful to know because political decisions about tariffs, quotas, investment incentives, and monetary controls are based in principal on assumptions contained in these theories. For example, Congress might vote for an increase in tariffs on imported oil based on the belief that it will stimulate domestic producers to bring larger quantities to market at higher prices. These principles then provide insight into the behavior of firms in the world marketplace and into the external environment that influences their behavior.

### The Law of Comparative Advantage

It should be apparent that a basic motivation of any exchange is that each party hopes to gain more from trading than from not trading. This is the principle upon which the law or doctrine of comparative advantage is based. If a country's climate is not well suited to growing wheat, then it can make better use of its resources by growing something else and trading that for the wheat it wants. If each country specialized in producing products in which it was most efficient, and then traded them for products which it did not make as efficiently, the whole world would have a higher standard of living. Each country would be able to have more variety of goods and more of each kind. These are the principles of the doctrine of comparative advantage:

1.  Every region (country or firm) should specialize in producing the goods in which it has the largest comparative advantage.

**FIGURE 3–8** United States' trading partners.

| | 1977 | | 1978 | | 1979 | | 1980 | |
|---|---|---|---|---|---|---|---|---|
| | U.S. Imports | U.S. Exports | U.S. Imports | U.S. Exports | U.S. Imports | U.S. Exports | U.S. Imports | U.S. Exports |
| Canada | 19.9%c | 21.2% | 19.4% | 19.5% | 20.0% | 18.0% | 15.8% | 15.7% |
| Western Europe | 18.7 | 27.9 | 21.2 | 27.7 | 20.2 | 29.7 | 19.0 | 30.5 |
| Japan | 12.6 | 8.0 | 14.2 | 8.9 | 14.8 | 9.7 | 10.8 | 9.4 |
| CACMa | 1.0 | 1.2 | .8 | 1.1 | .8 | .9 | .7 | .8 |
| LAFTAb | 9.0 | 11.5 | 9.4 | 12.2 | 12.9 | 12.7 | 9.0 | 14.6 |
| Communist Europe | .6 | 2.0 | .8 | 2.5 | .9 | 3.1 | .5 | 1.7 |
| Asia | 33.5 | 26.3 | 33.8 | 27.6 | 32.3 | 26.9 | 32.7 | 27.4 |
| Australia/Oceania | 1.0 | 2.0 | 1.0 | 2.4 | 1.4 | 2.4 | 1.0 | 2.2 |
| Africa | 11.6 | 4.6 | 9.8 | 4.1 | 11.8 | 3.5 | 13.0 | 4.1 |
| Middle East | 8.7 | 8.3 | 6.8 | 8.6 | 8.3 | 6.0 | 6.2 | 5.3 |

*Source: FT 155 Annual, FT 455 Annual* (Washington, D.C.: Bureau of the Census, U.S. Government Printing Office, 1977–1980), Schedule B.

aCentral American Common Market Countries.

bLatin American Free Trade Association Countries (now called Latin American Integration Association)

cNumbers should be read as "19.9% of U.S. Imports came from Canada in 1977".

2. Every region (country or firm) should then trade those goods for products in which it has a comparative disadvantage.

3. A trade price will naturally evolve that will benefit both parties and motivate them to engage in trade.

4. All regions will have, as a result, higher standards of living.

What happens if one country produces everything more efficiently than another? Is there no motivation to trade if one party has an absolute advantage in production over another one? The answer is that it depends on the products of comparative advantage that each country has. An example should illustrate this subtlety of the doctrine of comparative advantage.

Let's contrast Mexico and Canada. Mexico has low-cost labor, land that must be irrigated for agriculture, high capital costs and inflation, and a large unskilled and semiskilled labor force. Canada, on the other hand, has comparatively lower inflation and capital costs, a highly educated and skilled labor force, and large amounts of arable land. Mexico's resources are most efficiently used in producing labor-intensive products that do not require a sophisticated labor force. Canada's resources are best used in capital-intensive production and processing of more complex products. It is likely that Mexicans can produce the same quality of shoes cheaper than Canadians because shoe manufacturing requires a lot of semiskilled labor. On the other hand, Canadians can assemble automotive parts of a desired quality at a lower price than Mexicans because their labor force is better trained for that type of precise engineering. Let's further assume (unrealistically) that Canadians and Mexicans are each able to produce and consume only shoes and automotive parts—a two-commodity economy in each country.

Look at Figure 3–9.[2] If Mexico did nothing but produce shoes, it could have 240 million pairs; if it produced only automotive parts, it would have 200 million. Canada, with its resources, can produce either 360 million pairs of shoes or 400 million automotive parts. Canada has an absolute advantage because it can produce more shoes or automotive parts than Mexico. For every pair of shoes that Mexico makes it must forego .83 auto parts; in Canada, for every pair of shoes produced, Canadians are unable to produce 1.1 auto parts. These prices reflect the comparative advantages of each country. Mexico's most efficient use of resources is in shoe production; auto parts are therefore more expensive than in Canada. Canada is more efficient in producing auto parts than shoes; auto parts are cheaper than shoes in Canada because for every auto part it costs .9 pairs of shoes, but for every pair of shoes produced, 1.1 auto parts are sacrificed.

---

[2]This example is adapted from one used in Stefan H. Robock, Kenneth Simmonds, and Jack W. Zwick, *International Business and Multinational Enterprise,* rev. ed. (Homewood, Ill.: Richard D. Irwin, 1978).

FIGURE 3–9    Dual economies in Mexico and Canada.

| PERCENT OF TOTAL PRODUCTION | | MEXICO | | CANADA | |
|---|---|---|---|---|---|
| *Shoes* | *Auto Parts* | *Shoes (millions of pairs)* | *Auto Parts (millions)* | *Shoes (millions of pairs)* | *Auto Parts (millions)* |
| 100% | 0% | 240 | 0 | 360 | 0 |
| 75 | 25 | 180 | 50 | 270 | 100 |
| 50 | 50 | 120 | 100 | 180 | 200 |
| 25 | 75 | 60 | 150 | 90 | 300 |
| 0 | 100 | 0 | 200 | 0 | 400 |

"Price" of Shoes in Mexico          = .83 auto parts
"Price" of Auto Parts in Mexico     = 1.2 pairs of shoes
"Price" of Shoes in Canada          = 1.1 auto parts
"Price" of Auto Parts in Canada     =  .9 pairs of shoes

Canadians would do well to produce auto parts and trade them for Mexican shoes. This is because shoes costs only .83 auto parts in Mexico, but 1.1 auto parts in Canada. Likewise, Mexicans would like to have Canadian auto parts because the price (in shoes) is only .9. Thus, if Mexico were to trade its shoes for Canadian auto parts it would have more of both than if it tried to produce them itself. Let's assume that the Mexicans and Canadians agree to trade one pair of shoes for one automotive part. This is reasonable because both parties will benefit. Mexicans can now obtain auto parts at a cost of one pair of shoes instead of 1.2 pairs if they produce the auto parts themselves. Canadians will have one pair of shoes for one auto part instead of 1.1 auto parts. Let's assume that each country can only consume 150 million auto parts.

Now look at Figure 3–10. In order to meet demand for 150 million auto parts in each country, each country will have to produce that amount if there is no trade. Under Condition 1 (no trade), Mexico will have 60 million pairs of shoes and 150 million auto parts, while Canada will have 225 million pairs of shoes and 150 million auto parts. You should again note Canada's absolute advantage in production. However, both countries can have more shoes available for consumption if they trade with each other. Under Condition 2 (trade at 1:1), Mexico will have 90 million pairs of shoes and 150 million auto parts; Canada will have 240 million pairs of shoes and 150 million auto parts. In effect, each country has increased its standard of living by specializing in production of goods in which it has a comparative advantage and trading those goods for other products.

The example used to illustrate the law of comparative advantage was unrealistically simple: Each country could produce only two products, there were no economies or diseconomies of scale, nor were there tariffs

**FIGURE 3–10**  Benefits of trade in dual economics.

| | MEXICO | | CANADA | | TOTAL | |
|---|---|---|---|---|---|---|
| | Shoes (millions of pairs) | Auto parts (millions) | Shoes (millions of pairs) | Auto parts (millions) | Shoes (millions of pairs) | Auto parts (million) |
| *Condition 1* No trade; demand of 150 million auto parts in each country | 60 | 150 | 225 | 150 | 285 | 300 |
| *Condition 2* Trade at 1:1 and demand of 150 million in each country | | | | | | |
| Production | 240 | 0 | 90 | 300 | 330 | 300 |
| Export | − 150 | | | − 150 | | |
| Import | | + 150 | + 150 | | | |
| Amount For Consumption | 90 | 150 | 240 | 150 | 330 | 300 |

or transportation costs. These types of refinements are made by economists and politicians when determining the effects of international trade on the domestic economy and when they are developing trade regulations. However, the basic point remains: Specialization and trade can benefit all parties. Trade theory also can be used to explain and predict differences in wage rates among countries (due to relative productivities of labor forces) and differences in monetary values (due to differing amounts of resources and efficiency in use of resources).

The value of the law of comparative advantage is in predicting what products in what amounts will be entered into international trade. However, in our complex world of national protectionism, differing political ideologies, special-interest groups, and needs for national defense, actual trade patterns do not always follow the direction predicted by trade theory. Language and other cultural barriers are not taken into account by the theory. Furthermore, the theory is based on commodities trade, and not that of manufactured, branded products. It does not explain intracompany movements of goods across national boundaries, such as when Ford sends automotive parts from a plant in Michigan to another plant in Argentina for further processing.

In spite of the problems in using trade theory to predict actual trade patterns, the theory continues to be an important basis for regulating international trade. Most countries try to maximize their benefits from international trade and to minimize disruptive or negative consequences for their domestic economy. To do so, they must understand the "natural" structure of trade patterns. International marketers would also do well to select products in which their firms have a comparative advantage in production, marketing, finance, or management, for entry in foreign markets.

## Product Life Cycle of International Trade

An alternative explanation of international trade patterns and motivations is the product life-cycle model. A major advantage of the product life-cycle model over traditional trade theory is that it accounts for foreign production decisions as well as exporting and importing. Furthermore, it acknowledges the importance of advantages in technology and marketing know-how as sources of comparative advantage.

The argument of the product life-cycle model is that foreign investment and marketing decisions are a function of the evolution of a product. The introductory period for a major new product is a critical period for its sponsor. Such a firm seeks large, accessible markets and easy, quick communication with suppliers. In most cases, cost considerations are not as important as early market acceptance. Raymond Vernon, one of the proponents of the life-cycle model,[3] suggests that large markets like the United States fit these criteria. Therefore, products tend to be introduced in developed economies with large potential markets. Foreign demand is serviced by exporting, but is not a focus of the innovator's attention during this stage in product evolution.

When the product moves into the growth stage of the life cycle, the domestic market continues to be the center of marketing strategy within the industry. Even with increased competition, demand is growing in the domestic market. Maintaining or capturing a large share of the growing demand is still dependent on easy communication with buyers and improved product designs and technical refinements. Again, exports to foreign markets are peripheral to the industry, although foreign demand may be expanding at a fast rate.

In early maturity, production technology tends to become standardized within an industry. It is easier at this stage of development to transfer production to other developed economies. Simultaneously, individual firms within an industry are scrambling for ways to retain any differential advantages they might have. Foreign demand has usually expanded sufficiently to justify production in such advanced countries as Western Europe, Japan, Australia, or Brazil. The decision is often made in early maturity to produce in other advanced countries in order to protect the firm's share of

---

[3]See, for example, Raymond Vernon, "International Investment and International Trade in the Product Cycle," *Quarterly Journal of Economics*, May 1966, pp. 190–207; or, L. T. Wells, Jr., "Test of a Product Cycle Model of International Trade," *Quarterly Journal of Economics*, February 1969, pp. 152–62.

the growing foreign market and to compete more aggressively there against potential imitators and other domestic competitors.

When a product reaches the late maturity stage of the life cycle, cost efficiencies in production are a preeminent concern of producers. While production technology has become routine throughout the industry, only those firms that are efficient in production and innovative in marketing can survive the inevitable price competition. Production tends to be shifted to low-cost labor markets in the less-developed economies. These sites are used to serve growing demand in less-developed countries and the replacement markets back in the United States. Thus, production decisions are initially based on market access criteria, later on the defense of differential advantages, and finally on cost considerations. Market decisions during the life cycle are first oriented to the largest group of most likely buyers, next to foreign buyers with similar abilities to buy, and last, to markets with lower per-capita potential.

The product life cycle of trade is a fairly good explanation of U.S. firms' foreign marketing patterns. For example, John Deere, International Harvester, and other major producers of agricultural equipment have duplicated this pattern. An even more obvious example is the American electronics industry. Initially, televisions were produced in the U.S. and sold mostly to the American market. In the 1960s, American firms' sales in the U.S. peaked and they faced increased competition, in Europe and in other countries, from local producers. Production was decentralized. In the 1970s production of televisions was virtually abandoned in the U.S. and was switched to lower-cost assembly sites in Taiwan and other developing countries. These factories served demand in the U.S. and elsewhere.

The product life-cycle model of trade does not seem to be as applicable to European or Japanese firms' international marketing strategies. Volkswagen, for example, was able to produce its Beetles in Germany and still compete effectively in the U.S. automobile market. Its decision to produce in the U.S. was prompted more by U.S. tariff changes and the increased value of the German mark, than by a desire to protect its competitive position. Perhaps the greatest weakness of the product life-cycle model of trade is that it does not explain the behavior of firms with truly global product development strategies. Certainly, there are many firms today of various nationalities that plan product and market strategies simultaneously in multiple national markets.

There are other theories of international trade and international business. Direct investment theory, for example, explains capital flows from one country to another according to the marginal productivity of capital.[4]

---

[4]See, for example, Giorgio Ragazzi, "Theories of the Determinants of Direct Foreign Investment," *IMF Staff Papers*, July 1973, pp. 471–98.

Interest rate parity theory uses differentials in short-term interest rates to predict international movements of short-term capital.[5] And, the oligopoly model states that foreign investment is motivated by a firm's desire to exploit whatever quasi-monopolistic advantages it has in technologies, capital, products, management techniques, or marketing strategies.[6] All these theories contribute to our abilities to predict, explain, and monitor the dynamic world of international marketing.

## SUMMARY

Historical world trading patterns continue to affect international business today. International trade has always been used by countries to meet economic as well as political, social, or other goals. The age of economic imperialism left many countries with fears of foreign economic exploitation. Industrial development positioned the lesser-developed countries as resource suppliers to the developed countries, who in turn provided manufactured goods to the rest of the world. These fears or residuals of old trade patterns are the foundations for public policies that regulate international businesses today.

In recent times, international trade has changed in several important ways. Developed countries trade most with each other and account for the largest share of world trade. Developing countries are becoming major producers of manufactured goods, which they supply to both developed and developing countries. A growing portion of international trade includes intracompany movements of goods and services and does not always involve actual product sales. The United States is still the largest single world trader, but its position has been diminishing in recent years. We can recapture some share of world trade by increasing the diversity and destinations of U.S. exports.

The law of comparative advantage is a theoretical explanation of the motives for and nature of international trade. Its basic assumption is that production specialization and trade will generate higher world standards of living, if every country specializes in trade of the products in which it has a comparative production advantage. Comparative advantage suggests which products, and in what amounts, will be traded between countries. There are problems in using the law of comparative advantage to predict

---

[5]See, for example, Alan R. Holmes and Francis H. Schott, "The New York Foreign Exchange Market," *Federal Reserve Bank of New York,* 1965; or Peter Gray, *International Trade, Investment and Payments* (Boston: Houghton-Mifflin Company, 1979), pp. 427–32.

[6]See, for example, Richard E. Caves, "International Corporations: The Industrial Economics of Foreign Investment," *Economics,* February 1971, pp. 5–6.

actual trading patterns, but it is the basis upon which trade regulations are structured.

The product life cycle of international trade is another useful tool for understanding world markets. In the early stages of a product's life, production and marketing decisions are most influenced by the innovator's needs for access to easy transportation and communication networks and a large potential market. Later, cost considerations and access to markets in similar economies become essential to production and marketing. Ultimately, as costs of production become preeminent in location decisions, the original market in an advanced country is often served from an underdeveloped one.

## DISCUSSION QUESTIONS

1. In what ways has the role of international trade stayed the same throughout world history?
2. What is economic imperialism? How does it affect international business today?
3. Why are lesser-developed countries primarily resource suppliers for developed ones? Can you think of any exceptions to this general pattern of trade? (Use the figures in the chapter.)
4. Explain economic development.
5. How have the principal imports and exports of the countries shown in Figure 3–1, developed and developing, changed since 1979? (Use a current version of the same source.)
6. What factors have contributed to diversification of trade patterns since 1970?
7. How have trading patterns changed since 1970?
8. Why do developed countries trade so much with each other?
9. Describe why you believe centrally planned economies have increased their share of world trade since 1950 (Figure 3–4).
10. What factors will increase or decrease U.S. businesses' role in world trade in the 1980s?
11. How can U.S. participation in world trade be increased?
12. Using the basic data in Figure 3–7 on U.S. exports and imports, find out the composition of current exports and imports and discuss any trends or changes that you note.
13. Explain the law of comparative advantage. What are its strengths and weaknesses in predicting trade patterns?
14. Using the data below, answer the following questions.

| % OF RESOURCES | | XANADU | | PARADISE | |
| --- | --- | --- | --- | --- | --- |
| Baskets | Corn | Baskets *(million)* | Corn *(million bushels)* | Baskets *(million)* | Corn *(million bushels)* |
| 100% | 0% | 100 | 0 | 40 | 0 |
| 75 | 25 | | | | |
| 50 | 50 | | | | |
| 25 | 75 | | | | |
| 0 | 100 | 0 | 80 | 0 | 60 |

a) What are the "prices" of baskets and corn in each country?

b) Assuming each country needs 30 million bushels of corn, how much of each product could each country produce without trade?

c) Is a trade price of 1:1 a reasonable one? Why or why not?

d) If the two countries did trade at 1:1 and each needed the 30 million bushels of corn, how much could each have of both products if it specialized in the products of its comparative advantage?

15. Discuss whether or not the product life cycle of trade applies to the computer industry.

16. What factors influence production and marketing in different stages of the product life cycle?

# CASE 3 DERIVADOS DE LECHE SA ENTRY OF MULTINATIONALS IN A DEVELOPING COUNTRY

Derivados de Leche SA, founded in 1968, was the first firm to market yogurt in Mexico. It distributed yogurt under the brand name Delsa only in Mexico City, primarily in a limited number of upper-income areas. The company was family-owned and the capital was all local. For the first five years, Delsa was sold in food stores, particularly in the newly developing supermarkets, without any advertising or other promotion. Yogurt was a new, unfamiliar food product in the Mexican market, but Delsa depended primarily on word of mouth to provide product recognition.

During the next four years, the structure of the yogurt market changed dramatically with the entrance of three large multinational firms. In 1973, a number of laws regulating foreign investment in Mexico were modified under a single new "regulation of foreign investment" law. According to this law foreign investors were welcome in Mexico on a joint-venture basis so long as the foreign ownership share did not exceed 49 percent. Labor-intensive industries that helped to decentralize population were particularly welcome. All three of the multinationals entering the yogurt market operated on this joint-venture basis.

The first new brand, Chambourcy, was introduced by a joint-venture subsidiary of Nestlé which had operated in Mexico since 1935. This company, Industrias Alimentacias Club SA, was a major Mexican food producer with 7,000 employees. Chambourcy was launched with a strong promotional campaign and wide distribution. The following year, in 1974, a subsidiary of the French food firm, BSN-Gervais, launched their Danone yogurt in the Mexican market. Danone was also heavily supported with promotion. Finally, in 1976, a third multinational entered the market. Productos de Leche SA, which was 51 percent owned by Mexican capital and 49 percent by the Borden Company of the U.S.A.; it entered the Mexican market with two brands of yogurt, Darel and Bonafina.

By 1977, the management of Derivados de Leche SA was becoming concerned about their future position in the yogurt market. All three of the multinational competitors were aggressive marketers and promoters and were strong financially. Although the foreign ownership was a minority (49 percent), management was dominated in each case by the minority ownership, so that management was competent and professional. In the short term Delsa benefited from the primary demand creation activities of the multinationals. In 1974, Delsa sales almost doubled to 800 tons, and by 1977, it was 1,900 tons. But Delsa's market share had dropped from over

95 percent in 1972 (there were some other very small Mexican-owned competitors) to only 21 percent in 1977. The three multinationals divided 77.5 percent of the market among them. If the trends continued it was feared that Delsa's share of the market might drop so low that it would provide very little product recognition. And, it was feared that ultimately sales volume would stabilize and perhaps even decline.

By 1977, Delsa management was faced with the grim reality of competition from financially strong and aggressive, professionally managed multinationals. Although Delsa had been pulled along in the market by the initial marketing efforts which were designed to create a primary demand for yogurt, marketing efforts of the competitors were now focused almost entirely on selective brand-name promotion. Delsa management had concentrated its efforts on getting the product in retail outlets and maintaining good relationships with dealers; no effort had been made to create a consumer recognition and franchise through advertising and other promotion. Management was made up of the family members who owned the company; they brought little professional training to the job. New capital investment was needed to enlarge production capacity, and serious consideration needed to be given to investing in a promotional campaign to build and maintain Delsa brand recognition.

## QUESTIONS

1. Is the management of a small domestic firm at an advantage or disadvantage in competing with the professional management of a multinational who enters its market?
2. Would customers for a product like yogurt be likely to prefer a domestic brand or a foreign-related brand?
3. Is the local firm badly handicapped because of limited capital when competing with multinationals?

# chapter 4

# BUSINESS RELATIONSHIPS IN INTERNATIONAL MARKETING

Proctor & Gamble's *Pringles,* a form of potato chip, were an instant success when they hit Japan two years ago. Sales had soared to $50 million when suddenly Japanese customs announced a change. Pringles were dropped from the "processed foods" category, subject to a 15.5 percent import duty, and reclassified as a "confection" bearing a duty of 35 percent. Company officials complained to a joint trade committee of the U.S. Commerce Department and Japan's Ministry of International Trade and Industry. Last year, Pringles were once again listed as processed food on the customs books.

The Pringles battle is one of the rare victories won by American exporters in their effort to narrow an ever-growing U.S. trade deficit with Japan that reached $9 billion last year. American businessmen complain that they're up against formidable odds in selling to the Japanese who, they say, have devised a wide range of rules and practices designed to insulate domestic business from foreign competition. "No matter where you go in Japan," says Assistant Secretary of Commerce Frank Weil, "you find some regulation to control the marketplace, to maintain harmony in the economy."*

## INTRODUCTION

Businesses are social institutions; they have codes of conduct that are based on tradition, culture, law, and personal ethics, just as other social institutions like bureaucracies or churches have codes of conduct in the

*"Japan: Why It's A Hard Sell", *Newsweek,* May 15, 1982, p. 112. Copyright 1982 by Newsweek Inc. All rights reserved. Reprinted by permission.

same environment. The codes of conduct are not always clear and are constantly changing. Business firms themselves are agents of social change and are also affected by changes in their social and cultural environments. The codes of conduct dictate how businesses are organized as well as what a business' social obligations are. They also spell out who will be a business' managers and owners in a nation and what these persons' decision-making styles will be.

The business environment and rules for business conduct not only vary among nations, they vary from city to city and region to region. Two farmers in rural Kansas might seal a contract for $1 million by shaking hands; in New York City a $1 million deal is more likely to involve formal negotiations and a written contract. The pace and formality of business relationships in Chicago is faster and more formal than in San Antonio or Phoenix. Yet, because all these situations are American, it is easier for an American to interpret the differing rules for acceptable business behavior than it would be for a French businessperson. The cues are much harder to read when a businessperson superimposes his or her own cultural prescriptions for business activity and relationships.

International marketing managers face a difficult task. They must understand the rules for conducting business in environments quite alien to their own business environment. It is not just a question of making operations go more smoothly; it may be a prerequisite to closing the first sale in a foreign market. If the manager is not sensitive to issues such as differences in authority or decision-making styles, he or she may never make the first sale.

In this chapter we will try to alert you to some important areas where business organization and conduct vary in different countries of the world. First we focus on business structures and organization, ways in which the internal operating environment of business may differ from what you may be accustomed to. Next, we turn to the areas of business contact with external parties—competitors, partners, buyers, the general public. While it is hard to make generalizations about any of these, the examples should sensitize you to possible problems you might face in conducting business in a foreign environment. Last, we suggest some ways your firm can improve its ability to behave acceptably in foreign business environments.

## BUSINESS STRUCTURES AND ORGANIZATION

The corporate form of business ownership has been a principal factor in the increased size of business firms and the broadening scope of individual firm operations. The corporation dominates economic activity in advanced countries and in modern sectors of developing economies all over the world. Nevertheless, other forms of business organizations, such as the family firm, still thrive even in the most advanced countries. In international markets you are likely to encounter environments where the corporate form of business ownership is not the predominant one. You need to become familiar with other types of business ownership and how they can affect the way business is conducted. These firms may be your suppliers, competitors, distributors, customers, or even partners.

Even within the corporate form of business, managers and their decision-making styles differ significantly across cultures. For example, American managers tend to be ambitious, but participatory; Japanese managers are more likely to be company-loyal and use consensus decision making; Latin American managers are more authoritarian and use centralized decision making. Furthermore, the kinds of people attracted to business management and ownership are different in different cultures. These are the topics we will explore in this section.

### The Family Firm

Until the nineteenth century, when the public stock corporation appeared as a source of equity capital, friends and family resources were the limits of an entrepreneur's investment capital. Personal resources and loans remain as the way most new ventures are financed in the world. But as ongoing businesses grow and profit, they often look to outside sources of capital to finance expansion, and family firms become corporations. This process, whereby businesses change their form of ownership with growth, is not culturally universal. It requires acceptance of the corporate form of ownership as a customary form of business, and positive attitudes toward growth at the expense of entrepreneurial control.

In many countries the public stock corporation is still an anomaly. Most businesses are family-owned and operated; others are privately held corporations, products of growth in family-owned companies. The custom is to finance expansion through debt capital as opposed to dilution of ownership. This may be the case because other investors are scarce, because the country does not have an effective marketplace for buying and selling corporate stock, or because of tradition and personal preference. In some countries, only a few families control the majority of business enterprises. In others, family firms dominate certain industries, such as the Krupp's in German steel or the Rothschild's in French banking. In Mexico, the Garza-Sada family controls the major industries of Monterrey—steel, glass, and beer. These family-dominated enterprises are as professionally managed and as open to business opportunities as any public corporations. Nevertheless, control is tightly held and it may be important to know this when doing business with these companies.

Other family firms are unwilling to grow if it means that family members cannot effectively control all areas of management. Most successful small firms reach a critical point in growth where managerial skills become more important than entrepreneurial ones. Some family firms simply are not able to make this transition. Therefore, many family-owned firms remain small and conservative. Their owners want an acceptable level of income but are uninterested in further growth, or do not have the specialized skills required to adapt to growth.

The type of business with an untrained owner-manager and family employees is the one that predominates in underdeveloped countries and in less-progressive sectors of advanced economies. The international firm may be dependent on these businesses to get its products to foreign markets. Every international marketer should recognize that these firms' abilities to provide support for an integrated market strategy are limited. More training, credit, selling aids, and other services may be necessary to effectively implement market strategy. In other cases, the marketer must identify the relative power and dominance of families in business life in order to gain market access.

### Public and Cooperative Enterprises

Governments are sometimes major players in a country's business community, not as regulators but as active competitors. Government-owned organizations that act with more autonomy than agencies or ministries are called public enterprises.

There are of course many reasons why governments form public enterprises. The motive in some countries is strictly ideological and is consistent with the political philosophies of socialism or communism. In some cases the government wishes to control strategic industries such as petroleum or communications; in others, it may wish to provide industries (such as steel) that are necessary for other industrial development in the private sector. Yet another reason for direct government activity in business is to provide goods or services that may not be profitable enough to attract private investment.

It is important to understand the government's view of the purpose of public enterprises. In some situations, increasing government takeovers and ownership of businesses are preludes to socialism or communism, which would preclude all future private business activity. In other cases, public enterprises are just an accommodation to inadequacies in the private sector and they may be expected to operate just as private business would. Alternatively, public enterprises can be impossible competitors if they have access to continuing subsidies from government funds. Public enterprises are significant types of businesses in Europe and Latin America. The international marketer is likely to find them as suppliers, competitors, or buyers in many countries of the world.

Another form of business common in many countries is the cooperative. A cooperative can be buyer-owned, labor-owned, or a coalition of producers within an industry. Some cooperative businesses behave just as corporations or other businesses; others have quite distinct decision-making styles and organizational structures. For example, in Germany workers frequently participate in management decisions and sit on corporate boards of directors. In Scandinavia consumer-owned cooperatives, especially in the food industry, are active in retailing. Agricultural or producer coops are common in Europe and even in the United States.

Both public and cooperative enterprises must account to owners who may have very different interests from the owners of corporations. They are more likely to be active in management decisions and to consider the community impact of business decisions. The international marketing manager should anticipate doing business with both of these types of businesses in many foreign markets.

### Management Values

Managers throughout the world bring their own national and cultural values to their jobs. Therefore managerial values are a reflection of cultural values, beliefs, and traditions. In most countries management education consists of on-the-job training. There is no universal management "culture." The people who are attracted to or have access to careers in business come from very different backgrounds in different countries, somewhat depending on the status that business people have in each culture. The personal and career goals of managers also vary, as do their abilities or desires to advance in their careers.

Business careers have status in relation to alternatives such as careers in teaching, government, the church, farming, and so on. In countries like the United States, successful businesspersons have traditionally been accorded respect and community leadership; they are symbols of the American dream. In Latin America, careers in politics, the church, or landholding have been the historical routes to community status. Those persons who went into business were the ones to whom the traditional careers were closed (immigrants and religious minorities).[1] In Africa, service in government or politics has the highest community status for men; retailing has been considered a woman's occupation.[2] In India certain business occupations have been reserved for members of a particular caste, and in general, status is determined by caste membership not by success in business.

These examples illustrate the differing roles that business and business careers have played in different countries. It follows logically that the attraction of business careers will be proportionate to the relative status of business in society. In Japan, managers often come from the ranks of

[1]Flavia De Rossi, *The Mexican Entrepreneur* (Paris: OECD, 1975).

[2]Marvin P. Miracle, "Market Structure in Commodity Trade and Capital Accumulation in West Africa," in Reed Moyer and Stanley C. Hollander, *Markets and Marketing in Developing Economies* (Homewood, Ill.: Richard D. Irwin, 1968), pp. 209–27.

workers, who are in turn drawn from virtually all groups in the population. In the U.S., they are likely to come from business schools, available again to a broad group within the population. Managers in Europe, on the other hand, are more likely to come from elite groups. And in Latin America, they are likely to be friends or contacts of the business' owners, who are in turn part of an industrial elite. Suffice it to say that the background of managers in different countries will affect the knowledge of modern management techniques they bring to the job and their relationships with other employees.

Another difference among managers in different countries is the relative value they place on work and its relationship to personal happiness. The Japanese, for example, see work as the center of their lives; they are loyal to the companies they work for and expect to stay with one company for their entire working lives. Americans also value work as an end in itself; nevertheless, they are very willing to be mobile and to switch companies to meet personal success goals. Europeans place less emphasis on their work lives but do tend to be company-loyal. Latin Americans are more likely to value work for the income it generates and to seek intellectual stimulation in social and leisure pursuits.

These examples are by necessity stereotypes and generalizations. There are plenty of exceptions in every country to these overall value orientations, but they do provide managers with information about what to expect from their work environment. Japanese, European, and Latin American managers tend to be more patronistic than American ones—managers involve themselves in the nonwork lives of employees and the firms try to enrich employees' nonwork lives. American managers are more likely to restrict their social and nonwork relationships with co-workers.

## Variations in Decision-Making Styles

Management style results from a combination of training, personal preference, organizational structure, and cultural tradition. The broad differences in how decisions are made, even in the same company when it operates in several national environments, are often attributable to cultural influences.

A useful concept that isolates many of the ways in which culture influences managerial decision making is analysis of the relative importance of language, or verbal messages, in the communication of managers with superiors, subordinates, and peers. Edward T. Hall uses this relationship to classify countries on a continuum between high- and low-context cultures.[3] In a low-context culture, messages are direct and explicit regardless of the receiver's status relative to the sender, and words contain most of

[3]Edward T. Hall, *Beyond Culture* (New York: Anchor Press–Doubleday, 1976).

**FIGURE 4–1** Contrasts in managers' decision-making styles.

| AREA OF DECISION MAKING | U.S. FIRMS[a] | MEXICAN FIRMS[a] | JAPANESE FIRMS[b] | MIDDLE EASTERN FIRMS[c] |
|---|---|---|---|---|
| Delegation of authority | Yes; believed to be essential in increasing subordinate's capabilities | No; authoritarian style to meet needs for manager's individualism; subordinate development is not manager's responsibility | Yes; subordinate development is a primary management function; worker suggestions for improvement are sought and accepted | No; authority rests at the top, delegation depends on personal relationships |
| Participation in decision making | Yes; subordinates contribute to decisions; believed to improve motivation and performance | No; may indicate to subordinates that manager is unsure of own job; maintaining social distance is important | Yes; subordinates participate in and initiate decisions; consensus of all employees is sought | No; chain of command is rigidly followed |
| Importance of planning | High; problem solving is valued, planning is an indispensable tool for making good decisions; emphasis on short- to medium-term planning | Low; plans appear to restrict the manager's personal expression | High; planning is valued as in U.S. firms; more emphasis on long-term planning | Low; ad hoc planning |

| Emphasis in communication style | Direct and frank | Maintenance of pleasant relations; avoidance of difficult issues | Polite, respectful; patience in difficult topics | Tone depends on position, power, or family influence |
|---|---|---|---|---|
| Performance evaluations | System focus is on objective criteria and whatever will contribute to organizational effectiveness | Criticism is not viewed as constructive; evaluations are based on personality rather than performance | Employee on-the-job training and development are essential parts of job; mentor system is institutionalized; few employees are fired | Routine checks on performance but without comprehensive evaluation system; it varies from one employee to another |
| Commitment to firm's objectives | Doing well for the firm is an essential component of career success | Career success is based on personal relations with superiors | Firm's and manager's goals are one and the same; manager identifies with firm | Reluctance to take risks inherent in decision making; success dependent on contacts and being of the "right" social position |

[a]Adapted from, Eugene C. McCann, "Anglo-American and Mexican Management Philosophies," *MSU Business Topics*, Summer 1970, pp. 28–37.

[b]Adapted from William Ouchi, *Theory Z: How American Business Can Meet the Japanese Challenge.* © 1981, Addison-Wesley, Reading, Massachusetts. Reprinted with permission.

[c]Adapted from M. L. Dadawy, "Styles of Mideastern Managers," *California Management Review*, Spring 1980. Copyright 1980 by the Regents of the University of California. Adapted from Volume XXII, No. 3, pp. 51–58 by permission of the Regents.

the information to be sent. In a high-context culture, the context of the message—who is sending or receiving it, how the message will affect their relationship and the relationship with others, hidden or suggestive meanings that may be alluded to indirectly—may be more important than the words themselves. Managers in a low-context culture such as Germany or the United States may find it easier to make decisions according to objective criteria. This would of course influence their employee evaluations, their reports to superiors, as well as all their marketing decisions. Managers in a high-context culture such as the Middle East, Latin America, or Japan, are more sensitive to the impact of messages on personal relationships and the long-term significance implicit in minor operational decisions. They may also seem as interested in knowing or understanding a client's values and background as they are in negotiating a contract with the client.

There are many other ways that decision making varies in companies in different cultures. Centralized decision making is standard in Latin America and Middle Eastern firms. The Japanese are noted for consensus decision making that includes employees from the bottom to the top of a firm. Hiring and firing decisions in U.S. firms are dominated by objective qualifications and performance criteria; while European managers depend more on labor union rules to make these decisions. Figure 4–1 shows some specific ways that decision making is believed to vary in companies in different parts of the world. The differences shown are best considered tendencies rather than absolutes of decision styles. They should alert you to areas of possible misunderstanding with subsidiaries or joint venture partners, and they should provide some insight into how the internal environment of foreign firms might differ from yours.

## BUSINESS AND COMPETITIVE RELATIONSHIPS

Business organization and structure, as discussed in the last section, have a strong impact on the firm's relationships with external parties—clients, suppliers, competitors, intermediaries. When a firm's decision making is highly centralized, only top management can make external commitments of the firm's resources. Likewise, these people expect to do business only with the top managers of other companies because they are viewed as the only decision makers with the necessary authority to complete negotiations. As an example of the effects of communication style on business relations, intermediaries in Latin America might be less likely to notify an American manufacturer of problems because their style is one of maintaining pleasant relations. In Japan, competitors may compete in a more "polite" way than happens in American firms.

In this section we will focus on the variable rules of conduct for businesses and external parties. This includes an introduction to "the silent language of overseas business" and to differing views of acceptable competitive practices. We will also explore the different expectations of business responsibility to government, to consumers, to labor, and to the general public. Last we will discuss the touchy subject of business ethics in the international marketplace.

### Relationships Among Businesspersons[4]

Many years ago Edward T. Hall observed that business people had a significant number of problems in international business dealings because they were unaware of a "silent" code of conduct. He called this "the silent language in overseas business." It is not a language of words but one of subtle rules for communicating your expectations or intentions—without words—to someone else. Knowing the existence of this language can help an international marketing manager to interpret the behavior of a foreign businessperson without interjecting the manager's own cultural bias.

The first element of Hall's silent language is the language of time. We use time to say many things—a delay in response can indicate disinterest in the topic; giving someone a deadline could mean you are being overly demanding; being late for an appointment suggests the appointment may not have been important. However, these meanings are all culturally biased. In other countries being late might signify the importance of the meeting and a delay in response might be in proportion to the topic's significance. "There is a time and a place for everything" is especially true in international business. People in some countries simply will not commit until they have given the "proper" amount of time to considering a topic; and these topics may require different amounts of time in different cultures. Time simply has different meanings for people in different countries. Knowing this can keep international businesspersons from misinterpreting a foreigner's intentions.

The language of space refers to the ways we use space to communicate with each other. Americans and Scandinavians are comfortable talking business at distances of three to eight feet, and feel invaded when persons of another culture move in closer. Different situations can provoke a sense of being "crowded"—a small office with four employees may seem crowded to an American but spacious to a Latin American. We also use space to connote status; the size of our office, its location in the building, even what floor it is on, suggest the spheres of influence and authority of American managers. In the Middle East, these are poor indexes of status. It is improper to discuss business at social occasions in India but perfectly

---

[4]This section is drawn from Edward T. Hall, "The Silent Language in Overseas Business," *Harvard Business Review,* May/June 1960, pp. 87–96.

acceptable in Europe. All of these situations illustrate how the use of space says something distinct in different cultures.

The use of material possessions or the "language of things," as Hall calls it, is yet another important form of international business communication. Since we live in a socially mobile society, Americans are apt to use possessions such as cars, houses, and clothing to judge another person's status. In other countries, family ties and friendships are better indicators of status. Money is also less likely to buy loyalty in this context. High salaries or bonuses may motivate foreign businesspersons, but not for the same reasons or to the same extent as in the United States.

The language of friendships is a particularly important aspect of "the silent language." It governs our rules for who are acceptable as business partners and what our obligations are to these people. Americans have few lifetime friendships, have limited obligations to friends, and are perfectly comfortable doing business with casual acquaintances. Friendships may take longer to form and last longer in other countries. Friends may be expected to anticipate your needs—financial and other—and to do this without any expectations of reciprocity, as is the case in India. Likewise, Latin Americans and Arabs prefer doing business with friends and are less trusting of casual acquaintances. It may take years to build the necessary friendship as a precursor to business dealings. The opposite is true in the United States; business associations often develop later into social friendships.

The last element Professor Hall discusses is the language of agreements. Over and beyond legal rules for contracts, there are subtle customs that must be followed in business negotiations. Most American and European firms negotiate in order to arrive at a signed, written contract; it terminates negotiations. Arabs may value the spoken agreements of negotiators more than what is on the piece of paper. Greeks see the contract as only a beginning; each partner's obligations will be negotiated until the work is completed. Even in minor matters the language of agreements can confuse. The American who takes a cab ride in Latin America without negotiating the price first is fair game for anything the driver wishes to charge. There is an implicit understanding in some cultures that the price of services is negotiated before they are performed and bargaining afterwards is simply not allowed. All these situations indicate the dangers of cultural bias in the language of agreements: We sometimes commit ourselves when we do not know it, and in other situations, we may believe we have a commitment when we do not.

### Views of Competition

Through games we play as young children, we learn the subtle but complex rules for competition. The fact that children's games vary in different countries is a good sign that we have different views of acceptable competitive behavior in business. The inherent value placed on competition itself is often reflected in a country's laws regulating business. The importance of U.S. and European antitrust laws suggests the positive benefits we believe are derived from a freely competitive business environment. On the other hand, Japan has no such rigorous antitrust laws, but the Japanese are fierce competitors in world markets. These differences are better explained by cultural beliefs about the value of competition and what is acceptable behavior between competitors, than by laws.

Competition is viewed as wasteful of limited economic resources in some environments. In many Latin American and African countries this prevailing philosophy is seen in the protections (even licenses) that are given to limit the number of competitors in specific industries or regions of a country. Even in Europe, many industries operate as informal cartels whose members agree on pricing, market shares, and product development. Japanese firms in world competition may be aggressive, but among themselves they prefer to seek new markets rather than engage in more intense competition for current markets. "Japan, Inc." is a synonym for the cooperative relationship between business and government in Japan that goes far beyond government support of business. Through joint planning efforts, economic growth is assured by restricting the intensity of direct competition between Japanese firms; instead, their resources are concentrated to win markets from foreign competitors.

As competition for world markets intensifies, it is becoming more difficult to avoid it even where limited competitive behavior is the preferred mode of business. New competitors, especially foreign ones, and new techniques for competing, are likely to lead to cries of "foul play." Local firms in countries like Brazil and Mexico have for years accused American firms there of being too aggressive. While they were watchdogging U.S. subsidiaries, the Japanese silently but systematically, through cooperative efforts, became their most active competitors for local markets.

Firms who are accustomed to controlling prices and markets with their competitors may find it unfair for a newcomer to compete aggressively with tools like heavy promotion spending, discounting, new channels of distribution, or a continual stream of new products and improvements. In some countries, competition is based on rules similar to those in a "gentlemen's agreement," and new tactics in competition are simply not acceptable.

Some businesses may value friendships more than market growth if the two are in conflict. Long-term channel relationships may be based on such beliefs. Trying to lure away a competitor's intermediaries with financial incentives could backfire and endanger the firm's relationships with its own channel members. Friendships often lead to reciprocal deals between buyers and sellers and once reciprocity is established, competition is no longer between two sellers but is between personal relationships they have with potential buyers. Wherever friendships are considered essential to business relationships, competition will be restrained.

## Differing Roles of Business in Society

Businesses as social institutions must be responsible to different groups in society. Many of these are shown in Figure 4–2. They include consumers, labor unions, government and its agencies, the general public, and so on. The relative importance of each of these groups will not be the

**FIGURE 4–2**   Major constituencies as identified by international business.

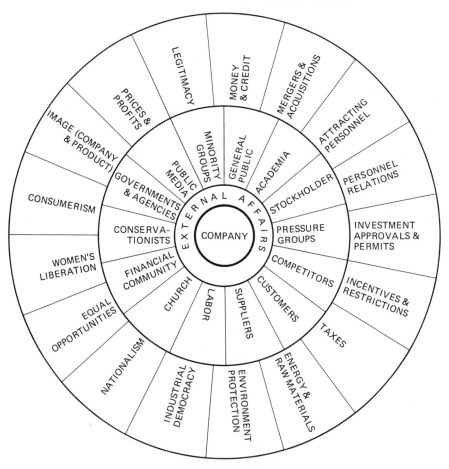

Source:   "The Management of International Corporate Citizenship," *Top Management Report.* The International Management and Development Institute and the U.S. Department of State, 1976. Bureau of Educational and Cultural Affairs (now Intl. Comm. Agency's Assoc. Directorate for Educational and Cultural Affairs).

same in different national environments. For example, in the United States and Europe environmentalists are a powerful constituency because they influence public opinion about corporations, and their lobbying efforts may determine companies' regulatory environments. In Asia and Latin America, environmentalists do not have equivalent power in their social systems. This is not to suggest that firms operating there need not be concerned with environmental issues, but any interest in the firm's safety and pollution records will likely be expressed by other social groups such as government agencies.

Government is a particularly important external party that affects everything about a business firm's operations. In Mexico, government is quite centralized and virtually all authority rests in Mexico City. As a result, the national hub of business activity is also Mexico City, in spite of many incentives to locate elsewhere. It is simply not practical for businesses in Mexico to be too distant from the important government offices with which they must interact frequently. In Japan, businesses are expected to coordinate their long-term planning with government plans for economic growth; but in the United States, government and businesses work independently at their planning tasks. Consortia of business and government executives work on industry problems in Canada and Europe, while in Latin America government-business ties are based on personal relationships. In the Middle East, government is a major source of all investment capital, while in most other countries, firms must depend on private sources of capital. Needless to say, business relationships with governments run the gamut from mutual suspicion to partnerships in a country's economic life.

International businesses must also cope with a variety of different roles for labor unions in world markets. In countries like Mexico or Argentina, labor unions have considerable political clout, and labor laws are quite protective. Firms may find they spend considerable time and money negotiating contracts in one country because labor unions are powerful or because there is a strong tradition of labor activity. In other situations, as in many European countries, labor unions expect to be included in management decisions or as members of the board of directors. The focus of a firm's interaction with labor may be over salaries, working conditions, other financial benefits, or provision of amenities to improve employees' nonworking lives. Workers in Japan are not unionized but expect more concern for their total lives than do workers in the United States. And, in some cases a business firm may find itself in the middle of demands from government (e.g. equal opportunity policies) and labor (e.g. discriminatory seniority systems). Whatever the situation, the international manager should learn what is expected in terms of the firm's interaction with labor unions in different national environments.

Buyers are another external group with whom the business firm relates. In Europe and the United States, forces of consumerism are organized, active, and cannot be ignored by either international marketers or local firms. Through their own organizations and their pressure on governments, they demand a high level of social responsibility from business firms. In some countries consumer boycotts are a frequent way in which buyer interests are expressed. Wherever consumers are active, they press for informative and truthful advertising, safe and reliable products, and honest trade practices.[5] Even where consumerist efforts are not yet organized, the public expects a higher degree of contribution to community well-being than in the past. This can take the form of more expensive product liability settlements or simply more attention to plant openings and closings and to the new products being introduced to the market. The general worldwide climate today is one of more scrutiny by the public of the social impact of business operations.

## INTERNATIONAL BUSINESS ETHICS

When developing a framework for ethical decision making in international markets, many managers are at a loss. There are few clear standards for everyday transactions at home and abroad, and the manager faces different rules. For example, in the U.S. it is acceptable to take a buyer from a private company to an expensive lunch, but not to give him or her an expensive gift. If the buyer were a purchaser for a government agency, it would not even be permissible to entertain him or her at lunch. What about tips for efficient service? We give them to waiters, even consultants, but we cannot offer a tip to a customs agent. In other countries these may not only be acceptable behaviors, they may be expected as an essential part of a business transaction.

In all situations, a marketing manager must draw on multiple sources for guidance in making ethical decisions. These are shown in Figure 4–3.[6] Law only sets the outermost parameter for ethics; a person's individual conscience and values establish the bottom line for their own personal ethics. In between, guidance can come from several sources. One of these is the individual manager's technical expertise and training. The better he or she understands marketing concepts, the easier it will be to anticipate the effects of marketing decisions. Knowledge of buyer needs and preferences gives the firm a better opportunity for buyer satisfaction. The firm's reporting structure and policy statements also help make clearer what is acceptable and what is not. An example of one company's rules for conducting foreign business is shown in Figure 4–4. The tighter a firm's financial or communication controls and accountability to top management, the less

---

[5]For more detail on worldwide consumer interests, see E. Patrick McGuire, *Consumer Protection Implications for International Trade* (New York: The Conference Board, Inc., 1980).

[6]This section is drawn from Earl Clasen, "Controlling Marketing Behavior in the Large Firm," in *Ethics in Marketing*. Minneapolis: The University of Minnesota, April 1966.

**FIGURE 4–3** Sources of guidance for ethical decision-making in international business.

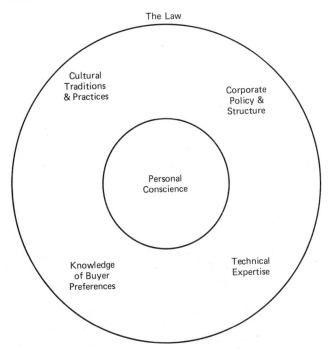

Adapted from Earl Clasen, "Controlling Marketing Behavior in the Large Firm," in *Ethics in Marketing*. Minneapolis: The University of Minnesota, April 1966.

likely it is to be surprised by questionable practices of its employees or agents.[7]

In international marketing, one of the most important sources of guidance for ethical decision making is knowledge of each country's culturally accepted business customs. For example, in many underdeveloped countries, low-level government functionaries are paid very low salaries in the expectation that the client should help pay, through tipping, for the services the employee performs. In Mexico this is called the *mordida* or *bite*; it is an accepted practice and inevitable cost of doing business there. It is simply an accepted custom in many parts of the world that performance of services is reimbursed before the service is performed—to "grease the wheel" as some people say.

On the other extreme, large payments to highly placed government officials for the purpose of acquiring favors or getting the official to "look the other way," are not condoned in any country. Over eighty-five American firms—among them Gulf Oil, Lockheed, Northrup, Boeing, and ITT—

[7]"Innocents Abroad? How a Multinational Avoids Paying Bribes Overseas—Probably," *The Wall Street Journal*, April 14, 1976, pp. 1, 16.

**FIGURE 4–4**  Conduct of business in foreign countries.

I.  POLICY

It is the policy of ABC Industries to conduct its business in foreign countries in accordance with all applicable laws and regulations of said countries. It is further the policy of ABC Industries not to seek to secure or accept business resulting from or connected with payments to officials of the government from whom the business is secured, unless the situation meets with all the conditions of Paragraph II. D. below.

II.  IMPLEMENTATION

A.  No fees, commissions or other payments are to be made to foreign organizations or individuals without a formal agreement approved by the Corporation's Comptroller, General Counsel and President.

B.  Before any commitment is made to pay a fee or commission, the identity of the proposed representative, as well as a justification for his employment, is to be provided in writing to the General Counsel's office for review.

C.  Each representation or consulting agreement involving activity in a foreign country shall be on the form specified by the General Counsel's office, which form shall contain specific provisions warranting that no portion of the fee, commission or other payment involved has been or will be paid to an official of a foreign government.

D.  Nothing in this policy shall prohibit the execution of a valid sales representation or commission agreement with an organization or individual who may be an official of a foreign government where such agreement is permitted by the laws or regulations of that foreign government and, provided, further, that the name of the representative or agent and the terms of the agreement are disclosed in writing to the appropriate entity of the foreign government involved. Such agreements shall be approved in writing in advance by the General Counsel's office.

were embarrassed in the 1970s with disclosures that they had made such payments in foreign markets. Some of the companies defended themselves by claiming the payments had been responses to extortion requests. Others argued that their competitors were willing to pay if they did not. This is undeniably true in some cases, and continues to be a problem for firms competing in world markets. What is also undeniable, however, is that such payments are not officially sanctioned and the guilty firm is likely to face negative political and media attention as a result. Political payoffs are a risky proposition and must be considered in light of possible consequences at home and abroad. The firm must also judge the cost of not making such payments when competitors will do so, and the effect is the restriction of the company's future growth.

In some countries it is legal for a business firm to make payments to directly support specific political parties. Business payments to political parties are illegal in the United States but legal in Canada. However, even where political party support by business firms is legal, the international firm should be careful. The multinational may be seen as an arm of its home country's government and its foreign policy; as a result, party support could generate negative public opinion. In 1973, ITT was discovered to have helped covert CIA operations in Chile by funding an opponent of Salvador Allende. When Allende was overthrown, ITT then came under the suspicion of governments in other countries for destabilizing activities.

Perhaps the most difficult aspect of international marketing ethics concerns the fees and commissions that are paid to a firm's agents or distributors in foreign markets.[8] Since markups, margins, and services performed by these agents vary throughout the world, there is no easy way to determine what is an "acceptable" commission. Furthermore, agents are independent businesspersons and thus a foreign manufacturer cannot as easily control what they do with their commissions, as would be possible with a sales force. And yet, in countries like Saudi Arabia firms are required to use local distributors in order to enter the market.

We conclude this discussion of international business ethics by reiterating the importance of strong auditing and financial controls as well as close communication with representatives in various parts of the world. At the least, the firm will not be surprised to learn it has participated in practices of which it disapproved.

## FITTING INTO THE BUSINESS COMMUNITY

In order to give you a feeling for the possible variations in business environments you might face in international marketing, we have committed the most serious mistake *you* could make: we have used stereotypes. For example, we have made generalizations about how American managers make decisions, about how Middle Easterners organize their firms, and about how Latin Americans tolerate bribes. It is easy to see what a mistake this can be when looking at your own culture because we are so aware of the situations that do not fit the mold. In a foreign culture however, we usually do not have as much information; thus, we find the stereotype useful as a way of making behavior meaningful. The first step in fitting into a business community is to avoid using stereotypes.

In this section we will explore two further ways in which a firm can adjust to local business practices. The first of these is cultural adaptation and it focuses on the task of identifying areas where the firm must "do in Rome as the Romans do." The second technique concerns introducing change into the foreign business community. Since the international firm is

[8]Jack G. Kaikati, "The Phenomenon of International Bribery," *Business Horizons,* February 1977, pp. 25–37.

very often a change agent in foreign markets, it must determine the most effective way to transfer ideas and processes into that environment without jeopardizing its position there.

## Cultural Adaptation

Understanding and knowledge of a country's culture as well as its business structure and codes of behavior are essential to fitting into the business community. The next chapter will discuss tools to use in cultural analysis. Business customs can be learned only through observation and experience, so it is important to use many sources of information when building knowledge of a foreign business environment. The best ones are personal visits to the country, complemented with interviews and questioning of business practitioners with bicultural backgrounds, such as home-country expatriates or other expatriates living in the country of interest. Most of us find it difficult to analyze and describe our own culture and customs with objectivity since we are unaware of differences from other cultures that would be of interest to a foreigner. Therefore, other persons or managers who have been through the processes of cultural analysis and adaptation are more sensitized to the significant differences, and are therefore an invaluable source. Some firms actually use foreign consultants more to observe their business style and contacts than for their technical expertise.

A personal visit to the country without some form of cultural interpretation can be disastrous. In that case, a manager is apt to give meaning to business behaviors that are explainable only in the context of his or her own culture. There are two things to do to reduce the possibilities of misinterpretation. One is to try to analyze situations without the manager's "self-reference criterion (SRC)."[9] There are four steps to this process.

> *Step 1:* Define the business problem or goal in terms of your own cultural traits, habits, or norms.
>
> *Step 2.* Define the business problem or goal in terms of the foreign culture's traits, habits, or norms. Make no value judgments.
>
> *Step 3.* Isolate the SRC influence in the problem and examine it carefully to see how it complicates the problem.
>
> *Step 4.* Redefine the problem without the SRC influence and solve for your optimum business goal situation.

Simply becoming aware of how your own culture affects your interpretation of foreign business customs is not enough. The international marketer must also assume an attitude of "different but equal" when adjusting

---

[9]James A. Lee, "Cultural Analysis in Overseas Operations," *Harvard Business Review,* March–April 1966, pp. 106–14.

to another country's codes of business behavior. The manager must be open to different styles of decision making and sensitive to foreign businesspersons' values and aspirations. While it is almost impossible not to make comparisons across cultures, it is defeating to make value judgements. The international marketer requires curiosity, openness to change, flexibility, and respect.

Knowledge and understanding of foreign business customs lead to the next stage of cultural adaptation. This stage requires development of a style for fitting into the community. It means deciding which customs of the host country the firm must adopt, which ones the firm should not adopt, and which ones it will choose to adopt. These are called cultural imperatives, exclusives, and adiaphora.[10] Cultural imperatives are behaviors that foreigners must adopt in order to be accepted into a foreign business community. For example, in the United States, Latin American businesspersons must be prompt for appointments or their American counterparts will not view them as dependable. Culturally exclusive behaviors are reserved for citizens; if a foreigner were to adopt them it would offend persons of that culture. For example, Christians should not participate in the Muslim prayers toward Mecca that might take place in the middle of a meeting; to do so would not be appropriate. In between imperatives and exclusives, the firm and its management will find cultural adiaphora—behaviors that are not necessary to adopt but are helpful in reducing the firm's "foreign" profile. When deciding which customs to conform to and which ones not to adopt, the manager must look to the firm's market goals, the possible effects on communications within the firm, and to how these behaviors will affect his or her own managerial effectiveness.

### Introducing Change: Technology Transfer

Most international firms derive their competitive advantages in foreign markets from their ability to introduce something new—new products, new organizational styles, new management or marketing techniques, or new production processes. The simple introduction of anything new to another culture is a transfer of resources to that culture, but the effects of those resource or technology transfers are not always clear or initially beneficial to the recipient culture. As a result, the international firm must develop a plan for introducing change.

There are three areas that receiving countries are concerned about when new ideas, products, or technologies are transferred to them via international businesses. The first of these is the cost of the transfer; in other words, the direct effects of the transfer in terms of foreign exchange, employment, income, exports, or productivity. The second issue centers

[10]Philip R. Cateora, *International Marketing,* 5th ed. (Homewood, Ill.: Richard D. Irwin, 1982), chap. 5.

around the appropriateness of changes or technologies in relation to the economic, social, or cultural structure of the country. In recent years many lesser-developed countries have begun to take a closer look at their own import substitution policies because they may have encouraged capital-intensive development in economies that are rich with unskilled but umemployed labor. They are questioning whether such production techniques are appropriate. The third concern of recipient countries is the indirect effects of business technologies on social, cultural, and political institutions. They may resist adoption of modern management methods, for example, if that will disrupt social or political ties.

It is important to understand these concerns because they form the basis on which an international firm's contributions to the local community are judged. Specifically, the firm's contributions are its products, organization structure, management style, production techniques, and other know-how. If such changes are resisted because members of the business or political community do not recognize their potential contribution, then the international firm will be ineffective in that environment. What is necessary is recognition of the impact that changes will have and a plan for disseminating information about their possible benefits.

## SUMMARY

In this chapter we have reviewed some of the ways in which business customs and practices vary throughout the world. Business activity does not have the same rewards or status in different cultures. This affects both internal and external relationships of businesses and managers.

Business ownership in many countries is dominated by family firms; in others, public or cooperative enterprises are important in economic life. Managers themselves bring to their jobs many culturally influenced values that affect their own managerial styles and the importance they place on jobs and careers. Values also determine the relationships that managers have with others in business organizations.

Culture and accepted business customs are the source of rules for business behavior when dealing with external parties. Competition is encouraged in some countries and restrained in others, depending on the perception of the benefits of free competition. Competitive intensity depends on varying views of acceptable styles of competition. Rules for interaction between businesspersons are often written in a silent language by which we communicate our purpose or intentions to others. The ways in which we use and interpret time, space, material possessions, friendships, and agreements comprise this silent language. There are also different expectations of business' responsibility to buyers, government, labor unions, and the general public in different countries. Likewise, what are considered acceptable ethics in one environment may not be acceptable in others. International firms have particular difficulty with political payoffs and payments to sales agents.

Last, the firm must assess its local environment and develop a strategy for "fitting in." It must understand and accept foreign ways of doing business, as well as decide which customs it will adopt. It will also need to estimate the impact of the changes it introduces on a foreign business environment; it can then present those changes in a manner that is acceptable and beneficial to the local community.

## DISCUSSION QUESTIONS

1. Why does a firm's business environment vary from country to country? Why is it more difficult to analyze the business environment in a foreign country?
2. Explain how family-owned firms are likely to differ from public corporations.
3. How can association with family-owned firms in an underdeveloped country affect a firm's international marketing strategy?
4. Why do governments form public enterprises to compete with private firms?
5. How do public and cooperative enterprises vary from corporations in goals and community relations?
6. How do cultural values affect the attractiveness of business careers?
7. Show how American and Japanese business managers are each influenced by their own cultural values with respect to career patterns and decision-making styles.
8. Explain how the differences between low- and high-context cultures affect decision making in business firms.
9. Why is the "silent language of overseas business" silent?
10. Review situations which you feel illustrate the relative importance of time and space in your own environment.
11. How can the "language of agreements" cause misunderstandings in international business?
12. Discuss how differing views of acceptable competitive behavior might impact on an American firm's attempts to develop markets in Japan, Venezuela, and Italy.
13. Using Figure 4–2, point out several issues that would be important to each of a business firm's constituencies. How might these issues differ in different countries?
14. Define a bribe.

15. Evaluate the strengths and weaknesses of the company's ethical policies shown in Figure 4–4.

16. Explain why commission payments to independent sales agents or distributors can cause ethical problems for the international firm.

17. Develop a set of guidelines for a firm wishing to adjust to its local business environment.

18. Define cultural imperatives, exclusives, and adiaphoras. Give an example of each for your own culture.

19. Why do countries resist new technologies?

# CRAWFORD ENTERPRISES:
# WHEN IN ROME
# DO AS THE ROMANS DO,
# BUT
# NOT IN THE UNITED STATES

In October 1982 the United States Justice Department brought action against Crawford Enterprises and Gary Bateman, former marketing vice-president of Crawford Enterprises, for bribery and corruption of two PEMEX officials. PEMEX is a petroleum production and distribution monopoly owned and operated by the Mexican government. The indictments charged that the parties involved had obtained purchase orders from PEMEX through payoffs to officials of the Mexican oil monopoly.

While such action is not legal, Mexico's political and business infra-structures have permitted monetary "subsidies" to influence and/or dictate transactional decision-making. Known as the "mordida" or "bite", public corruption has permeated throughout all socio-economic levels, becoming a "way of life" among Mexicans. Since bribes are effected in various forms, no country is immune to their existence. In Mexico, however, payoffs are conducted more openly—a catalyst for prompt, assured action.

While corruption has been over-emphasized as the cause for Mexico's current state of the economy, the new administration in 1983 was striving for a "moral renovation" which would include an attempt to reduce waste and political graft.

Late in 1981, Gary Bateman, former Marketing Vice-President of Crawford Enterprises of Houston, Texas, pleaded guilty to making payoffs totaling $342,000 US in bribes to Guillermo Cervera, Administrative Secretary to the Chief of Purchasing at PEMEX.

When fired from Crawford Enterprises on February 9, 1979, Bateman opened his own business—Applied Process Products Overseas, Inc. with the idea of transacting business with PEMEX. Bateman had offered to pay Cervera 30% of Applied's gross profit in exchange for assistance in obtaining business. Cervera presumably agreed and became "administrator and handler" of the money, which would be divided with other PEMEX officials. Bateman's company obtained approximately $5 million dollars in purchase

This case was prepared by Carol G. Spindola

orders from PEMEX until March 1981, when Bateman signed a cooperating agreement with the U.S. government bribery investigation in return for minor offense charges.

However, the U.S. government stated that while Marketing Vice-President at Crawford Enterprises, Gary Bateman handled company dealings with PEMEX and usually carried large amounts of currency from Houston to Mexico City. This led to further investigation and in October of 1982, the U.S. Justice Department alleged that a bribery scheme was set up by Crawford Enterprises paying $10 million in bribes to two former PEMEX officials to secure orders for gas-compression equipment totaling $225 million between June 1977 and March 1979. The U.S. government contends that Crawford Enterprises funneled cash to a Mexican intermediary company, Grupo Industrial Delta, to be passed on to the PEMEX officials.

Crawford Enterprises Inc., has been accused of representing the additional interests (in submitting bids to PEMEX) of Solar Turbines International, a subsidiary of Caterpillar Tractor Co., and Ruston Gas Turbines Inc., a subsidiary of General Electric England, Ltd. However, Crawford Enterprises has denied any wrongdoing in connection with the allegations.

The Mexican government formally charged and subsequently dismissed three PEMEX officials for accepting the over $342,000 in bribes from the U.S. firms.

## QUESTIONS

1. Is bribery the same thing as corruption? A bribe is defined as "money or favor given or promised to a person in a position of trust to influence his judgement or conduct; something that serves to induce or influence." Corruption is defined as "the impairment of integrity, virtue or moral principle; morally degenerate and perverted."
2. Do businesses bribe "corrupt" governments or are business representatives "corrupt" when they attempt to bribe? How should we describe the party receiving the bribe?
3. How are ethics established and whose ethics prevail in a foreign environment?
4. Who is the guilty party in the Crawford-PEMEX case, and why? Can Bateman's actions be justified?
5. Must foreigners comply with local customs or can traditional business practices be challenged? Consider the historical roles of U.S. marketers as "change agents" in foreign markets.
6. What is considered bribery in the United States? Are U.S. business/political practices more "ethical" than those of Mexican businesses? Explain.
7. If you were a marketing manager competing for foreign contracts worth millions of dollars in sales, what would your ethical parameters be?

# chapter 5

# THE SOCIAL-CULTURAL ENVIRONMENT FOR INTERNATIONAL MARKETING

American companies are giving new attention to international communications, no longer taking for granted that either their executives or their marketing campaigns are going to be automatically understood in foreign countries.

International faux pas can be costly and embarrassing. General Motors could not have been excited to learn that one of its most successful models, the Nova, translated in the Spanish-speaking market as "it doesn't go."

Friedl Scimo, the Austrian-born director of St. Louis Languages Services, says that such errors occur because Americans assume that a product is a product, and that patterns of thought carry over from one language to another. She recalls translating a shoe company's slogan into German:

"Obviously, the marketing department of that company overlooked the fact that advertising copy is highly psychological. Unless you understand how the people of a particular country think, you cannot attempt to sell them anything. It is perfectly all right to market your product in the United States as 'the fashion shoe.' But to a German the word fashion implies flimsiness and poor quality. And Germans hate anything that sounds flashy or gimmicky. I don't mean to suggest that Germans are not concerned with being fashionable, but to a German the most important thing is quality. So I had to convince the marketing director at the shoe company that what he needed was not a translation of his ad but an ad that was suitable for the German market."*

*Williams, Lorna V., "Around the World in 80 Phrases," *American Way*, November 1981, p. 97. Reprinted by permission of *American Way*, inflight magazine of American Airlines, copyright 1981 by American Airlines.

"If the Japanese removed every barrier tomorrow, we'd still have a very hard time selling over there."

Wham-Bam Business: For one thing, would-be exporters to Japan have a habit of making embarrassing mistakes. A few weeks ago, a delegation of buyers arrived from Japan to comb the U.S. for goods to import. One buyer was offered doormats by a salesman who apparently was unaware that the Japanese remove their shoes before entering a house. For another, in the words of Commerce's Frank Weil, Americans are "a wham, bam, thank you Ma'am kind of people." They can be too impatient to take the time for satisfactory arrangements. When Frigidaire began selling refrigerators in Japan, for example, the company refused to fit them with converters for Japanese electric current. And some manufacturers have assumed that because Japan's products are sometimes cheap, the Japanese must want cheap products. On the contrary, many exporters have found that their high-priced items—like Wilson golf clubs at $1,000 for a set of items—are the brisk sellers.**

## INTRODUCTION

People who live in different societies or cultures are different from each other in many easily recognizable ways. All you need to do is see or hear Englishmen, Scotsmen, Australians, and Americans to recognize how different and easily identifiable each of these groups can be. Even though some individuals from the United States may be more like Englishmen than other Americans, the average American is different from the average Englishman. These differences are obvious even among these four groups with their common language and racial heritage; differences are even more marked when comparing Americans with Frenchmen or Japanese. Yet, individuals of French or Japanese heritage who are born and raised in the United States have most of the same behavior patterns as other Americans.

Cultural and social behavior patterns are not inherent: they are learned behaviors.[1] Yet they are just as important in governing the behavior of people as are inherited traits. Culture determines what we see and feel. It explains why the Japanese prefer different cuisines from the French, why the Arabs conduct their business affairs in a different manner from the Chinese or Europeans, and why Italians dress differently from Indians or Pakistanis. Since large portions of human behavior are culturally influenced, most of our consumption behavior is also culturally influenced. Marketing strategy attempts to understand and influence consumption patterns. International marketers need to know what elements in a culture

**"Japan: Why It's a Hard Sell," *Newsweek,* May 15, 1982, p. 115. Copyright 1982 by Newsweek, Inc. All rights reserved. Reprinted by permission.
[1]Edward T. Hall, *Beyond Culture* (New York: Anchor Books, 1977), pp. 15–17.

have the greatest influence over consumption behavior in general and consumption of their type of product specifically. It is also important for marketers to understand the extent to which they may be able to generalize about the effect of particular cultural patterns across cultures. Measuring cultural similarities and differences are then the task of the international marketer.

## ELEMENTS OF CULTURE

Culture is defined as a group of people's learned responses to various stimuli. This interrelated set of responses is not innate; it is acquired through association with other members of the culture. Although different cultures may share many characteristics in common, each culture possesses unique traits that set it apart and allow it to be identified as a separate culture. The essence of any culture can be seen in a number of important factors that interact to determine cultural patterns. They include language, religion, cultural institutions, class structure, aesthetics, and social patterns.

### Language and Culture

Language, as the primary means of communication between civilized people, is perhaps the most important single cultural input. Language is the medium we all use to make meaning from environmental stimuli. Clumsy or careless language-use may result in inaccurate communication. Translation of ideas from one language to another must be done with great care to insure an ungarbled transmission of ideas. The nuances of meaning for particular words may vary from language to language, and a literal translation may change the entire meaning. For example, the verb *love* in English can mean a strong preference or actual love. In many languages, only the second meaning applies. So an advertisement in English reading "I love Krispy Krunchy cereals," when literally translated into French or Spanish means "I am in love with Krispy Krunchy cereal."

One of the most quoted examples of such confusion relates to the famous old General Motors motto "Body by Fisher," which was translated into several languages as "Corpse by Fisher." (See other translation blunders in Figure 5-1.)

Marketers who find it necessary to communicate in a foreign language should make use of a truly bilingual interpreter who will make certain that the meaning is not lost in translation. It can be dangerous for people with an elementary knowledge of a foreign language to act as their own interpreter. They can miss subtle meanings in written correspondence that may affect interest in a product, or even a possible sales contract. The same kind of traps exist in oral communication. Spanish-speaking businessmen were not amused by the American attempting to greet them with "Good

**FIGURE 5-1**    Examples of translation blunders.

| | |
|---|---|
| "Body by Fisher" | "Corpse by Fisher" (Flemish) |
| "Come Alive with Pepsi" | "Come out of the grave with Pepsi" (German) |
| Braniff's 747 Rendezvous Lounge | Braniff's 747 "Meet-your-Mistress" Lounges (Portuguese) |
| Exxon's Engros fertilizer | Exxon's "in bulk" Fertilizer (French) |
| "Accessories for the closet" | "Accessories for the toilet" (British) |

day, gentlemen" *(Buenos días, caballeros)* but who actually said "Good God! Horses" *(Buenos Dios, caballos).*

Language has a subtle role in our lives. It directs our thinking and constrains us. Linguists emphasize the predominance of action verbs in English (especially American English) as compared to other languages. Far-eastern languages are comparatively rich in terms to describe abstract concepts and philosophies. Spanish-speakers are able to draw from a rich vocabulary of terms to present ideas without revealing the speaker's true feelings. These examples serve to illustrate the difficulty of expressing equivalent ideas in different languages. The more alike languages are (such as the Romance or Chinese families of languages), the more likely are the peoples of those related languages to "think" in similar ways. If our vo-cabulary does not allow us much latitude in expressing certain concepts, we are not likely to engage in such "thoughts." The point is that language reflects our cultural priorities.

Differences in language usage among cultures does not only apply when the languages are different. The English language has different word usages and subtly different meanings in different English-speaking coun-tries. Words that may be innocuous in Great Britain may have different, even offensive meanings in the United States. Examples are "to throw up a cake," (to make a cake), and "to knock you up," (to knock on your door). At the same time, Americans use words such as "closet" and "bloody" in an entirely different manner than the British. The same kinds of misinterpretations take place with French-speaking countries such as France, Belgium, Switzerland, and Canada; or with Spanish-speaking countries such as Spain, Mexico, Argentina, and Peru.

The international marketer should be aware of the obvious differ-ences in language as well as the more subtle influence it has on thinking and cultural identities. In Chapter 8, we discuss the back-translation method—a useful tool in ensuring that written messages are equivalent in meaning when translated into another language.

## Religion and Culture

Religion establishes moral codes and taboos for the behavior of its adherents, and consumption behavior is one such aspect. Particular reli-gions may frown upon some kinds of business practices or certain types of consumption. For example, Moslems are prohibited from drinking alcoholic beverages or eating pork; Jews are prohibited from eating pork or shellfish; and Brahmin Hindus are prohibited from eating meat. Other activities affected by particular religions include social behavior, manner of dress, ways of doing business, and relations between people. The major religions of the world vary considerably between, and even within, cultures, and their impact on each culture may vary accordingly. There are many variations within the Moslem religion, the Hindu religion, the Jewish religion, and the Christian religion. Even within denominations, the variations can be great. The Roman Catholic church in Latin America, in French Quebec, and in Italy varies significantly in the kinds of influence it exerts over its members. The marketer must keep these differences in mind when planning a marketing strategy that may affect or be affected by the church in any of these markets.

Not only does religion establish taboos and moral standards within a culture, it also reflects the principal values of a people. Social mobility and the achievement ethic in the West are supported by the Christian values of self-determination and the importance of work. The Hindu religion emphasizes reaching Nirvana through a combination of inherited status and a contemplative life. It is no surprise then that many Indians continue to recognize family as a source of status and do not emphasize personal achievement in "worldly" activities. Furthermore, religion can be expressed through institutions, such as the church, or through secular and noninstitutionalized value systems. The moral values of a culture derive from a combination of these sources, and they may be in conflict or in concert. The difference between two cultures (the U.S. today and the U.S. of 1900) may lie in the relative dominance of one or more of the sources of principal values, institutional or secular.

## Cultural Institutions

Each culture develops institutionalized bases for determining the relationships between individuals in their day-to-day lives. The international marketer needs to know these relationships in order to understand and predict buyer behavior. These institutions include the family, the educational system, the influence and place of peers and peer groups, and the role of women in society.

*The role of the family.*    The family is an important social institution in any society. It always has responsibilities for nurturing small children and passing on to them some of the values of that society. In primitive and/or rural societies, the family is the all-important social focal point, providing food, clothing, shelter, education and acculturation, and a social center. In some of the more-sophisticated urban societies, the family may provide little more than food and basic acculturation. All other activities have been partially or totally transferred to other groups, especially peers and educational institutions. In such societies, when both parents have full-time jobs, even meals at home may be restricted to the evening meal, and much of this may be prepared and brought in ready-to-eat. Clothing and housing are purchased from outside sources. Education, entertainment, and even much of acculturation come from outside media, either in the home (radio and television) or outside of the home (in schools and through peers). In modern societies, the family has less influence over buying decisions than in the traditional society, and marketing strategies must be adjusted accordingly. The traditional areas of important family influence are in transmitting saving-versus-spending ethics and in establishing the importance of consumption as it reflects personal goals and status. In the traditional family, there are also likely to be more influences and consumption role-modeling via the extended family—multigenerations of consumers who learn from each other.

*The educational system.*    Every culture devises some way to transmit its important values to the young. This is the major thrust of its educational system, although it is also intended to prepare persons for roles to be assumed within that society. The educational "system" itself may take many forms. In the industrialized world, it is synonymous with schools. In some African countries, however, schools are more often limited to the role of preparing students for lives in the modern world. Elders and oral historians transmit traditions and values to young people in those cultures. Whatever form the educational system takes, it has a significant impact on the international marketer.

Formal education through schools has a strong relationship to literacy levels within a society. In those countries where schools are provided for the broadest possible group, literacy levels tend to be highest. Compulsory education in the U.S. generally requires completion of at least the eighth grade; in other countries, such as Mexico, it requires only completion of primary grades. Well-educated persons tend to want more sophisticated information about products and tend to use more sources of information when making purchase decisions. The marketer is severely limited in communicating with a market when literacy is low.

Even within industrialized countries, the role of schools as part of the cultural education system varies. In Western Europe, university education continues to be reserved for the social elite and the exceptionally bright members of society. In contrast, by 1985 over 40 percent of adult Americans will have some university education. In some countries, schools are the responsibility of the church and, as you might expect, in such a system there is relatively more emphasis on transmitting the values of society than on providing the individual with skills. In communist countries, schools are the major means of indoctrinating the people with socialist values; schools are a medium for propaganda. Even within the U.S., schools are assuming an increasing role as "transmitters" of cultural values, as the church and the family decline in importance. In all these cases, it is important for the marketer to understand the nature of the formal educational system, to whom it is available and at what levels, its relative importance in transmitting cultural values compared to other institutions, and its philosophical purpose.

*Peers and peer groups.*   The peer group includes persons with whom an individual has regular contact. Peers can be co-workers, friends, fellow-students, neighbors, members of athletic groups (tennis, aerobic dance, surfing, hiking), or social groups (bridge clubs, gourmet cooking clubs, Bible study, professional associations), to name a few. These types of reference groups have the strongest influence on consumption patterns in sophisticated and urban societies, and especially for products that are visible when consumed (automobiles, clothing, beverages). In less-sophisticated societies, the relevant peer groups may be limited to the family, church, and close friends. The important characteristic of peer groups to remember is that they sanction consumption behavior through group acceptance or approval and they illustrate appropriate life styles.

*The role of women.*   The role of women varies widely from society to society. In some cultures women are little more than chattel owned by men; in others they may have dominance over many or all facets of life. Women are not allowed to drive in Saudi Arabia, but they are the dominant merchants in public markets. The marketer is particularly interested in the amount of influence women exert over economic factors. Women affect the economic environment both as workers and as consumers. In those societies where women work primarily in the home, they contribute only indirectly to family buying power by making the things (like clothes) which, if purchased, would decrease family buying power. However, even in these societies, women may have a particularly important role as the family purchasing agent in consumption decisions and actual buying. In societies where women are a part of the paid labor force, they contribute to total family purchasing power, but their dominance over family buying decisions may actually be reduced because they do not have the time to be the specialized family purchasing agent. In designing any marketing strategy, it is necessary to start by identifying the prospective buyer and learning what factors or persons affect his or her buying decisions.

## Class Structure and Social Mobility

Every society has a class structure which relegates individuals to different levels of social status and power. Even the communist societies, which describe themselves as "classless societies," actually have a class structure with the party elite at the top, professionals, artists, scientists, and managers at the next level, and the proletariat at the bottom. American society is usually described as a three-class-level society, divided into upper, middle, and lower,[2] with identifiable differences in the consumption patterns of each class. One area where this is particularly noticeable is in housing and home furnishings. Members of each class generally live in different types of homes and purchase different kinds of home furnishings. And these differences are not simply explainable in terms of the difference in level of income between the classes. Lower-class (blue-collar) families in the U.S. often have as high an income as middle-class (white-collar) families, but the lower-class families spend less money on housing and home furnishings. These class differences apply in a great many consumption categories. The types of food and alcoholic beverages consumed, the kind of clothing worn, the kind of entertainment pursued, all vary widely among the classes in the United States.

One notable characteristic of class structure in the United States, however, is social mobility. Persons born and raised in the so-called working class can easily move into the middle class via education and occupational achievements. In India, class structure is less fluid; a person's inherited class determines the educational and occupational opportunities he or she might have. The kinds of things one owns are much more likely to be different across social classes in India than in the United States.

The degree of social mobility is generally highest in Western democracies, such as the United States, where the rags-to-riches tradition describes the opportunity for lower-class individuals to move upward in society. The degree of social mobility is important to the marketer of products that are visibly consumed in public. In socially mobile societies, people's social status is often measured at least to some extent by where they live, what they wear, what kind of car they drive, and what clubs they join. Depending on the degree of social mobility in each society, the same product might require a different marketing strategy to succeed in different markets.

Not only is social mobility an important dimension of class structure, but the relative size and number of distinct classes within a society is also significant. Figure 5–2 illustrates five different societies in terms of the relative sizes of different social classes (the top rectangle shows the size of the upper class relative to middle and lower classes for each society in the figure). As Ernest Dichter has noted, upper classes in almost all countries

[2]In an attempt to describe American society more precisely, W. Lloyd Warner divided each of the three classes into an upper and lower, resulting in six class levels. This structure is more precisely descriptive, but it makes it more difficult to draw the dividing line between individuals. See W. L. Warner and P. S. Lund, *The Status System of a Modern Community* (New Haven: Yale University Press, 1942), pp. 88–91; and for consumption patterns, see Robert D. Hisrich and Michael P. Peters, "Selecting the Superior Segmentation Correlate," *Journal of Marketing*, 38 no. 36 (July 1974), pp. 60–63.

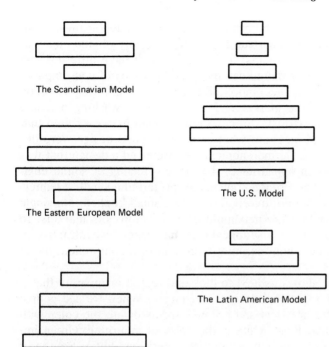

**FIGURE 5–2** Class structure in different societies.

seem to be more similar to each other than they are to the rest of their own society. Lower classes tend to be more culture bound; that is, they are less aware of other cultures or of these cultures' solutions to the problems of life. They are, therefore, more distinct from each other in the ways they dress, the food they eat, and how they spend leisure time and discretionary income. Middle classes are more apt to do cultural "borrowing" when there is some social mobility from lower to middle class and within the middle classes. Therefore, the larger the upper and middle classes, the more likely a market is to buy products and services that are not culture bound—food, clothing, household items, personal care products.[3]

### Aesthetics and International Marketing

Aesthetic values or preferences in the arts, music, and design, vary widely among societies. These are the areas of cultural difference that are often most noticeable to the casual observer. The Japanese have different preferences in art and design, music, and cuisine than do Americans.

[3]Ernest Dichter, "The World Customer," *Harvard Business Review*, 40, no. 4 (July–August 1962), pp. 113–23.

Americans often feel Japanese homes are "barren," while Japanese comment on the sterility of the American home. It is equally obvious that Indians, Chinese, Russians, Germans, and Spaniards all have differing aesthetic values that affect their day-to-day living and patterns of consumption. Even between cultures that seem more alike than these, differing aesthetic values are important to the marketer. For example, a washing machine manufacturer serving the British, French, and German markets found that the generally accepted ideas about what constitutes good design were different in each market. The German homemaker preferred a design that was larger and more sturdy in appearance, that gave a feeling of sound engineering and durability. The French homemaker preferred a smaller, lighter-appearing machine that did not overly dominate a small kitchen. No single compromise design would allow maximum penetration in both markets. In the same way, a visual advertising appeal that may seem very attractive to potential buyers in some countries, may seem dull or incomprehensible in other cultures.

Since our culture shows us how to look and feel, it is apparent that it shapes our tastes for art, color, design, and music. When we see people dressed in black, westerners feel sad because we associate the color with mourning. In the Middle East, white is the color of mourning. Green implies things that are cool and natural to most Americans, but in Southeast Asia it is most associated with the dangers of the jungle. Music from other cultures often sounds discordant or monotonous. In Japan, workers begin each day singing the "company song" in unison. Can you imagine an "IBM" song? Even cities and buildings are planned to reflect a culture's aesthetic preferences. Christians expect a church to have a certain form and we have used this same form worldwide, to the consternation of other peoples throughout the world. The international marketer must be sensitive to cultural preferences for aesthetics in design of products, packages, promotion, logos, brand names, symbols, company buildings, and in the use of music.

Modern communication has increased the understanding and appreciation of aesthetic values from other cultures in most parts of the world. A variety of ethnic restaurants are found in almost any major city, and these restaurants are patronized as a welcome novelty or change of pace. However, the impact of these foreign foods upon the basic cuisine of each society is generally very small. Aesthetics of other cultures are viewed as a source of cultural enrichment but not as agents of change. In the long run, aesthetic values may be changed through contact with other cultures, but in the short run they change hardly at all.

### Social Patterns

A society dictates how its members should behave in many kinds of personal relationships. A pattern of traditions and rules of behavior evolve in each society, and people who ignore these rules are considered naive, crude, or uncaring. These patterns of social usage vary from society to society, but they all have the common purpose of facilitating and structuring communication between individuals.[4]

In American society, separate sets of relationships have developed for business and social situations, and the levels of acceptable behavior vary widely in the two kinds of situations. Americans wouldn't think of telling social acquaintances that they disliked them, their taste in clothing, or their homes. Yet in business relationships the same individual would "tell it like it is" with no embarrassment at saying the product is inferior, service is below par, or the price is too high. In social situations Americans would consider it very rude to admit a dislike for the people involved, or to state the fear of boredom as the reason for avoiding a relationship or an invitation; instead they would consider it more polite to plead a prior engagement. Yet these same people, in a business situation, would not hesitate to say, "No, I don't want to do business with you."

In many societies the rules of social usage are the same in all personal relationships, whether of a business or personal nature. The Arab businessperson may apply the same rules of hospitality to a business caller as to a visiting friend. Japanese businesspersons consider it impolite to flatly turn down a business proposal; instead they merely suggest that there are too many difficulties. Latin American businesspersons would not think of hurrying a business deal any more than they would think of hurrying a conversation with a friend. Foreign businesspersons must adjust to local rules of social usage if they expect to compete successfully in the local market; otherwise, they may be perceived as boors. For example, continuing to try to close a deal with a Japanese businessperson who has suggested "difficulties" would be perceived by the Japanese as tantamount to trying to force a social relationship with an individual who has tactfully shown a lack of interest.

## PATTERNS OF CULTURAL INFLUENCE

Sociologists and anthropologists have developed a rich body of knowledge which helps to explain how culture affects members of a society. Studies among primitive and sophisticated societies have identified patterns of behavior that make it possible to predict the actions of individuals in a specified situation. However, this information is based mostly on intracultural analysis; there is very little cross-cultural behavioral theory. We may be able to predict how individuals will react to certain situations in Samoa, how individuals will react to other situations in Japan, or how individuals will react to still different situations in Spain, but we have little evidence

[4]Susan Douglas and Bernard Dubois, "Looking at the Cultural Environment for International Marketing Opportunities," *Columbia Journal of World Business,* Winter 1977, p. 103.

to help us predict how individuals will react to the same situation in all three cultures.

The lack of cross-cultural behavioral theory makes it necessary for the marketer to analyze each cultural situation in which he or she wishes to sell products almost from scratch. The first step in such an analysis should be to evaluate the general sociological climate toward business, foreigners, and new products. Measures of such a climate are national ideology, views toward foreigners, the nature and extent of nationalism, and attitudes toward and the process of diffusion of innovations.[5]

## National Ideology

The national ideology represents the way the citizens of a particular country think about and react to various stimuli. We can frequently predict how the typical Frenchman, Irishman, or Italian will act in certain situations. Even though all three of these countries are predominantly Roman Catholic, the Irishman will react much more strongly to infringements on the role of the church than will the Frenchman or Italian. The French have a much stronger sense of national pride and unity than the Italians or the Irish. As a consequence they are less willing to substitute a foreign-made product for a French product, at least in areas that reflect national expertise. Thus, after the initial development of the atomic bomb in the United States and Russia, France was the only European nation that felt the need to develop and test its own bomb. And, France produces its own armaments and munitions to a much larger extent than other neighboring nations.

Economic philosophy is an important element in national ideology. Sweden has a strong national commitment to socialism and has for several decades permitted greater and greater government involvement in business and economic affairs. Such massive governmental involvement in economic affairs has been resisted in the United States in recent years, and would be in other countries operating under a capitalistic ideology. Yet the American ideology is strongly opposed to restriction of free competition and monopoly, and Americans submit willingly to government controls aimed at protecting competition. Sweden sees nothing wrong with monopoly per se and does relatively little to control it.

The national ideology is strongest and most consistent in countries that have a long cultural identity. There is a strong, easily identifiable national ideology in a country like Egypt, which, even though it has not consistently had political independence in recent centuries, possesses a long and consistent cultural history. However, some of the newer black nations in central Africa have not had separate identities long enough to have de-

---

[5]See R. N. Farmer and B. N. Richman, *International Business: An Operational Theory* (Homewood, Ill.: Richard D. Irwin, 1976), pp. 109–27.

veloped strong national ideologies. Instead, different subgroups within these nations reflect the ideologies of the subgroups or tribes from which they descend.

Even in countries with strong national ideologies, these ideologies represent a general cross-section or average. Not all individuals fit the pattern. Even though some Australians can easily be picked out of a crowd of other nationalities, other Australians are more like the typical American or Englishman. Nevertheless, it is important to the marketer to know the general national ideology so that he or she can fit the product and its marketing strategy into the local environment.

### View Toward Foreigners

All people view that which is foreign as different and potentially threatening to existing patterns of action and behavior. In some countries this reaction toward foreign peoples and ways is reflected in a fear of contamination or change from outside. An extreme example of this fear was the policy of the Chinese government in its early years, when foreigners and foreign products were unwelcome. As the Chinese government has consolidated its own position and cultural patterns, it has gradually opened its doors to foreign visitors and products.

Yet even when foreigners and foreign products are not perceived as a threat to the local economy, they may still be perceived as different and/or inferior. It is for this reason that international businesses often play down their foreignness and try to blend in with the local scene. Few Americans even realize that Shell Oil products, Norelco razors, Nescafé products, or Seiko watches are not made by American firms. For many products this strategy of "blending into the local scene" may be the best one from a marketing standpoint.

Not all attitudes toward foreigners and foreign products are negative. Highly sophisticated and talented individuals may be perceived as interesting rather than just "different" by the nationals of other countries, particularly by those of similar education and talent. Foreign products of high quality are often viewed in the same light. Belgian lace, French wine, Japanese cameras, and German microscopes are all viewed as distinctive and of extra-high quality in world markets. In these instances, the foreign identification actually provides an advantage in the marketplace. Success in a foreign market, then, may depend on the marketer's ability to blend in with the local scene and develop a domestic identity or the ability to convince local buyers that "foreign" means better.

### Nature and Extent of Nationalism

Nationalism is a relatively recent development in human history. Great empires have developed as a result of conquest. Examples of this include Alexander's empire, the Roman empire, the Chinese empire, and the Islamic empire—but these only lasted a few generations and then dissolved into small nation-states. Strong national states have emerged only in modern times. Even as recently as the nineteenth century, Italy and Germany were still governed by a large number of small principalities. Nations are usually built up by combining groups of people with common language and cultural heritage. In such nations, it is necessary for the international businessperson to learn to adjust operations to local customs and usage. National pride dictates that foreign businesses conduct their affairs in recognition of the uniqueness of the market and its methods of operation. Failure to adopt national norms may result in economic disaster for the foreign firm.

Some nations, through historical accident or political expediency, combine more than one language and cultural group. Such is the case with Belgium, Switzerland, Canada, Great Britain, and the United States. In the United States and Great Britain, the subgroups have been to a large degree absorbed into a large majority, but in the other nations just mentioned, each group has maintained linguistic and cultural distinctiveness. The foreign business operating within markets such as these must recognize the need to adjust marketing strategy to each subnational group.

The nations which have become independent in the twentieth century, and those that are haunted by fears of foreign domination, frequently present the greatest problem to the foreign marketer. They are often struggling to develop a strong nationalistic feeling among their citizens, and therefore feel threatened by external economic influences. Such countries may specifically restrict the operations of foreign business within their boundaries. For example, Mexico and several other Latin American countries require that 51 percent of the ownership of enterprises operating within the country be locally owned, and require that some minimum number of employees and executives be locals. These policies have economic advantages but also meet political purposes. Such restrictions tax the resourcefulness of foreign businesses that hope to operate within these nations.

In the more drastic instances, emerging nationalism may make it impossible for a foreign business to penetrate a particular market. Some of the new nations developed from former colonies, and they have boundaries that were created politically with no relationship to peoples and cultures. Indonesia, a former Dutch colony, is an amalgam of several different cultures on separate islands. Some of the black African nations divide tribes in half. The rulers of such nations may be hostile toward foreigners who seem to threaten the fragile national character. In such nations there may be strong anticolonial feelings that are manifested in hostility toward whites or toward any foreigners.

## Attitudes Toward Diffusion of Innovations

Frequently when a foreign firm enters a market, it is introducing a product or service that represents an "innovation" in that market. If a product is sufficiently different from other products in a market, local consumers may see it as something entirely new. If a company proposes to introduce an innovation into a new market, it must try to anticipate how consumers in that market will react to change. If local citizens show a strong resistance to change, some other less-resistant market may prove to be more promising. Even where the introduction of a new product seems promising, it is important to understand the process through which changes are introduced and accepted.

Although research on the factors that influence acceptance of new products has not been conclusive, it is apparent that the way consumers perceive an innovation has a strong impact on how quickly it is adopted. An innovation that consumers see as being clearly superior to other ways of meeting their needs will be adopted faster than those products or services that do not have such relative advantage. If it is easy for consumers to understand the functions of an innovation and it can be "tried" or "explained," this product will also be adopted quickly. It follows that products or ideas that are less costly and more compatible with cultural values and traditional ways of doing things will be adopted faster than others. International marketers need to be aware that they must communicate these qualities to markets when the product or service is seen as new.

The process of diffusion of innovations within a social grouping has been studied in some detail in the United States. The early studies were made by rural sociologists, who studied the acceptance of new products and ideas among farmers. Results showed that most users of a new product do not adopt it simultaneously. Products are first tried by a group of innovators and then are gradually adopted by other groups of consumers over a period of time. This process of adoption is illustrated in Figure 5–3. In U.S. studies of the acceptance of new consumer goods and industrial technologies, these different adopter groups have also appeared.

Studies in the American market have identified five clearly different adopter groups. The *innovators,* who comprise only 2.5 percent of the potential market, like to think of themselves as trend setters. Of the five groups, they are generally the youngest, have the highest social status and wealth, and are frequently more cosmopolitan—that is, they have contacts outside their own immediate social circles. The *early adopters,* who constitute about 13.5 percent of users, are the really important factor in the adoption process. Out of the many items that are tried by innovators, early adopters select the items that will ultimately be adopted by the broad population. Early adopters are usually opinion leaders, but they restrict their contacts mostly to their own local groups, where they enjoy high social

**FIGURE 5–3**    Classification of adopter groups.

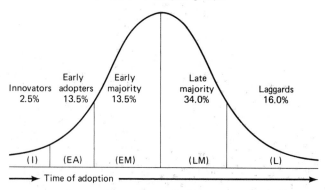

Source:    E. M. Rogers, *The Diffusion of Innovations* (New York: The Free Press, 1962), p. 76 copyright © 1962 by The Free Press of Glencoe, a Division of Macmillan Publishing Company.

status. They are usually younger than the groups that follow. Those in the *early majority* group (33 percent) are deliberate in their decision making; they will not consider adoption of a new product until a number of their peers (the early adopters) have done so. People in the *late majority* (33 percent) will not buy a product until it is in common usage. The people in this group have below-average income and social prestige, and they tend to be older than the groups who precede them. The *laggards,* who constitute the remaining 16 percent of users, have still lower income and social status.[6] By the time they have adopted a product, many of the users in the earlier groups may have moved on to something new. This entire process of diffusion may take only a few months with high-fashion items such as clothing, or it may take as long as ten years, for durable items such as television sets.

The American marketer is able to predict the process of diffusion of new products and can develop a marketing strategy that will reach each group of potential users by anticipating what their characteristics and values are. Unfortunately, little research on the diffusion of innovations has been conducted in other cultures, so the international marketer does not know the extent to which the American experience can be applied in foreign markets. Everett Rogers conducted a diffusion study in India in the early 1970s under the auspices of the Indian government. He learned that in the dissemination of birth control (in this case, vasectomies) to rural communities, there were innovators, early adopters, and later groups. In that instance, the innovators were the village leaders. In the absence of additional research of this nature, the international marketer may find it use-

[6]E. M. Rogers, *The Diffusion of Innovations* (New York: The Free Press, 1962), p. 314.

ful to apply knowledge of the American market to foreign markets on an experimental basis.

## SOCIAL STRUCTURE AND THE ROLE OF CONSUMPTION

The formal and informal structure of relationships between individuals and the effects of the actions of some individuals upon the actions of others not only varies between societies but may vary over time within one society. David Riesman identifies stages in the development of social structures through which societies may move.[7] His three stages of social structure evolution are traditional societies, inner-directed societies, and other-directed societies. To the extent that societies throughout the world can be described by such a classification, it is a useful comparative device for the international marketer.

### Traditional Societies and the Family

In the eighteenth century, European and American societies were essentially "traditional." Social practices and institutions were strongly affected by the way things had been done in the past. A number of societies throughout the world today are still primarily influenced by tradition. The Moslem states located on the Arabian peninsula are a good example of traditional societies. In a traditional society the influence of primary peer groups is particularly important: The family exerts strong influence over the actions of its members, and the paternal figure is usually dominant. In such societies, the family has a much stronger influence over the acculturation and education of its younger members; and the family is also an important center of social activities, particularly for women. In traditional societies, religion affects many more aspects of the life of society than in inner- or other-directed societies. The old ways of doing things are considered to be the good ways, and the opinions of the elders are considered most important. Patterns of consumption do not change rapidly or easily, so that marketing efforts are largely concerned with relating to the status quo.

### Inner-Directed Societies and Individualism

The inner-directed society is usually found in nations that are experiencing rapid economic development. This society is usually dominated by rugged individualists—the economic giants who own the new industries and financial institutions. Traditional values and relationships are breaking

---

[7]D. Riesman, N. Glazer, and R. Denney, *The Lonely Crowd* (New Haven: Yale University Press, 1950).

down, and the new social leaders tend to be the industrial leaders and their families. These leaders are characterized by a strong tendency toward individualism: they set their own standards of conduct—ranging from innovative to bizarre—and their patterns of consumption reflect these standards.

Many of the developing nations throughout the world have inner-directed social structures. The foreign marketer who seeks to sell products in these markets must identify the social leaders and adjust strategy, at least to some extent, to their wants and desires. The extent of the necessary adjustment depends on the impact of social factors on consumption behavior for the particular products. Thus, publicly consumed products might require more adjustment than privately consumed products.

### Other-Directed Societies and Conformity

An other-directed social structure is usually found in only the most highly developed and affluent societies. As the name implies, individuals are strongly affected by the actions and values of others. These "others" are described as reference groups—people with whom the individual wants to be compared. The reference groups will vary with individuals, and even at different times with the same individual. Thus, college students (or high-school students) identify with other students and want to dress like them, eat the same food, listen to the same music, and so forth. When these students leave school, they identify with an entirely different reference group—usually other people with whom they work or the superior whose job they someday hope to have. These same individuals' behavior away from the job may be influenced by entirely different reference groups, such as hobbyists with common interests (other golfers, tennis players, surfers, and so forth).

The marketer selling in an other-directed market has a more difficult job of identifying buying motives of target markets. Such markets are highly segmented, since the reaction of each individual toward a particular product depends on the relevant reference group or groups involved.

### The Role of Consumption

The social structure of a society affects the place that consumption has in that society. In a traditional society consumption is viewed as a means of serving basic human needs, but not as a contributor to one's role in the society. In such societies, big business and excessive consumption may be viewed as undesirable, and social sanctions may be declared against them. In an inner-directed society, consumption can serve as a means for the individual to establish a unique identity, and business is the means by which the individualist increases his or her impact. In an other-directed society consumption provides a means of identification with peer groups. Business can be a useful contributor to consumption, but it may be deemed as a target for regulation when its impact becomes too great.

## CULTURAL ANALYSIS: INTERPRETING
## THE IMPACT OF CULTURE  ─────────────────

The task of interpreting culture's impact on a group can be overwhelming. Cultural influence is both pervasive and subtle. Furthermore, our own culture always gets in the way of our understanding of another culture because we must understand the other culture in terms of how it is similar to or different from our own. This is called the self-reference criterion.[8] So, where is the international marketer to begin?

### Limits of Cultural Analysis and Cultural Universals

An important caveat must be made for the person who is considering marketing products in a foreign environment. First, differences often stand out more than cultural similarities. The fact is that culture is simply each society's solution to problems presented by life. Our solution to the need to satisfy hunger is tempered by our own resources, skills, and knowledge. Products and services must solve problems and meet consumer needs in order to be viable. It is important that the marketer understand whether a need met by a product is a recognized one within a particular culture. If it is, then the cultural difference (current or alternative ways of meeting that need), is not as relevant as the similarity of needs.

There are several barriers to overcome in estimating cultural impact. Of foremost importance is the need to recognize the influence of one's own culture in interpreting another. Second, cultural differences tend to stand out more than similarities; yet it is the similarities that may be more important to a marketer. More significant in many cases is the fact that all people have similar needs. Figure 5–4 illustrates some of these "cultural universals." Third, since culture is learned behavior, it is, by definition, individual. Therefore, any generalizations about a culture must recognize the variation *within* a culture as much as the differences or similarities between that one and any other.

### Tools for Cultural Assessment

Earlier sections of this chapter have provided an overview of the elements of culture and the areas to analyze as patterns of cultural influence. In most situations, a businessperson may not have the ability, time, or money to familiarize him- or herself with the subtle intricacies of a culture. Is there any shortcut system for estimating cultural impact on demand for a product or service? The method of analysis proposed by Edward T. Hall may not be a shortcut to cultural understanding, but it can help give focus to a cultural study for international marketing decisions.

---

[8]James A. Lee, "Cultural Analysis in Overseas Operations," *Harvard Business Review*, 44, no. 2 (March–April 1966), p. 47.

FIGURE 5–4    Cultural universals.

| | | |
|---|---|---|
| age grading | food taboos | music |
| athletic sports | funeral rites | mythology |
| bodily adornment | games | numerals |
| calendars | gestures | obstetrics |
| cleanliness training | gift giving | penal sanctions |
| community organization | government | personal names |
| cooking | greetings | population policy |
| cooperative labor | hair styles | postnatal care |
| cosmology | hospitality | pregnancy usages |
| courtship | housing hygiene | property rights |
| dancing | incest taboos | propitiation of |
| decorative arts | inheritance rules |     supernatural beings |
| divination | joking | puberty customs |
| division of labor | kin groups | religious rituals |
| dream interpretation | kinship nomenclature | residence rules |
| education | language | sexual restrictions |
| eschatology | law | soul concepts |
| ethics | luck superstitions | status differentiation |
| ethnobotany | magic | surgery |
| etiquette | marriage | tool making |
| faith healing | mealtimes | trade |
| family | medicine | visiting |
| feasting | modesty concerning | weaning |
| fire making |     natural functions | weather control |
| folklore | mourning | |

Source: George P. Murdock, "The Common Denominator of Cultures" in *The Science of Man in the World Crises*, ed. Ralph Linton (New York: Columbia University Press, 1945), pp. 123–42.

Hall's basic premise for understanding culture is that it consists of systems for structuring the interaction within a society. Interaction can be person with person, person with things, person with environment, person with outsiders, man with woman, and so on. Hall has organized this view of culture into a framework which identifies "primary message systems," or cultural rules for human activity. These primary message systems are shown in Figure 5–5.

By exploring each of the ten areas identified in the figure, the international marketer is better able to isolate him- or herself from the self-reference criterion and to understand the complexities of another culture. This level of analysis would be appropriate for a more comprehensive cultural understanding. However, in most cases such intense cultural understanding is not necessary; marketers need only know the culture's impact on their specific concerns: demand or use of a product, influences in the purchase decision, organization structure and relations with employees, and so forth. To perform this level of analysis, Hall suggests that we investigate the "intersection" of message systems. If we want to understand

**FIGURE 5–5**   Primary message systems of Edward Hall's *Silent Language.*

| PRIMARY MESSAGE SYSTEM | DEPICTS ATTITUDES AND CULTURAL RULES FOR: |
| --- | --- |
| 1. Interaction | The ordering of man's interaction with those around him, through language, touch, noise, gesture, and so forth. |
| 2. Association | The organization (grouping) and structuring of society and its components. |
| 3. Subsistence | The ordering of man's activities in feeding, working, and making a living. |
| 4. Bisexuality | The differentiation of roles, activities, and function along sex lines. |
| 5. Territoriality | The possession, use, and defense of space and territory. |
| 6. Temporality | The use, allocation, and division of time. |
| 7. Learning | The adaptive process of learning and instruction. |
| 8. Play | Relaxation, humor, recreation, and enjoyment. |
| 9. Defense | Protection against man's environment, including medicine, warfare, and law. |
| 10. Exploitation | Turning the environment to man's use through technology, construction, and extraction of materials. |

Material adapted from *The Silent Language* by Edward T. Hall. Copyright © 1959 by Edward T. Hall. Reprinted by permission of Doubleday & Company, Inc.

how people's attitudes about work are formed in a culture, for instance, work messages are related to each of the other message systems. How do people interact in work situations? And, how do work roles structure the way people interact? How do people learn about work? What work roles are reserved for instructing others? And so on. Each message has an intersection with each other one (subsistence impacts on learning and learning impacts on subsistence messages).

### Example of Analysis for a Toy Manufacturer

To apply such analysis to specific business purposes, all that is necessary is to choose a message system with which to begin. A toy manufacturer might choose to study the interaction of "play" with other message systems; cosmetic marketers might use the "bisexuality" message system; and a chemical firm might use the "exploitation" message system to study its impact within the culture on use and demand for its products. An example of the framework for such analysis for the toy manufacturer might look like Figure 5–6.

Hall's framework for cultural analysis is only one method to use in cultural analysis. Its advantage is that it can be as specific or as comprehensive as the decision maker needs. It suggests whether or not a firm should adapt a product when introducing it to a new culture. The next step is for the firm to assess its resources and objectives in a market, given the results of cultural analysis; then it can decide if the effort is worthwhile.

**FIGURE 5–6**    A business application of Edward Hall's map of culture.

| INTERSECTIONS OF PLAY AND OTHER PRIMARY MESSAGE SYSTEMS | SAMPLE QUESTIONS CONCERNING CULTURAL PATTERNS SIGNIFICANT FOR MARKETING TOYS AND GAMES |
|---|---|
| 1. Interaction/play | How do people interact during play as regards competitiveness, instigation, or leadership? |
| 2. Play/interaction | What games are played involving acting, role playing, or other aspects of real world interaction? |
| 3. Association/play | Who organizes play and how do the organization patterns differ? |
| 4. Play/association | What games are played about organization; for example, team competitions and games involving kings, judges, or leader-developed rules and penalties? |
| 5. Subsistence/play | What are the significant factors regarding people such as distributors, teachers, coaches, or publishers who make their livelihood from games? |
| 6. Play/subsistence | What games are played about work roles in society such as doctors, nurses, firemen? |
| 7. Bisexuality/play | What are the significant differences between the sexes in the sports, games, and toys enjoyed? |
| 8. Play/bisexuality | What games and toys involve bisexuality; for example, dolls, dressing up, dancing? |
| 9. Territoriality/play | Where are games played and what are the limits observed in houses, parks, streets, schools, and so forth? |
| 10. Play/territoriality | What games are played about space and ownership; for example, Monopoly? |
| 11. Temporality/play | At what ages and what times of the day and year are different games played? |
| 12. Play/temporality | What games are played about and involving time; for example, clocks, speed tests? |
| 13. Learning/play | What patterns of coaching, tuition, and training exist for learning games? |
| 14. Play/learning | What games are played about and involving learning and knowledge; for example, quizzes? |
| 15. Defense/play | What are the safety rules for games, equipment, and toys? |
| 16. Play/defense | What war and defense games and toys are utilized? |
| 17. Exploitation/play | What resources and technology are permitted or utilized for games and sport; for example, hunting and fishing rules, use of parks, cameras, vehicles, and so forth? |
| 18. Play/exploitation | What games and toys about technology or exploitation are used; for example, scouting, chemical sets, microscopes? |

This illustration is drawn from Robock, Simmonds, and Zwick, *International Business & Multinational Enterprises,* 2nd Edition, Irwin Publishers, 1977.

## INTERNATIONAL CULTURES

Even though each culture has unique characteristics that differentiate it from other cultures, separate societies may also share cultural characteristics in common. These similarities may be the result of geographic proximity and frequent contact. We find many cultural similarities between Canada and the United States, and among the Scandinavian countries. Or the similarities may result from long-term political ties, as is true for former colonies. People of Australia, New Zealand, and Great Britain express many cultural similarities. Even the black African countries, whose cultures are very different from the European cultures, still share some cultural characteristics (such as language) with their former mother countries.

In some situations, when countries have no geographic or political ties, they may still share certain kinds of cultural ties. Reference groups sometimes transcend national boundaries and are truly international. A good example is the world youth culture, which expresses common preferences in music, clothing, and recreation. Abba, a Swedish rock group and the Spaniard Julio Iglesias, sell more records worldwide than any other composers or performers. Levis or similar types of jeans are in great demand throughout the world, including the communist countries. The marketers of such products need only promote their products carefully in order to ride an international wave of popularity.

An "international" culture is also strong among businesspersons. People who conduct business affairs at international levels frequently identify closely with other international business people. Their personal behavior and business buying decisions may be strongly influenced by these peers. The international marketer must remember, however, that business people are also influenced by their own cultures and will not necessarily mirror international counterparts. Further, businesspersons whose primary reference group is other local businesses, may have culture-bound behavior even when they are active in foreign marketing.

## SUMMARY

Culture is a pervasive aspect of human behavior and motivation; it naturally influences buyer preferences and product usage patterns. Culture is learned from association with members of a group. The features that best differentiate one culture from another are language, aesthetics, religion, and the roles of family, educational systems, peers, women, class structure and mobility, and social interaction patterns in a society.

Cultural influence also directly affects the climate for business in general and international business in particular. National ideology determines how members of a culture view the role of business and how strong the culture's identity is. These factors in turn determine attitudes toward foreigners, foreign products, and foreign ideas. They also set the stage for nationalism, a collection of attitudes or policies designed to protect the group's cultural identity and independence. New ideas or products must be culturally compatible and that occurs when they are perceived as having an advantage over other ways of meeting a need. Nevertheless, some cultures are more resistant to changes than others. And, from what we know about diffusion of innovations in the United States, not all groups in a society are likely to adopt new products at the same time. The different groups have different demographic and status characteristics as well as values.

Social structure is another cultural variable that influences buyer behavior and motivation. There are distinctive values in traditional, inner-directed, and other-directed societies that determine attitudes toward the importance of, and change in, consumption behavior.

An important concept in analyzing the impact of culture is the role of cultural universals—the basic needs shared by all peoples. How those needs are met define cultural differences. In most cases, international marketers have little need to understand all the ways a foreign culture may differ from their own. A skeleton of cultural differences could be built by studying a culture's primary message system; however, in order to focus on the impact of culture on use or demand for a particular product or service, the manager can choose a critical message system and study how it intersects with the others. Last, it must be noted that some cultures are truly international today.

## DISCUSSION QUESTIONS

1. How do people acquire culture? How does culture affect us?
2. What are the elements of culture?
3. How does language affect our thinking patterns?
4. Discuss how the relative roles of institutional and secular values have changed in your culture over the last fifty years.
5. How does the role of the family vary in different cultures?
6. Explain several different types of, and purposes for, educational systems in a society.
7. How do roles of women in the work force affect buying behavior?
8. Using Figure 5–2, discuss how different class structures might affect consumption patterns in Sweden, the U.S., and Peru.
9. How might our cultural values in aesthetics affect our product preferences?

10. Explain national ideology and the way it influences attitudes toward international businesses and their products.
11. What factors contribute to cultural nationalism?
12. Discuss the differences among the adopter groups shown in Figure 5–3.
13. How can the international marketer minimize resistance to new products in foreign markets?
14. Differentiate between traditional, inner-directed, and other-directed societies and the role of consumption in each one.
15. What are the problems faced by international marketers in estimating the impact of culture in a foreign market?
16. What are cultural universals?
17. What is meant by a culture's "primary message systems"?
18. Assume you are analyzing the Mexican market for cosmetics. Show how you would construct a "map" of how Mexican culture would affect demand for your products.
19. Aside from the examples given in the text, what are some possible "international cultures"?

# SOPA

In November 1981, Milton Shayer, managing director of SOPA, was faced with the problem of developing a new product strategy. SOPA, Sociedade Productora de Alimentos, Ltd., was formed by the Campbell Soup Company in 1978 to enter the Brazilian market. Campbell, an established part of the American culture, had dominated the American soup market for decades with its familiar red-and-white labels available in every food outlet. Over the years, it had moved into a number of foreign markets with careful planning and a consistent record of success. Campbell had never withdrawn from a market anywhere in the world.

In the mid-1970s Brazil appeared to be a promising new market for canned soup. Consequently, in 1978 Campbell joined forces with a Brazilian-owned meat producer, Swift-Armour Industria e Commercio, to form SOPA. Campbell invested $6 million for a 65-percent interest in the new company, appointing Philip Beach as managing director. Mr. Beach decided to enter the Brazilian market with a limited line of soups. The line consisted mostly of vegetable and beef combinations and was offered in extra-large cans to serve the particular needs of the Brazilian market. Larger average family size and a preference for soup as a regular part of the diet dictated the need for a larger unit of sale.

Information about Brazilian soup consumption habits was obtained through a market survey in the southern city of Curitiba. The results were exciting to SOPA management. The respondents indicated that soup was a regular part of the Brazilian diet rather than an occasional diet item as is true for most United States consumers. The market potential seemed very promising.

The new product line was launched in 1979 with considerable fanfare and initial success. The initial advertising budget of $2 million gave the product almost immediate recognition in the marketplace. Packaging retained the Campbell red-and-white label adapted for the Brazilian market. The well-planned and coordinated introductory marketing campaign received two awards from the advertising industry. Sales grew rapidly, and SOPA sold over 200,000 cases of soup in the first year. However, this market success was short-lived. Repeat sales failed to materialize at a successful level. At the end of the first fiscal year, the company had suffered a loss of $1.2 million. In May 1981, production was sharply reduced.

In November 1981, the new managing director, Milton Shayer, set himself the task of determining what had gone wrong so that he could decide the direction of future marketing strategy. At that time SOPA's production was restricted to packaging soup for lunch programs in the Brazilian schools. He first learned that the potential market for SOPA's soup products had been greatly overestimated because the market survey had been restricted to a single city in the temperate south. It had become apparent that in the tropical northern provinces per-capita consumption of soup was lower. In addition, canned soup was not acceptable to the Brazilian home-maker as a regular part of the menu. Canned soup is a finished food product ready to dilute, heat, and serve, with no creative input from the home-maker. A psychologist retained by the company discovered in a series of in-depth interviews that Brazilian homemakers did not feel they were fulfilling their role if they did not serve a soup they had made themselves. They were perfectly satisfied to use the dehydrated packaged soups, such as Knorr and Lipton, because they used these products as a base with addition of ingredients of their own. They saw the SOPA product only as a useful item for the emergency shelf. This explained why initial sales were so good. Once the pantries were stocked, the repurchase demand was very low.

Mr. Shayer was faced with several possible decisions. First, should Campbell remain in Brazil? He wanted to make this decision by the end of the year. Second, if he decided to continue in the Brazilian market, he must decide what kind of products to offer—a modified soup line, sausage and beans (a basic part of the Brazilian diet), or some entirely different food product.

## QUESTIONS

1. Would you expect the culture to be the same with respect to soup consumption in rural Brazil and in the north?
2. How could SOPA soup be adapted to more successfully serve the Brazilian market?

# ELIOT GREETING CARD COMPANY

Thomas Eliot is the president of Eliot Greeting Card Co., a firm which was established by his father in the early 1950's in a medium-sized midwest city. Although the company only had about four percent of the US greeting card market, it had been profitable since its beginnings and had shown modest growth in a market environment dominated by Hallmark Company (which maintained about 50 percent of the market) and several smaller ones which also had double-digit market shares. Eliot had been successful largely by carving for itself a niche, marketing lines of specialty cards for which the other firms seemed to have little interest.

Recently, however, the greeting card market had been experiencing a period of (at least temporary) flat sales. This was seen to be the result of both the relatively weak economy and a dramatic increase in telephone advertising, urging consumers to "reach out and touch someone" at the expense of sending greeting cards. This had led to rather intense marketing efforts by the larger greeting card companies in order to gain percentage points of the relatively sluggish market. It was becoming obvious that the competition was turning its attention to the special lines that Eliot had been able to use to its advantage for so long.

For the first time in its history, Eliot Greeting was faced with a decline in its modest share, each point of which was worth several millions of dollars in sales. At a brainstorming session by the firm's board of directors, President Eliot suggested that one possible solution to the problem would be to develop an export market for their products in order to avoid the high costs of head-to-head competition for US customers. He reasoned that it would be easier for the company to design and make cards for English-speaking consumers in countries like England and Australia than to continue to slug it out with the market leaders. Bill Yates, Vice-President for Sales, had an alternative suggestion. He had recently returned from a tour of the US Southwest where he had become aware of the large number of Hispanic Americans, who were, according to his sales representatives, beginning to improve their traditionally low economic status. Yates' idea was to create and market a line of greeting cards for this largely Spanish-speaking group of Americans for whom greeting card sending was at a comparatively low level, compared to the general population. He argued that, rather than expanding its efforts to approach foreign customers, the firm

This was was prepared by Dr. Joel Saegert, Associate Professor of Marketing, The University of Texas at San Antonio.

would be better able to take advantage of its existing production and distribution system to develop this relatively untapped market at home.

Some preliminary demographic data were gathered and seemed to support the feasibility of Yates' proposal. For example, the 1980 census estimated conservatively that Hispanics numbered nearly 15 million in the US and that their growth rate was much higher than that of the population at large. It was speculated both because of immigration and high fertility rates that by the year 2,000 Hispanics would surpass blacks in numbers in the US and hence become the largest minority group. Yates was placed in charge of conducting secondary research into the idea and he hired the consulting firm of Lorca and Associates, specialists in the US Hispanic market. Yates requested that the firm provide recommendations concerning general consumer behavior of the Hispanic population so that decisions could be made about what the company would need to do to design and market greeting cards to the Spanish-speaking market in the US.

### The Consultant's Report

José Lorca, president of the consulting firm, presented a review of the literature pertaining to the consumer behavior characteristics of US Hispanics. He took some pains to point out that empirical data about this subpopulation were very meager, and that much of the information came from articles in trade periodicals which, while reflecting experience by firms who had been interested in the Hispanic market, did not report much of the hard data which would normally be expected to support the conclusions made about the subgroup. He expressed a desire for more extensive consumer research to verify the speculations made in attempts to characterize the Hispanic market. However, with this caution in mind, Lorca reported his interpretations, which were based on some 30 reports of Hispanic characteristics found in the literature. He extracted seven themes from these studies which to him summarized the traits attributed to Hispanic consumers:

1. A preference for locally-owned, Spanish-speaking businesses as well as a preference for Spanish ethnic products.
2. A high degree of brand loyalty and susceptibility to brand influence.
3. A tendency for purchases to be influenced by pride in Hispanic heritage.
4. A high degree of price consciousness and careful shopping characteristics.
5. A high degree of influence from "family" in making purchase decisions.
6. Preference for Spanish-language media, especially radio and TV.
7. A tendency to become "acculturated" with rising affluence.

Thus, the firm was confronted with the prospect of developing the use of greeting cards among a relatively provincial and traditional group of potential consumers who appeared to be heavily dependent upon their cultural background for purchase decisions. Moreover, as these individuals became more economically secure, they tended to become more like typical American consumers.

Lorca pointed out several other problems with developing the Hispanic market. First, it could not be said that the consumers in the overall Hispanic market were homogeneous. In addition to the acculturation characteristic (Hispanics were not alike at different economic levels), US Hispanics represent a number of different ethnic subgroups, depending on their national origins. These include Mexican Americans (59%), Puerto Ricans (15%) and Cubans (6%), as well as Hispanics with origins in other Central and South American countries and Europe (20%). These groups differ widely in cultural traits, especially in the particular dialects of Spanish spoken. It was also pointed out that nearly all of these people speak a kind of Spanish which is considerably different from the classical Castillian Spanish typically taught in Spanish courses offered at US high schools and universities. This fact seemed particularly important to the creation of Spanish verses for greeting cards, especially in light of the uniquely personal nature of messages used.

## QUESTIONS

1. Contrast the two strategies proposed. What are the benefits of developing an export market for English-language greeting cards compared to a market for Spanish-language cards here at home?
2. What issues will have to be addressed prior to the development of the Hispanic greeting card market?
3. Suppose that the company decided that primary consumer research would be needed to support the conclusions of the literature on Hispanic buyer behavior. How would such a study be done? What information would be needed before the company could begin marketing to Hispanic consumers?
4. Isolate the probable impact of "culture" on Hispanic preferences and purchasing patterns for greeting cards.

# chapter 6

# INSTITUTIONS OF THE INTERNATIONAL ECONOMIC ENVIRONMENT

Publication of the World Bank's 1981 World Development Report last week offered fresh food for thought and cause for comment. In it, the bank's economists stress—as they have in other years—the need for industrialized countries to keep their protectionist tendencies under control. Leaving their markets open is one of the most effective ways, the bank reiterates, in which the richer countries can help the poorer ones. But the battle against protectionism is too often seen only in terms of industrial goods, on which, with a few flagrant exceptions, the developed countries' record is fairly respectable. It is agriculture, as the World Bank says, where a new attack is needed on protectionist barriers.

Most industrialized countries protect their farmers from cheap competition by erecting tariff barriers that are lifted or reduced only for strictly limited quantities of Third World produce. These countries seem to believe the Third World should be encouraged to feed itself. But by closing off their own markets they eliminate the profit motive, the most potent factor in achieving agricultural efficiency. Many countries, indeed, compound this situation by overencouraging their own farmers and subsidizing the sale of resulting surpluses on the world market, thus depressing the prices available to Third World producers.*

· · ·

Battle lines are taking shape for another international trade conflict, this time over services.

*"Toward Free Trade Down on the Farm," *Financial Times of London,* August 24, 1981, World Business Weekly, p. 63.

U.S. officials have compiled a 210-page list of more than 2,000 instances of barriers to the free flow of services among nations, and the restrictions are multiplying almost daily. Examples of discrimination are diverse and widespread.

—Australia won't let foreign banks open branches or subsidiaries.

—Sweden bars local offices of foreign companies from processing payrolls abroad.

—Argentina requires car importers to insure shipments with local insurance companies.

—Japanese airliners get cargo cleared more quickly in Tokyo than do foreign carriers.

—And, if a U.S. company wants to use American models for an advertisement in a West German magazine, it has to hire the models through a German agency—even if the ad is being photographed in Manhattan.

"If we have restrictive protectionist tendencies in services," says Geza Feketekuty, a U.S. assistant trade representative, "it's bound to spill over to goods, and it would become increasingly difficult to maintain the open trading system."**

## INTRODUCTION

When a firm becomes involved in foreign marketing, it will encounter some unique institutions that strongly affect its marketing strategy. These institutions can help or hurt its ability to profitably penetrate foreign markets. For example, while a market exists for U.S.-made autos in Germany, prohibitive import tariffs may make exporting an unfeasible entry strategy for that market. In another situation, a profitable subsidiary may be unable to send dividends to its headquarters because the subsidiary is unable to acquire foreign exchange currencies. In other cases, common markets make joint ventures and foreign production more attractive because they can serve regional markets without economic barriers. These are all examples of how international economic institutions affect marketing strategy decisions.

In this chapter we introduce concepts such as the balance of payments, and organizations such as the International Monetary Fund. Their roles are important in determining the potential profitability of international markets. Next, we review the various ways countries engage in economic cooperation with each other. Economic cooperation creates multinational markets and can change the firm's market opportunities and competitive environment. The last section of the chapter is an overview of barriers to

**Laura Wallace, "Rising Barriers, Global Trade Skirmish Loom as Restrictions on Services Multiply," *The Wall Street Journal*, October 5, 1981, p. 1. Reprinted by permission of The Wall Street Journal, © Dow Jones & Company, Inc. All Rights Reserved.

worldwide marketing and the political and economic reasons for these barriers. These institutions place limits on foreign market entry strategies, organizational structure, and specific marketing decisions about products, pricing, distribution, and promotion.

## INTERNATIONAL MONETARY FRAMEWORK

One of the first questions that firms have when entering foreign markets is: How do I get paid? Other questions that frequently come up are: What is the International Monetary Fund? How does it affect me? What is the balance of payments of a country? How can I use the balance of payments in planning foreign marketing strategies? This section of the chapter should help to answer these questions. No international marketer is adequately prepared unless he or she understands the financial environment and institutions that impact on international marketing decisions.

### International Monetary System

It may seem surprising, but there is no such thing as an international system of exchange for different currencies. Most countries in the world have their own currencies and the value of each currency depends on the individual government's current and past monetary and fiscal policies. There are over one hundred fifty countries in the world and over one hundred national currencies whose values are controlled independently. This is an important fact for international marketers because it is the source of exchange risks, as discussed in Chapter 2. Exchange risks increase the uncertainty and costs of pursuing foreign market opportunities.

The "market" for foreign currencies is not an organized market in one location or with fixed hours. There are no central places for exchange of currencies as there are for commodities, such as Chicago and Zurich, or for stocks, such as New York and London. However, it is easy to identify the institutions that compose the "international money market." Figure 6-1 shows very simply how this market operates. Individuals or businesses may exchange currencies with foreign individuals or firms directly, but this is most prevalent in situations where the objective is to avoid legal exchange controls ("black markets"). Most common are transfers of currencies through commercial banks in different countries, many of whom have correspondent relationships. Firms or individuals can initiate this process by having their bank send a letter of credit to the foreign bank of the person or firm to which they wish to transfer funds. The letter of credit guarantees that funds are available for transfer from the person or firm's account. When payment is due, funds are then wired or credited to the foreign bank account. Letters of credit significantly reduce the risks of col-

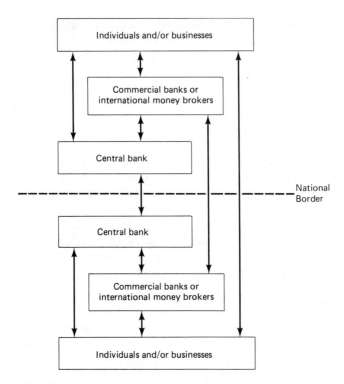

**FIGURE 6-1**   International transactions in different currencies.

lecting from foreign buyers, although there are still exchange risks on such transactions.

The completion of the transaction actually depends on yet another institution, the central bank. The foreign commercial bank takes its foreign currency credits to its own central bank, which in turn presents a request for that amount of currency to the central bank in the original country.Central banks buy and sell international currencies for their clients, who are either commercial banks, money brokers, or private businesses. The international exchange of currencies works only because central banks are willing to buy and sell foreign currencies at rates agreed upon by each other. Ultimately then, the central bank is involved in most transactions where one national currency is exchanged for another.

The International Monetary Fund (IMF) was established in 1947 to help stabilize foreign currency exchange rates. Member countries of the IMF have agreed to deposit reserves with the IMF to support the value of their currencies in relation to reserves of other members. In the past, member countries gave the IMF the power to set par values for their currencies. Today we have "freely" floating currencies, but the IMF still plays a clearinghouse role in establishing currency values. In recent years, the

IMF has forced Israel, Argentina, and Mexico, among others to reform their internal monetary policies in order to retain the international value of their currencies.

One of the real advantages of the current international monetary system is the development of "key" currencies, such as the U.S. dollar, Japanese yen, German deutsche mark, Swiss franc, and British pound, that various countries keep as reserves with the IMF in addition to their own currency and gold reserves. Key currencies allow companies and countries to engage in international trade without having to use their own currency to pay for those transactions. For example, a firm in Nigeria may buy something in Thailand and pay for it in U.S. dollars, transferred from Nigerias's IMF reserves to those of Thailand. Key currencies normally do not carry as much exchange risk as other ones; thus, overall trade is stimulated by the ability to use key currencies for commercial payments. Another advantage of our current IMF agreements is the ability to use SDRs (Special Drawing Rights) as reserves, thus freeing the currency reserves for international commercial payments.

### The Balance of Payments

The balance of payments is an indicator of the economic health of a country. A poor balance-of-payments position indicates a possible weakening of that country's currency in international money markets. For that reason, it is especially important that international marketers learn to use this information as a diagnostic tool, just as they might consider the impact of domestic economic conditions on a possible market opportunity at home.

Figure 6–2 shows the balance of payments for the United States for the twenty-one-year period between 1960 and 1981. Using it as an example, you can begin to identify the important accounts in a country's balance of payments. Exports and imports of goods or services, as well as military transfers, international tourism, fees and royalties, and gifts, constitute the "current account" items in the balance of payments. They are shown in lines 1 through 36 of Figure 6–2. When the value of imports exceeds that of exports, a country's balance of payments is said to have a "deficit," or, more precisely, a "trade deficit." The other major types of accounts, capital flows (lines 43–55 and 64–73) and changes in the value of official reserve items (lines 38–42, 57–63, and 74) must "finance" the deficit in the flow of goods or services. When a country has persistent deficits in its trade balance with other countries, it must "use up" its reserves to pay foreigners, and thus its own reserves are threatened. A devaluation may result if other steps cannot be taken domestically. This happened to the United States in the 1970s. On the other hand, a persistent surplus in the trade balance can force an upward revaluation of a country's currency, thus making it more expensive for other countries to buy their currency

## FIGURE 6–2

| LINE | CREDITS & DEBITS | 1975 | 1976 | 1977 | 1978 | 1979 | 1980 |
|---|---|---|---|---|---|---|---|
| 1 | Exports of goods and services | 155,729 | 171,630 | 184,295 | 221,021 | 288,925 | 344,667 |
| 2 | Merchandise, adjusted, excluding military | 107,088 | 114,745 | 120,816 | 142,054 | 184,473 | 233,968 |
| 3 | Transfers under U.S. military agency sales contracts | 4,049 | 5,454 | 7,351 | 8,096 | 6,669 | 8,231 |
| 4 | Travel | 4,697 | 5,742 | 6,150 | 7,186 | 8,335 | 10,090 |
| 5 | Passenger fares | 1,039 | 1,229 | 1,386 | 1,603 | 2,156 | 2,582 |
| 6 | Other transportation | 5,840 | 6,747 | 7,264 | 3,315 | 9,899 | 11,430 |
| 7 | Fees and royalties from affiliated foreigners | 3,343 | 3,531 | 3,383 | 4,705 | 4,980 | 5,695 |
| 8 | Fees and royalties from unaffiliated foreigners | 757 | 822 | 923 | 1,055 | 1,068 | 1,170 |
| 9 | Other private services | 2,920 | 3,334 | 3,806 | 4,130 | 4,187 | 5,207 |
| 10 | U.S. Government miscellaneous services | 446 | 489 | 557 | 620 | 320 | 382 |
|  | Receipts of Income on U.S. assets abroad: | | | | | | |
| 11 | Direct investment | 16,395 | 18,999 | 19,673 | 25,489 | 38,330 | 38,842 |
| 12 | Interest, dividends, and earnings of unincorporated affiliates | 8,547 | 11,303 | 13,277 | 14,115 | 19,358 | 19,845 |
| 13 | Reinvested earnings of incorporated affiliates | 8,048 | 7,698 | 8,396 | 11,343 | 18,965 | 16,998 |
| 14 | Other private receipts | 7,644 | 8,953 | 10,881 | 15,964 | 26,075 | 36,522 |
| 15 | U.S. Government receipts | 1,112 | 1,332 | 1,625 | 1,843 | 2,294 | 2,574 |
| 16 | Transfers of good and services under U.S. military grant programs, net | 2,207 | 373 | 203 | 236 | 305 | 635 |
| 17 | Imports of goods and services | -132,836 | -162,248 | -193,788 | -230,030 | -381,917 | -333,888 |
| 18 | Merchandise, adjusted, excluding military | -98,041 | -124,051 | -151,089 | -175,813 | -211,819 | -249,308 |
| 19 | Direct defense expenditures | -4,795 | -4,895 | -5,823 | -7,352 | -8,558 | -10,746 |
| 20 | Travel | -6,417 | -6,858 | -7,451 | -8,475 | -9,413 | -10,397 |
| 21 | Passenger fares | -2,263 | -2,368 | -2,748 | -2,896 | -3,184 | -3,087 |
| 22 | Other transportation | -5,688 | -6,852 | -7,874 | -8,911 | -10,415 | -10,896 |
| 23 | Fees and royalties to affiliated foreigners | -287 | -293 | -243 | -393 | -523 | -515 |
| 24 | Fees and royalties to unaffiliated foreigners | -186 | -189 | -198 | -214 | -234 | -254 |
| 25 | Private payments for other services | -1,551 | -2,096 | -2,190 | -2,566 | -2,820 | -3,222 |
| 26 | U.S. Government payments for miscellaneous services | -1,044 | -1,227 | -1,358 | -1,545 | -1,718 | -1,769 |
|  | Payments of income on foreign assets in the United States: | | | | | | |
| 27 | Direct investment | -2,234 | -3,110 | -2,834 | -6,357 | -6,357 | -9,336 |
| 28 | Interest, dividends, and earnings of unincorporated affiliates | -1,046 | -1,451 | -1,248 | -1,628 | -2,402 | -3,147 |
| 29 | Reinvested earnings of incorporated affiliates | -1,189 | -1,659 | -1,586 | -2,583 | -3,955 | -6,190 |
| 30 | Other private payments | -5,783 | -5,681 | -5,841 | -8,980 | -15,803 | -21,326 |
| 31 | U.S. Government payments | -4,552 | -4,520 | -5,512 | -8,674 | -11,076 | -12,512 |
| 32 | U.S. military grants of goods and services, net | -2,207 | -373 | -203 | -236 | -305 | -635 |
| 33 | Unilateral transfers (excluding military grants of goods and services), net | -4,613 | -4,998 | -4,617 | -5067 | -5,593 | -5,056 |
| 34 | U.S. Government grants (excluding military grants of goods and services) | -2,894 | -3,146 | -2,787 | -3,183 | -3,536 | -4,659 |
| 35 | U.S. Government pensions and other transfers | -813 | -934 | -971 | -1,086 | -1,180 | -1,303 |
| 36 | Private remittances and other transfers | -908 | -917 | -859 | -798 | -878 | -1,094 |
| 37 | U.S. assets abroad, net (increase/capital outflow(–)) | -39,703 | -51,269 | -34,785 | -61,070 | -62,639 | -84,776 |
| 38 | U.S. official reserve assets, net | -849 | -2,558 | -375 | 732 | -1,133 | -8,155 |
| 39 | Gold | – | – | -118 | -65 | -65 | – |
| 40 | Special drawing rights | -66 | -78 | 1,121 | 1,249 | -1,136 | -16 |
| 41 | Reserve position in the international Monetary fund | -466 | -2,212 | -294 | 4,231 | -189 | -1,667 |
| 42 | Foreign currencies | -317 | -268 | 158 | -4,683 | 237 | -8,472 |

**FIGURE 6–2** Continued

| | | | | | | | |
|---|---|---:|---:|---:|---:|---:|---:|
| 43 | U.S. Government assets, other than official reserve assets, net | −3,473 | −4,214 | −3,963 | −4,644 | −3,787 | −5,165 |
| 44 | U.S. loans and other long-term assets | −5,941 | −6,943 | −6,445 | −7,470 | −7,676 | −9,812 |
| 45 | Repayment of U.S. loans | 2,475 | 2,396 | 2,719 | 2,942 | 3,893 | 4,367 |
| 46 | U.S. foreign currency holdings and U.S. short-term assets, net | −9 | 133 | 33 | −115 | 16 | 280 |
| 47 | U.S. private assets, net | −35,380 | −44,498 | −30,717 | −57,159 | −57,739 | −71,458 |
| 48 | Direct investment | −14,244 | −11,949 | −11,890 | −16,056 | −23,949 | −18,346 |
| 49 | Equity and intercompany accounts | −6,196 | −4,253 | −5,494 | −4,713 | −4,984 | −4,348 |
| 50 | Reinvested earnings of incorporated affiliates | −8,048 | −7,696 | −6,396 | −11,343 | −18,965 | −16,998 |
| 51 | Foreign securities | −6,247 | −8,885 | −5,360 | −3,582 | −4,332 | −3,340 |
| | U.S. claims on unaffiliated foreigners reported by U.S. nonbanking concerns: | | | | | | |
| 52 | Long-term | −368 | −42 | −99 | −53 | −3,026 | −2,653 |
| 53 | Short-term | −991 | −2,254 | −1,814 | −3,800 | | |
| | U.S claims reported by U.S. banks not included elsewhere: | | | | | | |
| 54 | Long-term | −2,357 | −2,362 | −751 | −33,653 | −26,213 | −46,947 |
| 55 | Short-term | −11,173 | −19,096 | −10,676 | | | |
| 56 | **Foreign assets in the U.S., net (increase/ capital inflow (+))** | 15,670 | 36,518 | 51,218 | 63,948 | 38,946 | 39,251 |
| 57 | Foreign official assets in the U.S., net | 7,027 | 17,693 | 36,816 | 33,369 | −13,757 | 15,492 |
| 58 | U.S. Government securities | 5,563 | 9,892 | 32,338 | 24,221 | −21,972 | 11,870 |
| 59 | U.S. Treasury securities | 4,653 | 9,319 | 30,230 | 23,555 | −22,433 | 9,683 |
| 60 | Other | 905 | 573 | 2,398 | 686 | 463 | 2,187 |
| 61 | Other U.S. Government liabilities | 1,517 | 4,627 | 1,400 | 2,379 | −133 | 636 |
| 62 | U.S. liabilities reported by U.S. banks, not included elsewhere | −2,138 | 969 | 773 | 3,559 | 7,243 | −139 |
| 63 | Other foreign official assets | 2,304 | 2,203 | 2,103 | 1,430 | 1,135 | 3,143 |
| 64 | Other foreign assets in the U.S., net | 8,643 | 18,826 | 14,403 | 30,187 | 52,703 | 34,769 |
| 65 | Direct investment | 2,603 | 4,347 | 3,728 | 7,897 | 11,877 | 10,854 |
| 66 | Equity and intercompany accounts | 1,414 | 2,687 | 2,142 | 5,303 | 7,921 | 4,864 |
| 67 | Reinvested earnings of incoporated affiliates | 1,189 | 1,659 | 1,386 | 2,583 | 3,955 | 6,190 |
| 68 | U.S. treasury securities | 2,590 | 2,783 | 534 | 2,178 | 4,820 | 2,679 |
| 69 | U.S. securities other than U.S. Treasury securities | 2,503 | 1,284 | 2,437 | 2,253 | 1,334 | 5,384 |
| 70 | Long-term | 406 | −1,000 | −347 | −190 | 2,065 | 3,109 |
| 71 | Short-term | −87 | 422 | 1,332 | 1,967 | | |
| | U.S. liabilities reported by U.S. banks not included elsewhere: | | | | | | |
| 72 | Long-term | −280 | 231 | 373 | 16,441 | 32,607 | 10,743 |
| 73 | Short-term | 908 | 10,739 | 6,336 | | | |
| 74 | **Allocations of special drawing rights** | − | − | − | − | 1,139 | 1,152 |
| 75 | **Statistical discrepancy (sum of above items with sign reversed)** | 3,753 | 10,367 | −2,323 | 11,398 | 21,440 | 29,540 |
| | **Memoranda:** | | | | | | |
| 76 | Balance on merchandise trade (lines 2 and 18) | 9,047 | −9,306 | −30,873 | −33,759 | −27,346 | −25,342 |
| 77 | Balance on goods and services (lines 1 and 17) | 22,893 | 9,382 | −9,493 | −9,008 | 7,008 | 10,779 |
| 78 | Balance on goods, services, and remittances (lines 77, 35, and 36) | 21,475 | 7,531 | −11,323 | −10,392 | 4,930 | 8,382 |
| 79 | Balance on current account (lines 77 and 33) | 18,280 | 4,381 | −14,119 | −14,673 | 1,414 | 3,723 |
| | **Transactions in the U.S. official reserve assets and in foreign official assets in the United States:** | | | | | | |
| 80 | Increase (−) in U.S. official reserve assets, net (line 38) | −849 | −2,558 | −373 | 732 | −4,133 | −8,155 |
| 81 | Increase (+) in foreign official assets in the U.S. (line 57 less line 61) | −5,569 | 13,896 | 35,416 | 31,202 | −13,629 | 11,856 |

*Source: Summary of Current Business, U.S. Government Printing Office*

(and products). While a surplus is not as critical to correct as a deficit, both trends are indicators of possible future changes in currency values.

When managers analyze the health of a firm, they use financial ratios such as net earnings per share, stockturns, and assets-to-sales. Likewise international managers are able to use the balances in a country's balance of payments to estimate its economic health. The U.S. Department of Commerce calculates some of these and they are shown in lines 76–81 of Figure 6–2. The Balance on Current Account (line 79) is particularly important. This indicates the "net" of all flows of current-account items. When it shows a negative balance, that indicates pressure on the country's reserve items. The reserve balances (lines 80 and 81) also show whether foreigners are acquiring large amounts of that country's reserves.

For further detail on analyzing a country's balance of payments you should consult an international finance textbook. It is sufficient here to note that the balance of payments is an effective tool for understanding a foreign country's general economic environment. If the economic environment appears unstable, market opportunities there may not be as attractive as those in more stable environments.

## INTERNATIONAL ECONOMIC COOPERATION

As the law of comparative advantage showed us in Chapter 3, there are many reasons for countries to trade with each other. The promise of increased economic benefits has stimulated a broad array of activities as countries have tried to strengthen their international trading positions. Some countries have signed trade agreements with others to exempt specific products from tariffs. Other have formed common markets to integrate their economies. Still others have formed producers' agreements to increase their control over international prices and supplies of commodities. In this section we will discuss the major types of international economic cooperation and their advantages and disadvantages.

### Regional Agreements

The major advantage of regional economic cooperation is the creation of larger markets that will promote the efficient use of resources among the signer countries. However, there are a number of different forms that regional economic cooperation can take. Figure 6–3 shows the major types of economic cooperation and their characteristics.

The simplest type of agreement, the creation of a free trade area (FTA), only requires that its members remove barriers to trade within the participant countries. Ideally all goods and services can move from one member country to another without tariffs, quotas, or other barriers. The

**FIGURE 6–3**    Forms of economic integration.

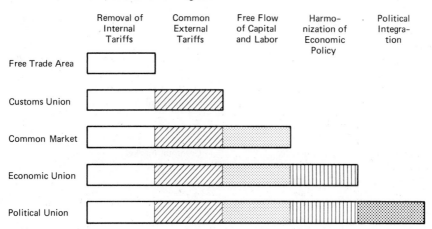

*Source:*    Ruel K. Kahler and Roland L. Kramer, *International Marketing,* 4th ed. (Cincinnati: Southwestern Publishing Company, 1978), p. 131.

European Free Trade Association (Austria, Iceland, Norway, Portugal, Sweden, Switzerland, and Finland) is an example of a free trade area where the agreement applies only to manufactured products. The major problem in a free trade area is that each country retains its own tariff structure with outsiders. Incoming products face different tariffs depending on which country they use to enter the free trade area. Inevitably, rules must develop for internal product movements to keep outsiders from entering a free trade area through the lowest-tariff member country. Other examples of active FTAs are shown in Figure 6–4.

In a customs union, members agree to free trade internally and to establishment of a common external tariff. The common tariff eliminates one of the problems of the more loosely organized free trade area, but it is often difficult to negotiate if the prospective signers start out with widely disparate tariff schedules. Belgium, the Netherlands, and Luxembourg constitute the most well known customs union—the Benelux countries. This customs union was superceded by the European Common Market when the Benelux countries joined it.

A common market has few internal trade barriers, a common external tariff, and the free flow of capital and labor among member countries. It is a major step toward regional economic integration because all factors of production can move freely within the common market countries. This aspect is its most attractive feature, but also one of the most practical problems in making a common market work. If one country within a common market suffers from high unemployment and is powerless to retain available jobs for its own citizens, it may suffer population loss through emigration to other countries in the common market. Membership in a common

**FIGURE 6–4**    Major regional economic associations.

| NAME & DATE OF FORMATION | MEMBER COUNTRIES | TYPE OF ORGANIZATION | MARKET SIZE (POP. IN MILLIONS) |
|---|---|---|---|
| *Europe* | | | |
| Benelux (1952) | Netherlands Belgium Luxembourg | Customs union | (24) |
| EC: European Community (1958) | Benelux France Germany Italy U.K. Greece Ireland Denmark Spain Portugal Turkey (Assoc.) | Common market | (308) |
| EFTA: European Free Trade Area (1959) | Austria Iceland Portugal Norway Sweden Switzerland Finland | Free trade area | (41) |
| Joint Trade Area (1977) | European Community EFTA | Free trade area for most commodities | (350) |
| Comecon: Council for Mutual Economic Assistance (1954) | USSR Poland Czechoslovakia Hungary Rumania German Dem. Rep. Cuba | Political union | (308) |
| *Latin America* | | | |
| LAIA: L.A. Integration Association (1980) (Formerly LAFTA, 1961) | Peru Paraguay Argentina Brazil Colombia Bolivia Mexico Venezuela Uruguay Chile Ecuador | Partial free trade area | (275) |

**FIGURE 6–4**    *Continued*

| NAME & DATE OF FORMATION | MEMBER COUNTRIES | TYPE OF ORGANIZATION | MARKET SIZE (POP. IN MILLIONS) |
|---|---|---|---|
| ANCOM: Andes Common Market (1961) | Bolivia<br>Peru<br>Ecuador<br>Colombia<br>Venezuela | Common market | (76) |
| CACM: Central American Common Market (1961) | Costa Rica<br>Guatemala<br>El Salvador<br>Nicaragua<br>Honduras | Common market | (17) |
| Caricom: Caribbean Common Market (1973) (Formerly CARIFTA, 1965) | Barbados<br>Guyana<br>Jamaica<br>Trinidad-Tobago | Common market in theory with rights to exceptions | (4) |
| *Asia/Middle East*<br>ASEA: Association of Southeast Asia (1967) | Thailand<br>Indonesia<br>The Phillipines<br>Singapore<br>Malaysia | FTA with planned economic cooperation (cooperation in expanded economic, political, and social fields) | (266) |
| Arab/Middle East Arab Common Market (1964) | UAR<br>Iraq<br>Jordan<br>Syria<br>Sudan<br>Yemen | Common market | (94) |
| Mahgreb Economic Community (1966) | Algeria<br>Libya<br>Tunisia<br>Morocco | Common market | (50) |
| *Africa*<br>ECOWAS: The Economic Community of West Africa States (1975) | Benin<br>Cape Verde<br>Gambia<br>Ghana<br>Guinea-Bissau<br>Ivory Coast<br>Liberia<br>Mali<br>Mauritania<br>Niger<br>Nigeria | FTA with ultimate goal of a common market | |

**FIGURE 6–4** *Continued*

| *NAME & DATE OF FORMATION* | *MEMBER COUNTRIES* | *TYPE OF ORGANIZATION* | *MARKET SIZE (POP. IN MILLIONS)* |
|---|---|---|---|
| | Senegal | | |
| | Sierra Leone | | |
| | Togo | | |
| | Upper Volta | | (115) |
| East Africa Customs Union (1967) | Ethiopia Kenya Rhodesia (Zimbabwe) Sudan Tanzania Uganda | Common market | |

market, as with other forms of economic cooperation, carries with it some loss of sovereignty over economic matters and the vulnerability to economic conditions in other member countries.

The most famous common market is, of course, the European Community (formerly European Economic Community) whose members are listed in Figure 6–4. The advantage of producing within a common market should be obvious: access to a large market with few barriers. Equally apparent should be the competitive disadvantages that common markets create for outside firms that want access to national markets within the economic community. When the EC was formed, some U.S. exporters with considerable sales success in Europe found themselves shut out due to new larger-scale competitors located within the common market. Other companies, U.S. and European alike, found themselves with small plants in several countries, none of which were designed to serve the larger common market. Nevertheless, the EC has been relatively successful because its members have diversity in their endowments of labor, capital, and technological expertise. Membership has been economically beneficial for most EC countries; however, there has been much discord over trade of certain products such as food and wines. Other common markets listed in Figure 6–4 do not have such diversity and have been less successful in promoting internal economic benefits.

Two other forms of regional economic cooperation are economic and political unions. Members of an economic union agree to all the requirements of forming a common market, but in addition they make efforts to coordinate their internal monetary and fiscal policies. Because such agreements require subjugating domestic economic policy to policies of the economic union, they represent true economic integration. That also means loss of sovereignty or control over domestic economic matters and is the major barrier to the formation of economic unions. Even though the EC has created some supranational coordination with respect to antitrust laws, corporate charters, environmental regulations, and consumer protection, it has still not achieved the status of a true economic union. A political union requires complete integration of political and economic entities among member countries. To date, the closest approximation of a political union is COMECON (Council for Mutual Economic Assistance), which is the trade agreement between the Soviet Union and its satelite countries in Eastern Europe. The USSR has centralized some aspects of planning related to trade and defense, but the satelite countries remain stubbornly nationalistic and oppose further efforts at political integration. Furthermore, some members of COMECON, such as Hungary, have developed their own trading arrangements with Western countries.

### Bilateral and Multilateral Agreements

In addition to regional forms of economic cooperation among countries, bilateral and multilateral trade agreements offer further opportunities for reducing barriers to international trade. Bilateral agreements involve only two countries and usually concern specific product exchanges. The U.S. has several such agreements with Canada, one of which is the 1965 Automotive Products Agreement. This concessionary agreement allows free movement of automotive parts between the two countries, and thus provides the benefits of specialization and larger-scale production for both countries.

Bilateral agreements frequently are the basis on which trade is conducted between the U.S. and nonmarket countries such as the USSR. Because such countries do not always have convertible currencies, barter arrangements are negotiated by our government and by individual firms to stimulate a two-way flow of products. Sales of U.S. grain during the 1970s were made possible by bilateral agreements that ensured compensation in gold and convertible currencies as well as in products. Other forms of bilateral agreements include counterpurchases. These are discussed in more detail in Chapter 12.

The two most significant multilateral agreements affecting international trade are GATT (General Agreement on Tariffs and Trade) and UNCTAD (United Nations Conference on Trade and Development). Multilateral agreements typically have signer countries from multiple regions of the world, and their overall purpose is the reduction of tariffs and other barriers to world trade. GATT was signed by twenty-three countries in 1947, but now has over one hundred members and associates. Its signers account for over 80 percent of total world trade. The main provisions of GATT were to commit its members to immediate reductions in tariff barriers and to future multilateral negotiations. A major aspect of GATT membership is that member countries must practice nondiscrimination in import duties—all concessions granted to one member must be extended to other GATT members. This is also called the "Most Favored Nation" clause. GATT provides a forum in which member countries can discuss trade problems and consult with each other about possible trade-policy changes. Under the auspices of GATT, eight major tariff conferences have been sponsored since 1947. They have led to significant reductions in tariff duties and thus have been a major factor in the expansion of world trade since 1947. However, in recent talks, during the 1980s, attention has turned to reduction of nontariff barriers such as those used by Japan. Negotiations over nontariff barriers have not been too successful to date.

UNCTAD was formed in 1964 as an agency of the United Nations. It has 147 member countries, but its main focus is to promote the interests of developing countries, in trade and other matters. Its main success has been in negotiating nonreciprocal concessions from the industrialized nations. In other words, products from emerging countries face lower tariffs than manufactured imports from industrial countries. In theory, these concessions contribute to the industrial development and exports of the less-developed countries. UNCTAD has also promoted international commodity agreements in sugar and coffee, among other products, in hopes of stabilizing their world prices. However, without authority to control supplies of such products, these agreements have not been very effective. Nevertheless, UNCTAD continues to be a lobbyist for changing world trade patterns and a voice in favor of the less-developed nations.

### Producer Agreements

Cartels and combines are agreements among producers to control prices, supply, exports, sales territories, or other aspects of production and distribution for a product. Combines are similar to cartels but usually involve more stringent means of enforcing the agreements. Either type may be entered into by businesses or governments. An example of a business combine is that of the DeBeers Consolidated Mines, Ltd. in South Africa, which controls about 95 percent of the world diamond trade. Governments have signed agreements to control supplies and prices of such commodities as coffee, tin, sugar, and petroleum. While cartels and combines have the effect of increased cooperation for producers, they obviously restrict competition and the operation of normal demand-and-supply forces. In their favor, we must note that they have the potential of lowering production and marketing costs by coordinating those activities and by making volumes of supply predictable.

OPEC (Organization of Petroleum Exporting Countries) is the most powerful producer agreement in effect today. It was formed in 1960 by oil-producing nations who wanted more power to influence policies of the large international oil companies, Today OPEC nations (and producers such as Mexico who adhere to OPEC prices) control over 80 percent of the world trade in crude oils. The 1970s success of OPEC in forcing oil consumers to pay higher and higher prices for the commodity may have been its undoing, and is a good example of the limits of cartels and combines. As prices became higher, consuming nations created competition for OPEC through increased exploration at home, and through development of alternate energy sources. Likewise, conservation efforts have reduced total demand and have reduced the monopolistic powers of OPEC. Furthermore, in the early 1980s individual OPEC members began asserting independence from OPEC pricing policies and export quotas, in order to finance their national projects with petroleum sales. Ultimately then, the limits to the power of cartels or combines come from competing products, from nonsigners to such agreements, and from the divergent goals of member countries or businesses.

## ECONOMIC BARRIERS
## TO INTERNATIONAL BUSINESS

Essentially every nation in the world has unique resources and unique ideas about how those resources should be used. For these reasons, each nation develops its own policies to assert control over its economic resources. As a result, most countries attempt to regulate business activity within the country and trade with other nations. In this section we will discuss the reasons for regulating international business activity and the different tools that are used to do so.

### Rationale for Trade Restrictions

As American automobile producers saw their share of the U.S. auto market decline in the 1970s and early 1980s, they joined with labor unions to pressure the Carter and Reagan administrations for protection from foreign producers. They wanted higher tariffs on Japanese automobiles, but they settled for voluntary import quotas. American consumers may ultimately have fewer product choices and pay higher prices for protecting American industries like automobile manufacturers, but American jobs will have been preserved.

This example is a classic illustration of the rationale of economic protectionism. Restrictions on foreign trade, especially on imports, help protect the national economy. By making foreign products more expensive or inaccessible, jobs and capital are kept at home. During the Great Depression, tariff and nontariff barriers to trade were at their highest levels in the twentieth century. High rates of inflation and unemployment in the 1970s and early 1980s once again created pressure on governments to impose protective barriers to insulate and protect domestic economies. While trade brings economic benefits and higher standards of living in the long term, the short-term effects of high import levels can be devastating. Therefore, in the world of political economies, the economic benefits of trade must be measured against their political effects.

In underdeveloped and developing countries, we can see other purposes for creating barriers to imports. These nations often need to build basic industries, such as steel, so they can supply industrial development that will increase their competitiveness in world markets for manufactured goods. Since the national markets for such products are usually small, these industries cannot develop economies of scale for low-cost production. They are therefore vulnerable to foreign producers and must be protected through trade barriers. Less-developed countries also want to preserve their holdings of foreign exchange for purchases of materials and equipment that will contribute most to future industrial development. By imposing high trade barriers to the importation of nonessential goods, they can force substitution for imports from local sources of supply. This contributes to the diversification of their local economies and makes them less dependent on fluctuating world commodity prices (their usual way of earning foreign exchange).

In all countries of the world, dependence on foreign sources of supply reduces national sovereignty. For security and defense purposes it makes sense to promote self-sufficiency where possible or reasonable. For example, if the U.S. had continued to increase its dependence on foreign supplies of oil in the 1970s, our military and foreign policy autonomy could have been jeopardized. European nations and Japan, who receive over 70 percent of their oil supplies from Arab countries, are much less able to act independently in Israeli-Arab confrontations in the Middle East.

To summarize, the overall purpose of trade barriers is protection of the national interests over international ones. Currently, most major world traders are committed to reductions of trade barriers, but negative domestic economic and/or security conditions could prompt policy reversals. Most recently, nontariff barriers, such as import quotas, have been expanding even while we continue to negotiate tariff reductions.

### Tariff Barriers

There are three types of tariffs that can be imposed on imports or exports. A specific tariff is a tax based on the physical amount of the product being imported or exported. This type of tariff is often imposed on commodities such as grain or oil, and might take the form of one dollar per ton or per barrel. Ad valorem tariffs are set according to the value of imported or exported goods. When products arrive at customs, a sales invoice or other document must be presented to establish the value of the shipment. A tax is then levied according to the determined value. Ad valorem tariffs are most common for manufactured and processed goods. The third type of tariff is a combination of specific and ad valorem tariffs. A tax would be imposed based on both weight and value of a shipment.

A country's tariff schedule is the listing of all tariffs for imported or exported goods. Most countries use tariffs for imported products, but rarely impose them on exports since exports earn foreign exchange. More often exports face a variety of nontariff barriers. In addition, if one country prices its exports very low, the country into which they are imported may impose antidumping penalties or countervailing duties based on the original country's import duties.

## Nontariff Barriers

Firms involved in international business often find nontariff barriers to be a more serious restraint than tariffs on their international activities. Import or export quotas provide a good example. When a firm's access to a particular foreign market is restricted to a certain quantity or value of shipments, its success in penetrating the market or in building buyer loyalty is truly hampered. Quotas can be discriminating too; that is, there may be limits set on imports of a particular product from one country, but no restrictions on the same products from another country. For example, in the 1970s, Japan and the United States agreed to voluntary import quotas for imports of Japanese automobiles and televisions. The agreement was intended to reduce the flow of goods from Japan to the U.S. and to reduce the overall imbalance in trade between the two countries. No such limits were imposed on German autos or Mexican televisions. Export quotas are imposed on essential goods when domestic price controls could make world sales more attractive so that domestic producers export all they produce, leaving nothing for local consumers.

Even more pervasive as barriers to world trade are licensing requirements. In the United States, for example, an import license is required for shipments of significant value of all products in commerce. Export licenses are only required for specific products such as firearms and for high-technology goods like computers or airplanes. However, these categories are not as straightforward as they appear. Many of the companies that supply parts for products seemingly unrelated to strategic or defense-related industries, occasionally find that they are faced with licensing restrictions on their international activities. In 1982, Westinghouse and several other U.S. companies faced prosecution from the Reagan administration because their European subsidiaries were supplying the Soviet pipeline then under construction in Europe. The administration's argument was that this was an illegal export of U.S. technology (transferred via the European subsidiaries) to the Soviet Union. In many countries, including the U.S., licensing may be granted only for products destined to certain countries. Import licenses are sometimes granted only to local citizens, thus restricting a foreign firm's intracompany transfers of products.

In addition to quotas and licensing there are a myriad of other barriers facing international businesses. A country's regulatory framework for domestic business can discriminate against foreign producers. For example, U.S. law requires that clothing be labeled in English with the origin of the product, its contents, and cleaning instructions. Imported foods must meet all U.S. laws regarding standardization, grading, and labeling. Environmental regulations for production, distribution, and product quality pose other barriers to imports and exports.

Business customs and market structure can also make it difficult for foreign firms to compete in a domestic market. In Japan, for example, access to the market is almost always contingent on a successful joint venture with one of the large Japanese trading companies, because the distribution structure there is lengthy, complex, and dependent on long-term relationships. American and other firms have found it almost impossible to break into the market without local expertise and ties.

Government monetary policy can also be a direct threat to international business activities. In order to preserve holdings of foreign exchange, all foreign currency transactions can be blocked. Purchases of foreign currency may be available only for approved debts or purchases of foreign goods. Likewise, domestic price ceilings or controls can change a market into a losing one. Credit may be made available only to locally owned companies or only for approved investments. Last, tax penalties may be imposed on firms viewed by a government as having an excessive dependence on imports, or tax subsidies may be granted only to local competitors.

## SUMMARY

International marketing exposes the firm and its marketing strategy to a unique group of economic institutions. The first of these is the international monetary framework. The system that has evolved for exchange of currencies has no one marketplace, but is composed of individuals, firms, commercial banks, currency brokers, and central banks. The International Monetary Fund plays a clearinghouse role in stabilizing currency values. Its member countries keep reserves at the IMF in the form of gold, their own currency, holdings of key currencies, and SDRs. The balance of payments of a country summarizes each country's international currency transactions and the state of its IMF reserves. Trends that can be seen by analyzing a country's balance of payments are indicators of its overall economic health and the relative strength of its currency on world markets. Balance-of-payments analysis is an important tool in assessing economic conditions in a foreign market.

There are many forms of economic cooperation that impact on foreign market opportunities. Regional economic cooperation in various forms—free trade areas, customs unions, common markets, or economic and political unions—can facilitate exports and imports between member countries, and can increase the size of the potential market. Bilateral agreements facilitate trade between two specific countries, but they are usually product-specific. Multilateral agreements such as GATT commit their signers to negotiate for reduced trade barriers. Producer agreements, such as the OPEC cartel and DeBeers combine, are intended to coordinate supply and distribution of a particular commodity, but their effectiveness is limited by the levels of world demand and competition for their products.

In order to preserve independence in economic matters, and sovereignty over critical industries, many countries place restrictions on international trade. Trade barriers protect national interests at the expense of international ones in the short-term, but in the long term, protectionism can be harmful to a national economy. Trade barriers take two forms: tariff and nontariff barriers. Tariff duties can be assessed on the physical amount (specific) or value (ad valorem) of either exports or imports. They are more often assessed against imports since most countries want to encourage exporting. Exports can face countervailing tariffs or antidumping duties in foreign markets. The most significant nontariff trade barriers are quotas and licensing requirements. These regulations can be placed on either imports or exports and have become an important focus of recent worldwide trade negotiations because of their impact on trade imbalances between countries. Other nontariff trade barriers are domestic business and environmental regulations, labeling requirements, business customs, and domestic monetary policies.

## DISCUSSION QUESTIONS

1. What are the major economic institutions of the international environment for world marketing?
2. Explain why there are over one hundred separate currencies in the world.
3. What is meant by the international money "market"? Who are its principal participants?
4. How can firms reduce the risks of collecting payments from foreign buyers?
5. Study the letter of credit shown in Appendix C. What are its most important parts?
6. What is the IMF and what does it do?
7. Explain "key" currency and give an example.

8. Using Figure 6–2, discuss the following trends:
   a. U.S. merchandise exports and imports during the 1970s
   b. U.S. foreign direct investment, 1960–1981
   c. U.S. reserve assets and holdings of different reserve items
9. What is meant by "deficit" in the balance of payments?
10. How can you use a country's balance of payments in analyzing its market potential?
11. Differentiate between free trade areas, customs unions, common markets, and economic and political unions.
12. What are the strengths and weaknesses of the European Community?
13. Explain how bilateral agreements have helped expand trade between the United States and the USSR and its satelites.
14. What is GATT?
15. Explain a cartel and the ways it differs from a combine.
16. What are the limits on the powers of cartels and combines?
17. Discuss the rationale for restrictions on international trade.
18. Describe the different types of tariffs.
19. What are quotas? How do they operate as trade barriers?
20. Explain how licensing requirements are used to restrict international trade.
21. Develop a list of domestic business regulations which you feel adversely affect imports into the United States.

# TRADE BARRIERS: ADVANTAGEOUS OR ABORTIVE?

When the General Agreement on Tariffs and Trade (GATT) Treaty was negotiated in 1947, its general purpose was to promote world trade among member countries by reducing tariffs and trade restrictions. Boasting over 60 member countries today, periodic conferences are held in Geneva to consult and negotiate trade barriers on a bi- and multi-lateral basis. However, there always exists the possibility of a trade war initiation among member nations since no legal council exists to "enforce" agreements. The possibilities increase during a slow-growth world economy—when nations with high unemployment rates protect their industries from competition.

Multi-lateral trade networks established the concept of "one huge marketplace" and subsequently, the idealism of unlimited trade opportunities. Unfortunately a dismal world economy in the 1980's has activated protectionist measures among industrialized nations in an effort to relieve economic stagnation and maintain a favorable balance of payments.

A prime example of market protectionism are the recent Japanese trade barriers enacted against U.S. cigarettes. While President Reagan warned Prime Minister Nakasone that Japanese trade barriers would increase protectionist sentiment in the U.S., the $10 billion-a-year cigarette market remains virtually impenetrable by U.S. marketers.

Japan Tobacco and Salt Public Corporation, the state-owned tobacco monopoly, controls all production, distribution, marketing, pricing and advertising of tobacco products. Japan is a large potential market for U.S. cigarette marketers since there are an estimated 35 million smokers in the mid-20's to mid-30's (40% of the adult population).* Since the tobacco monopoly controls all facets of the industry, bureaucratic regulations restrict distribution and advertising of foreign brands resulting in a limited U.S. market share of 1.4% of all cigarettes sold. Because import tariffs favor domestic brands (usually local versions of popular American brands), price differentials between American and Japanese brands have been as much as 50 cents a pack.

Of Japan's 250,000 retailers which sell tobacco products, only 20,000 are supplied with American brands. The tobacco monopoly supplies these dealers with foreign brands once a month while supplying Japanese ciga-

*Jack Burton, "Japan Sparks to U.S. Cigarette Attack", *Advertising Age,* October 18, 1982, p. 56.

This case was prepared by Carol G. Spindola.

rettes on a weekly basis. American companies have provided ample surpluses to Japan's Tobacco and Salt Corp. but the monopoly does not actively promote the foreign brands to retailers. While Tobacco and Salt doubled the number of outlets for U.S. brands in March 1983, half the dealers were located in small rural towns and none in the prime Tokyo and Osaka markets.

Japan has stated that it must protect its tobacco farmers who are key supporters of the incumbent Liberal Democratic party. The state monopoly subsidizes Japan's 110,000 tobacco growers (2% of the country's farmers) by purchasing their low-quality leaf at triple the prices of the finest tobacco in the world.** It has been estimated that the monopoly imports a third of its tobacco needs from the U.S., which it then mixes with its own.

Due to U.S. pressures, Japan has agreed to reduce cigarette tariffs from 35% to 20%. Furthermore, the Japanese government is addressing a series of proposals directed at easing import restraints as well as allowing increased advertising expenditures by foreign brands. The U.S. hopes that with Japan's implementation of reduced trade barriers to the American tobacco industry, the continually rising trade deficit with Japan can be significantly reduced. Some U.S. officials believe that over-protecting the inefficient state-owned monopoly does not justify damaging U.S.-Japanese relationships—especially with growing anti-Japanese sentiment by the U.S. steel and automobile industries.

**EXHIBIT 1**

| U.S. WORLD TRADE (1982) | |
| --- | --- |
| Exports | 212.2 billion |
| Imports | 244.0 billion |
| Deficit | ⟨31.8 billion⟩ |

| U.S. TRADE WITH JAPAN (1982) | |
| --- | --- |
| Exports | 21.0 billion |
| Imports | 37.7 billion |
| Deficit | ⟨16.7 billion⟩ |

## QUESTIONS

1. Discuss the political implications of trade barriers on international trade.
2. Discuss the economic arguments (pro and con) of trade barriers in the case of cigarette sales between the United States and Japan.

**Louis Kraar, "Japan Blows Smoke About U.S. Cigarettes," *Fortune,* February 21, 1983, p. 105.

3. While tariff barriers are more explicit, how can American cigarette marketers address the nontariff trade barriers imposed by Japan's state-owned monopoly?
4. Given the existence of a state-owned (monopolistic) industry, what available foreign entry strategy could a U.S. marketer pursue?
5. When do trade barriers become advantageous or abortive in meeting a country's needs?

# chapter 7

# THE POLITICAL-LEGAL ENVIRONMENT FOR INTERNATIONAL MARKETING

When General Motors was considering last fall whether to reopen an assembly plant in Buenos Aires, Gordon Rayfield, a political-risk analyst on GM's staff, was asked for an opinion. Argentina's economy was collapsing, Rayfield told the corporate brass; there was widespread labor unrest and the ruling military regime might try to reassert its shipping authority by railing against some "foreign threat." All things considered, GM decided to drop its plans for Argentina. Six months later the Falkland Islands invasion was launched. "I was not surprised," says Rayfield. Fortunately, neither was GM.

In fact, many multinational corporations were forewarned about events in Argentina, usually by in-house analysts like Rayfield who try to predict where political crises will occur—and how they might affect big businesses. Until the Iranian revolution, only a few banks and oil companies had formal risk-analysis departments. But now most big corporations hire political experts to advise them on the growing uncertainties of investing abroad. "The problem is to relate the political environment to business conditions," says Stephen Blank of Multinational Strategies, a New York–based risk-analysis consulting firm. "We try to predict what political changes will mean to corporations—and to tell them how to adjust."*

---

*"The Risk Analysts," *Newsweek*, June 7, 1982, p. 59. Copyright 1982, by Newsweek, Inc. All rights reserved. Reprinted by permission.

## INTRODUCTION

Business and governments need each other. Business can only prosper when there are stable economic and political environments; these are prerequisites for business planning and risk taking. Governments need a source of revenue to support their endeavors in administering the public interest. In many countries, they see business as the major source of economic opportunities that determine citizens' standards of living. Unfortunately, mutual dependence does not always generate mutual respect or trust. Businesses resent government regulation of their activities, and governments suspect businesses of subverting their economic goals and of exploiting resources without societal contributions.

There is fruitful ground for misinterpretation and misunderstanding between businesses and governments. Foreign business exacerbates the potential for mutual suspicion. Attitudes about the role of business in a country's economic life, as well as what relationships should exist between business and government, vary throughout the world. The differences in attitude may be due to different political structures or to party philosophies, history, and tradition; the roles of interest groups or the political elite; an unstable political environment; forces of nationalism; or any number of other reasons. When a firm develops policies that establish a workable relationship within its home political environment, it may find these same policies at cross-purposes with those of a foreign government. In fact, the international firm may find it necessary to adjust its profit goals, decision-making processes, and operating standards in each country in order to have continued permission to operate.

This chapter focuses on the elements of a firm's political and legal environment that affect its operations and goals. Analysis of foreign market opportunities must include assessment of the country's political and legal impact on the ability to exploit those opportunities. The tools needed to make this assessment are covered in the following sections. They are

1. An awareness of attitudes toward business, foreign business, and the multinational corporation
2. Analysis of political forces affecting international marketers
3. Knowledge of different legal systems and their effect on decision making and operations

We will also suggest ways in which the international marketer can minimize political and legal risks.

## THE IMPACT OF PUBLIC POLICY AND LAW ON INTERNATIONAL MARKETING

### Public Policy and Business Interfaces

Public policy defines the rules for business operations, ranging from the kind of legal identity a firm can have to what it can charge different buyers to how many hours a day its employees can work. All domestic firms must evaluate their political and legal environments and then develop marketing strategies that accommodate these complex, subtle, and changing "rules of the game." At the domestic level, government policies may vary widely, even given a consistent view of the roles of business and government. For example, the philosophy of "government as watchdog over anticompetitive practices" can be implemented by antitrust laws in one country and by cooperation with industry self-regulation in another country. Over time, different implementation policies are often tried in the same country, thus creating a changed political and legal environment for business firms. Philosophies of "business versus government responsibilities" are also variable. Government may be the benefactor of business, a watchdog, or both. Therefore, two sources of risk in marketing strategy formulation are changing public policies and differing philosophies about the responsibilities of business firms.

### Special Position of the Foreign Firm

In international business, two additional sources of risk confound the marketing manager's task in developing strategy. The first of these concerns the alien status of foreign businesses. Each sovereign country puts the interests of its own citizens above those of others, and its government has the prerogative to develop public policies that will achieve this goal. These policies can affect foreign business firms at two levels.

First, legislation and policies can be established that discriminate against foreign firms in favor of local ones in domestic matters. Certain industries may be foreclosed to foreign investors—for example, banking, mining, oil refining, telecommunications. Government purchasing may be limited by law to locally owned suppliers, thus restricting the foreign firm's market access. This type of discrimination may take the more subtle form of "policies" rather than laws. There may be special agencies that police foreign firms' business practices, while local firms are allowed more freedom in pricing, hiring, use of technologies, and other such matters.

A second way in which foreign businesses may be treated differentially from local firms is in the area of international transfers of goods, money, personnel, and know-how. Exporters clearly have a disadvantage over local producers because they must pay customs duties and submit products for inspection as they enter a country, both of which increase the cost and time of getting a product to market. In order to encourage foreign-owned producers to buy supplies locally, they are sometimes charged extra duties or taxes that are not assessed to locally owned importers. In many Latin American and African countries, licenses are required for acquisition of foreign currency. A subsidiary of a multinational company may be unable to purchase necessary parts for production if it is not granted a license to purchase the foreign currency needed to pay for the parts. Some countries have used these currency licenses to force multinationals to invest in local industrial development. International transfers of personnel are also restricted by the visa-granting powers of individual countries; this usually has more significant impact on foreign-owned firms than on locally owned ones. In the area of technology acquisition and transfer, the foreign firm may also face discriminatory policies. In Mexico, for example, a petition must be filed before firms are granted permission to acquire and register foreign-developed technologies. This agency makes no secret that it grants preference to requests from Mexican-owned firms. And Levi Strauss found the Italian courts to be excruciatingly slow in prosecuting Italian firms that were violating Italian copyright-trademark laws in their copies of Levi's blue jeans.

The second way in which public policy causes risk for international firms is the inexorable link between international business activity and international relations between countries. When two national governments have good relations with each other, there is a supportive framework for trade and investment by businesses in the two countries. However, political forces often prompt drastic and immediate changes in international relations, and these changes can have negative effects on business flows between those countries. A good example was Iran's taking of American diplomats as hostages in 1979. To create pressure for their release, President Carter froze all Iranian assets in American banks. Several U.S. businesses that had orders or production ready for delivery to Iranian subsidiaries or distributors were severely affected by this international conflict.

A further complication in the international political environment is the absence of international organizations that can resolve international business disputes. The World Court will hear cases of disputes between two national governments, but it is not empowered to consider commercial cases. This is also true of other international organizations, such as the United Nations or the Organization for Economic Cooperation and Development (OECD). As a result, the international firm has no advocate that can put aside political pressures in either its home or host country and mediate conflicts over international business issues.

We do not mean to imply that the interactions of foreign business and government are always negative or threatening. The goals *are* often divergent; yet, foreign firms are in a unique position to benefit many governments. They bring in valuable foreign exchange, train local managers, introduce new products that increase the variety of choice for buyers, and introduce new managerial and technical know-how. These assets, while not easily measured and not without costs, contribute to the economic and competitive well-being of recipient countries.

## The MNC and National Sovereignty

In Chapter 2 we discussed the multinational corporation as a new social institution of the twentieth century. It developed before or in spite of political institutions that remain national in scope. This is an immediate source of potential conflict—national interests versus those of the transnational corporation. Due to the multinational's ability to move resources internationally, it can threaten the sovereignty of national governments in controlling business activity within their own borders.[1] Theoretically, a multinational subsidiary has access to financial assets that can upset a country's balance of payments or its anti-inflation policies. Other international assets of the multinational could affect a country's industrial development plans, employment levels, holdings of foreign exchange, or national security.[2]

The MNC is most threatening to smaller, less-developed countries; but advanced countries, such as the United States, have also developed policies to restrict the operations of multinational enterprises. Various U.S. laws affect capital, technology, and personnel movements within international companies.

Less-developed countries have devised their own restrictions on the operations of MNCs, but most recently they have joined together to increase their bargaining power vis-à-vis international companies. A major arm of their joint efforts has been the New International Economic Order (NIEO), a resolution passed by the United Nations. The NIEO promotes a restructuring of economic power in the world by transferring more resources to the less-developed countries and by giving them a united voice in negotiating with MNCs.[3] Whatever the ultimate achievements of the

[1] For more detailed discussion of multinational corporations and the issue of national sovereignty, see Raymond Vernon, *Sovereignty at Bay* (New York: Basic Books, 1971); Joseph S. Nye, Jr., "Multinational Corporations in World Politics," *Foreign Affairs,* October 1974, pp. 170–80; Peter P. Gabriel, "The MNC and the Public Interest," *Journal of World Trade Law,* Jan.–Feb. 1971, pp. 26–28; Louis T. Wells, Jr., "Social Cost-Benefit Analysis for MNC's," *Harvard Business Review,* March–April 1975, pp. 36–48.

[2] Stefan H. Robock, Kenneth Simmonds, Jack Zwick, *International Business and Multinational Enterprises,* rev. ed. (Homewood, Ill.: Richard D. Irwin, 1977, pp. 200–202.

[3] Joel Davidow, "Multinationals, Host Governments and Regulation of Restrictive Business Practices," *Columbia Journal of World Business,* Summer 1980, pp. 14–19; and Jack N. Behrman, "Transnational Corporations in the New International Economic Order," *Journal of International Business Studies,* Spring/Summer 1981, pp. 29–41.

NIEO, it has encouraged individual member countries to be more assertive in capturing economic benefits from international businesses.

It should be clear at this point that international marketing abilities are intricately tied to international and national political and legal environments. Now we will review the forces that ultimately determine a firm's vulnerability to political and legal risks in international marketing. We also propose strategies that can be applied to reduce exposure to such risks.

## POLITICAL FORCES AFFECTING THE INTERNATIONAL MARKETER

The task of the marketing manager is to assess the political forces that comprise the firm's political environment and to analyze their impact on marketing strategy. Figure 7-1 presents a checklist of questions that can guide this process; it also outlines topics covered in this chapter.

**FIGURE 7-1**  Checklist for analyzing the political-legal environment.

1. What is the country's political structure?
2. How do citizens, political parties, and special-interest groups participate in political decision making?
3. What is the current government's political philosophy? How is it implemented?
4. What are the philosophies of opposing political forces?
5. What role does the current government see for foreign business?
6. Is foreign business treated differentially from local firms in public policy? If so, how?
7. What is the country's history in dealing with different types of foreign businesses?
8. What is the process whereby changes in public policy are made?
9. What are the current and foreseeable trends in relationships between government in this country and in my home country?
10. What general role does government see for private business in this country's economic life?
11. What restrictions on international transfers of resources will affect my firm's operations in this country?
12. What are the major trends in the regulatory environment?
13. What incentives does the government give to private business and foreign investors?
14. What are the trigger points for increased nationalistic feelings in the host country?
15. How does the government assert its economic sovereignty?
16. What are the specific risks of loss of ownership or control of assets?
17. What are the chances of political harassment and what forms is it likely to take?
18. What tools can we use to build a mutually beneficial relationship with this country's government? Will they survive a possible change of government?
19. What are the possibilities of a change in government or other expressions of political instability?
20. Are my firm, my industry, and/or my products likely to be politically vulnerable? (See Fig. 7-3.)
21. What is the basis of this country's legal system?
22. Will my firm's activities violate any of the home or host countries' extraterritorial laws?
23. What areas of my marketing strategy will be affected by the host country's legal environment?

## Political Structure and Philosophy

A good place to begin an analysis of a country's political environment is to study its political structure and decision-making processes. The basic structure is determined by the roles of citizens, political parties, and special-interest groups in the power structure and in political decisions. In democracies, all these groups have comparatively high participation in decision making; in monarchies and dictatorships, these groups play minimal roles, except for the military, which, as a special-interest group, may be important in selecting a dictator. In communist political structures, the political party is central to decision making, while citizens and other interest groups are less important. It is helpful then to know *who* participates in decisions about political structure and policy.

Each of the models of government—democracy, monarchy, dictatorship, socialism, and communism—can vary greatly in the way it is practiced. For example, in democracies, executives can be elected directly (the United States), chosen by the dominant political party (Great Britain or Canada), chosen by a coalition of political parties (Italy or France), or chosen by the outgoing executive (Mexico). These aspects of transferring political power tell a lot more about the political environment than voter participation rates.

As important as knowledge of a country's political structure is an understanding of the significant political philosophies that guide policy. Conservative governments usually promote a broad role for private business in the country's economic life with a minimum of restrictions on its activities. Leftist governments, on the other hand, may encourage public ownership of business and a more comprehensive and restrictive regulatory environment. It is important to understand the philosophy of the government in power, as well as those philosophies that guide opposing political parties and other significant political forces in a country.

International firms are often viewed differently from local businesses as participants in a country's economy. A government that encourages private investment in general may discourage importation or foreign ownership of local businesses. For example, in the 1960s and 1970s, Canadians became concerned about foreign ownership of a significant share of their oil, forestry, and manufacturing industries. Both the Labor and Conservative parties developed platforms that called for strict rules regarding future takeovers of locally owned firms. Japan is perhaps the most obvious example of a government that supports domestic industry but creates barriers to foreign firms wishing to penetrate the Japanese market. In some countries the prevailing philosophy may be that imports are to be discouraged but foreign investment in manufacturing is good for the country; in other countries, only joint ventures find government support. The international marketer must discover what the perceived role is for foreign business activity in a country.

Not all political philosophies can easily be classified on the conservative-moderate-liberal-leftist continuum. Governments that are committed to industrial development or diversification of their economy have a "development" philosophy. The government of Mexico, for example, does all of the following: gives incentives for domestic or foreign investment in some industries, while reserving other industries for public enterprise; restricts foreign ownership to 49 percent in some industries, and allows full ownership in others; controls some industries by government ownership, others by regulation, and leaves still others relatively free of restrictions. These seemingly conflicting policies make it difficult to classify some political philosophies within a standard conservative-leftist framework.

Another important topic in analyzing a country's political structure and philosophy is the continuity of government policy. Change is the main source of political risk, and radical change causes the most difficulty for business adjustment. Because change in a government or its political philosophy can lead to unknown consequences for business, it is more disrupting than a constant but antagonistic relationship between business and government. The international marketer should become aware of the processes whereby policy changes are instituted. More detail on identifying inherent political instability is given in a later section.

### Nationalism

Nationalism to the outsider or analyst is an irrational force. It causes governments to view the world from a "we versus they" perspective and to dismiss possibilities of mutual benefit and cooperation. Nationalistic feelings are behind policies that generate "psychic income" at the expense of real income or benefits. For example, takeover of a foreign-owned business that local citizens do not have the expertise to operate effectively, may create the "psychic income" of giving control to national citizens, but it will be at the expense of productivity and contribution to the country's GNP.

On the other hand, nationalism is a necessary and rational force in a world of nation-states. The mutual interests and identity of a group of people must be translated into a "public interest," and institutions must be formed to administer the agreed-upon public interest. This is the basis of a nation-state. The sovereignty of every nation-state lies in its government's ability to preserve and protect its citizens from foreign domination or control. Therefore, nationalism is the force which cements a people with their government.

Nationalism is expressed, even stimulated, in a variety of ways. For example, we encourage national identity in the United States through recognition of national heroes, national holidays, the Pledge of Allegiance, and flying the flag, among other activities. These things make us feel patriotic and protective of what we perceive to be American. We also identify things as being as "American as apple pie and motherhood" even though these are surely not exclusively American. A new way of competing, new products, new types of stores, different rules for subordinates and superiors, or even different business and government relationships can be seen as jeopardizing a people's national identity. Not too many years ago, the French were so threatened by the "Anglicizing" of their language that political leaders forbade the use of terms such as *le parking* or *le super*. In 1976 Mexico passed a law forcing the "Mexicanization" of brand names registered there. National pride and national identity are expressions of nationalistic feelings.

A somewhat more threatening form of nationalism for international businesses is economic sovereignty. The foreign-owned firm, particularly the multinational corporation, responds to directors that are outside the control of the host country. This gives rise to the view that foreign business takes away control over the economic resources of a country. Mining and petroleum, in which considerable foreign investments have been made in various countries, represent physical and tangible exploitation and removal of a country's resources, even if there are economic benefits in terms of employment, technology transfer, and revenues for the government. As a result, these industries are vulnerable to local feelings of nationalism in the form of pressure to domesticate ownership. Economic sovereignty is the force behind policies that restrict profit repatriation, domestic ownership or equity rules, requirements to use local sources of supply, and restrictions on the use of foreign personnel or technology.

The international marketer needs to know the likely trigger points for increased nationalistic feelings in a country. They may be issues related to national pride, identity, or economic sovereignty. It is also helpful to determine if any political parties or interest groups have strong nationalistic philosophies and what the country's history is with respect to expressions of nationalism. The next section reviews some of the risks that may be associated with increased nationalism.

### Political Risks and Harassment

The risks that an international firm faces from the political environment can be significant. At one extreme the firm can lose all control, ownership of assets, and market access; on the other hand, the firm may simply face customs delays or problems in getting visas for needed foreign consultants. Whatever the extent of political risks, they can reduce the firm's operating effectiveness in foreign markets.

A firm can lose total ownership of foreign assets in one of four ways: confiscation, expropriation, nationalization, or domestication. The first two are likely to be immediate, while domestication may take years and may even have the foreign firm's cooperation and assistance. Nationalization may affect both domestic and foreign business. Confiscation requires nothing more than a government decision to take control of a foreign firm's assets in its country; no payment is made to compensate the firm for its loss. Expropriation differs only in that *some* compensation is given for the firm's assets. Either one of these two political actions has the effect of discouraging future foreign investment, but they may meet the country's perceived needs for more secure national defense, economic independence, or "psychic income."

When the revolutionary government of Iran took power in 1979, it confiscated many foreign firms' assets. The confiscations covered firms in a variety of industries. In contrast, the most publicized confiscations in the past have been of firms in mining, petroleum, transportation, communication, and utilities. These industries appear particularly vulnerable to the risk of confiscation, expropriation, nationalization, or domestication. For a list of some U.S. firms that have had assets expropriated since 1960, see Figure 7–2.

Very few firms feel satisfied with the compensation given when their assets are expropriated. In most cases, the payment is not negotiable; but even when a government is willing to discuss compensation with a firm, they are likely to disagree on the basis for valuing the firm's assets. When the Cerro mining assets were expropriated by Peru in 1973, the Peruvian government considered the firm's initial investment and additional assets less all profits over the history of the firm's operations in Peru. The Cerro company felt this was inadequate because it did not compensate for income contributions to the Peruvian economy, appreciation of assets, or loss of future income.

Nationalization is the process whereby a government decides to take over ownership of an industry for its own control. Both local and foreign-owned firms may be affected. The socialist president of France, Francois Mitterand, nationalized French banking in 1981 and both foreign banks and French bankers were stunned. Government ownership and management of an industry may give it more control over the country's economic life and is usually tied to issues of economic sovereignty, national defense, or control of strategic industries.

Domestication represents a variety of pressures that can be placed on a foreign-owned firm to transfer ownership and/or control to local citizens. At one extreme, a foreign investor may be forced to sell shares of stock to local investors at a predetermined price. Alternatively, the firm may be asked to develop a plan for divestment over a certain time period, but the business is allowed to determine how the transfer of ownership will occur. Other examples of domestication policies that might affect foreign operations are pressure to employ nationals at top decision-making levels; permits required for importing equipment, parts, personnel, or technology; and, requirements to sell a portion of the firm's production in export markets.[4]

[4]Philip R. Cateora, "The Multinational Enterprise and Nationalism," *MSU Business Topics,* 19, no. 2.

**FIGURE 7–2**   Expropriated companies.

The list of companies below is taken from recent State Department reports. These companies are cited in the reports as having experienced some form of foreign government interference since 1960. It should be stressed that most, but not all, suffered an overt expropriation.

Alcan
ALCOA
Allied Artists
Allied Chemical
American Eastern Tankers
Amerada Hess
American Insurance
American International Insurance
American Life Insurance
American Metal Climax
American Smelting and Refining
Aminoil
Anaconda
Argentine Southeastern Drilling
Armco Steel
Atlantic Richfield
Bank of America
Bethlehem Steel
Boise Cascade
Brown & Root
California Asiatic Oil
Cargill
Cerro
Chase Manhattan Bank
Citibank
Cities Service
Coca-Cola
Columbia Pictures
Continental Oil
Continental Telephone
Corning Glass Works
Crown Cork & Seal
Diamond Distributors
Dow Chemical
Dresser Industries
E.I. DuPont de Nemours
El Paso Natural Gas
Engelhard Minerals & Chemicals
Exxon
Firestone Tire & Rubber
Ford Motor
General Cable
General Electric
General Mills
General Motors
General Tire & Rubber
Georgia-Pacific

Getty Oil
Giddings & Lewis
Goodyear Tire and Rubber
W.R. Grace
Grace Petroleum
Great American Insurance
Gulf Oil
Gulf Resources & Chemical
Hanover Insurance
Hartford Fire Insurance
H. J. Heinz Starkist
Holiday Inns
Home Insurance
Hunt International Petroleum
International Basic Economy
International Flavors & Fragrances
International Railways of Central America
International Telephone & Telegraph
Johns-Manville
I.S. Joseph
Kaiser Industries
Kellogg
Kennecott Copper
Kerr-McGee
Marathon Oil
Marcona
Marine Construction & Design
Metro-Goldwyn-Mayer
Mobil Oil
Morgan Guaranty Trust
Morrison-Knudsen
NCR
Occidental Petroleum
Olin
Panamerican Sulfur
Paramount Pictures
Parsons & Whittemore
Phelps Dodge
Phillips Petroleum
Procter & Gamble
Ralston Purina
Raytheon
RCA
Republic Steel
Reynolds Metals
Sinclair
Singer

**FIGURE 7–2** *Continued*

| | |
|---|---|
| Standard Oil of California | Universal Pictures |
| Standard Oil (Indiana) | Warner Brothers |
| Sterling Drug | H.B. Zachry |
| Sun Company | |
| Tenneco | |
| Texaco | |
| Textron | |
| Twentieth Century-Fox Film | |
| Union Carbide | |
| Union Oil | |
| Uniroyal | |
| U.S. Steel | |

*Source:* Reprinted by permission of the Harvard Business Review. Excerpt from "Managing Against Expropriation" by David G. Bradley (July–August 1977). Copyright © 1977 by the President and Fellows of Harvard College; all rights reserved.

Political harassment is a less significant, but more insidious political risk than loss of ownership. It can affect exporters as well as companies that enter foreign markets via foreign production, joint ventures, or licensing. Harassment can take many forms and can affect all areas of business operations, from labor relations to customs duties to product design or pricing. The foreign firm may be singled out for harassment, or an entire industry may be the target of new, restrictive regulations.

Any government's powers to license are a source of political risk and can be used to harass a business firm. A license may be required for business incorporation, acquisition of foreign exchange, purchase of imports, change in prices, hiring or firing of personnel, or sales to government agencies or enterprises. Changes in tax policy can also be used to capture more revenue and to penalize businesses.

Another source of political risk that may result in harassment of the foreign firm is social unrest. Internal rebellions or domestic violence can disrupt operations even if they are not targeted at the foreign firm. Political terrorists in Europe and Latin America have increasingly used kidnappings of business executives to publicize their demands and fund their causes. Damage to property from riots or insurrections can be significant.

Many of the political risks discussed in this section are foreseeable, if not predictable. In some cases, all foreign businesses will face the same risks; but in others, the risks will have differential impact. Nationalization of a country's oil industry may have no impact on foreign automobile manufacturers. A soft-drink company may face domestication because of its dominance in the industry, but a foreign-owned utility may be seen as the best way for the country to acquire up-to-date technology. In the next section we will suggest some tools for identifying political risk and measuring vulnerability to political risk.

## STRATEGIES TO REDUCE POLITICAL RISK

Change in the firm's political environment is the major source of political risk. Therefore, the international marketer must be able to anticipate political instability as a precursor to change in the political environment. Another technique for anticipating change in the firm's political environment is an assessment of the firm, industry, and product vulnerability to political risk. A long-term strategy for positive business-government interfaces is yet another tool for minimizing political risk.

### Measuring Political Instability

There are several sources the international marketer can use to measure political instability. The first is the use of personal consultants. These may be private individuals, embassy personnel, persons currently or formerly active in the country's political life, personnel in other firms with interests in that country, or State Department personnel in the firm's home country. The advantage of personal consultants is that they can evaluate the possibility of political instability in a country as it would impact upon a specific firm; they may also have sources of information not accessible to the firm in other ways. Their disadvantages center around problems of objectivity and timeliness of their opinions.

An alternative way of measuring political instability is for the firm to use one or more of the indexes of instability that political scientists use and publish. These indexes are developed for the purpose of comparing political instability in different countries of the world, and are particularly useful when international marketers wish to compare two or more foreign market opportunities and believe that political instability is a key factor in assessing market potential or market-entry decisions.

A good example of a political instability index is the one developed by Feierabend and Feierabend.[5] The index is actually a three-digit score based on the severity of the most destabilizing event in recent political history and the frequency of destabilizing activities within the country. Examples of political events covered in their index are shown in Figure 7–3. Any firm can calculate the index for countries for which it wants to estimate instability, given sufficient information about political events. Like other indexes, however, it must be interpreted for applicability to the specific risks the individual firm might face.

A third technique is the use of a service company that specializes in analyzing political instability and risk. Business International is a consult-

---

[5] Ivo K. Feierabend and Rosalind L. Feierabend, "Aggressive Behavior in Politics, 1948–62: A Cross-National Study," *Journal of Conflict Resolution*, Fall 1966, pp. 249–71.

**FIGURE 7–3**

*EVENTS CONSIDERED IN THE FEIERABEND INDEX.*

| | |
|---|---|
| 1. Elections | 16. Arrests of significant persons |
| 2. Vacation of office | 17. Imprisonment of significant persons |
| 3. Significant change of laws | 18. Arrests of few insignificant persons |
| 4. Acquisition of office | 19. Mass arrests of insignificant persons |
| 5. Severe trouble within a non-governmental organization | 20. Imprisonment of insignificant persons |
| 6. Organization of opposition party | 21. Assassinations |
| 7. Governmental action against significant groups. | 22. Martial law |
| | 23. Executions of significant persons |
| 8. Micro strikes | 24. Executions of insignificant persons |
| 9. General strikes | 25. Terrorism and sabotage |
| 10. Macro strikes | 26. Guerrilla warfare |
| 11. Micro demonstrations | 27. Civil war |
| 12. Macro demonstrations | 28. Coups d'etat |
| 13. Micro riots | 29. Revolts |
| 14. Macro riots | 30. Exile |
| 15. Severe macro riots | |

*Source:* Ivo K. Feierabend and Rosalind L. Feierabend, *Cross-national Data Bank of Political Instability Events (Code Index),* (San Diego: Public Affairs Research Institute, 1965), pp. 2A–10A.

ing firm that will do detailed analysis of a firm's exposure to various types of political risk in a foreign market. As part of its analysis, this firm will estimate the probable impact of political instability on the client's current or potential investments in a country. Services such as the one offered by Business International are justified when the firm's investment in the foreign market is substantial.

### Identifying Political Vulnerability

Changes in the political environment do not always come from obvious instability in the political system. As discussed earlier, even an orderly change of government can lead to a drastic change in public policy. Also, some firms, industries, and products are simply more vulnerable to changes in public policy. For various reasons, a government may have a strong interest—negative or supportive—in a company's operations.

The international marketer may find it useful to use Richard D. Robinson's checklist, reprinted in Figure 7–4, for identifying political vulnerability. Some of the factors he identified that increase a firm's vulnerability are existence of local competition, dominance in an industry, products that are dangerous to the user or are critical to defense or mass communication. Other factors that might lead to vulnerability touch sensitivities related to a country's need for economic sovereignty.

### Establishing a Positive Political-Business Interface

The surest long-term strategy for minimizing political risk is to acknowledge the importance of positive interfaces with host governments. Some firms implement this by reminding personnel that they are "guests" in foreign markets and that continued permission to operate is contingent on showing the benefits the firm brings to host countries. Four important types of benefits are resource transfers, balance-of-payments additions, employment or income contributions, and social or cultural benefits.[6]

The international marketer brings new capital, manpower, and managerial and technical know-how to host countries. Even though these resources have costs, the net benefits are certainly of interest to the host government. Foreign investment can also improve a country's balance-of-payments position through foreign exchange earnings and increased exports. Foreign firms employ substantial numbers of local citizens and, when these firms buy locally, they provide income to other local firms. Social and cultural benefits can accrue in the form of support for local cultural institutions; building of roads, schools, or housing; employee training and development; or involvement in local community activities. All these

**FIGURE 7–4**    Measures of political vulnerability.

1. Is the availability of supply of the product ever subject to important political debates? (sugar, salt, gasoline, public utilities, medicines, foodstuffs)
2. Do other industries depend on the production of the product? (cement, power machine tools, construction machinery, steel)
3. Is the product considered socially or economically essential? (key drugs, laboratory equipment, medicines)
4. Is the product essential to agricultural industries? (farm tools and machinery, crops, fertilizers, seed)
5. Does the product affect national defense capabilities? (transportation industry, communications)
6. Does the product include important components that would be available from local sources and that otherwise would not be used as effectively? (labor, skills, materials)
7. Is there local competition or potential local competition from manufacturers in the near future? (small, low-investment manufacturing)
8. Does the product relate to channels of mass communication media? (newsprint, radio equipment)
9. Is the product primarily a service?
10. Does the use of the product, or its design, rest on some legal requirements?
11. Is the product potentially dangerous to the user? (explosives, drugs)
12. Does the product induce a net drain on scarce foreign exchange?

*Source:* Richard D. Robinson, "The Challenge of the Underdeveloped National Market," *The Journal of Marketing,* October 1961, pp. 24–25.

[6]This section draws on Stefan H. Robock, Kenneth Simmonds, and Jack Zwick, *International Business and Multinational Enterprises* (Homewood, Ill.: Richard D. Irwin, 1977), chap. 9, pp. 183–97.

activities have an impact on the firm's political interfaces and can be the basis for mutual support.

International firms use a variety of techniques to institutionalize their efforts to have a supportive political environment. One of these is the social audit. British Oxygen Company uses a social audit that covers the areas shown in Figure 7–5.[7] The formal audit assures that host country personnel will be apprised of the firm's impact on a country in specific areas such as pollution, public safety, safety and health of employees, and profits.

Another tool for building a positive political environment is the development of a "balance sheet" showing benefits and costs of the firm's activities in a specific country. Figure 7–6 shows a checklist that Business International uses to help clients prepare their balance sheets.[8] The balance sheet is particularly helpful when a firm has some history of operations in a country; it should be updated at regular intervals.

Yet another approach is to hire local consultants to prepare the balance sheet or other reports summarizing the firm's impact on the local

**FIGURE 7–5**  British Oxygen Company social audit.

1. Safety and health of employees.
2. Mental health.
3. Employment policies.
4. Education and training.
5. Retirement benefits.
6. Leisure. (Can the company, should the company, guide employees in their use of leisure time?)
7. Civil rights, including the special needs of minorities.
8. Treatment of women.
9. Welfare (dealing with employee problems outside the workplace).
10. Employee attitudes.
11. Pollution.
12. Public safety.
13. Waste.
14. Physical environment.
15. Use of land.
16. Participation in community affairs.
17. Government relations.
18. Consumer relations.
19. Profits.
20. The company's business image.

*Source:* Orville L. Freeman, "The Management of International Corporate Citizenship," *Top Management Report,* International Management and Development Institute and the U.S. Department of State, 1976.

[7]Orville L. Freeman, "The Management of International Corporate Citizenship," *Top Management Report,* by International Management and Development Institute and the U.S. Department of State, 1976.

[8]Ibid.

**FIGURE 7–6** Social balance sheet checklist.

| CAPITAL CONTRIBUTIONS | OTHER CONTRIBUTIONS | NEGATIVE FACTORS |
|---|---|---|
| 1. *Original capital, loans from parent, and reinvested profit,* added to local capital accumulation, speed development, strengthen the local balance of payments. | 1. *New ideas* represent inputs of technology, new products, marketing organization, business experience. | 1. *Remittances of dividends,* royalties, fees, interest, and other payments detract from balance of payments. |
| 2. *Trademarks, patents, and know-how* bring in years of research and development. | 2. *People trained locally.* Both local managers and technicians, as well as skilled workers, are developed, creating stable middle class, speeding economic development. | 2. *Materials and components imported,* while cutting import bill for finished products, generally increase overall bill as more semi-manufactures and raw materials are required. |
| 3. *Local loans* channel savings into wealth-producing projects, stimulate savings. | 3. *Output.* A new venture supplies goods, otherwise unavailable or available at greater expense and/or in smaller quantities, develops local resources. | 3. *Damper on local investors.* Fear of "big and powerful" foreign investors sometimes creates antagonism in local manufacturers, who worry about their competitive position. |
| 4. *Local equity capital* channels savings into wealth-producing operations, strengthens the stock market. | 4. *Import savings* displace foreign exchange losses otherwise incurred to bring in finished goods. | 4. *Lack of local understanding.* Foreign subsidiaries generally are managed in world-wide terms rather than in the interest of any one country (but foreign firms know that success of local operations depends on the stability and strength of the local market). |
| | 5. *Exports* contribute to country's foreign exchange earnings, provide worldwide marketing network. | |
| | 6. *Taxes paid* finance government and development. | |
| | 7. *Wages and salaries* raise employment and living standards, create purchasing power, add tax revenue. | |
| | 8. *Purchases from ancillary industries* spur local industry, develop diversified local suppliers, in turn raising incomes, tax revenues, and development. | |
| | 9. *Other local expenditures* stimulate all types of service industries, from insurance and banking to shipping and advertising, raising incomes, tax revenues, and development. | |

10. *Local dividends paid* strengthen purchasing power, savings.

11. *Stimulus to other foreign investors.* Capital inflow shows confidence in country and encourages further inflow or slows capital flight.

12. *Stimulus to local investors.* A foreign venture enlarges the local market, provides skilled managers, technicians, and workers through transfers among companies; often sets efficiency model, creates confidence in the economy.

13. *Contributions* to charities, education boost social infrastructure.

14. *Working conditions.* Foreign-owned plants usually set standards for worker facilities, plant improvement.

15. *Standard of living.* Foreign ventures make more and better products at lower cost.

*Source:* Orville L. Freeman, ''The Management of International Corporate Citizenship,'' *Top Management Report,* by International Management and Development Institute and the U.S. Department of State, 1976.

economy and society. Reports prepared by outsiders have the advantage of perceived objectivity. Whatever technique is used, building a positive political-business interface is simply an integral part of international marketing management.

## THE LEGAL ENVIRONMENT
## FOR INTERNATIONAL MARKETING

Law is the ordering of activity; it spells out the rules of the game. In different countries not only are the "rules" for business different, but the ways they are applied vary. This variation presents an exceedingly difficult environment for international marketers because they must understand complex legalities in each and every national environment before determining an appropriate marketing strategy. In this section we will try to point out the most common legal issues that a manager needs to understand.

### Absence of International Commercial
### Legal System

International business is seriously hampered by the absence of international court or legal systems. Just as political institutions remain national in scope, courts and laws regulating business activity have only national jurisdiction. While there are some important treaties between countries, there is no international arena in which to enforce business conflicts, and foreign marketers must abide by the individual laws regulating their operations in each national market.

Only nations can have international disputes with each other. If a foreign-owned firm has a conflict with private or public parties in a foreign market, it must solve it in the court system of that country if it wants to ensure enforcement. And yet, the foreign firm is often at a disadvantage in using another country's legal system. It may find public opinion hostile or experience discrimination in judgments because it is "alien." Perhaps this phrase summarizes the international marketer's precarious position: "Engaging in business transactions in a country other than one's own is a privilege and not a right."[9] What should be added is that legal discrimination against the foreign firm is the rule—with some exceptions. The foreign firm may have the option of settling an international dispute within its home-country legal system, but enforcement of the decision will then be a problem.

One of the key issues in international disputes is determining jurisdi-

[9]Robock, Simmonds, and Zwick, *International Business,* p. 150.

cation in the absence of international commercial law.[10] Three bases are used in deciding which country's laws have jurisdiction over the dispute:

1. Jurisdictional clauses in business contracts
2. Country where the contract was negotiated
3. Country where the provisions of a contract were performed

Unfortunately, these bases do not always lead to a clear decision about jurisdiction because the contract could have been negotiated and signed in one country, but performance may have taken place in another. As noted in the last section of this chapter, the clearest rule is when the original contract itself spells out jurisdiction.

### Extraterritoriality of Laws

While laws and legal systems are national in scope, there are some situations in which nations apply these laws to activities outside their borders. This concept is called the extraterritorial application of law. It holds, for example, that even if an American business is operating outside the territorial jurisdiction of U.S. courts, those courts still have jurisdiction if the operations produce effects within the U.S.[11]

One area where the concept of extraterritoriality frequently applies is trade with enemies of the home country. For example, wholly owned subsidiaries of U.S. firms in Europe were anxious to sell technology to the USSR to facilitate the natural gas pipeline the Russians were building in 1982. The U.S. government threatened sanctions against their parent companies because it believed this technology could be used for military purposes and thus the sale was a violation of the Trading with the Enemy Act. The U.S. is not the only country with laws that forbid aiding and abetting an enemy country. An international firm may find itself in violation of these laws as world alliances and hostilities constantly change.

Host governments find it difficult to treat a foreign firm like a local one, especially when that firm must adhere to its home country's foreign affairs policies, and thus appears to be an arm of its home country's government and a threat to the host country's economic sovereignty. A French subsidiary of the American Freuhauf Corporation faced this situation prior to 1971.[12] The French subsidiary signed a contract to sell equipment to the People's Republic to China. The U.S. parent forbade the subsidiary to fulfill the contract since it was a violation of the U.S. Trading

---

[10]Philip R. Cateora, *International Marketing,* 5th ed. (Homewood, Ill.: Richard D. Irwin, 1983), pp. 195–96.

[11]Andre Simons, "Foreign Trade and Antitrust Laws," *Business Topics,* Summer 1962, p. 27.

[12]Cateora, *International Marketing,* p. 208.

with the Enemy Act. In response, the French government seized the subsidiary, forced compliance with the contract, and then returned it to its French owners.

Another dilemma faced by international firms is the extent of home-government protection they want. Under the Hickenlooper Amendment, U.S. law requires cutting off foreign aid to a country where U.S.-owned assets or personnel have been seized without restitution. While it may seem to protect American firms from political risks, it presents its own problems. For example, American tuna boats were seized by Ecuador and Peru for violating their 200-mile international boundaries. The U.S. recognized only a 12-mile international boundary, so the Hickenlooper Amendment was invoked against the two countries. And yet, the American fishermen had clearly violated Peruvian and Ecuadorian law. The "long arm" of U.S. law can complicate the international firm's request to be treated the same as local firms and to be seen as independent of its home government.

Antitrust laws are also applied extraterritorially. When subsidiaries of U.S. firms engage in mergers in Europe or in other countries, they may find the U.S. Justice Department ruling them illegal. Gillette was disallowed purchase of a German firm that held Ronson patents in the U.S. IBM has been prosecuted for violating antitrust laws of the European Community. The major problem with extraterritorial application of antitrust laws is that they judge the effects of joint ventures, licensing, and mergers only in terms of their domestic effects on competition. Such activities may increase world-level competition, but have a negative effect in one market. Again it seems that international firms are unduly hampered by the national scope of laws regulating their activities.

## Major World Legal Systems

Two major structures have guided the development of legal systems in most countries of the world. Common law is the basis of law in countries that have been at some time under British influence. Common-law countries do not attempt to anticipate all areas in the application of a law by writing it to cover every foreseeable situation. Instead, cases in common-law countries are decided upon the basis of tradition, common practice, and interpretation of statutes. Civil- or code-law countries have as their premise the writing of codes of conduct that are inclusive of all foreseeable applications of law. Codes of law are then developed for commercial, civil, and criminal applications. Precedents are important in understanding common law as it is or has been interpreted. The laws themselves are the important factor in understanding the legal environment in civil- or code-law countries.

Even in common-law countries there are often codes of law. The Uniform Commercial Code in the U.S. is a good example of a code of law governing business activity. However, common law does not differentiate between civil, criminal, and commercial activities, and thus a business may be liable under any of these laws. Code-law countries separate the three types of activities, but there are always areas where codes are not sufficiently specific and must be interpreted by courts. Most countries use either common or code law as the basis for their legal system, but they rely on a combination of the two in applying the legal system to actual disputes.

Perhaps the best example of how common and code laws differ is in the recognition of industrial property rights. Industrial property rights include trademarks, logos, brand names, production processes, patents, even managerial know-how. In common-law countries, ownership of industrial property rights comes from use; in code- or civil-law countries, ownership comes from registering the name or process. The implications of this difference are obvious: A company may find itself in litigation in a code-law country to gain the rights to use its *own* names or logos, and it may not win!

There are many other ways in which code- and common-law systems affect the legal environment of the international marketing manager. Some of these are liability of the business firm for product damages; requirements for an effective contract; defenses for noncompliance with a contract; and liability of business owners. Suffice it to say here that good legal counsel is an essential component of effective marketing in foreign markets.

## Different Legal Perspectives
## of Marketing Activities

The legal environment that requires marketing activities is so broad that we cannot hope to cover all areas for all countries in this space. However, we can point out a few differences in the way marketing strategy in some countries is affected by the legal environment. For example, we have already discussed antitrust laws as they affect joint ventures, mergers, and licensing as market-entry strategies. Antitrust laws can also affect territorial restrictions on dealers or the granting of exclusive territories. Exclusive territory provisions in U.S. contracts are not enforceable, but they are allowable under most conditions in Latin American countries. Other distribution activities such as tying contracts, resale restrictions on dealers, reciprocity, full-line forcing, functional discounts, franchising, or other forms of vertical integration may be prohibited in some countries and permissible in others.[13]

Pricing by the international firm is likely to be affected in a variety of

---

[13]For a full discussion of these distribution activities, see a text such as C. Glenn Walters and Blaise J. Bergiel, *Marketing Channels*, 2nd ed. (Glenview, Ill.: Scott, Foresman, 1982).

ways by the legal environment in different countries. Price maintenance laws may prevent the firm from using discount stores or from offering quantity discounts or other price concessions. Some countries have minimum price laws and others may require licenses for price increases. Pricing may have to be pegged to inflation indexes in some situations; in others, the firm may be prevented from raising prices in a highly inflationary environment, and thus will face declining profitability.

Promotion is the area of marketing strategy where the impact of varying legal rules is particularly obvious. In Germany, for example, advertisements cannot claim that a firm's products are the "best" since that is interpreted as violating a law that forbids disparaging competitors. Comparative advertising messages (direct comparisons with competing products) may not be permitted. Sales promotion tools, such as push monies, consumer giveaways, sampling, coupons, contests, trading stamps, or "two-for-the-price-of-one's" are illegal in many countries; in others, these practices are strictly regulated. Taxes may be levied on store windows or displays. In Chapter 13 we discuss the restrictions that limit the firm's media choices.

Product development and introductions must conform to laws that regulate units of measurement, to quality or ingredient requirements, to safety or pollution restrictions, and to industry standards. This may force the firm to modify its products in every national market in order to meet varying legal rules. Labeling and branding also face a myriad of laws regulating their use. Product liability is yet another area of adjustment; the differences in interpreting implied and express warranties, as well as product returns, are special areas of concern to international marketers. One ingredient in a product may be the cause for special taxes in one country, but not in others.

## STRATEGIES TO MINIMIZE INTERNATIONAL LEGAL PROBLEMS

There is no way a textbook can totally prepare the international marketer for the variety of laws he or she will face in foreign markets. We have tried to make you aware of areas that are likely to be affected by differing legal environments, but good legal counsel in each market is an essential input into the development of international marketing strategy. In the following sections we will note some more specific steps that can be taken to minimize legal problems in international marketing.

### Elements of a Good International Contract

The use of specific terms that are not bound to one culture, is most important to the international marketer when writing a contract for business in a foreign market. Consider the problems that might be caused by terms such as *premium, first-rate quality, grade A,* and *commercial grade* when a different country's cultural and legal perspectives will be used to interpret such terms. Conflict can also arise when units of measurement such as weight and length are not sufficiently clear. Standard contracts that are used in domestic markets are often inadequate in international marketing because they make too many assumptions about the interpretation of terminology. The marketing manager should make every effort to make international contracts free of cultural misunderstandings caused by the use of terminology that is imprecise within another cultural context.

A good international contract should also specify jurisdiction in case of a dispute. The jurisdiction clause should state which country's laws will apply, as well as which court system would be used to judge the case. Both these phrases are important because they facilitate enforcement of a decision. In a conflict between a Canadian importer and U.S. exporter, the Canadian might specify that Canadian laws will apply to the contract provisions. On the other hand, the importer may prefer to file the case in U.S. courts to improve the chances of collecting from the American exporter in the event the case is decided in the Canadian's favor. If it was not specified in the contract, U.S. laws would, of course, be the basis for any judgment in American courts. Some courts will only interpret their own country's laws, but others look to the original contract for guidance. Thus, a jurisdiction clause should be specific about whose laws and courts will be used to judge a dispute.

### Advantages of Arbitration

Many firms engaging in international business further protect themselves from legal problems by including an agreement for arbitration in their international contracts. An arbitration clause commits all parties in a contract to an agreement that they will take disputes to an arbitrator before pursuing other legal recourses.

In international business there are clear reasons for preferring an independent, third-party arbitrator to litigation. First, as noted earlier, there is no court for international commercial conflicts. Thus, at least one of the parties will have to face the vagaries and whims of a foreign legal and/or court system, and such litigation can also be extremely expensive. Second, the foreign firm may face prejudice in the courts simply because it is foreign owned. Even if the bias is not intentional, the issues may be too complex for interpretation based on laws that are only national in scope. Third, it may be difficult to enforce, in one country, judgements that are made in another country; and legal proceedings may be even more extensive than anticipated. Fourth, litigation is very time consuming. If the dispute involved a shipment of industrial machines sitting in a customs warehouse, the machines may be useless by the time the case is decided. Last, legal proceedings often generate the kind of image an international firm most seeks to avoid in foreign markets. The avoidance of a high or negative profile is one of the best reasons for arbitration.

There are several sources of arbitrators for international business conflicts. The American Arbitration Association and the International Chamber of Commerce use different rules, but both will provide arbitrators for disputes worldwide. Other more regional arbitration courts also exist, for example, Inter-American Commercial Arbitration Commission, London Court of Arbitration, Moscow Foreign Trade Arbitration Commission.

### Knowledge of International Conventions

Another way to minimize the prospects of international legal problems is to be aware of and to use the international treaties and agreements that do exist. There has been a concerted effort worldwide to coordinate, if not standardize, the regulations related to customs, labeling, quarantines, units of measurement, and taxes. Many bilateral treaties help prevent double taxation of the international firm, but they are not worldwide. Other international agencies affiliated with the United Nations assure a smooth flow of transportation and communication between nations—a necessary infrastructure for international business activity.

Perhaps most important to international firms are the international conventions that help protect the firm's industrial property rights in foreign markets. The Convention of Paris established the International Bureau for the Protection of Industrial Property; this convention gives the person or firm which has filed for a patent in one country, twelve-months priority in applying for that patent in about eighty other member countries. The European Patent Office allows a firm's patent to be automatically registered in sixteen European countries. These international agreements help simplify the international marketer's task in minimizing legal problems in foreign markets.

## SUMMARY

When firms operate in foreign markets they often find it necessary to adjust to different, and sometimes hostile, political and legal environments. Businesses and governments are mutually dependent, but governments control the rules by which businesses operate. In some instances public policies prescribe an important role for business, even foreign-owned firms, in a country's economic life. One source of political risk comes from changing policies with regard to the respective roles of business and government.

The international firm is in a unique position in foreign markets with respect to host governments. There may be policies that discriminate against it in favor of local firms; or it may be treated differentially in international transfers of goods, money, personnel, or technologies. International relations between a firm's home-country government and the governments in host countries where it operates, also can create risk in the firm's political environment for foreign marketing. The internationality of multinational corporations can be viewed as a threat to the sovereignty of individual governments.

An important part of assessing the political environment in a foreign market is an understanding of the impact of differential political structures and philosophies on business operations. Different political structures—such as democracies, monarchies, dictatorships, socialism, and communism—determine market opportunities for private business. Even within the same overall political structure, subgroups such as conservatives, moderates, liberals, and leftists, view the business economic role in variable ways. Change in either structure or philosophy creates political risk—often directed particularly at international firms via nationalistic policies. Nationalism is a natural force that defines the interests of one citizen group, but it can create risk in international marketing. Political risks can mean threats to ownership or control of foreign operations. The most serious of these are the risks of confiscation, expropriation, nationalization, or domestication. Political harassment can affect even exporters through problems in acquiring licenses, domestic violence, or terrorism.

Not all firms face the same amount of risk in foreign operations. It is therefore important to estimate individual exposure to risk. The use of consultants and indexes of political instability are helpful tools in this task. It is also useful to assess the firm, its industry, and its products' political vulnerability. In international marketing it is especially important to establish a positive relationship with host country governments. The development of social audits or balance sheets that indicate the contributions of international firms to a country's economic and cultural lives, are a good basis on which to build such positive relationships.

In the legal arena, international marketers find they must conform to unique legal systems in every country. There are no international courts for commercial disputes and thus jurisdiction is a key issue in settling and enforcing legal conflicts. In the areas of national security and antitrust, one country's laws are sometimes applicable to the activities of a firm in other countries. The differences in common law and code law can affect a firm's market-entry strategy as well as all the other areas of marketing. To avoid legal problems, international contracts should use precise language, and avoid culture-bound terms; contracts should also include jurisdiction and arbitration clauses. Furthermore, the knowledgeable international marketer can take advantage of international standards and conventions to reduce the possibilities of legal problems in international markets.

## DISCUSSION QUESTIONS

1. Why is there sometimes an adversary relationship between business and government?
2. How do public policies affect business differently over time in one country? Give an example from your own political environment for business.
3. What are the unique sources of political risk faced by foreign firms?
4. Describe how international relations between countries affect the political environments of international firms.
5. Why does the multinational corporation appear to threaten the national sovereignty of countries?
6. What is the NIEO and what is its purpose?
7. Use the checklist in Figure 7–1 to analyze the political-legal environment for Apple Computers, which is thinking of producing in Mexico for Latin American markets.
8. Differentiate between political structures and philosophies.
9. What is meant by a "development" political philosophy?
10. Why is change in political structure or philosophy the main source of political risk?
11. Define nationalism.
12. What is psychic income? Give an example of its impact on international business.
13. Differentiate between confiscation, expropriation, nationalization, and domestication as political risks.
14. What is political harassment?
15. How can different firms face different exposure to political risk in the same country?
16. Describe two ways of measuring political instability and the advantages and disadvantages of each.
17. Using the Feierabend Index in Figure 7–3, develop a comparative profile of political instability in Italy, France, and Great Britain.
18. What are the factors that increase an international firm's exposure to political instability?
19. Describe the areas covered by a social audit.
20. How is international business hampered by the absence of international court or legal systems?
21. Explain what is meant by extraterritoriality of laws. How does it affect international business activity?
22. Differentiate between common law and code law as legal systems.

23. Give an example of how each area of marketing decision making may be affected by different legal systems.
24. What are the elements of a good international contract?
25. Why is arbitration an important option for resolving international legal disputes?

# CASE 8     G. H. MULFORD PHARMACEUTICAL CO.

In 1943, George Mulford leased a portion of an abandoned textile mill in Fall River, Massachusetts to manufacture aspirin. His aspirin, which was introduced under the brand name, Blue Seal, was positioned to sell at a price of one-third lower than that of Bayer, the industry leader. During the next twenty years, he added antacid tablets to the line and gradually spread his market throughout northeastern United States. In 1960, his son, Daren, joined the firm. Concerned with the company's dependence on two mature products that might at anytime become obsolete, Daren persuaded his father to develop a research division and introduce antibiotics and other prescription drugs. By 1983, Mulford was marketing a line of seventeen drugs. Although Blue Seal Aspirin still accounted for 42 percent of sales, sales of prescription drugs were steadily increasing as a share of company volume. In 1982, Mulford had a 1.7 percent share of the American pharmaceutical market.

In 1971, Bailey and Sons, a Boston export agent, suggested that they could find a market for Blue Seal Aspirin in Argentina. The market proved to be profitable, and ultimately Mulford opened a sales office in Montevideo serving both Argentina and Uruguay, and a second South American office in Sao Paulo, serving Brazil. In 1982, Daren Mulford investigated the possibility of launching the full line of prescription drugs in the Latin American market. He discovered that it would probably be necessary to design a very different promotional program in the Latin American market than the one used in the United States.

In the United States, physicians obtain information about drugs from the *Physicians' Desk Reference,* a standard reference book providing information on all ethical drugs. The statements found in this reference book reflect the official attitudes of the FDA and its expert consultants. Each manufacturer must submit statements about its drugs to the U.S.A. Food and Drug Administration for approval. It is from these statements that the descriptions in the *Physicians' Desk Reference* are drawn and also, all package inserts, medical journal advertisements, and all other labeling and promotion are drawn. The Food and Drug Administration requires full disclosure of unpleasant, dangerous, or potentially lethal side effects. In general, American manufacturers have welcomed these disclosure requirements as both clinically essential and socially desirable, but also as an important protection in product liability litigation.

The situation is very different in South America. Although the extent of government protection of drug consumers varies somewhat from country to country, the level of control is much lower. The standard reference books, commonly called PLM *(para los médicos)* by the doctors, allow much more extensive and unsupported statements about the drugs, and the listings of hazards are curtailed, glossed over, or totally omitted. The same is true of advertising, both to the physicians and to the patients. There is much more use of hyperbole and omission of undesirable facts.

The medical reference book for Brazil indicates that the information was provided by each manufacturer based on texts approved by the government's Servicio de Fiscalizacao de Medicina e Farmacia, but apparently Brazilian law does not require that the promotional material be subjected to government approval. The situation in Argentina is quite different. The texts of *Therapia Vademecum* were written by the staff from material contributed by the manufacturers, and the material was not submitted to laboratories for approval.

The Director of Advertising in Fall River recommended that the promotional and informational copy prepared for the United States market be translated into Spanish and Portuguese and used unchanged in the Latin American markets. The manager of the Montevideo office objected strenuously. He believed that Mulford products would not be able to compete in the local markets unless he was allowed to follow competitors' practices of overstating potential benefits and understating hazards or limitations. Daren believed that such action was not only unethical and immoral, but it also provided no protection from litigation by injured customers.

## QUESTIONS

1. What promotional action should Mulford take in the South American markets?
2. Should they get local legal advice?

# PART III

# MANAGEMENT TOOLS IN INTERNATIONAL MARKETING

OVERVIEW _____

In this section of your text we address two major areas that are central to the management and development of international marketing strategy. In Chapter 8, we focus on the tools that are available in gathering and analyzing information about foreign markets. The material there is supplemented by Appendix B of your text, which lists some of the more useful sources of information on foreign markets. In Chapter 9, we turn our attention to the organization of international marketing activities. This chapter addresses the issues and problems inherent in centralizing or decentralizing marketing decisions, as well as the effects of different organizational alternatives on market entry strategies.

# chapter 8

# INTERNATIONAL MARKETING RESEARCH AND INFORMATION

Japanese women—four of them dressed in kimonos, the other 66 in western-style clothes—sit impatiently, staring at the rice crackers and cups of green tea in front of them.

They're part of JMRB's Tokyo field force, and they are waiting for one of our regular research "gripe sessions" to start.

At normal briefing meetings, the interviewers do more listening than talking; today, on the other hand, it's the interviewers' turn to make their complaints, suggestions, and other observations known directly to the senior staff of the agency.

Motohiro Shiraki, field department head, starts off the meeting. In his speech of welcome, he emphasizes that the interviewers shouldn't pull any punches but should speak their minds frankly and openly.

He needn't have worried. These ladies are no shrinking violets. They need to be tough to do the work they do, and they have plenty of strong opinions, which come across loudly and clearly through the honorifics and polite phrases that make up a Japanese woman's language.*

## INTRODUCTION

The international marketer has the same basic need in each foreign country for information about markets and reaction to marketing activities; but the specific types of information needed and the methods used to get it vary

*Andrew Watt, "Consumerist Views Reflected in Woes Cited by Japanese Field Researchers," *Marketing News*, October 6, 1978, p. 12. Published by the American Marketing Association.

from country to country. The domestic marketer knows the local environment instinctively, and makes little attempt to incorporate such information into the marketing information system; but the international marketer, when entering a new market, must learn how the environment differs from the home environment.

The environmental differences among countries were discussed in earlier chapters of this book. They include

*Cultural factors*—differences in social institutions, food and dress, language.

*Legal factors*—structure and application of laws affecting marketing.

*Political factors*—type of government, stability of government, governmental attitudes toward business and foreign business.

*Economic factors*—wealth and productivity, extent of industrialization and commercialization, distribution of income.

*Financial factors*—value and convertibility of the currency, sources of trade and consumer credit, repatriation of funds.

*Geographic factors*—differences in climate and topography, accessibility.

*Multinational economic markets*—existence of trade zones, common markets, or other economic agreements.

*Stage of economic development*—underdeveloped to affluent, effects on extent and nature of demand.

*Business customs*—how business is conducted, types of business organization, views of competition.

Environmental information might need to be collected in new and different ways from other marketing information. Nevertheless, the organization and structure of an information system will essentially be the same in foreign markets as in the domestic market.

## THE INTERNATIONAL MARKETING INFORMATION SYSTEM

Ideally, marketing information systems make use of four kinds of data: internal operating data, market intelligence, sales forecasts, and marketing research. Each kind of data is necessary to the development of a successful marketing strategy, and the use of each in the information system should be optimized in terms of need, availability, and cost.

### Internal Operating Data

The most accessible and least expensive source of international marketing information is internal operating data. This invaluable, but sometimes neglected, source of information is as close as the company's own records. It is also available (with an adequately planned system for information retrieval) on very short notice. In a study of information sources for multinational companies, internal sources provided 40 percent of all information used.[1] Such information tells the way a product has performed in each country or region, the comparative performance of different products in the line, the comparative performance of individual selling units, and the relative demand and preferences of different customers and channels. Only when internal sources of information have been exhausted should management turn to sources outside the company.

Since internal data make use of records of past performance, they are not available in a new market. When first planning to enter a new foreign market, the marketer must rely on external information about that market. However, company data concerning performance of the same or similar products in the domestic market or in other foreign markets can often provide some forecast of what might be expected to happen in the new market.

### Marketing Intelligence

Marketing intelligence can provide a vast amount of global information to the decision maker. Such information comes from two sources: direct human contact and printed or recorded material. Human sources are more popular with many executives. They prefer the personal opinions of a few individuals on the spot to pages and pages of written material. In a study of global business information, human sources (three-quarters of which was face-to-face) provided 67 percent of all information gathered.[2] Use of human sources of information requires that the information seeker maintain access, either directly or through subordinates, with individuals who are knowledgeable about the countries involved. Such information does not flow into the organization automatically; a procedure must be established to identify sources, and to encourage the inflow of relevant data.

There are no sure-fire rules for identifying the key persons with reliable information about foreign markets and their environments. They may be found in the home country—expatriates of the foreign market, industry or company colleagues with experience in the foreign market, or other persons who have lived or travelled there. These sources often have the disadvantages of dated and/or superficial understanding of the foreign environment. Embassy personnel, such as commercial attachés, are often good contacts within the foreign market; other persons that can be helpful are

---

[1]Warren J. Keegan, "Multinational Scanning: A Study of the Information Sources Used by Headquarters Executives in Multinational Companies," *Administrative Science Quarterly,* September 1974, p. 418.

[2]Keegan, "Multinational Scanning," p. 418.

members of trade associations, personnel of other international companies, consultants, potential competitors, and home-country expatriates.

With the revolution in communication and information throughout the world, documentary sources of information have proliferated in recent years. News media, government bureaus, international organizations, and trade associations are just a few of the organizations providing information about particular countries or parts of the world. Many of these sources are listed in Appendix B. Frequently, the flow of information is so great, and demands on the time of executives so confining, that much of the information that flows over their desk is never read. Although much of it is probably not important enough to be read, there is always the danger that really valuable material may be missed. It is for this reason that international marketers need a strategic intelligence system to process such information.

The strategic intelligence system, instead of relying on random personal contacts, establishes a procedure for regular monitoring of news media, trade organizations, and other information sources in the markets to be served. The responsibility for routine collection and summarization of such information should be delegated to a local employee in each foreign market served. If local personnel are either not available or do not have the time for intelligence gathering, the job can often be contracted out to a "clipping service". This intelligence information should be summarized and forwarded to responsible executives on a regular basis. The sheer volume of published information makes it impossible for top marketing executives, particularly those in the home offices, to monitor information personally. As a consequence, they rely almost entirely on internal sources of marketing information.[3] A good strategic intelligence system will ensure that important market information is regularly fed to the executive as a part of the internal information system. The large multinational corporation is in particular need of an intelligence system. Without a system to assess, collect, and evaluate the vast amount of information from the international environment, the decision maker may not be adequately aware of the factors which make each foreign market unique.[4]

Still another facet of international marketing intelligence is the covert collection of information about competitors and their products. Businesses have taken a lesson from government and used spying, theft, and bribery to obtain important information about competitors and their products. In 1983, for example, a Japanese computer firm was caught in the United States using such techniques to obtain technical data from IBM.

---

[3]Keegan, "Multinational Scanning," pp. 415–16.

[4]Ralph H. Kilman and Kyung-Il Ghymn, "The MAPS Design Technology: Designing Strategic Intelligence Systems for MNCs," *Columbia Journal of World Business,* Summer 1976, pp. 35–46.

## Sales Forecasts

The starting point in marketing planning and strategy is a sales forecast. How much a company hopes to sell will determine the allocation of resources and the development of a strategy to achieve its goals. In domestic markets the forecasting procedure is largely an economic or econometric one because environmental factors are essentially static and assumed given. With the broad variation in international environments, the preparation of a forecast must be adjusted to local conditions in each market. The penchant for secrecy among international businesses makes it difficult to identify important economic changes at the international level. There was little warning for the onslaught of the energy crisis in the 1970s, or for the development of double-digit inflation in many parts of the world. The enormous size of multinational corporations compared to some of the nations they serve, also results in situations where businesses must assume that their own plans affect the future as much as the future affects their plans. Andre Van Dam[5] proposes a series of questions to be used in the preparation of forecasts at the international level:

What is the outlook for the world economy?
What is the impact of world trends and events upon the business cycle?
Which governments will interfere with which market opportunities?
How will the emerging international monetary system affect our equity?
Will the New International Economic Order affect our inputs and outputs?
Will the business environment allow free competition or plan the market?

In the domestic market, the planner can often make use of general economic forecasts prepared by government or trade-association planners; but no comparable organization exists for forecasting at the international level. Each company must compile its own forecasts from basic data.[6]

## Marketing Research

Whereas internal-operating-data analysis and marketing intelligence involve the collection and/or retrieval of existing information, marketing research involves the collection and analysis of information not previously available. Marketing research is the systematic gathering, recording, and analyzing of data about marketing problems. Its purpose is to facilitate decision making. This important source of external information focuses on

---

[5]Andre Van Dam, "The Future of Global Business Forecasting," *Business Horizons*, August 1977, pp. 46–50.
[6]One useful source of international information for forecasting is *Predicasts Forecasts* (a publication of Predicasts, Inc., Cleveland, Ohio) which gives tables of statistics and forecasts for products (price, production, growth rates) in various parts of the world.

the relationship of the firm to its environment and to its potential markets. The specific problems of marketing research in foreign markets are described in the sections that follow.

## INFORMATION COLLECTION

One reason many firms never enter foreign markets and, consequently, restrict their potential growth, is that the job of collecting marketing information about these areas appears to be terribly costly and time consuming. However, there are a number of inexpensive ways to explore foreign markets without leaving home or spending a lot of money. The local library is a good place to start; a surprising amount of information—including directories of foreign importers and descriptions of selected foreign markets—is available in libraries. The government is another important source of market information; in the United States, the Departments of Commerce and State provide a wealth of information about foreign countries as markets. Present customers who are subsidiaries of firms headquartered in foreign countries may also be able to provide considerable information about their home countries. International banks, located in a number of large cities, can often provide useful information about markets with which they have contact. Manufacturers' agents who sell in foreign markets are often seeking new lines, and in any case, they can provide useful information about the markets they serve. Ultimately, however, if the commitment to foreign marketing becomes very large, the marketer must seek to collect a broader range of information, frequently in the form of primary data.

Market information gathered in one market may prove to be inadequate or even deceptive when applied to a new foreign market. For example, a successful American manufacturer of dishwashers who is thinking of exporting to Norway will need to know many things about that market, such as:

> compatability of electric current,
> availability of outlets in kitchens,
> availability of extra space in kitchens,
> feelings of homemakers about the need for sterilization of dishes,
> availability of household help,
> fragility and durability of chinaware,
> who normally does the dishwashing,
> availability of hot water.

Even though demographic studies of the Norwegian population indicate that an adequate number of households should be able to afford a dishwasher, answers to some of the questions above may demonstrate that a market does not exist. The marketer will probably find it necessary to do some exploratory research so as to define the market and its basic views and usage of products. Thus, before it is possible to even design a market survey for a product such as bicycles, it is necessary to know whether the market uses them primarily as transportation or as a means of recreation.

### Secondary Data

Whenever possible, the marketing researcher tries to locate and make use of data already available from an outside source; this is called secondary data. Since the collection of primary data is both costly and time consuming, it should be sought only as a last resort. Also, the market being considered may be too small to justify the cost of a study.

*Problems with secondary data.* The information needed may not be available at all from secondary sources. For example, government censuses often prove to be a valuable source of demographic information, yet the government of Oman has never conducted a census. Even when census data are available they may be so dated that they prove useless. Before 1982, the last census conducted in the People's Republic of China was in 1953; the population has obviously changed markedly since then. Another problem with secondary information is accuracy. Even the United States Census, which involves a large amount of funding and very careful planning, admits to errors in undercounting low-income and minority people. Censuses and other government statistics from nations where funding is less than adequate, and where statisticians may be unskilled or uncaring, may be quite inaccurate. Still another problem is the unreliability of secondary information. Statistics from one year to the next may not be comparable because base-comparison periods or methods of evaluating data change from time to time. Also, if data come from government sources, they may be inflated or deflated at different times for reasons of political expediency.

*Sources of secondary data.* Even though secondary data may be flawed, they are still available quickly and at low cost. Often a foreign market may be too small to justify the cost of a special study, and secondary data, if used with caution, can provide useful information. Secondary sources of information on foreign markets, as shown in Figure 8–1, include the United States government; international organizations; foreign governments; and trade, business, and service organizations. More specific secondary sources are outlined in Appendix B.

**FIGURE 8–1**    Sources of information on international markets.

*United States Government*
**Trade Lists**
**World Trade Data Reports**
**Commerce America**
**Marketing Handbook**
**Overseas Business Reports (by countries)**
**U.S. Trade Center Reports**
**Foreign Commerce Handbook**

*International Organizations*
**United Nations Statistical Yearbook**
**Organization for Economic Cooperation & Development**
**Pan American Union**
**European Community**

*Foreign Governments*
**Government Censuses and Statistical Services**
**Chambers of Commerce**

*Standard Reference Sources*
**Business International—weekly news service**
  *Business*
  *Investing Licensing & Trading Conditions Abroad*
  *Financing Foreign Operations*
**CIS**
  *Statistical Reference Index*
  *Europe Yearbook*
  *Exporters' Encyclopedia*
  *International Financial Statistics Yearbook*
**Predicasts**
  *World-Product-Casts*
  *World-Regional-Casts*
  *Statesman's Yearbook*
**World Bank**
  *World Tables*
  *World Development Report*

*Trade, Business, and Service Organizations*
**International and foreign marketing research agencies**
**Trade associations**
**Service companies**

## Defining the Problem for Primary Research

Before designing a survey, it is often necessary to make a preliminary analysis of consumption habits and patterns in order to avoid research blunders. *Readers Digest* made such a blunder in a study of consumer behavior in Western Europe. The researcher did not realize that most Italians buy pasta unbranded, from bulk supplies at the local store, whereas French and German consumers buy packaged, branded pasta as do Americans. As a consequence, the survey reported that French and German households consumed more pasta than the Italians.

Definition of the problem is the first step in any good research design. The way in which a problem is defined will have an effect upon the solution. In cross-cultural research, the problem may not be perceived in the same manner by all peoples. Even though all cultures may have similar interpretations of the concept of health maintenance and prevention of illness, in cultures where most citizens earn livings through hard physical labor, the concept of jogging or other recreational exercise seems ridiculous and unrelated to health. A similar example involves the concept of dieting; it is only in affluent cultures, where people can afford to overeat, that dieting has any meaning or relevance.

In order to define the research problem in a new culture, it is often necessary to engage in exploratory research. In the home market, the researcher can usually rely on personal experience as a guide; but in foreign markets it quickly becomes evident that introspection is not enough. Exploratory research need not have the precision or structure demanded of regular marketing research studies; it merely needs to identify very basic societal differences. Thus, before one can design a survey of the market for bicycles in the Netherlands, one must learn whether bicycles are perceived as a means of transportation or of recreation. A market survey designed for the United States, where bicycles are used primarily for recreation, may be ineffective in measuring market attitudes in the Netherlands, where bicycles are more often perceived as a means of transportation.

## Questionnaire Design

The most commonly used instrument for gathering primary data is the survey questionnaire. People in different countries react differently to questionnaires and to specific questions. Americans are more willing to answer questions of a personal nature, such as those about family relationships and financial matters, than are residents of many other countries, where such matters may be considered private and secret even from a supposedly confidential survey. Americans are also willing to spend more time with an interviewer, making it possible to use longer questionnaires. In Hong Kong, where the life style is very hectic, the questionnaire must be shorter. The reaction to and way of answering a questionnaire also affect the length of the questionnaire. In Brazil, where the respondent is likely to answer in great detail, often embroidering on the basic question, the number of questions must be limited.

Three central issues to the design of survey questionnaires are scaling, measurement, and wording. Common scales in marketing questionnaires are the semantic differential and *Likert* scales. When developing an instrument for use in another culture, the researcher should take care that such scales are understood and responded to in the intended manner; otherwise, interpretation of responses is meaningless. For example, Latin Americans are more likely to use the extreme points on a scale to express their individualism, while Indians may express similarly intense opinions using points around the midpoint of the same scale. Therefore, research instruments may need to be adapted to cultural variations in response styles or reasoning patterns in a foreign market.

As researchers, we are always forced to take concepts that are somewhat abstract and to give them arbitrary, operational definitions so that we can measure those phenomena. For example, brand loyalty is a concept that is sometimes defined as repeated purchases of a particular brand; at other times it is operationally defined as a positive rating of a brand on an attitude scale. In order for survey instruments to have conceptual equivalence—in other words, for them to measure what they are intended to measure—the researcher must first verify that a concept has meaning in the other culture. For example, brand loyalty may be meaningless to consumers who have never had significant product choices or who perceive little risk in product purchasing. Second, researchers may need to adjust their operational definitions of the concepts they are measuring to account for different economic, cultural, or market structure situations.

Wording presents yet another problem for the researcher studying foreign buyers and their attitudes. Many standard marketing survey instruments simply cannot be translated into other languages because the words do not exist to express precisely the same thought. Eskimos have many words for "snow" in their languages, while English has only one; *machismo* is a Spanish term describing a complex phenomenon, and would need many English words to express its full equivalent meaning. Perhaps the safest method of assuring that the terms used in one language have the same meaning when translated into another is the back-translation technique. Back translation of a questionnaire requires four steps: first, the instrument is constructed in the researcher's mother language; second, a bilingual person translates it into the desired language; next, a second bilingual is given only the foreign-language version of the instrument and translates it back into the original language. In the last step, all three persons get together and iron out any differences resulting from the various translations so that the foreign-language version of the questionnaire can be finalized. Short-circuiting the back-translation method by using only one translation can lead to serious errors in instrument equivalence.[7]

[7]Robert T. Green and Phillip D. White, "Methodological Considerations in Cross-National Consumer Research," *Journal of International Business Studies,* Fall/Winter, 1976, p. 15.

## Sampling

Marketing researchers have developed fairly precise methodologies for drawing samples of a population to be studied, but these sampling methods were devised for use in economically advanced nations, and are not always transferrable to other nations. If the researcher has good statistical information about the population to be studied—its composition and location—a sample can be drawn with predictable error and deviation from the universe. However, in less-developed countries, as mentioned earlier in this chapter, statistical information about the nation may not be available at all and when available may be highly inaccurate. Thus, the researcher in less-developed countries may have to rely much more heavily on judgment samples than on random samples.

The researcher must also design the sample to be representative only of that portion of the population that is a part of the potential market. In some countries, residents of the cities operate in a money economy while rural residents may be either self-sufficient or use barter to meet their needs. If this is the case, the sample used to measure the potential for a new product should be drawn only from the cities.

Other differences in countries' economies and cultures confound the ability of the researcher to compare results across national markets. Two samples of the "middle class" will have absolute income differences (thus purchasing power) in countries at different levels of economic development. Sales-force personnel and students are two other groups likely to have different economic and social status in different countries. Any differences found concerning their product attitudes or behavior may be due only to these status differences, although they may appear to be similar samples.

## Interviewing

Once the questionnaire is designed and the sample is drawn, a method must be devised for obtaining information from the people selected for a sample. Information may be obtained from observation, personal interviews, telephone interviews, or mailed questionnaires. These methods are not equally available in all countries. Telephone interviewing is a very useful source of information in the American market. It is fast and relatively inexpensive; it allows the research director to monitor interviews and check on interviewers; and it provides a certain anonymity to the interviewee when answering sensitive questions. However, even in the United States it cannot be used to survey a truly mass market because the lowest-income families may not have telephones. In many other countries, telephone ownership is so small that this interviewing technique is simply not available as an information-collecting alternative.

Observation as a research method requires familiarity with the respondent's culture. This is because the researcher must interpret the nonverbal as well as the verbal behavior of the respondent. As was pointed out in Chapter 4, and in "The Silent Language of Overseas Business,"[8] this is difficult for the foreigner. If observation methods are used, the actual observers need to be members of the local culture.

The use of mailed questionnaires is an inexpensive and easy method of collecting market information, although it has limitations with respect to the representativeness of returns. However, in a great many countries where the level of literacy is low, too many recipients of the questionnaires would be unable to read them. This method of obtaining information can only be used when the market segment to be reached is likely to be literate. In some countries, persons would not consider responding at all to a letter from an unknown individual. Last but not least, the postal service in many countries is unreliable. All of these factors work against the use of mail surveys as a viable research method in many foreign markets.

Thus, in many markets the researcher is limited to the information-gathering methods of observation and personal interviews, both of which are expensive and time consuming. The personal interview may also be limited by problems of access to the potential interviewees. In some countries—particularly Moslem countries, but also in some others, such as French Canada and southern Italy—women are not accessible for interviews by strange men. Women interviewers may not be available because such work is considered improper for females. If the person to be interviewed is a man, it may be difficult to reach him in the home; it may be necessary, instead, to arrange interviews in public places. It is also difficult in some countries to obtain trained interviewers who can approach the interviews objectively without introducing their own opinions or what they surmise to be the opinions of their employer.

## Analyzing and Interpreting Data

The researcher must have a high degree of cultural understanding to interpret data in a useful way. What consumers will interpret as important characteristics of a floor wax depends on the type of surfaces on which it is to be used. The important characteristics of a detergent will depend on whether the clothing is to be washed in boiling water, warm water, or cold water. Some level of cultural familiarity is obviously essential for effective data analysis and interpretation.

Timing is also important. It is generally considered good research methodology to conduct surveys in several markets at approximately the same time in order to reduce the bias from changes that may occur in mar-

[8]Edward T. Hall, "The Silent Language of Overseas Business," *Harvard Business Review,* May–June 1960, pp. 87–96.

kets over time. Yet, if the product is affected by the season—clothing, for example—a survey in Europe in July would measure summer consumption patterns, but in Argentina or Australia, it would measure winter consumption patterns.

The marketing researcher must adopt a creative approach in handling the job so that adjustment can be made for cultural differences; and such adjustments may need to be almost intuitive. Above all, the researcher must adopt a skeptical attitude toward all cross-cultural data, and must look beyond apparent differences to determine whether they represent real behavioral differences or simply differences in two cultures.

## Other Marketing Research Activities

Certain types of market information gathering are essentially unique to the international scene. Marketing intelligence work and market surveys are important in both domestic and international markets, but other factors are taken for granted in domestic marketing. For example, the political situation is a given; changes in political factors are much less likely to affect decisions to continue or discontinue marketing activities. Also, the analysis and comparison of new markets for entry, present unique information and research challenges to the international marketer.

*Measuring political risk.*    A major concern of international marketers is the fact that changes in the political environment, and resulting changes in governmental policies, may affect return on investment or even the safety of the investments themselves in foreign countries. Political risk can take many forms and these were discussed in Chapter 7. It can involve war and thus pose a threat to the firm's assets and/or disruption of income; it can imply nationalization or even outright expropriation; it can involve a change in convertibility of currency, with threats to repatriation of profits. Such risks may seem only minor in the present, but they could pose serious danger in the future. Thus, a program of creeping nationalization may be only a bother at first, but it could represent future loss of control and profit.

The most common method of assessing political risk is intuition. An on-site tour of the country in question provides the decision makers with a "feeling" for the political situation. The opinions of "experts," such as ambassadors or State Department employees, are often used to buttress the intuitive opinions. This method can be made more sophisticated by gathering intuitive information on a series of factors from several experts and averaging them to arrive at a consensus.

A still more sophisticated technique is to develop an index of political risk. In the Business Environmental Risk Index, for example, a group of experts are presented with a list of variables and asked to assign to each a score of 0 to 4. These variables include political stability, nationalization, monetary inflation, attitudes toward foreign investors, balance of payments, bureaucratic delays, and so forth. A problem with such indices lies in the interpretation of items such as political stability. In addition, even though it is systematized, the index still represents only the opinions of "experts."

Another method of measuring political risk is based on identifying the hidden political structure.[9] This is done by identifying the main groups able to exert political pressures in a society and assessing their relationships with each other and with the ruling bodies. These clusters are identified by interviewing individuals selected on a random basis. This method of analysis focuses not only on the current coalition in power and its attitude toward the foreign business, but also on the segments likely to form a new coalition if there was a change in the power structure. More details about assessing political risk were given in Chapter 7.

*Choosing among alternative markets.* Every time a firm makes the decision to expand foreign operations, it is faced with the problem of deciding which market offers the greatest marketing opportunity. The selection of potential new foreign markets is an information-gathering and screening process. It involves collecting data and passing the alternative country choices through a series of filters to eliminate the less-promising opportunities. The filtering process, which consists of four major steps, is illustrated in Figure 8–2.

The first step in the information-gathering process involves a macro-level look at the general market potential in each country. It includes analysis of economic statistics (for example, are there enough people with disposable income?), the political environment, the social structure, and geographic factors. A majority of the potential markets can be eliminated at this level. Any one factor, such as geographic inaccessibility or political instability, may be sufficient to eliminate the market from further consideration.

The second stage of data collection relates the general market to the product to be sold. It includes growth trends for similar products, cultural acceptance of such products, availability of market data, market size, stage of development, and taxes and duties. Again any one of these factors may be enough to drop a country from consideration. For example, high import duties will eliminate a market from consideration unless the marketer is willing to manufacture the product locally.

The third screening stage involves micro-level considerations. It involves collecting information about existing and potential competition, ease of entry, reliability of information, sales projections, cost of entry,

[9]See Jean-Pierre Ferrier, Patrick Gantes, Jean-Mathieu Paoli, "Opportunities and Challenges for Foreign Business: A Coalition-Oriented Methodology," *European Marketing Research,* September 1980, pp. 228–39.

**EXHIBIT 8–2**  A Model for Selecting Foreign Markets.

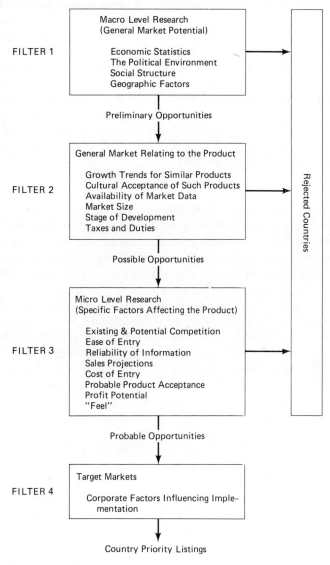

*Source:* R. Wayne Walvoord, "Export Market Research," *American Import/ Export Bulletin,* May 1980, p. 83.

probable product acceptance, profit potential, and "feel." Countries that pass this screen have a good probability of being profitable opportunities.

The fourth screen involves consideration of corporate factors affecting implementation of marketing plans. The remaining potential markets are arranged in priority order according to consistency with current marketing strategy. Thus, a country in Southeast Asia might be ranked below a country in Latin America because the company is already heavily involved in neighboring Latin American countries and has no markets in Asia.

## USE OF MARKETING RESEARCH AGENCIES

In international marketing, as in domestic marketing, the decision maker has the alternative of conducting marketing research in-house or using professional marketing research organizations located in the markets to be studied. Many firms maintain in-house marketing research departments to handle routine research such as analyzing internal data, monitoring intelligence information, and preparing forecasts; but for special market surveys which may require additional personnel and special expertise, they may turn to outside marketing research agencies for help. When seeking market information in foreign countries, the marketer is even more likely to benefit from the help of local marketing research agencies or international agencies with local offices. There are several reasons for this preference. First, the local agency has unique expertise. In addition to the technical abilities and facilities for handling complex statistical data which the marketer may possess in the home-office staff, the foreign agency can offer a thorough knowledge of the target country, its customs, attitudes, trade practices, and *a priori* knowledge of local industries, products, and contacts. Second, the foreign agency has the language expertise to cope with survey communication problems in the country to be studied. Third, the foreign agency may be more cost-effective, since it maintains research personnel and facilities and can spread their cost over several projects.[10]

Professional marketing research agencies are to be found in all developed and in many developing nations. They can be located in a number of ways, from directory listings, or from the recommendations of informed local consultants, trade associations, or other businesses. When a choice is available, it is important to identify the best agency with the two most important characteristics: integrity and ability. Since marketing research in-

---

[10]"Using Marketing Research Agencies," *International Trade Forum,* April–June 1981, pp. 24–25.

formation is easily faked, both by the research agency and by incompetent or poorly trained interviewers, it is important to know that the agency cares about the accuracy of data and has the competence to achieve accuracy.

## COMPANYWIDE INFORMATION SYSTEMS

The international marketing firm must design its marketing information system so that all regional and home-office personnel have the information necessary to make optimal marketing decisions. This requires the development of international data banks to integrate and process the information from each separate market. Internal operating data from each branch must be integrated with companywide data, and the system must provide automatic feedback of relevant information to each office.

Marketing intelligence provides a particularly difficult challenge. The problem is how a company with worldwide marketing operations, composed of individuals with limited information-absorbing capacities, can miminize its acquisition of irrelevant information and maximize its acquisition of relevant information. The system must be devised so that it scans information sources in each market on a regular basis, incorporating that which is relevant into the data bank and directing it to attention of those individuals concerned.

Analysis of relevant information should indicate where additional information is needed. If this information can be obtained through further review of current or new sources, the investigation should be conducted. If special marketing research is necessary, it should be implemented if its value is deemed to be in excess of the cost of obtaining it. Companywide access to and exchange of information is particularly important for international marketers. The range of choices about allocation of resources is broader than for domestic companies, and the physical and cultural distance between markets makes it more difficult for management to keep informed on an informal basis.

## SUMMARY

When developing international marketing strategy, there is often a need for broader information collection than in domestic marketing. Since environmental conditions vary in virtually all national markets, they are an important source of information about foreign market opportunities. New sources and research techniques are also part of collecting information about foreign markets.

The major information inputs for international marketing decisions come from four sources: internal operating data, market intelligence, sales forecasts, and marketing research. Each of these is a part of the firm's international marketing information system. Internal data are most often used by multinational firms, but they are unavailable when the firm has little or no foreign marketing experience. Marketing intelligence about environmental conditions can come from either personal contacts or monitoring of published materials. International sales forecasts are the basis for allocating resources. They must be derived from an interpretation of how world environmental conditions or events will impact on demand for a particular firm's products. There are external organizations whose statistics can be helpful in developing international forecasts.

When collecting information about foreign markets, one of the biggest problems is knowing what information to gather. Before conducting primary research, the international manager needs to know something about basic product views and usage patterns in a foreign market. And, as with any research project, he or she should review secondary sources of information first. While secondary data are sometimes unavailable, inaccurate, unreliable, or not timely for foreign markets, they still can provide some unique sources that are helpful in providing background information and in directing further research, if needed.

Many times international marketing research projects are exploratory and less formal than domestic ones. An alien culture makes it more difficult for the decision maker to define the research problem clearly. Survey instruments may have to be adapted in length, in scaling techniques used, in measurement of concepts, and in wording. The back-translation method is an important tool in ensuring an accurate translation. Sampling techniques must also be adjusted in foreign markets and judgement samples are more often used. There are limitations on the use of each method of gathering primary data—observation, telephone, mail, and personal interviews—in foreign markets. And even data analysis and interpretation require some familiarity with foreign market characteristics. In addition to the typical research needs, foreign marketing decisions often require information about political risks and foreign market structure and conditions.

One way to facilitate information gathering in foreign markets is the use of outside research agencies. They reduce the firm's need to acquire in-house expertise in cultural factors affecting the entire research process, and can minimize the associated costs. Further, by developing company-wide information systems, the international company can minimize acquisition of irrelevant and duplicate information, and can maximize the dissemination of relevant information to decision makers.

## DISCUSSION QUESTIONS

1. Why is the scope of international research usually broader than that of domestic research?
2. What are the components of an international marketing information system?
3. List examples of internal operating data that are useful for international marketing decisions.
4. What is global market intelligence?
5. Why are human sources used so frequently by multinational firms in gathering market intelligence?
6. Why are sales forecasts an input to international marketing decisions?
7. What is the strategic intelligence system?
8. Explain why information gathered about one national market can be in-effective in understanding demand in another.
9. What are the advantages and disadvantages of secondary data on foreign markets?
10. What are the major sources of secondary data on foreign markets?
11. Why is it difficult to define the problem when doing primary research in international marketing?
12. Describe how questionnaire design may be affected by a research project in two different national markets.
13. Explain the back-translation technique. What is its purpose?
14. Why are judgement samples more frequent in foreign research projects?
15. Discuss the limitations of each interview technique in international marketing.
16. Explain why effective data analysis requires cultural familiarity.
17. What is the Business Environmental Risk Index?
18. What is the first information need of the international marketer when choosing among potential foreign market opportunities?
19. Explain the systematic process for collecting information on potential foreign markets.
20. What are the reasons for using outside research agencies in foreign markets?
21. What is a companywide information system?

# HOW TO CONDUCT AN INTERNATIONAL INDUSTRIAL MARKETING RESEARCH STUDY

This case analysis of a major European marketing research study conducted for a division of a large industrial firm reports in detail the step-by-step procedure involved in complicated overseas marketing research.

The U.S. division manufactures and sells electrical termination products, such as motor timers, circuit breakers, switches, relays and terminal blocks, through distributors to manufacturers of industrial controls, electrical panels, turbines, generators, transportation equipment, machine tools, etc.

The task was to provide an operational marketing report for both the U.S. headquarters and the European manufacturing organization. Typically, the time pressure was enormous with a conception date of June 10, 1977, and a management report due date of February 1978.

### Objectives

An examination of secondary research uncovered a major 1974 study, *The European Electrical Market,* published in London. While it didn't cover all of the division's products, it was a good benchmark for extrapolations based on its findings. This study also provided a comparative basis for our objectives.

Several meetings with executives and researchers found agreement as to the study's expected results. The key catalyst was the division president who stamped his approval on the project, participated in all planning meetings, and fully supported the research team. This avoided one of the most common mistakes made by marketing research consultants and client staff concentrating on middle and technical management with only a few perfunctory meetings with senior executives, especially the president. The top one or two officers must know what they're buying to prevent the all too often heard remark at the final presentation. "I thought you were going to cover . . ."

The study's final objectives were:

To qualify the potential European market for specific major products, existing and planned. With hundreds of lines, we had to be selective and deal with primary products.

This case is taken from Richard L. Pinkerton, *Marketing News*, April 4, 1980, p. 4.

To identify the major European users by industry types; something like the U.S.S.I.C. code system.

To determine if and to what extent, national boundaries and customs segment the market.

To identify major competitors including their strengths and weaknesses.

To determine the proper marketing and promotional mix for converting potential into sales.

To ascertain technical specifications for the key product line including special and unique electrical code requirements (government, private, and engineering society).

To determine the direction of the technological trends, especially in solid state products.

## Research Methodology

Like most technical marketing research, the personal in-depth interview using a structured guide was the collection tool. Product samples and catalogues were also used during the interviews to facilitate interest and communication.

***Field interviewers.***    Fortunately, I had completed extensive training in data collection and field interview techniques with the division's engineering and product management force. This was a key factor because while we needed technically competent interviewers, we had to avoid the natural bias and selling tendencies of any good sales force.

When trained in questioning, listening, and other marketing research techniques, experienced industrial sales force members make excellent data collectors.

***The sample.***    Random statistical sampling for technical products can actually produce the wrong results because the research must often be targeted to specific industries, individual firms, and identified expert respondents in order to reach the early adopters, opinion leaders, heavy users, and cooperative respondents. Since we had no way of knowing the total population or universe, we used this representative and key opinion sample method.

Respondents were purchasing managers, engineers, planning managers, and product managers. Senior executives or "directors," as they are often called in Europe, were avoided except to direct us to the proper technical people who would have detailed knowledge and major buying influence.

The division's European sales and engineering reps, would select the interview list, and, since they were all foreign nationals, would also act as interpreters. While professional interpreters can be hired, they usually lack technical expertise.

The bonus of using your own sales force as field interviewers, is the tremendous training derived in market development and in the recommended role of any good sales engineer, that of a consultant–problem solver vs. the order taker. The U.S. and foreign sales force of this firm are, for the most part, holders of technical degrees, seasoned, and well trained.

Detailed instructions concerning the purpose and necessary sample were sent to the division's European reps and a final sample of 128 was selected in West Germany, United Kingdom, France, Holland, Italy, Sweden, Spain, Norway, Switzerland, Belgium, Austria, and Denmark.

*Questionnaire design.*    During July, the objectives were translated into a structured interview guide which eventually totalled 37 pages!

While only a rare interview would require all the data in this form, it had to cover all possibilities of respondent classification, 12 major products, competition, detailed technical specifications, buying procedures and influences, and promotion possibilities, such as trade and technical journals and potential trade shows. We also had a section to rate the interview reliability, degree of cooperation, follow-up, etc., using a simple rating scale.

Great care must be used in preparing such questions for overseas work. For example, Europeans use the word "turnover" rather than "sales."

Also, because of the distance and costs involved, the questionnaire had to be complete and ordered for proper question flow (one product question naturally leads to another in a similar category), plus adequate spacing for quick recording of responses. It would be impossible to conduct post interviews by telephone for clarification.

We would have but one opportunity and two hours per interview would be the limit. We were already on our third major revision.

*Pretest.*    In August, the manager of planning and I left for Europe to field test not only the questionnaire but also whether or not this entire study was feasible. A few key European sales engineers selected test interviews.

Much of Europe, however, goes on holiday for the month of August. This presented problems finding respondents to interview.

While we had no choice and were successful because of persistent efforts by our foreign colleagues, we don't recommend any marketing research be conducted in Central Europe during the late summer; England was not as difficult, but the same advice holds there.

We tested 14 interviews in six countries to check our question design, reception, ability to work with a translator, time per interview, travel time and arrangements, costs, reliability of responses, and adequacy of the results in view of the study objectives.

The results were positive and exciting although we found the one-night stands, constant travel, and mental strain in a foreign work environment to be totally exhausting. The few problems included some reluctance to give "turnover" or sales figures, but we returned home and wrote the fourth and final revision plus copious notes for the necessary training session.

*Field interviewer training session.* A quick meeting with the division president produced a "go" and while the sample selection continued in Europe, we selected our U.S. field team from product management, marketing specialists, sales engineering, and other executives—including the president.

On August 25, the manager of planning and I held a one-day training session. We reviewed the objectives, questionnaire, problem areas, how to show the sample products, and, in particular, how to work with an interpreter. Aside from the time lag while the translator rewords the question, great care must be taken to make sure both the questioner and translator are at the same place in the questionnaire.

Use of the translation adds about 30% to the interview time, but the interviewer can record the last answer while the translator and respondent are talking. Interviewers should never operate without the use of a translator unless they are fluent in the language.

Another common U.S. misapprehension is that French and West German businesspeople speak English, when in fact, few do. We didn't let the European sales reps conduct the entire interviews alone, because we didn't have time to train them in research and questioning techniques and would not have had immediate use of the completed interview. Another consideration was the loss of control over the research when using individuals in another division and overseas at that.

We emphasized the necessity for opening rapport with a slow, low voice and the proper opening as to why you are there. Europeans are more formal than Americans and great care and discretion must be exercised. Suggestions included:

*Do's:* present your card, assure confidentiality, talk about their country in positive terms, sample their food, and watch for facial and body communications, and check to see if they're talking in metrics, including temperatures, and in their currency (they usually do);

*Don'ts:* loud suits, jokes, politics, World War II stories (except in England and perhaps France, if appropriate), boasting about U.S. greatness, loaded questions, sales pitches, and first names, unless they suggest it.

As in all research of this type, we emphasized the necessity for the correcting and editing of the questionnaire that same evening while the memory is fresh. Each respondent was presented with an expensive pen set, and we also covered how to present this gift.

Business hours vary by country. For example, in Germany they run from 7:30 A.M. to 3:30 or 4 P.M. at the latest. To cover items such as the above, we developed our own Guide to Europe concerning customs, temperature, politics, history, money rates and conversion, medical questions, eating customs (Europeans take much longer to eat; most American don't dine, they "destroy" food, an insult to the host). We also included items such as Arthur Frommer's Guides, Michelin Guides and Maps, and other material.

The initial scheduling of various trips was done through a travel agency and interviewers were placed in first-class traditional European hotels. This is quite a task and requires at least two months to obtain reservations, passports, tickets, etc. Try to schedule the interviewing during the tourist off-season to obtain maximum discounts and avoid expensive first-class air travel.

All this detail is very necessary. Appointments must be planned in great detail with rather complicated travel arrangements in mind. In most cases, only one appointment could be scheduled in the morning and one in the afternoon.

In no case can cold calls be made. Advance appointments are mandatory in Europe. Europeans also have a habit of calling in "groups" of managers during the interview. This is helpful because you meet the many buying influences, but the interviewer and translator must be prepared for constant interruption.

**European training.**   The American team held a half-day training session for the European translator team but much of this preparation had been accomplished during the August field test. The European reps also had to brief the American team as to appointments, travel, and any special industrial information for specific countries and contacts.

"Translator team" may be misleading for these individuals did much more; they were the expert guides and sample selectors and helped analyze responses and allowed us to complete a rather complicated study in a short time.

**Actual field interviewing.**   All the detailed preparation paid off. Nine interviewers plus nine European counterparts successfully completed 128 interviews during September.

There was some difficulty with questions concerning future demand by number of individual units of various products, because Europeans don't seem to conduct detailed forecasts in the same manner as large U.S. firms, but the estimates proved to be reasonably accurate when checked with other secondary sources.

**Data analysis.**   From October through December, the huge amount of data was tabulated, analyzed, and compared with secondary information such as the 1974 *European Electrical Market Report.*

Jan Hansen, a Norwegian born and reared professor of economics and marketing at Capital University, was brought in to help the research analyst at the division headquarters. In mid-December, preliminary reports were prepared and presented to senior management for comment and direction.

*Formal Report Writing.* During January 1978, a first draft 100-page report was prepared with findings, conclusions, recommendations, and full documentation regarding all interviews and supporting data.

*Executives' Summary and Report.* On January 16, a preliminary report was delivered to the top division management with a slide and flip-chart presentation. Senior management asked for more analysis of specific data and the final written report was issued on March 17, 1978.

The real payoff, the implementation and translation of this market study into marketing plans, the final action step, is still going on. The direct cost of the study, excluding the salary allocation of division personnel, was approximately $60,000, including all travel expenses and consultant fees.

Only time will reveal its worth. Could this study be accomplished by a firm without a foreign national sales force? Yes, but at double the time and perhaps three times the cost because a European technical marketing research agency would have to be hired—a difficult selection task.

The critical last step in any marketing research project is follow-up. A study of this magnitude should have a yearly "audit" for two years after the study completion for the obvious reason—a market report only gives direction, managers make it happen.

## QUESTIONS

1. Evaluate the market survey with respect to:
   a) The sample
   b) Field interviewers
   c) Training of interviewers
   d) Use of translators
2. Would the client have been likely to get better results from the Pinkerton survey or from a survey conducted by a European marketing research organization?

# chapter 9

# ORGANIZING INTERNATIONAL MARKETING

Some 15 or 20 years ago in U.S. industries, highly paid senior executives made "state visits" to Europe and Latin America, concluded distributorship contracts with local importers in every country they visited, spent a reasonable amount of time shopping and eating well, and when they returned to headquarters they promptly sent copies of the contract down to something called an "export department" with the mandate to "get out there and sell!"

The "get out there" part of the mandate meant, however, that the exports manager possibly was permitted to make one trip a year. No one else in the department was allowed to leave headquarters.

Management tried, in those days, to rationalize such methods of operating by calling them "centralization." Centralization indeed is a reasonable way of conducting one's farflung business.

The conditions of doing business, however, have forced us to change these attitudes. Probably a foremost change resulted from the paradox that these export activities often were successful. International markets became more and more important, and better, personnel more properly trained, were assigned to local overseas markets. Slowly realization grew that there were certain better ways to accelerate this success. Or, the opposite might have forced the change of attitude—a total failure.*

*"Successful International Marketing Depends on Centralized Leadership," *Industrial Marketing,* March 1975, p. 54.

## INTRODUCTION

Organizational structure of a firm includes relationships between people, how they relate and react to each other; it also details who has authority over various activities and people. Since the people in an organization are constantly changing, their relationships also change, and the formal organizational plan, or organization chart, only approximates reality. Despite this dynamism, the formal organizational plan serves certain necessary purposes in an organization.[1]

As organizations grow, it becomes possible to develop specialization. Individuals in different positions become expert in some part of the total task, and the firm's overall efficiency is increased accordingly. The organization chart defines the role of each specialist and his or her relationship to other personnel. When there is only one manager in an organization, he or she is responsible for planning and controlling all activities. When an assistant is hired, there must be some formal division of responsibilities to ensure that everything gets done. When there are a number of assistants, it becomes even more important to divide responsibilities and allocate them among the individuals. The larger and more complex the organization, the more important it becomes to specify all necessary activities, to assign responsibility to specific people, and to assure completion of assigned tasks.

When responsibilities are divided among a number of individuals, some may end up working at cross-purposes with others. For example, when entering a new market, one executive may launch a big advertising campaign before another executive has achieved adequate retail distribution. The advertising dollars are wasted because the prospective customers who received the message are unable to find the product. A properly designed organization chart should build in a method of coordinating the activities of these executives.

In hierarchical relationships, there is little doubt about the location of authority; individuals higher in the organizational structure have authority over individuals beneath them. But as an organization grows in complexity, the number of staff specialists who may have some legitimate input into a particular decision also grows. A staff specialist, although lower in the hierarchical organization than a particular line executive, may have authority over certain aspects of the line executive's decisions—authority which has been delegated to the specialist from someone higher in the structure. Thus, although the line executives responsible for sales, advertising, and marketing in a company like Proctor & Gamble are ultimately responsible for decisions in their respective areas, they receive considera-

---

[1]See, Richard R. Still, Edward W. Cundiff, and Norman P. Govoni, *Sales Management: Decisions, Strategies, and Cases,* 4th ed. (Englewood Cliffs, N.J.: Prentice-Hall, 1981).

ble input, recommendations, and requests from product managers for individual brands such as Crest, Tide, or Pringles. The organization chart is designed to define such flows of authority.

Ideally, top management should spend its time setting goals and planning. In order to free time for this purpose, the routine execution and administration of plans must be delegated to subordinates. The organizational plan provides a formal mechanism for such delegation. It also helps subordinates know their relationship to other subordinates and to top management, as well as their designated duties.

In this chapter we discuss some of the complexities of organizing international marketing activities. We are concerned principally with the effects of organizational structure and the location of decision making as they affect marketing strategy. In the first section we review the unique aspects of international marketing that influence organizational structure. We do not try to identify one best way to organize international marketing responsibilities, only the effects of different situations on organizational alternatives. In the next section we discuss the advantages and disadvantages of centralized and decentralized international decision making. We also describe the characteristics of some common ways businesses have organized their international activities. Last, we explore the organizational requirements of different foreign market entry strategies. These were discussed in Chapter 2 in terms of their relative amounts of risk and control; here our focus is on their relationship to centralization and decentralization in decision making.

## UNIQUE ASPECTS OF ORGANIZING INTERNATIONAL MARKETING

The job of organizing marketing responsibilities, never an easy one, is still more difficult in a company engaged in international marketing. Size, in itself, presents a problem; the larger the organization, the more complex is the job of charting relationships among the people within it. Many international marketing organizations are huge multinational corporations, larger than average ones. In addition to size complexities, there are a number of specific problems unique to the international marketing environment that make organizational planning more complex.

### Communication Problems

Communication across national boundaries is likely to be slower, more erratic, and more unreliable than domestic communication. The extra distance alone is a complicating factor, since it can slow down the speed of communication between persons in different places within the firm. The efficiency of postal service varies widely among nations, affecting both the time required for delivery of messages and the reliability of delivery. Even within highly developed nations, there is a wide variation in postal service. One national system may take pride in providing "twenty-four-hour service anywhere in the nation," while another service in a country of equal size may require several days for domestic mailings. Even the most-efficient postal service may place a different priority on foreign mail; each national postal service operates under somewhat different rules. In the United States, for example, it is considered to be a public service that should never be interrupted. Postal employees are not allowed to use strikes in their collective-bargaining process. In contrast, the Canadian postal service is shut down completely for a number of weeks every two or three years while the employees are bargaining for better wages or working conditions. A strike in July 1981, as usual, shut down all postal communication within and outside the nation for more than a month. Although there are alternative methods of communication available when postal service is inadequate, they may not be as effective for specific jobs. For example, a written order from a customer provides legal evidence of a contractual relationship, whereas a telephone conversation provides no lasting evidence of the order. Even if it is recorded, the conversation may not be easily admissable as legal evidence.

Electronic communication media also vary in effectiveness from one nation to another. The telegraph is an important means of international communication, but the speed of service varies considerably. It is a very expensive medium if the message is long, and provides no opportunity for immediate response or feedback between most nations. International telephone service has increased enormously in efficiency with the use of communication satellites. It is possible to dial direct to many parts of the world today with very high quality transmission. Short-wave radio offers an electronic alternative when telephone service is bad, but since the air waves are available to the public, no confidential messages can be sent. Many corporations today are using their computer systems to speed communications with far-flung subsidiaries.

It is important for managers to meet periodically with subordinates on a face-to-face basis. When a subordinate is located thousands of miles away in another country and across a body of water, such meetings become very expensive and time consuming. Using air transportation, busy executives can be anywhere within their own national markets within a very few hours, even in the largest countries. But if they have to fly halfway across the world to confer with subordinates, it may take a day or more to reach the destination, and the resulting jet lag may impair work efficiency for another twenty-four hours. Such travel may be necessary for coordinating activities, but it adds to the cost of doing business. In general, internal communications are more expensive for the firm involved in international markets.

## Government Regulations

A firm's organizational structure may have to be adjusted to meet local governmental regulations. Although management might prefer to treat its operations within each foreign country as branches, equivalent to branches within the parent country, laws requiring a minimum percentage of local ownership may make it necessary to operate these offices as corporate subsidiaries. Local regulations may also require a minimum percentage of indigenous employees, thus complicating staffing and promotion patterns within the company, as well as creating problems for standardized hiring criteria and job qualifications. Tax laws and regulations about the repatriation of funds may also dictate the firm's organizational structure. Since government regulations are constantly changing, organizational structure within each market must be flexible. An international marketer may have operated for a number of years in a foreign market that had no restriction on foreign ownership, but a sudden change of government could result in laws restricting foreign ownership to a specified percentage of total capital. As a result, it would be necessary to completely restructure the organization in that market.

The firm's organizational structure can also affect its political acceptability within a nation. Norton International, Inc., a management agency for abrasive products manufacturers, has as its basic organizational philosophy the belief that you cannot operate as a United States firm on foreign soil without building bad relations in the long run. International firms must minimize their "foreign" profile and contribute to the nations where they operate—both in the public and private sector—in order to maintain an acceptable public image.[2]

## Movement of Human Resouces

Competent, experienced managerial personnel are a scarce resource in domestic marketing, but at the international level they are even harder to find, and more expensive to train and relocate. When a company first moves into international markets, it often turns first to its own domestic personnel as a source of managers abroad. If this source proves inadequate, the firm is likely to recruit international management trainees from regular domestic sources. These managers are familiar with the firm's domestic management techniques and have no language problem in communicating with top management.

However, this policy of exporting managers has a number of drawbacks. First, each individual must be given the necessary skills to operate in the new market. This involves learning about the foreign culture—the way business is conducted, the economic resources, and the government

[2]"How Norton Went POP—Basic Marketing Feedback Strategy Pays Off in New Worldwide Profit Opportunities," *Business Abroad*, April 1970, p. 21.

and political influences. This knowledge must be complete enough so that the individual can deal effectively with nationals. Training frequently involves instruction in a new language, because it is unusual to find an individual with the necessary managerial skills who is also fluent in the required foreign language. The individual needs to be fluent to ensure that communication is accurate. Language instruction is costly, time consuming, and may be unwelcome to the trainee who is more interested in managerial skills than in language skills.

Movement of an executive into a foreign market is costly and traumatic for the family. Professional managers have learned to accept mobility as a part of upward progression in their organizations, and often each promotion involves a move to a new location. Even in purely domestic organizations, such moves are expensive and difficult. The company sometimes must pay the cost of buying and selling homes and the costs of the physical move. And, such moves may be resisted or even refused in dual-career homes. International moves are much more costly and are more traumatic for the family. The cost of the physical move and subsequent adjustment will be much higher, and subsidies may have to be provided for such things as differential living costs, education of the children in boarding schools or special language schools, and periodic home vacations. Some families who would accept transfers within their own country will flatly refuse to move to foreign countries.

In addition to the language and family problems involved in moving a domestic manager abroad, there may be even bigger problems in the new market. If the local culture is too different, the expatriate manager may always be perceived as a foreigner and outsider with whom it is difficult to conduct business. The manager never becomes a part of the local "establishment." Countries like Mexico make such transfers even more difficult by specifying that only a certain percentage of employees, managerial and nonmanagerial, may be foreigners.

Some companies have tried to solve the problems arising out of moving personnel by developing local professional managers in each foreign market, or by hiring third-country nationals for foreign assignments. In highly developed nations this process may be a relatively simple one. If people can be found with managerial training and experience, they can be brought to the home office for a period of indoctrination in company operating and management procedures, and then sent to manage operations in a foreign market. In less-developed countries, experienced, competent nationals may not be available, and it may be necessary to provide extensive training for promising but inexperienced young people. When Creole Petroleum decided in the 1950s to develop a cadre of native managers in their Venezuelan operations, they found it necessary to send young Venezuelans to American universities to study engineering, geology, and management to give them a level of technical expertise sufficient to prepare them as management trainees. Such programs are costly and time consuming. The use of local nationals in management also reduces a company's flexibility. These people are just as difficult to move to a third country as are the managers in the home country. Hiring third-country nationals (for example, an American firm hiring an Australian for assignment in New Zealand), can be an effective alternative to either home- or host-country resistance to foreign assignments when they are available. They have already made a commitment to foreign employment.

Companies heavily involved in international marketing, with distribution in a number of countries, have found it useful to develop truly international managers with broad cultural backgrounds and language skills. With such managers nationality is irrelevant.[3] The company builds managerial quality and depth through worldwide personnel assignments and interchange. As an example of this, in 1981 the president of Coca-Cola at the home office in Atlanta, Georgia was an Argentinian. The problem is in persuading managers without previous foreign experience to get excited about an overseas assignment. It may not be easy to excite an Italian about the wonderful promotion to Brazil, or an Australian about the opportunities in European countries.[4]

### Effect of Foreign Sales Volume

Organization of international marketing activities is also affected by the proportion of the firm's total sales volume that comes from outside the domestic market. For example, until 1977, the Hershey company sold only a small portion of its billion-dollar annual volume in foreign markets. Their organization was simple; international exports were executed through export management companies and treated like domestic sales. In 1977, management decided to seek long-term opportunities overseas through direct investment or joint ventures. A new structure was needed to greatly increase international volume and to maintain marketing control at the same time. An international department headed by a vice-president–international was set up to develop these opportunities.[5] Other firms that are already heavily involved in international markets have had to create an organizational structure that integrates planning for both domestic and international markets.

### Effect of Product-Line Size

Simple product lines can usually be marketed abroad with simpler marketing organizations. The Hershey company is a good example. But a

---

[3]"International Executive Compensation: How To Make Pay and Benefits Fit the Job," *Business Abroad,* July 1970, p. 9.

[4]"How Norton went POP," *Business Abroad,* p. 21.

[5]"The Case of the Prosperous Exporter," *Distribution,* October 1980, pp. 84–85.

company such as AMF, with its large and diverse line of products, has developed a complex organization to handle worldwide sales. Its consumer products range from volley balls to yachts, and its industrial products range from electronic switches to bakery equipment to bowling alleys. Many products are exported, but others are manufactured abroad. The complexity of the marketing organization must respond to the needs of administering diverse product lines.

### Diversity of Human Needs

The needs of industrial buyers are fairly similar in all markets, so international marketers of industrial goods can often centralize their marketing activities. Copiers, computers, and machine tools can be sold in many foreign markets with little or no product adaptation. In contrast, the needs of consumers will vary a great deal from one country to another. In earlier chapters of this book, we explained how cultural, political, and economic factors affect human needs. Consumer goods designed for one market may have to be redesigned to satisfy another market. The entire marketing strategy may be subject to the same country-to-country variations. For such products the marketing organization needs to be much more decentralized to serve each market effectively. The Nestlé Company, with 209 factories located throughout the world and only 3 percent of its sales volume in its home country (Switzerland), learned long ago that it was impossible to make key marketing decisions at a central location. The Nestlé organizational structure is premised on the philosophy that "the closer the man is to the battle front, the better his decision is likely to be."[6]

## ORGANIZATIONAL ALTERNATIVES

The alternative ways of organizing marketing responsibility, even in a purely domestic firm, are many. In worldwide marketing, the potential for variation is even greater. Still there are generalizations that can be made about the organizational process in all markets. These are concerned with issues such as degree of centralization, participation of employees, and ownership of foreign facilities and offices.

### Degree of Centralization

Depending on the size and importance of foreign markets, the organization for foreign marketing may vary from a part- or full-time specialist in the home office, to an organization of all company operations on a worldwide basis.

[6]Norm Willst, "How Nestlé Adapts Products to Its Market," *Business Abroad*, June 1970, pp. 31–34.

*International specialists.*    Domestically oriented businesses that treat foreign markets as outlets for excess capacity or incremental volume are likely to rely on an international specialist to locate foreign customers. This type of organizational structure is illustrated in Figure 9–1. This individual or outside firm may be physically located in the home office, although many such specialists have their headquarters in cities like Washington or New York. International specialists frequently rely on export agents to implement the marketing plan in foreign countries. They are equivalent to "export departments" in most firms.

The overall role of the international specialist is determined largely by the structure of a corporation,[7] but there are several activities for which they are normally responsible. They maintain contact with embassies and embassies' supply missions, with important visitors from countries of interest, and with export financing agencies. They keep informed on current government regulations and programs, and maintain contact with the agencies whose policies and programs affect the overseas operations of the company. They act as liaison with international financing agencies. There

**FIGURE 9–1**  Organization using an international specialist.

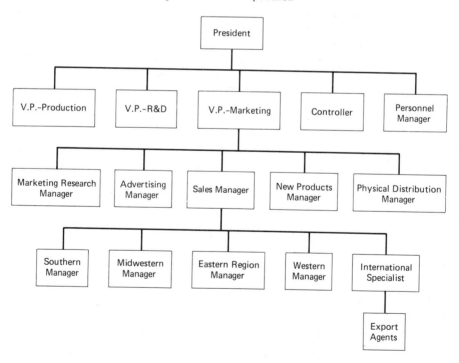

[7]"Washington's Elite Corps of International Representatives for Corporate Business Abroad," *Business Abroad,* April 1970, p. 17.

is very little centralization in planning international marketing in the firm that uses international specialists.

*International division.* As foreign sales grow and as the number of countries covered increases, management finds that international specialists, export departments, and export agents are inadequate to penetrate foreign markets effectively. The next logical evolutionary step is the establishment of an international division headed by a top-level executive who reports directly to the president. One such international division is portrayed in Figure 9–2. In this instance, the vice-president of the international division is responsible for marketing and manufacturing (when available) in the various foreign markets. The marketing executives in each foreign market report directly to the international marketing manager, but they can turn to staff specialists in the home office for help with such things as advertising and product development.

An international management consultant has suggested that the international division is the best organizational alternative when overseas business reaches 10 percent to 15 percent of domestic activity, but still does not represent a majority of total business. It would also be most appropri-

**FIGURE 9–2**   Organization using an international division.

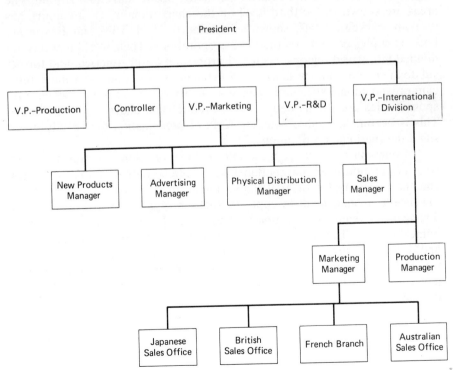

ate when the company's staff of international specialists who oversee foreign sales in separate markets, grows to the point that an organizational relationship must be established between them.[8]

The number of experienced international executives in this type of organization is still very small compared to the domestic operation. Even though total international sales volume and the number of countries covered may be small, an international division is particularly important in those situations where the overseas marketing strategy must be adapted from that in the United States. Its major advantage lies in the superior ability to coordinate and control foreign operations.

*International corporation.*    Ultimately, as international business grows in comparative importance, the entire organization must become internationally oriented. These truly international businesses may take many organizational forms, but the basic characteristic common to all is that top management—the corporate staff at headquarters—is world oriented. Figure 9–3 portrays one such organization. Each member of the corporate staff, shown as the second level, has worldwide responsibilities. The world market in this firm is divided into six geographic areas, each with its own staff; and the areas are divided into country offices. The European area might have subsidiaries in France, Germany, Spain, and Great Britain. The areas are shown as the third level on the chart. Finally, each country has its own marketing staff, shown as the fourth level. IBM and Exxon are both examples of such international corporations. Their world markets are divided into world regions, such as Europe and Latin America, and further subdivided into country markets. Westinghouse uses an even more intricate organizational structure—called a "matrix organization"—because responsibilities are subdivided by both product line and country or region. This is becoming a more common form of organization for heavily diversified international corporations.

Companies evolve from the international division structure to worldwide orientation when international sales volume outpaces domestic sales, and the necessity for diversification among markets makes it difficult for lower-level management to cope. In such an organization, the entire top-management team views problems and policy from a world rather than a domestic level. The need to adapt products to different market conditions and to adjust promotion efforts to different communication needs, requires top management's awareness of international differences. And, the problems of pricing between operations in different countries are particularly difficult in complex international organizations.[9]

---

[8]"Learning the Rules for Global Selling," *Business Abroad*, November 1969, pp. 43–44.

[9]"Learning the Rules," *Business Abroad*, p. 44.

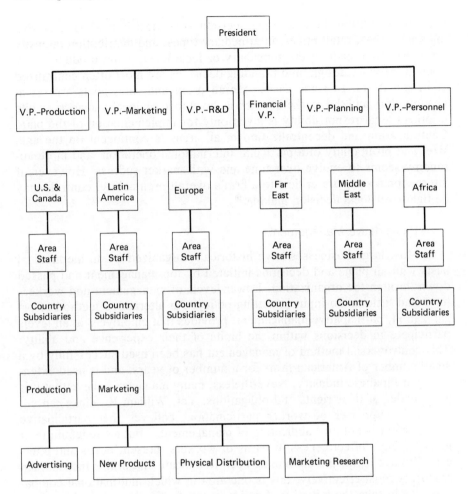

**FIGURE 9–3** Organization for total international orientation with world corporate staff.

The world orientation offers the most centralization because not only are marketing and manufacturing centrally planned, but the firm's financial and accounting systems are also organized to coordinate international operations and strategy.

Some business functions are more likely to be centralized than others in firms involved in international markets. Finance, research and development, new investments, and long-range planning are examples of these; while marketing and production decisions, as well as control over day-to-day operations, are more likely to be decentralized. However, industrial firms tend to centralize more marketing decisions than do consumer goods companies. Within the marketing decision area, decisions about advertising approaches, retail prices, intermediary types, and distribution intensity are most often made at the subsidiary or local level; while product development, product design, and branding decisions are most often centralized at headquarters. In some cases, overall profit and sales goals are set at headquarters and the marketing plan is developed by local managers, while in others local responsibility is given only for implementation of the plan. Centralization and decentralization of all areas is contingent on the age, size, and profitability of a particular international operation, and more autonomy seems to evolve over time and with market success. However, if international sales are critical to a firm's overall profitability, controls may be tight over local decision making.[10]

### Participative Management

Most large businesses have historically organized on an hierarchical basis with all plans and decisions initiated by top management and passed down through the organization. Lower levels of management and workers have had little or no input in setting policy. An alternative method of organization, participative management, provides that employees at all levels participate in decisions within the limits of their experience and ability. This controversial method of management has been used successfully by a small number of American firms for a number of years, and is used extensively in Japanese industry. Nevertheless, many managers believe that it is a surrender of their rights and obligations. Yet, William K. Zinke, an enthusiastic supporter of worker participation, believes that participative management is not an "abdication of management," but a "redefinition of management's effectiveness in terms of workers' present needs and interests."[11] Faced with the continuing need to allocate and utilize their human resources most effectively, this is one area in which multinational companies should take the initiative. Employee satisfaction is a critical factor in the success of international companies. As foreigners, they are likely to be resented as interlopers, and if such resentment becomes strong enough, it can lead to government restriction on foreign ownership and even to nationalization of facilities.

In several Western European countries, labor participation in management decisions is mandated by law. As we mentioned in Chapter 4, labor may even have seats on a company's board of directors, as is required in West Germany. When international decisions have a potentially negative

[10]R. J. Aylmer, "Who Makes Marketing Decisions in the Multinational Firm?" *Journal of Marketing,* vol. 34 (October 1970), pp. 25–30; and Randolph A. Pohlman, James S. Ang, and Syed I. Ali, "Policies of Multinational Firms: A Survey," *Business Horizons,* 19, no. 6 (December 1976), pp. 14–18.

[11]William B. Zinke, "Participative Management: Growing Need for Initiative by Multinational Companies," *Business Abroad,* December 1978, pp. 11–12.

impact on domestic labor, they may cause conflict and thus paralyze a firm's competitive efforts in world marketing. In countries where labor is a powerful political force, decisions may be shared between management, labor, and politicians or government agencies. Under such conditions, exporting may be the only acceptable foreign market entry strategy. Whatever the case, centralization of marketing decisions can often help avoid jurisdictional conflicts that impede meeting organizational goals. More employee-management sharing of decision-making responsibilities can be expected throughout the world.

The commitment to participative management may vary, but every company can take steps in the direction of codetermination. William F. May, Chairman of American Can Company, suggests several ways of making the job content more meaningful for all employees.

1. Talented local young people should be advanced more rapidly to provide them with a greater opportunity to make decisions and to share in management responsibilities.

2. The traditional organization pyramid should become more like a truncated cone with greater participation throughout the organization in less-important decisions.

3. Management should reorganize to create smaller, more independent, less-structured units within the corporate framework, reporting relationships to a management hub at the center of a wheel.

4. The relative stature of all functional management should decline relative to program management.

5. The future executive should be more concerned with being part of a team than an outstanding professional.[12]

### Ownership of Foreign Facilities

When a multinational firm moves into a new market, it is faced with a number of alternatives with respect to its ownership and control over local operations. Its marketing strategy may range from outright ownership of branches or subsidiaries, to management contracts. Each alternative may be advantageous in certain circumstances when entering a foreign market. These issues were discussed in Chapter 2, but will be reviewed here in the context of their implications for organizing international marketing.

*Sales branches and subsidiaries.* Branches are simply extensions of a parent company in new locations. A sales branch in Calcutta is no different from a sales branch in Chicago, in that both are totally owned and operated

---

[12]"The Human Factor: Key to Survival in Global Business," *Business Abroad*, October 1970, p. 10.

by the parent. The Calcutta branch may be operated quite differently because distance and differences in the culture may make it necessary to delegate more authority to local management. Branches are often the best way to control retail or direct-sales activities in foreign markets.

Subsidiaries are separate companies, frequently operating under separate names, but controlled by the parent company. Subsidiaries are not necessarily wholly owned by the parent company, but the parent does retain effective voting control. Minority local ownership decreases the likelihood of classification as a foreign concern and increases local identification with the company and its products. Opening the ownership of subsidiaries to local nationals also reduces the amount of financial investment a parent firm must make in the foreign market. Marketing decisions of subsidiaries are usually guided by policies set in the parent company; however, they tend to have more independence than branches in implementing marketing.

*Joint ventures.*    Joint ventures are popular among international companies as a way to enter new markets. Joint ventures involve a merging of two or more firms, at least one of which is local. A common arrangement is a fifty-fifty partnership between a local firm and a multinational company, with the local firm providing expertise in the local market, and the multinational providing management and marketing expertise. Familiarity of the local partner with local conditions can save the multinational both time and trouble in penetrating a new market. In addition, the joint venture can be politically desirable since the local involvement enhances national pride and reduces the firm's profile as an outsider.[13] Fifty-fifty ownership implies fifty-fifty managerial control, and international marketers are frequently unwilling to give up managerial control to local partners with less managerial experience and less total commitment. Various solutions to this problem have been devised, such as providing in the bylaws that the multinational firm will have a majority of board members, or providing for voting and nonvoting stock. In addition, they may work out agreements as to market strategies, market expenditures, profits, reinvestment, and dividends.

Managerial decision making, as well as ownership, are shared in most joint ventures. A multinational firm using joint ventures in various national markets may face more problems of coordination and control of marketing activities. Such firms are much more likely to have decentralized policymaking and implementation procedures. Industrias Pachacocha is a joint venture in Peru with Procter & Gamble and local capital. This firm's product mix includes some well-known Procter & Gamble products and some unique Peruvian ones as well. Such independence was necessary in deci-

---

[13]"Learning the Rules," *Business Abroad*, p. 43.

sion making to meet the needs of Peruvian consumers and environmental conditions. However, offering nonstandard products under the Procter & Gamble name has caused conflict, duplication of marketing effort, and a lack of standardized product image with Procter & Gamble products and pricing in other markets.

*International licensing.* Licensing provides an inexpensive way of entering new markets. Licensing may grant the right to manufacture and distribute under the licensor's trade name, as Schweppes (an English firm) has done in the American market with its line of mixers and soft drinks. Or, licenses may be granted for distribution of an imported product manufactured in the licensor's home country. The licensee assumes the entire marketing cost, and sometimes the production cost as well, in his or her own market. Licensing provides a way of developing markets in nations which restrict foreign ownership, and licensing provides the potential of stronger identification as a domestically owned business in all markets. Licensing is a good way of controlling marketing and manufacturing activities in markets where foreign ownership is prohibited or economically unfeasible. However, licensees are independent entrepreneurs and often rebel against standardized marketing or product designs, especially when these are inappropriate for the local market. Therefore, from an organizational point of view, licensees can be a big headache, threatening the firm's image and markets by changing the marketing mix; or they can help the firm by adjusting to local conditions. In cases where firms use licensees in multiple markets there must be liaison personnel at headquarters to provide licensees with technical support, and to supervise, cajole, and coordinate their activities.

*Franchising.* Some of the problems inherent in licensing arrangements are eliminated in franchise contracts. These contracts, of course, tend to be more comprehensive in specifying how the franchisee should operate and what the mutual rights and obligations are. Many franchises in services (Hilton, Avis) and fast foods (McDonald's, Kentucky Fried Chicken), not only provide management systems for supervising personnel, bookkeeping, and promotions, but they also ensure product development and site location expertise unavailable to the franchisee alone. Nevertheless, there is still the inevitable conflict over how and when to adjust marketing strategy for the local market. McDonald's, for example, sued its franchisee in Paris, France to cease operating under the McDonald name because of sale of nonstandard products (Big Macs are garnished with Béarnaise sauce) and because of substandard sanitary conditions. Again, it is important to have personnel whose principal responsibility is support, coordination, and supervision of franchisee operations.

*Management contracts.*  The management contract provides payment for the management and marketing expertise of large firms in markets other than their own. A firm with only minority ownership in a foreign subsidiary can obtain effective control through use of a management contract. Local owners may recognize that they lack the expertise to operate the enterprise in the most effective manner. This is also a way international firms have retained effective control over former subsidiaries that have been expropriated by local government. Exxon was expropriated in the 1950s in Venezuela, but through contracts it continued to run its operations there for over a decade. Payments may include management fees, share of profits, and even options to purchase.

### Ways of Dividing Marketing Authority

Multinational marketers who have moved beyond the use of an international division to a worldwide marketing organization have two basic alternatives in deciding how to divide marketing authority. The most commonly used method is by geographic specialization. In such instances, authority is delegated from the central office to a head marketing executive in each country served. Or, if the organization is very large, authority may be delegated to regional specialists who are each responsible for several countries, as illustrated in Figure 9–3. This geographic division of authority is most effective with low-technology products and where there is a need for local product adaptation or local marketing expertise.

The second alternative is to divide marketing authority on a product basis; that is, to establish an international marketing division for each major product. When a company produces high-technology products which require unique expertise in sales, installation, and servicing, and when servicing is very important to product success, division of authority by product makes sense. In large multinationals, marketing authority will normally be divided on both bases—the matrix form of organizational structure. Thus, IBM, which divides its world markets into regions and countries, also divides these markets between computer and office-equipment divisions.

### SUMMARY

Organizational structures are highly dynamic. As the people in an organization move or change, their relationship to others changes, so that an organization chart is more likely to describe historical relationships than current reality. Nevertheless, the formal organizational structure is important in defining authority, in providing coordination, and in assuring that all necessary activities are carried out. International marketing organizations must be designed to reflect the greater distances between people and markets, and the variations in impact of local governments—both of which affect the movement of personnel and the development of marketing strategy. And, the very size of the typical international marketer makes for a more complex organization. As companies become more involved in international marketing, their marketing organization evolves toward a total worldwide orientation.

The firm involved in international markets faces unique conditions that affect its organizational structure. Problems inherent in long-distance communications, government regulations, and hiring of personnel for international assignments are among these factors. The extent of a firm's involvement in international markets, as well as the diversity and nature of its product mix, also affects its decisions about how to organize international marketing activities.

If a firm needs to centralize marketing decisions, it is more likely to use international specialists in implementing its international marketing program. This could take the form of an export department or even the use of an outside service. The international division is an effective organizational form if the firm has moderate overall involvement in a growing number of foreign markets. The organizational form that offers the greatest potential for decentralizing decision making is an international corporation where responsibility for worldwide management decisions rests with the top corporate managers. Technically, the organizational structure may divide responsibility according to geographic area, product line, or a combination of these factors. Another important issue in organizing international marketing is the extent of employee participation in management decisions. Whether this is mandated by law or by worker needs, it is an important trend in world businesses for improving corporate effectiveness.

Last, different foreign market entry strategies offer different opportunities for the organization of international marketing. Sales branches or subsidiaries provide more standardization and supervision over marketing strategy. Joint ventures, licensing, and franchising provide local expertise and the ability to adapt marketing strategy where conditions require it, but the shared decision making implicit in these organizational options can be a source of conflict. Management contracts are useful in gaining decision authority where ownership is prevented in a foreign market.

## DISCUSSION QUESTIONS

1. What are the benefits of specialization and delegation of authority in an organization?
2. Explain why communication is more difficult in an international firm.

3. How do government regulations affect organization of international marketing activities?

4. What are the advantages and disadvantages of home- and host-country nationals as international marketing managers?

5. How does the extent of foreign sales volume influence a firm's organization for international marketing?

6. Give examples of the relationships between organization structure and size and nature of the firm's product mix.

7. Describe why international specialists offer the most centralization in decision making.

8. What is an international division? When is it most effective in organizing international marketing activities?

9. Differentiate between an international division and an international corporation with respect to responsibility for international decisions.

10. Why are distribution and promotion decisions more easily decentralized than product development ones?

11. What is participative management?

12. How can a firm institute participative management?

13. Differentiate between sales branches and subsidiaries as international organization structures.

14. What are the similarities and differences in managing joint ventures, licensing, and franchising?

15. What is the matrix form of organization for international marketing?

# AUNT SARAH'S FRIED
# CHICKEN

Early in March 1983, Jean Michel, President of Aunt Sarah's Fried Chicken–Europe, was faced with the problem of maintaining quality control among franchisers in Germany. He had received reports that several of the franchisers in Germany were serving potato pancakes instead of french fries. Also, there were reports of inconsistency in the size of the servings of chicken. Aunt Sarah's had built its reputation on its ability to offer a completely standardized product of high quality in every retail outlet.

Aunt Sarah's Fried Chicken was started by Sarah Browning in a little shop in Dallas, Texas in 1958. The great popularity of her home-style fried chicken led to expansion to other locations in Dallas and in neighboring cities. Because of limitations of capital, expansion to other American markets was accomplished through franchises. By 1970, Aunt Sarah's had 760 franchise outlets in the United States. In 1971, an entrepreneur in Paris, France sought and received the first franchise outside of the United States. As requests began to come in for other foreign franchises, it became necessary in 1973 to establish Aunt Sarah's Export Company, a wholly owned subsidiary. Aunt Sarah's chicken fitted into European eating preferences well as a popular foreign novelty item. It soon became evident that the European market was potentially large and should be actively cultivated. In 1976 the European division was set up with Jean Michel, a Belgian advertising executive, as the new director, with the headquarters office in Brussels. Michel was successful in establishing new franchise outlets at the rate of about ten per year. By 1980 there were 61 outlets in Europe, more than Michel could personally supervise. Since the Aunt Sarah reputation was based on high-quality food preparation and absolute consistency in the product offered for sale, it was necessary to maintain a careful supervision over the franchise outlets. Consequently, in 1981, Mr. Michel divided the European division into four regions: England, Benelux, Germany, and Italy, each headed by a regional manager. The Aunt Sarah organizational structure is illustrated in Exhibit 1.

From the start, the regional division managers had difficulty enforcing company operating procedures among the franchisees. Mr. Schmidt was having particular difficulty with the sixteen franchises in Germany. The franchisees had little confidence in Mr. Schmidt and resented his attempts to control their activities. Most of the franchisees had been with the firm longer than he had. Each had gone through a company training program, either in Dallas or in Brussels, and had subsequently operated his business without the help or advice of a German regional manager. During the period of min-

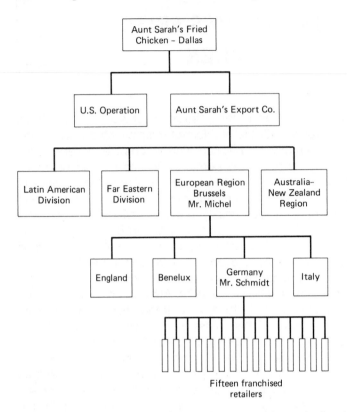

**EXHIBIT 1**    Aunt Sarah's Fried Chicken-Europe, partial organization chart. January 1983.

imal supervision, many had modified their product or service to fit what they felt were the unique needs of the local market. For example, three franchisees had decided that potato pancakes would be more popular than french fries in their parts of Germany. Two others had modified the carefully developed mixture of spices used in the chicken batter. Although these modifications had been accepted in the local markets where they were made (the franchisees involved had excellent sales performance), these aberrent outlets failed to present the standardized product and atmosphere expected by Aunt Sarah customers throughout the world.

Mr. Schmidt was a graduate of the INSEAD graduate program in business in Fontainebleau, France in 1978. Before joining Aunt Sarah's in 1981, he worked for a large department store in Bonn. He was bright, well-trained, and twenty-six years of age. The typical franchisee in Germany was in his forties and had worked in the restaurant or food business for a minimum of ten years. These entrepreneurs were reluctant to accept suggestions about how to run their businesses from Mr. Schmidt.

## QUESTIONS

1. Evaluate the organization structure of the international marketing subsidiary of Aunt Sarah's. Could it be reorganized for greater efficiency?
2. Would it be better to integrate international operations into the domestic marketing organization instead of operating a subsidiary?
3. How can Jean Michel help Mr. Schmidt in his relations with the German franchisees?

# PART IV

# BUILDING INTERNATIONAL MARKETING STRATEGY

## OVERVIEW

In this section of the text we concentrate on the factors that directly affect decisions about marketing strategies for international markets. Chapter 10 reviews issues that are preeminent in marketing consumer goods, such as when to standardize or adapt products for foreign markets, the varying relevance of specific product attributes, and the influence of country of origin on product image. Chapter 11 emphasizes the internationality of demand for industrial products, but it also addresses differences in industrial buyer behavior and preferences for product features. In Chapter 12 we cover some of the complexities of international price decisions. We refer to the unique environmental conditions in international markets that affect control over price, such as price escalations, dumping, transfer pricing, and the use of credit as a competitive tool. Chapter 13 focusses on international promotion. Here we emphasize the role of promotion tools in communicating with buyers, where differences in language, media, personnel and skills for the salesforce, legal restrictions on the use of sales promotion and advertising media, actually determine the promotion mix and its effectiveness. Chapter 14, the last one in this section, reviews distribution decisions in international markets. It identifies the most common types of middlemen in international markets and differences in their operating styles across different nations. This chapter also reviews physical distribution functions as to how they differ in foreign markets.

PART IV

# GUIDING INTERNATIONAL MARKETING STRATEGY

# chapter 10

# CONSUMER PRODUCT DECISIONS FOR INTERNATIONAL MARKETING

When Avon Products, Inc. began selling to Japan a decade ago, the giant US cosmetics, fragrances and costume jewelry manufacturer and distributor suddenly found itself deluged with complaints.

"Initially we came in with the same products that we were selling in the US, and we did badly," admits Malcolm Aylett, general manager (marketing) for Avon in Japan. "We soon learned that the needs here are significantly different, and so we started to adapt and change as fast as we could." For example, Japanese women lead the world in the use of skin care products, applying up to nine different cleansers and creams. Avon accordingly developed a range of new products to meet this demand.

In the US, Avon has been successful with a gift line of cosmetics and scents in decorative decanters. But these sparked no interest in Japan. In their place, Avon developed gift boxes of soap, elaborately packaged to meet the high Japanese aesthetic standard.

For all its products, notes Aylett, "we've had to upgrade our packaging for Japan."*

## INTRODUCTION

The businessperson who decides to sell products in foreign markets must carefully reevaluate his or her entire marketing strategy. This evaluation should begin with the product itself. A decision must be made whether to

*"Japan Changes Avon's Makeup," *International Management,* July 1979, p. 42.

export the product unchanged, or to adapt it to meet the needs of differing markets. Since consumer products and industrial goods are bought by very different markets, this process of product adaptation will vary for the two classes of goods. The remaining elements in a marketing strategy will also require the same careful evaluation before a product is launched success-fully in a foreign market. How should the product be priced to consumers? to the' middleman? How should it be promoted in light of differing buying preferences and different media availability? What kinds of marketing channels should be sought? How should the goods be physically distrib-uted in the new market? When the answers to these questions are put to-gether, the strategy that emerges may be very similar to the strategy al-ready in use in the home market, or it may be quite different, depending on the environmental context of the foreign market.

In this chapter we focus on the particular requirements of marketing consumer products in world markets. First, we discuss the relative merits of standardizing and adapting products, as well as criteria that are useful in deciding which approach to use. Next we look at some product and service attributes that are affected by different consumer preferences in foreign markets. We then turn to the role of the product life cycle in inter-national marketing management. Other sections of this chapter center on various behavioral and environmental situations that influence product mix decisions. An important area noted in this section is the affect of a prod-uct's country of origin on perceptions of its quality; this allows us to intro-duce the fifth ''P'' for international marketing strategy—production loca-tion—one of the unique areas of international marketing management.

## STANDARDIZATION VERSUS ADAPTATION

The international marketer finds it easiest to standardize products and, for that matter, the entire marketing strategy as much as possible. He or she is particularly reluctant to change the basic product, both because it is re-lated to the company's total image and market position, and because it is the most difficult of the marketing inputs to change. Each change in the marketing strategy to meet the needs of a foreign market moves the mar-keter farther from the familiar and reduces the gains from large-scale standardized operations.

### Marketing Strategies for Worldwide Marketing

The matrix in Figure 10–1 illustrates some of the alternative market-ing strategies that a firm might face entering more than one foreign market. Ideally, the marketer would seek Situation I, where product, promotion,

**FIGURE 10–1**   Strategy alternatives in foreign markets.

| *Marketing Strategy Inputs* | *ALTERNATIVE WORLD STRATEGIES* | | | | |
|---|---|---|---|---|---|
| | *I* | *II* | *III* | *IV* | *V* |
| Product | same | same | same | same | different |
| Promotion | same | same | same | different | different |
| Channel | same | same | different | different | different |
| Price | same | different | different | different | different |

marketing channel, and price all remain the same. The marketer might hope to find a number of foreign markets that would fit into Situation I because the firm will incur the lowest marketing costs. But in most instances, he or she would probably have to vary price (Situation II), because of variable costs of serving distant markets and local differences in buying power. In Situation III, the marketer finds it necessary to vary the marketing channel as well as the price. The different types of intermediaries found in foreign markets and the varieties of services performed, explain why price and channel must often be adapted. In Situation IV, only the product remains unchanged—acknowledging the need to adapt to foreign communication patterns, media and intermedia availability, and the resulting adjustments to the firm's variable costs. In Situation V it may be necessary to adapt each of the four strategy inputs to local conditions. At this point, the marketer may have lost any advantages from expertise gained in domestic markets and all the economies of scale. Although he or she is still selling ''widgets,'' they are different types of widgets, advertised and sold in a different manner, to different dealers, and at different prices. Most international marketers actually use Strategies II, III, and IV more frequently than either total standardization or total adaptation.

Another marketing strategy input—physical distribution—is almost always different in foreign markets. It is possible that an Austrian manufacturer selling in Germany, or a Canadian selling in the United States, would be able to use identical systems of transportation, materials handling, and storage; but, in general, physical distance and national boundaries require adjustment in physical distribution. It was for this reason the PD was not even included in the matrix in Figure 10–1.

It is rare that a firm is able to enter foreign markets without adapting its marketing strategy to some extent to meet local needs. Among the most successful at using a standardized strategy are the bottlers of soft drinks, Pepsi Cola and Coca-Cola, who sell their products pretty much the same way throughout the world. Even these firms have found it necessary to adapt to variations in local conditions, but the necessary amount of adaptation has been small. The factor of importance to the international marketer is not whether or not some adaptation is necessary—it almost always is; concern is with the degree of adaptation necessary. Volkswagen, for example, has found it necessary to adapt its autmobiles sold in the American market to meet local safety and emission standards. It has also adjusted promotion, distribution, and price; but none of these changes has been sufficient to change the basic image or strategic goals of VW in the market. It is perceived as pretty much the same kind of automobile in Germany as it is in the United States. In the post–World War II era when VW entered the American market, General Motors was selling in the German market. However, the General Motors products which were selling successfully in the American market were large, heavy gas guzzlers, which were not considered acceptable by any sizeable segment of Germans. Eventually General Motors found it necessary to design a totally different product for German and European consumers. Since the car was so totally different, it was even given a different name, Opel. Thus, in order to compete in European markets, General Motors lost the advantage of its expertise in building large cars, and the prestige from its highly successful American brand names. Adaptation of various elements in the marketing strategy is almost always necessary when moving into foreign markets, but if the required change is too great, the venture may not prove to be profitable.

### Criteria for the Standardization-versus-Adaptation Decision

The factors that influence decisions to standardize or adapt promotion, distribution, and pricing are discussed in later hapters. Since most firms have significant fixed costs associated with the products they develop and produce, this area is of particular importance in international marketing. Many firms are not willing to adapt products for foreign markets at all, because they view international sales as simply a "bonus" addition to their domestic marketing effort. To such firms, foreign market needs do not really influence product decisions as part of their marketing strategy. This type of firm will be more likely to use exporting as an entry strategy and to let intermediaries determine prices, promotion, and distribution in foreign markets. And when conditions are right, this approach may be quite effective and profitable. Those firms are not, however, truly international marketers.

The international marketer views product-adaptation decisions in the same manner in which domestic product-development decisions are made. Products are developed to exploit market opportunities, and a market opportunity exists when a firm has the resources and skills to satisfy specific consumer needs. The international marketer, then, just like his or her domestic counterpart, will first investigate market needs and conditions. A decision will then be made as to how to respond to the market, given the firm's objectives and resources. Market needs, market conditions, and the firm's objectives and resources are the criteria to use in deciding whether to standardize or adapt products for foreign markets.

*Market needs and conditions.* Products or services only have value to a market in their ability to meet consumer needs. People all over the world "need" transportation; that need is met, however, in a variety of ways, such as walking, using beasts of burden, bicycles, public transport, automobiles, trains, planes. How people meet their needs is determined by their surrounding conditions—how much money they have, what the distances are, what technologies are available, the existence of supporting infrastructure such as roads, and so on. So, while needs may be the same in two markets, conditions may be quite different. Peru has the same land area as France, Spain, and Britain combined, and is smaller than Colombia, another South American country. Peruvians are much poorer than the average European, so they are less able to meet transportation needs with personal automobiles. Colombians are on average even poorer than Peruvians, but Colombia's major cities are not separated by the geographic extremes (the Andes Mountains and Amazon Jungle) that separate Peruvian cities. So Colombians have more roads and as a result, more ways of transporting people and materials within the country. In this example, several market conditions have influenced how people meet their need for transportation. Figure 10–2 shows other conditions that affect consumers' abilities to meet their needs.

**FIGURE 10–2** Market conditions affecting product use and needs.

| MARKET CONDITIONS | POSSIBLE PRODUCT POLICIES |
|---|---|
| 1. Consumer incomes low | Product simplification (such as mechanical to manual) or innovation |
| 2. Different consumer preferences | Redesign physical product |
| 3. Different geographic conditions from domestic market | Redesign physical product |
| 4. Different language from domestic market | Adapt package and all written materials |
| 5. Product used to meet different consumer needs | Possible redesign of physical product, adjustment of communication strategy, and possibly innovation |
| 6. Different styling preferences | Adapt product appearance |
| 7. Users are mobile | Standardization of basic products across world markets |
| 8. User skill levels are low | Adapt product to reduce need for product-use skills |
| 9. Government regulations | Adapt product to meet regulations |
| 10. Different operating conditions for product (electrical current) | Adapt physical product |
| 11. Different distribution and purchasing conditions (longer shelf life) | Adapt package and package sizes; plus possible redesign of product |

Most products and services have multiple need-satisfying attributes. Automobiles meet the need for transporting both people and things. It is possible, therefore, for people in one country to emphasize the use of a product to meet a particular need, while people in other parts of the world use the same product to meet other needs. Consumer expectations concerning the purposes of products do vary in different markets. A classic case is the bicycle. In countries where there is high per-capita ownership of automobiles, the bicycle is used for recreation and exercise. Where ownership of automobiles is limited, bicycles play a primary role in personal transportation. Since bicycles are used for different purposes, the product may need to be adapted for each situation. A bicycle designed primarily for recreation will still meet the transportation need, but it will not meet that need as well as one adapted primarily for personal transport.

The bicycle example epitomizes the dilemma of the international marketer. A product-standardization policy restricts the firm's ability to compete in the long run in foreign markets because its products may not match market needs and conditions. It makes the firm vulnerable to competitors who introduce more appropriate products. Standardization is, however, less risky or costly to the firm, so it is often used to "test the waters" in an initial international marketing effort. Product adaptation, on the other hand, offers the most potential for market penetration and profits. Yet it may not be feasible if the firm has limited resources or foreign market size is limited.

*Constraints on product adaptation and standardization policies.*    Adapting products can mean as little adjustment as redesign of a package or as much as design of innovative products to match foreign market needs and conditions. The extent of product adaptation is constrained by the firm itself and its external environment. Put another way, national markets are simply "segments" of the world market. Whether a firm develops unique products for each of those segments depends on the firm's ability and desire to identify the needs and conditions affecting a market segment, whether a segment is accessible to the foreign firm, and whether or not the firm has the resources to adapt a product for a particular segment.

The firm's desire to meet foreign market needs has been alluded to earlier. International marketing may have the exclusive purpose of ridding a firm of excess domestic inventories. A firm may use foreign markets to "milk" more profits from products that are no longer in demand in the domestic market. Or, the firm may be guided by the ethnocentric belief that market needs and conditions are the same everywhere. Whatever the case, this type of firm does not have the ability to identify any unique market needs or conditions that might exist in a foreign market.

On the other hand, simply because market needs or conditions differ in foreign markets, the firm may still not choose to adapt its products. A market may be inaccessible to a foreign firm as a result of government regulations. International product standards for consumer goods are rare; local governments usually reserve the right to set their own product standards. Variation in regulations constrain the firm's access to foreign markets with standardized products. At the same time, a firm may choose to market only those products in its product line that are not subject to government regulation. For example, finished textiles (clothing) face variable labeling restrictions in different countries. Textiles not sold as "finished pieces" (for example, bolts of cloth, and wool) do not face such intense labeling restrictions. Small firms are able to sell standardized textiles in many countries when they are not sold as clothing; their international efforts would be much more limited if they had to label ("adapt") products for each market. So, while a textile firm may sell clothing in domestic markets, it might choose to sell "unfinished" textiles in foreign markets, even though it recognizes differing needs and conditions.

Government regulations or competitive conditions may also constrain a firm's choice of standardized or adapted product strategies. Rules concerning foreign ownership of business may force a firm to produce products locally in order to have access to a market. While this does not necessarily result in an "adapted" product policy, it is technically perhaps easier to do so. Intense competition, of course, also exerts pressure on a firm to adjust its products to market needs and conditions.

Last, the firm is constrained in its choice of product policies by its own objectives, traditions, and resources. When international markets play a minor role in achieving the firm's growth or profit objectives, the firm will find it difficult to make serious product adaptations for foreign markets. Even if international sales are important in meeting the firm's objectives, it may not have the requisite financial, production, or personnel resources for making product adjustments. And, of course, some firms find consumers expect their products to be the same, wherever in the world they buy them. Standardization is critical to the quality image of firms that make products bought by mobile consumers (photographic equipment, personal-care products, soft drinks, liquor, to name a few such products). These groups represent the growth of international market segments and provide an opportunity for successful product standardization.

In summary, the product standardization or adaptation decision must be contingent on a cost-benefit analysis. A firm needs to know what market needs and other environmental conditions differ in markets it is considering entering. It must then estimate sales and costs under the two conditions—introduction of a standardized product and development of an adapted product. Even with these data as inputs to the product-policy decision, the firm must also consider its long-term goals and other constraints on adapting or standardizing its products for foreign markets.

## PRODUCT ATTRIBUTE RELEVANCE

Product attributes that may be very important in one market may have little sales appeal or relevance, or may even hinder sales, in other markets. Recognizing a frequent need to adapt products to local needs, the marketer must decide whether the potential sales justify the costs of adaptation. Keeping this cost factor in mind, the marketer should consider which attributes products should or should not possess in each new market. What follows are some examples of how attributes vary in importance in international marketing.

### Convenience versus Price

Many modern products, especially American products, are designed to provide the consumer with maximum convenience and saving of labor. But, in some foreign markets the cost of labor or alternative sources of energy may be too low to justify the added cost of building these characteristics into a product. The sewing machine is a good example. The modern American and European sewing machine is a complex labor-saving device. First, its operation is motorized so that the operator need not apply human power to make it operate. Second, it has built-in mechanisms that make it possible to change the type of stitching with minimal effort. The resulting machine is expensive to buy and expensive to use in terms of energy consumption. Yet it is exactly what a large segment of the European and American markets want. In underdeveloped markets there is both a need and a demand for sewing machines—a need that is even greater than in developed nations where more clothing may be purchased ready-made. However, the sophisticated new machines cannot be sold in these markets because they are too expensive. In order to compete in these markets, the sewing machine manufacturer must simplify the machine. If this simpler machine provides a variation in stitches at all, it will be accomplished by a manual adjustment instead of a mechanical one. To sell in the most primitive markets, it may be necessary to provide a machine that is operated by human power, with a treadle, because of the unavailability or high cost of electrical energy.

### Durability versus Styling and Change

Different societies have different attitudes about how long a particular product should last. During a period of several decades before and after World War II, when the typical American considered an automobile purchase as a short-term matter, the typical Englishman considered an automobile a life-time purchase. The American, expecting to own a new car for an average of five or six years, looked for modern styling, new features, and high performance when making a selection. The Briton, who planned to keep a car for many years, looked for durability and comfort in the purchase. Americans keep their refrigerators an average of about fifteen years, at which time they feel that the new models have made the equipment obsolete; they don't expect refrigerators to last much more than fifteen years. European refrigerator buyers may consider a refrigerator a life-time investment and will buy a basically simple, very durable model. Americans buy freezers much as Europeans buy refrigerators. There is little expectation that they will become obsolete, and buyers may keep them for twenty-five to thirty years or more.

The international marketer must be aware of consumers' expectations about the products they sell. There is little likelihood that a single marketer can change traditional buying patterns in a culture. So, if consumers expect durability and long life in a product, the new entrant should emphasize products with those attributes. If the market expects high fashion and change, the product should meet these needs. If there are few similar products, the international marketer should try to anticipate consumers' attribute expectations by observing their demands for related products. If the market is large enough, there may be some presently unserved segments that can be reached profitably through products with different attributes than those of competing goods. Thus, in the 1950s and 1960s, even though most of the American automobile market was still committed to high styling and change, a number of European imports that emphasized durability and absence of change were able to profitably serve small segments of the American market.

International differences in design and styling preferences are well known. Many consumer products are clearly identifiable as Danish (furniture), as Chinese (decorations), as Mexican (pottery), and so forth. Even the design and styling of more functional products, like automobiles, varies among nations; British, Italian, and French cars each have unique design characteristics. The international marketer has two options with respect to styling: products can be adapted to conform to local preferences, or domestic styling can be retained and "foreignness" emphasized. Certain segments of the market in most countries like to use obviously "imported" goods, which may provide an image of being more expensive and exclusive.

## Product Size

Different markets prefer different sizes in similar product types. This variation in preference can be explained at least partly in terms of population density and standard of living. In sparsely populated lands, many goods come in comparatively large sizes. In the Western hemisphere, which generally has a low population density, consumers tend to want homes, automobiles, appliances, and recreation vehicles that are larger than those preferred in Europe or Asia. Income and standard of living also affect size preferences. In low income countries, housing space per capita is very small, and many other consumer goods, if they are purchased at all, are bought in small sizes. The liter or quart Coca-Cola bottle is popular only in countries with relatively high standards of living, and where storage space in the home is adequate.

Product size preferences are also affected by purchase patterns and cultural preferences. The French homemaker, who prefers to shop daily for foods to ensure their high quality, does not need as much refrigerated storage space as the Canadian homemaker. Canadians prefer to shop less frequently, and believe that frozen and other preserved foods are almost as good, or are willing to put up with their lower quality to save time. The refrigerator manufacturer must offer different-sized products to compete successfully in these two markets. A refrigerator that would seem "roomy" to the French would be rejected as too small in the Canadian market. Whatever the reasons for varying size preferences, the successful marketer must adjust products to the patterns and preferences of each market.

### Costs and Availability
### of Maintenance and Repair

In underdeveloped or less-developed countries there is usually a shortage of skilled service mechanics able to keep complex mechanisms in repair. Manufacturers who wish to sell products in such countries have two choices: they themselves can provide service facilities, or they can simplify the product so a local serviceperson could repair it. Since durable-goods manufacturers seldom sell direct to the consumer, it is a complex matter to provide adequately trained service personnel at the point of sale in foreign markets. For this reason it may be easier to adapt the product to the simpler servicing abilities of local repair personnel. Instead of a power lawn mower, a manual one could be offered in the market; instead of a heat-controlled electric toaster, a time-controlled toaster could be offered. In addition, of course, the simpler product will serve a bigger potential market in underdeveloped countries where purchasing power is lower.

At the other end of the continuum of economic development, servicing problems of a different type may develop. High levels of employment and demand for labor may attract many repair persons into higher-paying occupations and drive up the wages of those who remain. As the cost of keeping products in repair gets higher, the consumer may elect to replace old products that require frequent repairs with new ones. The marketer can deal with this problem by designing products so that they are easily repairable or so that worn or defective parts are replaced instead of being repaired. The firm might also take the initiative in redesigning products so that it is cheaper to replace a worn or broken product with a new one. The Swiss watch industry has lost market share in a number of foreign markets because competitors in the United States, and later in Japan, introduced pin-lever-movement watches that were cheaper to replace than to repair. Subsequently, digital watches, which were even cheaper to produce, cut further into the market for jewel-movement watches. Consumers in the developed countries, where it has become difficult and time consuming to get watches repaired, find that these newer watches are attractive, keep good time (in the case of the quartz digitals, better time), and are disposable when out of order.

### Compatibility

Products destined for foreign markets must be designed so that they are compatible with local needs and preferences. Historically, every nation has developed its own system of standards and measures, but during the past century an increasing number of nations have adopted "international standards." For example, the metric system is rapidly becoming an international standard. American manufacturers who are still operating on the English system of weights and measures find themselves at a disadvantage in international markets, because they must adjust their products to meet local demands while foreign competitors are already producing on metric standards.

Weights and measures are not the only product characteristics where compatibility is a necessary competitive factor in foreign marketing. Energy standards vary around the world. Electric power can be produced in a number of combinations of wattage and voltage. Products designed to operate on the American standard, for example, may not operate properly or at all from some foreign energy sources. Some manufacturers sell products that can be adjusted to operate on either 110 or 220 volts—the two most common standards—but differences in the current cycles may still make products inoperable outside domestic markets.

### Throwaway versus Reuseable Containers

For most products, the cost of the container is low relative to the cost of the product it delivers; but for a few products, the container cost may be as high as the material inside. For these products it is frequently deemed necessary to provide returnable containers. Soft drinks and beer provide good examples of this type of product. In highly affluent countries, where the cost of labor is high in relationship to the cost of materials, it may prove cheaper to bottle the product in throwaway containers (even though the container may cost as much as the liquid inside) than to pay the costs of handling returned bottles through intermediaries. In less-affluent nations, however, it may be cheaper in terms of total costs to use returnable bottles. In some societies there may be additional pressures to use returnable containers no matter what the comparative cost. A concern for resource use and/or pollution of the environment may result in the prohibition of products which, like aluminum, require more energy in their production or which litter the countryside. Thus, packaging policy must be adapted to each local environment.

## ADAPTATION OF SERVICES _____

Most services are so unique in character that they do not lend themselves to standardization from market to market. An income-tax advisory service is a good example. The tax structure varies so much from country to country that there is little carry-over of expertise into new markets. Yet some service industries have become truly international. American Express and Cook's offer travel service in most parts of the world. The basic service they offer remains unchanged; they do, however, provide personnel with local language proficiency in order to compete effectively in each market. Because of their wide international contacts, they frequently have a competitive advantage over local travel agencies in planning international travel. Consumer credit is another service area that is becoming truly international. A number of international credit cards have been introduced on the market during the past twenty years. Visa, Master Card, and American Express are accepted in lieu of cash in most parts of the world. The amount of adaptation necessary to make marketing of these services possible in other nations is not great. Insurance and banking services at the consumer level usually require considerable adaptation in foreign markets, primarily because of varying government regulations. For this reason their services tend to be adjusted to local conditions even when there is international ownership of the firms.

## THE PRODUCT LIFE CYCLE _____

The concept of the product life cycle is described in detail in most introductory marketing books.[1] For a quick review, the product life cycle describes the cycle of total industry sales and profit for new products introduced into a market. Sales in all new industries seem to follow the same general pattern of growth, as shown in Figure 10-3. The pioneering stage is a period of slow but gradually increasing growth in total industry sales, as the public is made aware of the new product and its benefits. The market growth stage is a period of rapid growth which gradually tapers off to no growth. Early in this period profits peak and gradually decline for the industry as a whole. The market maturity stage begins with stable sales, followed by a period of gradual decline and intense competition. In the stage of market decline, there is a continuing period of decline in sales until the product is discontinued. Industry profits may actually become negative during this period. The number of competitors in an industry increases rapidly during the growth stage and declines after that.

[1]William J. Stanton, *Fundamentals of Marketing* (New York: McGraw-Hill, 1973), pp. 200–202; E. Jerome McCarthy, *Basic Marketing*, 6th ed. (Homewood, Ill.: Richard D. Irwin, 1979), pp. 240–43; and Edward W. Cundiff, Richard R. Still, and Norman P. Govoni, *Fundamentals of Modern Marketing*, 3rd ed. (Englewood Cliffs, N.J.: Prentice-Hall, 1980), pp. 162–65.

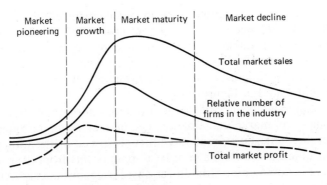

**FIGURE 10–3**    Product life cycle for an industry.

*Source:* Taken from Cundiff, Still, & Govoni.

### The PLC in International Marketing Management

The importance of the product life-cycle concept to the international marketer lies in the fact that not all markets throughout the world are at the same stage of the cycle. A product which may already have reached the market maturity stage with its squeeze on profits and downward trend in sales in the marketer's home country, may be only at the pioneering stage in some countries, and may not yet have been introduced to other markets. This enables a marketer with expertise in producing and marketing a particular product to launch the same product in new markets where the prospects for growth and profit are high and competition may still be small. This life cycle was discussed in Chapter 3 with respect to production and foreign market entry implications.

An important first step, then, in analyzing potential new markets abroad is to determine which stage of the life cycle a product is in, in each market. If the firm decides to introduce a new product in a new market at an early stage in the product life cycle, it must also try to become familiar with the process of diffusion of innovations in that market. The diffusion process (discussed in Chapter 5) will help determine what people to reach in the early stages of introducing the new product in the market.

### International Trade Product Life Cycle

Closely related to the product life-cycle concept is the cycle of international trade proposed by Louis T. Wells, Jr.[2] This concept suggests that many new products go through a cycle in which production is concentrated

[2]Louis T. Wells, Jr., "A Product Life Cycle for International Trade?" *Journal of Marketing,* July 1968, pp. 1–6.

first in the introducing country, then in other advanced countries, and finally in the less-advanced countries where production costs may be lower. Ultimately, the introducing country, instead of exporting the product to foreign markets, may become a net importer; whereas the less-developed nations start out as importers, they may eventually become exporters. This process is illustrated in Figure 10–4.

The major significance of the life cycle of international trade is its impact on long-term marketing strategy. The marketer who introduces a new product in the domestic market should try to spread distribution to foreign markets as quickly as possible in order to reap profits from the early period before there is competition from lower-cost foreign producers. At the same time, if the introducing firm initiates foreign production as early in the cycle as is technically feasible, this will provide the best long-term production and marketing strategy.

## PRODUCT USAGE PATTERNS AND POSITIONING

Different cultures use the same products in very different ways. In a number of Far Eastern countries, rice is the central portion of most meals, with other foods added in smaller quantities. In Western countries, rice is served as a side dish to complement a meat dish. Refrigerators are used in the U.S. primarily to store food, but in other countries they are used only to cool selected foods and drinks. Leather, plastic, or rubber sandals, which are used as regular footwear in many underdeveloped countries, are used as leisure wear in more advanced countries.

The manufacturer who hopes to sell products successfully in foreign markets must be careful to position them for optimum success in the market. The Japanese marketer who first exported zoris (rubber thong sandals) to the United States positioned them as beachwear, an entirely different role from their use in the Japanese market. American consumers accepted zoris as inexpensive and practical footwear for the beach and for other informal occasions, and the product was a success. There are many other examples of products which have been successfully repositioned to serve different market needs in foreign countries. These include foods adapted to different roles, clothing used for different purposes, and household items serving different decorative purposes. The challenge to the marketer is to find innovative uses for products that will make them attractive to consumers in a different culture.

The repositioning necessary to sell some products in foreign markets places the product in a much smaller market segment than that held by the product in the home country. Repositioning French table wine as a drink for special and festive occasions in Australia provides a much smaller market than if it could be sold as table wine to be consumed with every main

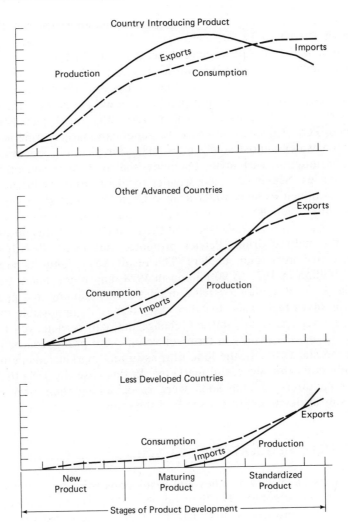

**FIGURE 10–4**  Product life cycle in international trade.

*Source:*  Louis T. Wells, Jr., "A Product Life Cycle for International Trade?"
*Journal of Marketing*, July 1968, pp. 1–6. Published by the American
Marketing Association.

meal, as is the case in France. However, the French wine exporters see no
real chance of affecting the low per-capita wine consumption habits of
Australians except in the long term. Positioning a product into a major consumption segment in a foreign market will yield a much larger potential
sales volume if it successfully penetrates that market segment. In order to
achieve such a change in product-usage patterns, the foreign marketer
must be willing to invest heavily in promotional efforts.

A successful example of such a positioning approach was the introduction of Perrier, a French carbonated water, in the American market. Carbonated water, usually called "mineral water" in Europe, is a popular item in a number of European countries to drink with meals or as a refreshing thirst quencher between meals. Many users buy it because they believe the combination of minerals in a particular brand is good for their health. Others drink it just because it is a light, refreshing thirst quencher. At the time when Perrier decided to enter the American market, Americans used carbonated water almost solely as a mixer for alcoholic beverages. Per-capita consumption was small, far below that of France and other European countries. Seeking a much broader segment of the American market, Perrier positioned its soda water against Coca-Cola and Seven-Up as a refreshing thirst quencher. In the American market no attempt was made to promote the mineral characteristics of the product, but it was positioned as a healthful, natural drink. Perrier promoted this image heavily to consumers, distributors, and retailers. The result was a jump in bottle sales from 14 million in 1977 to 90 million in 1978, and more than a tripling of dollar sales to $30 million.[3] Such a dramatic repositioning in a market obviously involves high risks. In other cases it may be impossible to change consumer usage patterns, and any change that can be achieved is expensive. However, the results in terms of volume and profits can be large, at least in the short run. In the long run, as in any market, competitors will eventually copy the successful marketer. In this case, by 1980 the American manufacturers of club soda were repositioning their own products against soft drinks to capture a share of the growing and lucrative market.

## GOVERNMENT REGULATIONS

Governments have varying rules and regulations regarding what products can and cannot be sold within their borders. Pharmaceutical products, for example, if not properly tested, can have side effects that may be more dangerous than the conditions they are designed to treat. Most nations ban specific drugs, or require evidence of testing for safety before their introduction is permitted. Among the most rigorous government regulations are those concerning the sale of automobiles in the United States. In an effort to improve passenger safety and reduce the automobile's negative effects on the environment, the U.S. government has promulgated a complex set of regulations and specifications to which an automobile must conform. The total cost-per-vehicle for safety and emission controls is well in excess of $500 per vehicle. Since these features raise the price of an automobile considerably, foreign manufacturers who sell in the American market usu-

---

[3]"Perrier Putting More Sparkle into Sales," *Sales and Marketing Management*, January 1979, pp. 16–17.

ally produce two lines, one for the United States and one for other markets. When American automobile manufacturers try to compete in world markets, they must either manufacture a second line without the safety and emission features, or try to convince the foreign consumer that these features are worth the added price. Another important area of government regulation in many countries is in the sale of foodstuffs. Laws have been passed to ensure that foods are pure, unadulterated, and that additives are not harmful. Almost any type of product is subject to government regulation in some part of the world, and the international marketer must take pains to learn of all such regulations before entering a new foreign market. A good source of information on product regulations are the commercial attachés in foreign embassies or consulates. Other sources are government publications, and secondary data as well as service companies active in international trade for their clients.

## THE CONSUMERISM MOVEMENT

For centuries, "caveat emptor" was the operating policy in markets throughout the world. The buyer and seller were considered equal in their ability to judge quality, value, and performance features. But as sellers have grown larger and more powerful and products have become sophisticated and complex, consumers feel they have lost equality in the marketplace. They have turned to organized efforts and to the government for protection.[4] This movement has taken many directions, from participation in consumer research groups (such as the Consumers Union in the United States) to lobbying for government protection.[5] Consumer groups try to provide their members with more information about complex products in order to help them make better buying decisions. This may be achieved through research efforts by their own organizations, or by gaining the cooperation of impartial news sources such as magazines. Pressure on governments has resulted in the enactment of specific laws to prevent particular abuses, and also in the appointment of consumer advocates within the formal government structure. The ombudsman in Sweden was one of the first of these. In other nations there are cabinet-level ministers of consumer affairs. In this new climate of opinion, the international marketer can no longer "cut corners" in dealings with consumers.

The international marketer will face vastly different consumerist climates throughout the world. In some countries, such as Sweden and the U.S., governments have institutionalized consumer representation through creation of industry "watchdogs" and through protective legislation. In

---

[4]"EEC Survey Reveals Deep Consumer Hostility toward Advertising," *Business International*, July 23, 1976, pp. 238–39.

[5]Ralph M. Gaedeke and Udo Udo-Aka, "Toward the Internationalization of Consumerism," *California Management Review*, Fall 1974, p. 87.

other areas the legislation may exist, but few resources are allocated to its enforcement. In yet other environments, the government may not recognize any consumer protection responsibility on its part. In general, the industrialized countries have the stronger government participation in protection of consumers. Governments in underdeveloped countries are less likely to intervene between business and consumers. The international marketer needs to be familiar with the organizational structure within which consumerism is expressed, and with the overall climate for consumer protection.

## INFLUENCE OF COUNTRY OF ORIGIN

Consumers often have stereotyped opinions about the products of nations, or about certain types of products from specific nations.[6] Americans, for example, have a strong positive stereotype about technical products from Germany. This generally favorable feeling predisposes Americans to expect high-quality performance from German products. This feeling has evolved from perceptions of durable and mechanical goods such as cameras, microscopes, and automobiles. Any new product of this nature exported from Germany to the United States should meet a favorable initial reaction from the market. If Germany should start exporting high-style and fashion goods to the American market, we might find that the favorable stereotype does not carry over, or that it is specific only to durable goods. In contrast, high-fashion goods from France enjoy a favorable stereotype in the American market, but their durable goods enjoy, at best, a neutral image. French automobiles, although well engineered, have made very little impact on the American market as compared to German cars.

The products of Sri Lanka have no positive or negative image in the American market because most Americans know nothing about the country and have never consciously been exposed to any of its products. Yet between any two countries that have regular contact and that exchange goods, there develops some type of stereotypical image, either favorable, neutral, or unfavorable. Robert Schooler studied the effect of "country of origin" on the perception of Guatemalan consumers concerning the products of neighboring Central American countries. Using identical products identified with different countries of origin, he found that Guatemalan consumers classified products from Costa Rica and El Salvador as inferior to domestic products and to Mexican products. Mexico, the more economically advanced neighbor, was even viewed as having products superior to

---

[6]Curtis Reierson, "Attitude Changes toward Foreign Products," *Journal of Marketing Research* vol. IV (November 1967), pp. 385–87; and Akira Nagashima, "A Comparison of Japanese and U.S. Attitudes toward Foreign Products," *Journal of Marketing*, vol. 34 (January 1970), pp. 68–74.

domestic Guatemalan products.[7] Akira Nagashima compared U.S. and Japanese businessperson's perceptions of products from their own and other countries. He found Americans to be very "jingoistic" about most types of products—we tend to see our own as superior. The Japanese also rated their own products high, but they indicated there was more prestige in owning American and German products. Both groups of businesspersons gave English and French products the lowest marks, but they stereotyped English goods as "old-fashioned" and French goods as having "style."[8]

Country-of-origin stereotypes, like other product images, are not immutable. If a negative stereotype exists, it might be changed through an effective marketing strategy. But if ignored, it can effectively prevent penetration of the foreign market. It is not an easy or fast process to change a stereotype; once consumers have decided a particular product is inferior, lots of education and promotional effort are necessary to change their opinions. An outstanding example of a change in stereotype is the perception of Japanese products in the American market. The first penetration of the American market by Japanese products was prior to World War II. At that time Japan exported large quantities of cheap imitations of American and European products to the United States and as a result, Americans developed a stereotype image of Japanese products as being "cheap," "imitative," and "shoddy." After World War II, Japan began exporting high-quality, originally designed and engineered products to the United States. One of the first successes was cameras, which gradually achieved acceptance as high-quality products. Japanese trading companies put on exhibits of Japanese art and design in American cities to expose Americans to Japanese talents in design and construction. Today, Japanese products enjoy a highly favorable image in the American market, but the job of changing this image has been slow. Years after World War II, in a study of American stereotypes of foreign products, Curtis Reierson found that even though Japanese products no longer had the strong negative image of prewar years, they were still seen by Americans as far inferior to German products.[9]

In many instances country-of-origin prejudices are quite strong and widespread. In such cases the foreign marketer can safely make use of this generally accepted knowledge—if it is positive. But in other cases, the prejudices may not be as strongly held; and it is not patently obvious that prejudices exist or how strong they are. Even a mildly negative stereotype may prevent or minimize the effectiveness of a foreign product entry. Not many studies of country-of-origin stereotypes have been made, but the methodology has been tested, and a marketer who has any doubts about the acceptance of products in a foreign market should spend the time and

[7]Robert D. Schooler, "Product Bias in the Central American Common Market," *Journal of Marketing Research,* vol 1 (November 1965), pp. 394–97.

[8]Nagashima, "Comparison of Japanese and U.S. Attitudes."

[9]Curtis Reierson, "Attitude Changes."

effort to make such a study. By moving assembly or production to countries having positive product images, the multinational corporation is able to develop a fifth "P" in its marketing strategy—production location.

There are some instances when domestic products face negative stereotypes in their own market. Foreign goods are seen as superior to locally produced ones. This phenomenon which has been observed frequently in underdeveloped countries, has been called the "paradox of Third World peoples." The paradox is the perceived superiority of products of industrial, developed countries by persons who simultaneously decry the "imperialism" of developed countries. A good example of this occurred with Winston cigarettes in Venezuela. Although Winstons were made locally with the same tobaccos and formula as American-made Winstons, many Venezuelans were willing to pay as much as $1 a pack for the imported Winstons. A national inferiority complex about a country's productive skills can lead to such preferences for foreign goods. This phenomenon does seem to prevail in developing countries where industrial production experience has been limited. But even in developed countries, large segments of the market occasionally have negative attitudes about their own products. Young people in the 1960s in the U.S. expressed some of their frustration with the Vietnam War by blaming American business; the German VW was lauded as representing good value and economy, something they believed was not relevant to American businesses and their products.

## COMPARATIVE PRODUCT STRATEGY

The introduction of a product or service into foreign markets requires a comparison of the differences and similarities in these markets. This will determine the extent to which the product or service needs to be adapted or changed to be marketed successfully. The differences or similarities which are important will vary from product to product. For General Motors, income in the new market is very important, but for Coca-Cola it is of little importance. In making product decisions, international marketers find again and again that comparison of groups of markets is valuable.

The firm that plans to penetrate worldwide markets faces more than a hundred different national markets. By comparing and grouping countries according to their needs for, uses for, and perceptions of products, the firm may find that there are only three or four different markets, and that three or four versions of the product will serve the needs of consumers in almost every nation in the world. A good place to start is to penetrate those markets which will accept products essentially unchanged. A "staging" strategy could then be used to introduce products successively to different markets, depending on the extent and costs of product adaptation.

## SUMMARY

There is a demand for consumer products in virtually all countries of the world. Nevertheless, products are used in different ways and under various conditions, to meet differing buyer needs. As a result, international marketers must analyze these factors and decide the merits of standardizing or adapting their products for foreign markets. At one extreme, a firm's entire marketing strategy might be standardized and used intact in foreign markets; at the other extreme, all strategic elements can be adapted to meet foreign market needs. In most cases, some adjustment of prices, channels of distribution, promotion techniques, and products must be made to meet different conditions in foreign markets. Products are often the most costly to adapt, but sometimes adjustments must be made because the product is used to meet different buyer needs, or because specific attributes of a product have no value or meaning in foreign markets. If a firm has limited resources or limited goals for foreign sales, it may choose to standardize its products even if demand for them will be limited. On the other hand, a firm may be forced to adapt products to meet demand, regulations, or conditions of use in order to achieve successful foreign market penetration.

In international markets, consumers often value different attributes of products. For example, price may be more important than convenience factors associated with product use; durability may be valued higher than styling in some markets; products may be too big or too small in size; replacement may be preferable to repair; compatibility with local operating conditions may be more important than up-to-date technology; and packaging may be valued for its reuseability. These are all possible areas of product adaptation. Even if the physical product is not changed, foreign marketing often calls for repositioning in terms of occasions for product use or target market. (Even government regulations and consumerists present situations that require adaptation.) Services, which by their very nature are more customer-specific, almost always need to be adjusted to meet local conditions and regulations.

Another important facet of managing international product strategy concerns the changing nature of world demand over the life of a product. The manager must recognize that the stage a product may be in varies across different markets. Furthermore, it may be advantageous to move production and marketing emphasis from developed to less-developed countries in order to retain competitive advantages.

One unique area of international product strategy is the influence that a product's country of origin has on buyer perceptions of it. Due to stereotypes about different countries' abilities to manufacture products, certain products can face negative or positive images in international markets. The multinational firm can adjust production locations to take advantage of such stereotypes. This adds a "fifth" dimension to its overall marketing strategy.

Comparative product strategy involves a comparative analysis of potential markets in terms of the needs for product adjustments. Countries can then be grouped and a staging strategy developed so that markets requiring the least adaptation can be entered first.

## DISCUSSION QUESTIONS

1. Why do companies resist product adaptation for foreign markets?
2. Under what conditions would each of the five international marketing strategies shown in Figure 10–1 be appropriate?
3. What are the major factors which influence decisions to standardize or adapt products in foreign markets?
4. Why would a firm decide to standardize its products even when market conditions differ in a foreign market?
5. Using Figure 10–2 as a guide, discuss how you might need to adjust the design and qualities of motorcycles introduced into Kenya.
6. What are the major constraints on a firm's standardization and adaptation policies in foreign markets?
7. Explain how price and convenience can be traded as product attributes in foreign markets.
8. Differentiate between durability, styling, and design as product features of importance to buyers.
9. In countries with low labor costs, how do products' maintenance requirements need to be adjusted?
10. What are international standards?
11. Why are services almost always adjusted in foreign markets?
12. Describe how the product life cycle affects international marketing of products.
13. Give an example of how repositioning can lead to successful foreign market penetration.
14. How do U.S. government regulations affect the international marketing strategies of American and Japanese automakers in different ways?
15. What are the implications of consumerism for international product strategies?
16. Explain what the fifth "P" is for international strategies of multinational corporations.
17. How do national stereotypes affect product images?
18. What is the "paradox" of product images in developing countries?
19. Explain how you would develop a comparative product strategy using "staging" for foreign market development.

# W.H. SCHWARTZ AND SONS, LTD.*

## Introduction

In the spring of 1974, Mr. R. A. Bureau, Vice-President of Marketing and Sales of W. H. Schwartz and Sons, Ltd., visited Australia to assess the possibility of Schwartz entering the Australian spice market. Mr. Bureau had to consider not only the volume potential of the Australian market, but also the strategy the company would use to enter the market, should the situation justify this.

## Company History

W. H. Schwartz and Sons, Ltd., is the oldest-established spice house in North America, having been founded in the port city of Halifax, Nova Scotia, in 1841. In the early days of the company, the son of the founder was the only salesman, travelling around Nova Scotia by stagecoach in summer and by horse and sleigh in winter. Later, he imported the first bicycle with pneumatic tires from England and travelled throughout Nova Scotia selling his products.

Formed as a family firm, the company is still privately owned and family run. The company was the first in Canada to sell pure spices. Formerly only compound spices, such as ginger mixed with flour and cornmeal, were available. Even though pure spices were more costly than compound spices, Schwartz was able to convince the public that pure spices offered better value than compound spices which lacked strength and flavor. This emphasis on quality has continued throughout the company's history and remains the basis of its worldwide reputation today.

Sales of spices were modest and confined to Nova Scotia until after the First World War. Beginning in the 1920's, the company expanded both its sales and product line. As the company grew, it acquired in 1930 Canada Spice and Specialty Mills in Saint John, New Brunswick. After this acquisition, the company's product line was extended to include peanut butter, flavoring extracts, and packaged dates and raisins. Later, in 1949, Schwartz purchased the second oldest Canadian spice company, S. W. Ewing Ltd. Within ten years this Montreal plant was replaced by a new facility which served all of Quebec, Ontario and the Western Provinces.

Over the years the company has demonstrated its ability to adapt to changing market conditions. Although coffee had constituted the bulk of their sales, the line was dropped when it was found that instant coffee was

---

*This case was prepared by Professor Philip Rosson and Janet Forrest of Dalhousie University. © 1977 by Philip Rosson. Reproduced by permission.

posing a serious challenge. The company adapted to the supermarket "revolution" by introducing specially designed racks for the display of their spices, and was a forerunner in pack design, being the first to introduce the apothecary-type glass spice jar. A new merchandising technique was also pioneered by the company. This involved using full-time female staff to service display racks, thereby reducing costs and improving retail servicing. So successful was this method that Schwartz's competitors very quickly emulated the pioneering company.

In recent years, Schwartz has further expanded their manufacturing facilities and they continue to expand their markets at home and abroad. In 1957, Schwartz entered the British spice market, where their high-quality pure spice was immediately recognized by the housewife. Initial losses were turned around and by 1972 Schwartz had become brand leader. This involved unseating its arch-rival, the large American McCormick organization, from the top-spot.

The company now sells in some 50 overseas markets, has gross sales of $27 million, and employs 300 people worldwide. Schwartz is optimistic about its future position in the spice market which accounts for 44% of sales revenues. As one of its managers commented " . . . we have the best quality in the world, the most attractive jar in the world, and the best method of merchandising in the world. How can we fail?"

### The Spice Industry

A great deal of the production of the world's spices takes place in the countries of the developing world, where, for example, chili peppers, ginger, nutmeg, sesame, cloves, and black and white peppers are grown. Spice production in more developed, non-tropical countries consists mostly of herbs like rosemary, thyme, basil, tarragon and sage.

The developed nations of the western world are the most important markets for spices. In most countries the spice trade is concentrated in the hands of a few importers and spice packers, and processing usually takes place in the importing country. The main users of spices are households and the food industry. In the household sector, only a few spices such as pepper, nutmeg, and paprika are important and the bulk of household consumption is accounted for by these spices. Most consumers are unfamiliar with spices such as turmeric, coriander, mace, and cardamom and the food industry provides the major market for these spices. In recent years, however, increased travel and greater numbers of foreign restaurants have led many households to experiment with the more exotic spices. There are in fact many spices and the principal companies may sell a hundred or more different varieties.

One principal problem of the spice industry is the frequent and wide fluctuations in the prices of most major spices, notably pepper, ginger and cloves in recent years. These fluctuations are caused by a number of factors including supply irregularities and speculative trading.

The packaging of spices is an important element in the marketing policy of the major packers. Traditional packs involved the use of a cardboard tube system with metal or plastic top, and the plastic drum or sachet. Schwartz and McCormick pack the majority of their spices in American style glass jars. Both companies utilize racks in self-service stores, using their own merchandisers to keep the display stocked. Advertising of spices is minimal, but various promotions such as spice rack offers and recipe suggestions are frequently used by the major companies.

### Trip to Australia

A variety of information was collected by Mr. Bureau on his visit to the Australian market. In overall terms the Vice-President felt that Schwartz should contemplate entering the Australian market but had to sell the board of directors on the concept. As well as an entry decision, Mr. Bureau had also to think in terms of a marketing strategy which showed the best potential for success in this market. For as his investigations had shown him, the market was "anticipated to grow approximately 20% per year in coming years," but some industry sources felt that "there was some indication that the spice market was proliferating with too many brands."

With a board meeting one week away, Mr. Bureau began to closely evaluate the data he had collected on the Australian market, which are shown in Exhibits 1–7.

**EXHIBIT 1**  Indicators of the market size for spices: Canada and Australia (Canadian dollars)

| Indicator | Canada | Australia |
| --- | --- | --- |
| Total population | 21,089,000 | 12,881,064 |
| Annual rate of population increase | 1.7 percent | 1.9 percent |
| Net migration gain | 127,000 | 123,000 |
| Percent population between 20–40 years of age | 33.1 percent | 28.3 percent |
| Percent population 40 years and over | 32.0 percent | 34.3 percent |
| Population growth (compared to 8 major developed Western economies) | Fastest | Second fastest |
| Urbanization | 22 percent population live in Metro Toronto and Montreal | 40 percent population live in Sydney and Melbourne |
| Gross National Product | $84.5 billion | $52.9 billion |
| National product per capita | $4,005 | $4,107 |
| Per capita disposable income | $2,541 | $2,477 |

**EXHIBIT 1** *(concluded)*

| | | |
|---|---|---|
| Total retail sales—all food products . . . . . | $7.5 billion | $5.0 billion |
| Per capita retail food sales . . . . . . . . . . . | $354 | $385 |
| Market size spices at retail . . . . . . . . . . . | $18.0 million | $10.2 million |
| Per capita sales spices at retail . . . . . . . . | $.85 | $.78 |

**EXHIBIT 2**   Grocery product sales and population

| | Grocery product sales | Percent | Population | Percent |
|---|---|---|---|---|
| *Australia:* | $2,008,575,000 | 100.0 | 12,957,000 | 100.0 |
| States: | | | | |
| **New South Wales and Australian Capital** | | | | |
| Territory . . . . . . . . . . . . . . . . . . . . . . . | 750,500,000 | 37.3 | 4,847,000 | 37.4 |
| Victoria . . . . . . . . . . . . . . . . . . . . . . . . | 578,675,000 | 28.8 | 3,564,000 | 27.5 |
| Queensland . . . . . . . . . . . . . . . . . . . . . | 280,450,000 | 13.9 | 1,890,000 | 14.6 |
| South Australia . . . . . . . . . . . . . . . . . . . | 161,950,000 | 8.1 | 1,205,000 | 9.3 |
| West Australia . . . . . . . . . . . . . . . . . . . . | 173,800,000 | 8.7 | 1,063,000 | 8.2 |
| Tasmania . . . . . . . . . . . . . . . . . . . . . . . . | 63,200,000 | 3.2 | 388,000 | 3.0 |
| Urban centers: | | | | |
| Sydney . . . . . . . . . . . . . . . . . . . . . . . . . | 462,000,000 | 23.0 | 2,717,000 | 21.3 |
| Melbourne . . . . . . . . . . . . . . . . . . . . . . . | 392,000,000 | 19.5 | 2,389,000 | 18.7 |
| Brisbane . . . . . . . . . . . . . . . . . . . . . . . . | n.a. | n.a. | 817,000 | 6.4 |
| Adelaide . . . . . . . . . . . . . . . . . . . . . . . . | n.a. | n.a. | 809,000 | 6.3 |
| Perth . . . . . . . . . . . . . . . . . . . . . . . . . . | n.a. | n.a. | 640,000 | 5.0 |

**EXHIBIT 3**   Competitive data (extracted from the trade journal, *Food Week,* Fast Facts, no. 12)

*Fast Facts Herbs and Spices:* McCormick Foods describes the market, what it did to it, how the company merchandises its products, and the cooperation it receives from retailers.

**Spice consumption rising 20 percent a year without any fall in margins.**   *In seven years, McCormick Foods has risen from a zero share of the Australian spice market and now claims to be volume market leader.* The company estimates that in 1966, the year it launched in Australia, the market was worth about $2 million, with the average supermarket offering the housewife a range of about 30 spice products. Today the market is worth between $7 million and $8 million and the average supermarket offers a range of over 120 items. *Ted McLendon,* managing director of McCormicks in Australia, said: "As world leaders in spices, we introduced the expertise necessary to develop the market and stepped into the quality void that existed. In 1966, our products were distributed by *Socomin,* the *Petersville* company. We opened our own manufacturing plant here and now handle our own sales in Sydney, Melbourne, and Brisbane, with Socomin looking after the other states. In 1976–77 we grew rapidly and now have in excess of 20 percent of the total spice volume sales: our share of the supermarket trade alone would be in excess of 50 percent. We're beginning to concentrate on the smaller food stores and I'm confident that the next two years will see us doubling our sales.

"*The market is one of the fastest-growing food sectors, with consumption growing an-*

**EXHIBIT 3** *(continued)*

*nually at about 20 percent.* Rivals in growth over the last five years would be frozen foods and soft drinks. And the potential of spices is excellent. On a per-capita basis, Australians consume probably less than half the spice intake of Americans. In Australia we're presently marketing 180 products and sizes in three basic ranges—gourmet, regular, and the one-shot aluminum foil pouch range of gravies, sauces, and spice blends. The foil pouch range is our fastest-growing section. It has been available on a limited scale in Australia since 1966 but it is only during the last year that it has really taken off. *One of the major trends* has been the move away from the cardboard tube container to glass or tin. Cardboard is a very poor spice container; in a relatively short period of time it absorbs the essential oils of the spice, leaving the housewife with a flavour-depleted cellulose. That's the major reason we have never used it as a container. Another trend is toward spice blends as distinct from traditional spices."

*Ted McLendon continued: "In Australia, spices sell according to areas and there's a lot more to servicing supermarkets than people realise.* We normally start in a supermarket by installing a standard range of products. Over a period of time we study movement and then stock accordingly, planning the right mix for the right area. While we're introducing new products all the time we rarely drop any of the old. Australians are becoming more spice conscious and we haven't yet reached the plateau where we have too many products. From the retailer's point of view, spices are a profit spinner. They don't lend themselves to specialising and we make sure he enjoys a handsome margin and emphasize this point to him. Now we find that more and more the retailer is beginning to appreciate the value of his spice section. Spices are impulse items and we do a lot of in-store demonstration work, which is quite expensive, to encourage the housewife to purchase."

*Fast Facts Herbs and Spices: Master Foods and Somerset College policies.*

**Van delivery service and merchandising reps help reduce out-of-stocks.** *Master Foods has 46 varieties of herbs and spices* and claims the biggest share of the dollar market. Master Foods started a retail van delivery service for herbs and spices and raised sales of some of its products by over 50 percent in a year. One reason why it started this service was caused by many out-of-stocks which retailers suffered with stocking over 100 items. Master Foods says most major chains now stock the company's range. Some use the van delivery service and some the company's merchandising service (company reps bring stock from the store's back room and restock the shelves themselves). Retailers usually carry either a two-shelf spice rack of 18–24 varieties, or a four-shelf rack of 46 varieties. *Master Foods estimates the market to be worth about $6 million at retail prices,* including all herbs, spices, flavoured sugar, seasoned salt, curry and mustard powder, pepper, and miscellaneous items such as meat tenderiser and monosodium glutamate. White pepper is the biggest commodity in the market. Parsley flakes, garlic salt, and garnishes are also volume-sellers.

*The market is in three segments: (1) health food sales,* which comprise mainly herbs and spices packed by the health food stores in cellophane packs; *(2) cannister and packet sales* of traditional herbs and spices such as peppers, cinnamon, and nutmeg, and *(3) the shaker-pack ranges* produced by Master Foods, McCormicks, and Somerset Cottage. Master Foods says the first two segments provide high sales but low margins. The shaker packs sell fewer units but have the highest dollar sales because of high unit price, and also have the highest margins and highest quality image. The market has good potential for expanding its distribution through butchers, health shops, and delicatessens, apart from grocery outlets. As people become more conscious of herbs and spices, cookbook sales, the art of cooking, newspaper and women's magazine coverage of the subject are all rapidly increasing. Master Foods says the market is rising at 15–20 percent a year, and should increase its growth rate in the future years. The company is using such promotional materials as a wall chart for the kitchen listing the herbs and spices to use for certain dishes. The increasing number of Continental restaurants in capital cities and major towns is making people more conscious of herbs and spices.

**EXHIBIT 3** *(concluded)*

*John Hemphill, managing director of Hemphill Herbs and Spices,* of Dural, N.S.W., says his *Somerset Cottage* range has maintained a steady growth rate in the 15 years he has been in business. There are now also more volume-selling lines. Many people use a jar of chives, onion flakes, garlic powder, or parsley flakes in a week or fortnight. "We have had a demand for larger sizes in these lines and did introduce them. But they weren't popular with the su-permarkets who felt they were too bulky," said Mr. Hemphill. Items such as nutmeg, ground ginger, and cinnamon continued to be bought at rare intervals because they last so long. Dried herbs have been the fastest-growing segment of the market. "Spices have always been around, but the herbs such as oregano, sage, and marjoram are just beginning to be noticed and are really jumping ahead. Certain spices sell better in some areas than others. "For in-stance, in the higher-income suburbs, herbs sell better, and in the poorer areas, items like garlic salt and onion salt sell well."

Other minor brands of spices available in Australia include Lawry's seasoning, Hoyts, Tasty, John Ball, McKenzie's, and Harper's.

---

**EXHIBIT 4**    Discussions with buyers in the grocery trade

**Meeting 1**

McCormicks has approximately 50–60 listings and without doubt had good control of the sections. The stores can adjust listings by deleting items which are listed at the head office. They also have a form which can request new products. These are then sent to head office and if the head office receives several requests, they usually list the product. He summarized the effectiveness of McCormicks by the following points:

1. Thorough approach to the market.
2. Good service.
3. Good lines.
4. Good stands and organization of the category for the first time.

Spice Island apparently tried to come into the market a couple of years ago, but were not thorough enough and failed.

The buyer indicated that frankly at this stage, he would not add another range because of the money tied up in relation to the return. This may be a point that would have to be clearly defined. He estimates a return of 6–7 times a year. He also pointed out that McCormicks did good stock rotation and gross profit return was satisfactory at approximately 25–30 percent. He was by no means suggesting that it would be easy or that his store group would even ac-cept another line. He indicated that Master Foods' spices were only being stocked in three of his stores and that they had them for six months and nothing much had come of it. Appar-ently, Master Foods has been aggressive with its new line only for a couple of years. He did indicate that service and supply might be a bit of a problem with McCormicks and left the door open on the basis that with a proper programme, they might well be interested as long as the price was right.

**Meeting 2**

The buyer indicated that his group is extremely happy with McCormicks. The market was developing satisfactorily and the gross margins were in the region of 30–35 percent. He indi-cated that specialist stores might be interested in another line of spices.

Apparently, his group tend to be somewhat diffident with suppliers and he was not at all keen to see me, so I was limited to a discussion on the telephone. After discussion with him,

EXHIBIT 4 *(concluded)*

he somewhat backed off and suggested that the market might be accessible, but he was not at all optimistic.

**Meeting 3**

This buyer indicated that the spice section, in his judgment, was becoming proliferated with too many brands. He agreed that there are essentially four elements: the bag; another section which we call the "tube section"; a third section, the regular McCormick-type product; and a fourth section, McCormick's gourmet which is also like Master Foods' product. It was apparent that this buyer intended to thin out the spice section and probably remove one of the major items, but it will not be McCormicks for whom he has a lot of respect as a result of their selling in the past few years.

He indicated that white pepper is a very big item by far and the tube product sells extremely well. There is a low margin on this line of between 16–18 percent. On the other items, there is a 25–30 percent markup. In his opinion, the market is overpriced and really, McCormicks should be selling between 20–25 percent markup.

He indicated that to do in-store demonstrations, which is quite good to move products in the spice section, costs $100 a store for demonstrator space. In addition to that, one has to pay for the demonstrators and the material.

It was obvious this buyer knew his business and was very willing to talk. He indicated by direct question that getting into the spice market may be difficult, but he believed that with the right pricing and promotion that it would not be impossible. However, this is in relation to the fact that the present spice market is probably already overserviced by a number of spice companies.

**EXHIBIT 5** Visits to grocery stores

**Store 1**

Spice section is 9 feet—6 feet of McCormicks and 3 feet of Master Foods—4 shelves of each of them.

**Store 2**

Six feet of shelving—3 of Master Foods and 3 of McCormicks. The gourmet 1½ ounce McCormicks was 55 cents. Cinnamon sticks gourmet were 99 cents.

**Store 3**

Spice section 6 feet, 3 shelves—1 shelf gourmet and the rest regular McCormicks. Regular peppercorns, 35 cents and gourmet, 53 cents. Regular size is 1¼ ounce and gourmet size is 1⅞ ounce.

**Store 4**

Spice section has only 1 shelf of gourmet and 2 shelves of regular—6 foot section. The 4-shelf unit has 37 varieties only.

**Store 5**

Store was approximately 10,000–15,000 square feet in size.

Two brands were represented, primarily Master Foods and McCormicks. The Master Foods shelves were 80 percent empty. A third brand was Somerset Cottage. The shelves were made of metal with shelf dividers. Division of shelves was as follows:

Master Foods: 4 shelves
Somerset Cottage: 3 shelves
McCormicks: 3 shelves

**EXHIBIT 5** *(continued)*

---

The length of the shelves were approximately 3 feet each.

Shelf prices were as follows:

| | | |
|---|---|---|
| Master Foods: | Ground cinnamon | 35 cents |
| | Sage | 28 cents |
| | White pepper wh. | 40 cents |
| McCormicks: | Garlic salt | 33 cents |
| | Garlic powder | 55 cents |

The McCormicks products were regular line not the gourmet line.

**Store 6**

McCormicks had a 2-foot section; Master Foods a 3-foot section; and Somerset Cottage, a 3-foot section. Again, Master Foods was very poorly serviced, but McCormicks and Somerset Cottage were in better condition. In the case of Master Foods and Somerset Cottage, there were 4 shelves for each and McCormicks had 7 shelves. Prices were as follows:

| | | |
|---|---|---|
| McCormicks: | Garlic powder | 49 cents |
| | Garlic salt | 29 cents |
| Somerset Cottage: | Garlic powder | 55 cents |
| | Garlic salt | 38 cents |

**Store 7**

This was a basement operation, similar to a North American department store gourmet section. This was in downtown Sydney, part of a complex called "Centre Point" which is a very up-scale shopping centre on several levels with stores all around. The food section in the store was quite messy, but may have been due to delivery that day. It had all the makings of a typical downtown store, so did not check prices on spices which might well have been different than the norm.

The spice section was round a pillar and included McCormicks' gourmet jars, regular tins and bottles, as well as Master Foods. It looked to me as if organization of the total spice section would not have been amiss in this store.

The Master Foods' and the McCormicks' stands were a little more modeled on the English-type stand about 3 feet each with 7 shelves made of tin, though the McCormicks was a gravity-fed metal affair looking like wood. Underneath each stand were two cupboards similar to the U.K. stands that we use. The McCormicks' 3-foot stand for the regular McCormicks product was a metal stand of white chrome. The single-shelf McCormicks' spice racks containing probably 6 or 7 bottles were also available in this store—priced at $8.95 each.

**Store 8**

8,000 square feet. Six feet of McCormicks—3 feet regular, 3 feet gourmet. 5 shelves double stacked of the regular and also about 6 feet of baskets of tub products.

**Store 9**

Five checkouts; this store has about 2,000—3,000 square feet. This store has Master Foods' and McCormick's gourmet, as well as regular—total of about 9 feet.

**Store 10**

It has 8 checkouts and is approximately 7,000 square feet. It is a clean store, much more like the regular American supermarket.

Nine feet of spices, 8 shelves high—including McCormick's gourmet, 2 shelves on the top; Master Foods, 3 shelves; and then baskets, 2 shelves below with the salt underneath. McCormick's gourmet is gravity fed.

**Store 11**

**EXHIBIT 5** *(concluded)*

A little store about 4,000 or 5,000 feet. A small Master Foods spice section—3 feet; only 4 shelves. Also a McCormick's section.

**Store 12**

About 10,000 square feet. Spice section is about 6 feet, very poorly serviced. McCormick's gourmet and regular.

**Store 13**

A department store with a food section. The section runs about 500–600 square feet. Small spice section, very empty—just the regular McCormicks; 3 foot, 2 shelves, only.

**Store 14**

There is a 3-foot McCormicks stand with 3 shelves gravity fed of the gourmet and 4 shelves doubled up with the regular underneath.

**Store 15**

There was a complete gondola, with spices all the way around with gravity fed McCormick's gourmet bottles. Below that were McCormick's regular items.

---

**EXHIBIT 6**   The spice market at the retail level (Australian dollars)

|  | *Bags/tubes* | *Regular* | *Gourmet* | *Total $s* |
|---|---|---|---|---|
| Dollars .................... | 3,000,000 | 2,000,000 | 1,500,000 | 6,500,000 |
| Percent .................... | 46 percent | 31 percent | 23 percent | 100 percent |
| Average unit price ............ | 19 percent | 29 percent | 49 percent | — |
| Trade margin percent ......... | 12–16 percent | 22 percent | 30 percent | 20 percent |
| Volume dozens ............. | 1,300,000 | 575,000 | 255,000 | 2,130,000 |
| Percent volume ............. | 61 percent | 27 percent | 12 percent | 100 percent |
| Profit to trade dollars ......... | 420,000 | 440,000 | 450,000 | 1,310,000 |
| Profit percent ............... | 32 percent | 34 percent | 34 percent | 100 percent |

Exhibit 7 follows.

## QUESTIONS

1. How should Schwartz position its range of spices?
2. If Schwartz enters the Australian market what market entry strategy should he use—direct export, joint venture, or direct investment in Australia?
3. What marketing mix decisions require resolution?
4. How successful is Schwartz likely to be?

EXHIBIT 7 Cost price comparisons—Schwartz and McCormick (Australian dollars)

| | SCHWARTZ REGULAR | | | McCORMICK REGULAR | | | | McCORMICK GOURMET | | | |
|---|---|---|---|---|---|---|---|---|---|---|---|
| Spice | Ounce | Wholesale price* | Retail price at 32 percent trade margin | Ounce | Wholesale price | Retail price | Trade markup (percent) | Ounce | Wholesale price | Retail price | Trade markup (percent) |
| Black pepper ground | 1¼ | 3.18 | 0.39 | 1 | 2.24 | 0.25 | 24 | 1½ | 4.56 | 0.55 | 30.9 |
| Cinnamon ground | 1⅛ | 5.63 | 0.69 | 1¼ | 4.40 | 0.49 | 24 | 1¾ | 8.20 | 0.99 | 31.0 |
| Curry powder mild | 1⁹⁄₁₆ | 2.37 | 0.29 | 1⅛ | 3.16 | 0.35 | 26 | 2 | 3.72 | 0.45 | 31.0 |
| Paprika | 1⅜ | 3.67 | 0.45 | 1⅛ | 3.52 | 0.39 | 26 | 1¾ | 4.72 | 0.57 | 31.0 |
| Bay leaves whole | ³⁄₁₆ | 7.26 | 0.89 | ³⁄₁₆ | 3.52 | 0.39 | 26 | ¼ | 9.68 | 1.17 | 31.0 |
| Nutmeg whole | 1⅛ | 4.00 | 0.49 | | n.a. | | | 1½ | 5.56 | 0.65 | 28.7 |
| Garlic salt | 2¹³⁄₁₆ | 4.00 | 0.49 | 2 | 2.96 | 0.33 | 24 | 3 | 4.56 | 0.55 | 30.9 |
| Onion salt | 2½ | 4.00 | 0.49 | 1¾ | 2.96 | 0.33 | 24 | 2¾ | 4.56 | 0.55 | 30.9 |
| Black pepper whole | 1¼ | 2.86 | 0.35 | 1¼ | 3.16 | 0.35 | 26 | 1⅞ | 4.40 | 0.53 | 30.8 |
| Parsley | ³⁄₁₆ | 3.18 | 0.39 | ⅛ | 2.96 | 0.33 | 24 | ¼ | 4.40 | 0.53 | 30.8 |
| Oregano | ¼ | 2.37 | 0.29 | | n.a. | | | ⁷⁄₁₆ | 3.72 | 0.46 | 31.0 |
| Red pepper | 1⅛ | 2.69 | 0.33 | 1 | 3.52 | 0.39 | 26 | 1⅞ | 4.40 | 0.53 | 30.8 |
| Allspice | 1⁵⁄₁₆ | 5.63 | 0.69 | 1½ | 5.32 | 0.59 | 25 | 1¾ | 7.36 | 0.89 | 31.0 |

*Price per dozen.

# chapter 11

# INDUSTRIAL PRODUCT DECISIONS FOR INTERNATIONAL MARKETING

A realistic appraisal of market conditions and a commitment to technical research and development were the major factors in the transformation of Sharp Electronics Corp. from a manufacturer of mechanical pencils to a giant in the electronics industry.

"It's important that you know where you want to go," observed Charles S. Grill, general manager–marketing communications for the Japanese company, whose U.S. headquarters are in Paramus, N.J.

"If you don't know where you're going, any road will take you there. We have a pretty good idea of our basic course, and we try to hew to that line.

"Technical research and innovation are the cornerstones of the company's philosophy. We spend a great deal of time and effort in researching and developing new technologies.

"Some of the products suggested by our research department become very successful, but many of them never see the light of day. We don't force a product onto the market just because it's state of the art."*

## INTRODUCTION

The industrial product is purchased for use in the operation of a business, not for individual or family use and satisfaction. The industrial marketer must learn how businesses in various nations make purchasing decisions

*"Marketing, Technical Research Lead Sharp from Pencil Pushing to $2 Billion in Electronics Sales," *Marketing News*, March 6, 1981, p. 1. Published by the American Marketing Association.

and the extent to which those decisions vary from country to country. Is the business organization as strongly affected by society and culture as is the family unit? Is it more influenced by local economic conditions or by international economic factors? Are industrial purchase decisions more or less affected by politics and the legal environment? These are questions the international marketer must answer to compete successfully in industrial markets abroad.

In this chapter we are concerned with the factors that affect the demand for, and the marketing of, industrial products in world markets. We first review the ways in which demand for industrial goods is similar and is different in various national markets. We then turn to specific differences in preferences for attributes and servicing of industrial products. Next we review some important trends in world industrial markets, including the declining U.S. monopoly in high-technology products and the dominance of multinational corporations in industrial competition. We then address specific areas that affect the overall industrial product strategy. These topics include identification of foreign buyers and patronage motives of industrial buyers in different buying situations.

## CHARACTER OF DEMAND
## FOR INDUSTRIAL PRODUCTS

### Universality of Demand

Authorities on management generally agree that the science of management is similar across cultures. Thus, one might expect industrial buying decisions to be more similar than consumer buying decisions in different countries. The professional purchasing agent has essentially the same obligations in any culture: He or she will be expected to provide the right product at the right time at the right price, to operate with professional competence, and to be prudent and honest. The purchasing agent's performance will be judged according to how well specific business needs are met and whether or not purchase decisions have contributed to the firm's overall goals.

The needs of businesses are generally more similar throughout the world than are the needs of individuals. Firms that are fabricating metal will require the same types of presses, lathes, and foundries no matter where they operate, although each firm's size and technology of operation may affect the degree of sophistication of the equipment needed. Similarly, all textile mills will require basic spinning and weaving machinery, although one mill may choose more complex or highly automated equipment than another.

Industrial buying is less affected by such cultural factors as language, religion, and social roles, than is consumer purchasing. The purchasing agent, whatever his or her cultural background, is more heavily influenced by product performance specifications, delivery dates, and price than is the consumer. Brand images and national product stereotypes are secondary to the perceived performance capabilities of products to be purchased. There are, of course, other factors that affect industrial buyer behavior and preferences, and we will address these later in the chapter.

## Level of Economic Development

Even though the demand for industrial products is more universal than the demand for consumer goods, there are still considerable variations among national markets. One important cause of these variations is differences in the stage of economic development. There is a close correlation between a nation's level of economic development and the sophistication of its industrial infrastructure. In general, highly developed nations have more complex and sophisticated industries, while less-developed nations have simpler, more basic industries. There are some exceptions, such as when a steel mill or refinery is built in a relatively underdeveloped nation to satisfy the government's status needs or development aspirations, rather than to serve the needs of current local industry and markets. In most cases, less-developed nations have neither the ability to operate complex industrial facilities nor the market to dispose of their products. A sophisticated industrial installation requires a pool of skilled workers to operate the facility and an infrastructure that will provide the capabilities of maintaining and repairing the equipment. The higher the stage of economic development in a nation, the greater are the resources to operate and maintain industrial facilities.

The industrial marketer must adjust product offerings to the stage of development in potential markets. One option is to concentrate efforts on markets at similar stages of development. If these markets are at the same stage as the domestic market, little or no product adjustment may be necessary. If the goal is to broaden the potential market, product features may need to be adapted to the needs of markets at other stages of development. For example, if the product is buses, the product line may range from very large, high-performance vehicles with a strong emphasis on providing rider comfort (luxury seating, heating and air conditioning, excellent visibility), to the small, simple vehicles that provide basic transportation at minimal cost. The machine tool manufacturer may offer lathes that range from huge, high-volume turret lathes with automated controls, to simple manually controlled lathes that may be powered by a person or by an animal.

Each product, from the simplest to the most complex, has a potential market in some part of the world. Any one nation may provide a potential market for a fairly wide range of product variations. In some of the less-developed countries, the level of development varies widely between urban and nonurban areas, and between accessible and inaccessible areas. In fact, economic "dualism" is a characteristic of developing economies because not all sectors of an economy develop at the same rate. Thus the manufacturer may find it necessary to offer a wider range of technologies in industrial products for foreign markets than are offered in the domestic market. International marketers who sell products in markets with a low level of technological development must make particular efforts to ensure that the technology is transferred satisfactorily.[1] Even though the product may be redesigned, simplified, and adapted to a new culture, the potential users may not accept it. The farmers in Sri Lanka may be unwilling to accept the changes in agricultural technology necessary for the use of mechanized equipment. Warehouse owners in China, with a plentiful supply of low-cost labor, may see little advantage in buying technologically advanced materials-handling equipment. In order to ensure success in such markets, the marketer must make certain that the ultimate users of a product find its technological level appropriate for their needs. Many times the industrial marketer is a change agent, introducing more advanced equipment or new ways of solving problems. Thus, marketing strategy for industrial products in foreign markets must include a provision for informing and educating the potential market as to the relative advantages of advanced technologies.

### Politics, Nationalism, and Development

The largest markets for industrial products can be found in those countries which have already invested in industrial infrastructure. Examples of such countries are Germany, Japan, Brazil, England, Canada, and the U.S. Industrial infrastructure consists of financial and transportation networks, among other things. In those nations that already have a large industrial base, industry constitutes a strong pressure group to provide access to needed products. Therefore, these countries may offer fewer barriers and minimal government interference to foreign sources of supply for industrial inputs. On the other hand, their mature industries (steel, textiles, electronics) are now not as efficient as those in developing countries. As a result there are increasing pressures for protection from foreign competitors.

The developing countries present a different market opportunity for international marketers. Very often their economic development goals must be met with limited resources. They must be selective about the use of their foreign exchange and the appropriateness of technologies that local businesses purchase abroad. These countries may also have formidable import duties for foreign industrial products. However, since they are eager to pursue industrial development, they may be willing to offer concessions, to purchase technologies, or to grant licenses and exemptions on a case-by-case basis. While there is likely to be more government involvement in industrial purchasing in the developing countries, there may also be less

[1]A. Coskun Samli, "5 Steps Can Help Industrial Marketer Transfer Technology to Third World," *Marketing News*, May 1, 1981, sec. 2, p. 6.

competition and more negotiable terms of trade. Furthermore, the government itself is a likely purchaser in some markets such as the Eastern European nations.

Foreign suppliers of industrial products may be treated differently than foreign suppliers of consumer goods, for political or development reasons. Often domestic consumer goods can be substituted for foreign-made products, whereas industrial products have no locally produced substitutes. In other cases, the government may support industrial development at the expense of consumer standards of living. As an example, many governments in recent years have pressured consumers to reduce their consumption of petroleum-related goods. In developing countries, however, oil for industrial use is considered strategically important to future economic growth. The company exporting petroleum to such a nation will find the industrial market is more promising and perhaps less regulated than the consumer market.

Another aspect of the political environment for industrial products is their role in national security. Computers, nuclear energy, armaments, measuring and tracking devices, and many other industrial goods, are considered essential in many nations for defense purposes. There are, as a result, restraints on companies that manufacture and develop these products. In some cases, sales to a commercial party in another country must be approved or licensed by the home government; in other cases, such sales are prohibited. The U.S. government uses both these policies to restrict exports of products it feels might jeopardize defense programs. It is important that the international marketer be aware that some of its products may not be eligible for international marketing.

The degree and level of nationalism in a foreign market is also important to the industrial marketer. Highly nationalistic governments tend to encourage economic self-sufficiency even at the expense of economic efficiency. Such nations are anxious to develop their own basic industries, and they encourage their nationals to buy domestic products in preference to imported products, with little reference to comparative quality or price. This kind of discrimination was discussed in more detail in Chapter 7. It is difficult for the international marketer to compete in such markets except in those countries where a lack of raw materials or of sophisticated expertise makes it impossible for domestic marketers to offer competitive products.

## PRODUCT FEATURES

Many features of industrial products need to be adjusted to meet the requirements of different foreign markets. Although industrial buyers are less influenced by sociological or cultural differences than are individual consumers, they still have needs that are sufficiently different, making necessary a careful reevaluation of product features before introducing an industrial product in any new market.

### Perception of Quality

Perceived quality is a subjective basis for evaluating a product or service. It is composed of the purchasing agent's expectations of performance, maintenance, durability, after-sale servicing, and appearance. One of the important decisions in positioning a product in any market is the determination of an optimal level of quality to satisfy the chosen market segment. In general, American industrial goods are of a rather high level of quality. They are designed to meet high performance expectations and to last for a considerable period of time. But the American definition of high quality may not be the same as that of industrial buyers in Bolivia or in Indonesia. The manufacturer of a fertilizer-spreading machine in the United States, for example, may find that farmers in less-developed countries have very different definitions of product quality. The American farmer may expect the spreader to be manufactured to close tolerances, with careful machining and finish. The farmer in Bolivia, on the other hand, may be satisfied with a machine where the welding of sections is somewhat rough and tolerances between moving parts are looser, as long as the machine is durable and foolproof in operation. The American farmer, who may equate the finishing details and smoothness of performance with operating quality, would not accept a spreader which might be deemed of satisfactory operating quality by the Bolivian farmer—who could not even afford the American version.

The perception of quality may be unrelated to the performance characteristics of a product. A machine tool, such as a lathe, may operate perfectly well with a hand-operated lever to turn it on and off. The addition of push-button controls in no way affects the performance of the machine. Yet buyers in highly developed countries who are accustomed to push buttons on machine tools, are likely to rate a hand-lever-operated machine tool as of lower quality. The professional purchasing agent may recognize that there is no real difference in performance, but he or she will still rate the push-button machine higher because machinists prefer it. The purchasing agent in a less-developed country will only be concerned with the operating performance of the machine and will accept the hand lever if it carries a lower price. Quality perceptions can also be affected by contracts for after-sale servicing; in one country this may be seen as a sign of a superior product value, while in others it may be viewed as a sign of lower quality.

### Variations in Performance

Industrial product users in different countries may require very different performance and operating characteristics. Railroad locomotives are a good example. American railroad companies are almost solely interested in locomotives for freight—machines that are durable but not particularly fast, and that are able to take the pounding from poor roadbeds. There is little demand for passenger locomotives, and those that are available also emphasize durability at the expense of speed. Railroad companies in Western Europe and Japan, with their well-maintained roadbeds, have less need for rugged durability. They have a greater overall demand for passenger equipment and a greater interest in the speed of the equipment.

The same kinds of product-performance variations between countries are found in many industries. The state of the roads dictates the necessary performance characteristics of trucks. Climatic conditions such as temperature, altitude, and humidity dictate the performance characteristics of many kinds of machinery. The cost and availability of fuel determine whether certain performance characteristics are economically justifiable. As a consequence, there is no one best standard of performance for most products. The manufacturer must adjust product performance levels to new markets, after carefully studying the factors in each market that will affect performance expectations.

## Service and Replacement Parts

The problems of providing adequate service and replacement parts for industrial goods increase in geometric proportions as the marketer moves farther from the domestic market.[2] Not all marketers find it necessary to provide trained service personnel to keep their products running, since industrial users are frequently willing and able to maintain their own equipment. Machine shop operators may prefer to keep their own machine tools in running order and may have the know-how to do so. The same is true for a great many users of industrial goods, from farmers to factories. They often feel they cannot afford the lost production time involved in waiting for the arrival of an outside repairperson to fix a piece of machinery. In addition, their own personnel may be technically oriented and trained to do their own repair work. However, in these instances it is still necessary for the manufacturer to make replacement parts conveniently and quickly available to customers who are prepared and willing to make their own repairs. This may require the maintenance of at least one stock of replacement parts in each foreign market. And if the market is geographically large, it may be necessary to maintain more than one parts depot. Some marketers have found that it is not feasible economically to maintain stocks of infrequently used parts in the foreign market at all. In these instances, the availability of air freight makes it possible to provide speedy service to customers. A truck manufacturer, for example, may find that the need for replacement axles is so infrequent in Denmark that it is impractical to stock replacements in Copenhagen. Instead, when an axle does

---

[2]Dick Berry, "Industrial Marketers Use Secret Weapons—Customer Service—for Marketing Success," *Marketing News*, May 1, 1981, sec. 2, p. 8.

break, an order is sent to the factory in Detroit by telephone or telex, and the part is shipped by air freight to arrive the next day. This same manufacturer when distributing in Peru, where the condition of the roads results in many broken axles, may find it necessary to carry a stock of replacement axles in Lima.

Not all industrial product users are able to maintain and repair their own equipment. The equipment may be too complex to be repaired by anyone but a factory-trained expert. Such is the case for computers and for many types of sophisticated electronic equipment. The operators may be technically proficient in the operation of the equipment, but they may know nothing about how to repair it. Other machinery operators may not be technically oriented at all. Bakers may know how to use sophisticated ovens and other baking equipment to make bread, but have no idea how to repair them. Users of typewriters and more complex word-processing equipment are not expected to know how to repair their equipment. In these instances the foreign marketer, in order to be competitive, must provide competently trained servicepersons within easy and rapid access of all major users of the equipment in the market. When the equipment is highly sophisticated it is often necessary to transport key service personnel from the foreign market to the home plant for training. An alternative to this is to send trained service personnel from the home market to the foreign markets. But with the high cost of relocating personnel and their families to a foreign location, and the problems of language and cultural adjustment, most firms choose to train foreign nationals for maintenance jobs at a central point in the organization. Maintaining a competent staff of nationals trained as servicepersons is not an easy one. Personnel turnover, and product improvement and modification, require an almost continuous job of training and updating of personnel.

## Universal Standards

The international marketer benefits enormously from product and performance standardization among markets. Otherwise, the problem of manufacturing a separate line of products for each market and maintaining separate stocks of replacement parts would be overwhelming. Perhaps the most important single set of international standards is the standard of measurement. Over the years, measurements in most parts of the world have been standardized under either the English system or the metric system of measurement. Gradually during the past fifty years an ever-increasing portion of nations have shifted to the metric system, so that the United States stands alone as a user of the English system. The costs of changing to the metric system have been a barrier to change in the U.S., as have buyer habits. Even the British shifted to the metric system during the past decade. American exporters are at a competitive disadvantage in most foreign markets if their products are not metric. For this reason, a growing number of American marketers who sell extensively abroad have shifted individually to use of metric measurements.

The need for standards is just as important for many other kinds of product characteristics. The textile manufacturer must establish such product characteristics as thread count, weight, and washability, so that foreign buyers have common bases for comparing competitive offerings. Steel mills must establish product standards; chemical manufacturers must agree on common characteristics of the chemicals and plastics they produce; pharmaceutical manufacturers should agree on the ingredients in their generic products. Energy needs can be just as important as product characteristics. A product designed to operate on fifty-cycle current may be inoperable in a nation where the electric current is sixty cycle, and a product designed for ethyl gasoline may not perform satisfactorily with standard or unleaded gasoline.

The international marketer should first seek to determine the extent, if any, to which standards have been applied to his or her products in each foreign market. If there is no standardization in the foreign market, it is best to adopt the most common international standards if it is at all possible to pursuade local users to accept them. Some producers prefer not to manufacture to broadly accepted standards because they feel they can bind their customers to them alone so as to maintain compatibility in their equipment. However, potential new customers may be unwilling to commit themselves to products that are not interchangeable if they have the option of buying competing products that do meet international standards. In general, it is to the advantage of the international marketer to conform to available international standards and to take leadership within an industry to develop standards where they do not exist.

### Services

Like physical products, services may have to be adapted to the unique needs of different markets. For example, when banks move into the international arena, they usually find that their offerings must be adjusted to meet local customer preferences and regulations. The local regulatory bodies may exercise control over reserve requirements, interest rates, and extension of credit, and preferences of local borrowers may affect the methods of processing loans and collecting interest.

Management consulting firms find that their methods of dealing with clients must be adjusted when they move into new markets. The consultant-client relationship tends to be a very personal one, so it can be strongly affected by the cultural differences and business customs that affect relationships between individuals. Management service firms of all types find that differences in the infrastructure and cultural mores require them to adjust their offerings. International advertising agencies, for example, must tailor their campaigns to local media. A campaign heavily oriented toward television in one market may have to be shifted to other media because of a particular market's absence of commercial TV. International marketing research organizations find that the research methodologies and services they offer will depend on availability of secondary data, reaction of local residents to personal surveys, and availability of communication media such as a reliable postal service. The challenge to the service marketer is to adjust the services offered enough to serve local needs and yet retain a common international image that carries the benefits of recognition in new markets.

The relative importance of services in a country's economy is correlated with level of economic development, just as in the case of industrial demand. Therefore, services are more significant and diversified in the more advanced countries of the world. This is true of the financial, publishing, communications, research, education, legal and professional, insurance, advertising, and transportation industries in the United States, and other developed countries, as compared to the same industries in developing countries. They account for over 40 percent of the U.S. gross domestic product; corresponding percentages for Europe and Southeast Asia are 30 percent and 11 percent. Services are still growing in the United States, and have become one of our most important exports. The sales of industrial services in foreign markets by American firms contribute significantly to reducing our trade deficits in merchandise.

## TRENDS IN INDUSTRIAL MARKETS

International industrial markets are dominated by firms that are willing to invest heavily in research and development and to take the risks of innovation. By the time the "me-too" firms enter a market, competition is often reduced primarily to a price basis. The market for transistors in the 1950s and 1960s is a good example. The innovator, Texas Instruments, had almost a monopoly in the early years. But after production techniques were perfected and markets opened up, many new competitors entered the market, and competition gradually shifted almost entirely to a price basis.

The high-technology firm that enters foreign markets often has a short production cost advantage compared to local firms due to economies of scale in large, established production facilities in the home market. However, high costs of physical distribution may make the delivered costs of their products high. In addition, to this must be added the costs associated with developing demand for a product in a new market. The local competitors that are often attracted to the field because of the foreign producer's high cost structure may have lower production and marketing costs over time. The innovating firm must drastically pare costs (through local production and reduced marketing) or abandon the product and concentrate on more profitable new innovations.

## The Declining U.S. Monopoly

During the period immediately after World War II, a large majority of the high-technology innovative firms in world markets were American. This dominance has gradually declined as high-research-oriented firms have developed in other nations, particularly Germany and Japan. American firms have maintained leadership in some industries, such as computers, air frames, and chemicals, where they continue to dominate world markets. However, in a number of industrial product categories, competition is now truly international, with major competitors from a number of the highly developed industrial nations. And because industrial strength is sometimes perceived as a measure of economic strength and level of development, even some developing nations have invested scarce capital in major installations such as steel mills and oil refineries for export to world markets.

When American firms dominated world trade in the production of sophisticated industrial goods, there was an advantage inherent in U.S. production. Buyers throughout the world were impressed with the quality, performance, and uniqueness of American products. Today, however, that inherent competitive advantage is gone. This happened partially because American firms did not keep up with technological developments and partially because foreign firms aggressively developed competing technologies. Now, not only do U.S. industrial producers have to compete on an equal footing with firms in such countries as Brazil, Canada, and Germany, but they also find that in many cases these firms have lower production costs, cheaper means of transportation, better terms of trade, and/or more home government support. Today, competition—even in highly technical product categories—is truly international. Figure 3–5 showed the declining share of U.S. firms as world investors.

## The Position of Multinational Firms

In general, multinational corporations are more involved in the marketing of industrial products than consumer goods. Although there are notable exceptions, such as soft drinks, appliances, and automobiles, consumer goods have been most frequently manufactured and marketed by local domestic firms. A great many of the companies that market industrial goods are truly international in scope, viewing the world, or at least portions of it, as their real markets. Figure 11–1 shows the nationalities of the major world companies. You may also wish to refer back to Figure 2–4 for the names of the major world companies. While a domestic firm develops marketing strategy in terms of the size and restrictions of the local market, a multinational sees potential markets wherever they might exist and develops its marketing strategy accordingly. Its loyalties are to its shareholders, employees, and customers—not to any particular nation.

Multinationals have long been important in the production and distri-

**FIGURE 11–1**    World's top 100 and 500 industrial corporations, by nationality.

| | *TOP 100* | | | *TOP 500* | |
|---|---|---|---|---|---|
| **1963** US | 67 | | **1963** US | 300 | 60.0% |
| UK | 7 | | UK | 54 | 10.8 |
| Japan | 3 | | Japan | 37 | 7.4 |
| Germany | 13 | | Germany | 33 | 6.6 |
| France | 4 | | France | 25 | 5.0 |
| Canada | — | | Canada | 13 | 2.6 |
| Other | 6 | | Other | 38 | 7.6 |
| | 100 | | | 500 | 100.0% |
| **1971** US | 58 | | **1971** US | 280 | 56.0% |
| UK | 7 | | UK | 48 | 9.6 |
| Japan | 8 | | Japan | 53 | 10.6 |
| Germany | 11 | | Germany | 36 | 7.2 |
| France | 5 | | France | 25 | 5.0 |
| Canada | — | | Canada | 11 | 2.2 |
| Other | 11 | | Other | 47 | 9.4 |
| | 100 | | | 500 | 100.0% |
| **1979** US | 47 | | **1979** US | 219 | 43.8% |
| UK | 7 | | UK | 51 | 10.2 |
| Japan | 7 | | Japan | 71 | 14.2 |
| Germany | 13 | | Germany | 37 | 7.4 |
| France | 11 | | France | 27 | 5.4 |
| Canada | — | | Canada | 19 | 3.8 |
| Other | 15 | | Other | 76 | 15.2 |
| | 100 | | | 500 | 100.0% |

*Source:* John Hein, *Major Forces in the World Economy: Concerns for International Business,* (New York: The Conference Board, Inc., 1981).

bution of raw materials. Among the strongest and earliest true multinationals are the international oil companies, with production and distribution facilities throughout the world. Multinational corporations have also been important in mining and forestry, and in the agricultural area as distributors rather than producers of foodstuffs. The other area in which multinational corporations are important is in the production and marketing of high-technology products. Communications equipment, electronics, and computers, for example, are products that require a commitment to research and development and sophisticated production facilities. The firms that manufacture such products are large and wealthy and tend to be headquartered in the most highly developed nations. They compete with each other in the wealthy markets, as well as in the less-developed nations where they have an enormous potential advantage over local competition.

The dominance of multinationals in worldwide industrial marketing represents both an opportunity and a challenge to smaller, less-experienced international firms. The challenge they offer is in competing against firms that are quickly becoming worldwide oligopolies. The opportunity they provide for smaller firms is to develop products that are not economically feasible for the large multinationals, and to meet local demand better in selected markets.

### Foreign Investment

Marketers of industrial goods frequently find themselves heavily involved in direct foreign investments. This is particularly true with raw materials where the sources of supply are often in less-developed countries, while the major markets are in industrial countries. The major reserves of petroleum products are in the Middle East, Africa, and Latin America. The major sources of forests and mines are also located outside the developed countries of the world. The local demand for such products may be very small or nonexistent, so most of the production there is for export. Production or processing often requires technical expertise and heavy investments of capital. As a consequence, production facilities for these raw materials are usually developed by foreign investors. Such investments may be welcome at first by local residents and governments because of the infusion of capital and employment opportunities. In the long run, however, the investors frequently come to be resented as exploiters. The ultimate result may be rigid government restrictions or even expropriation. In order to avoid the almost inevitable negative feelings, these producers must take particular pains to reduce their "foreignness' and try to become identified as local business, through employment of nationals and joint local ownership. Other ways of fitting into the business community and minimizing political risks were discussed in Chapters 4 and 7.

Marketers of raw materials are not the only ones who invest heavily in foreign markets. Producers of products that are bulky or heavy in relation to their value, may find it necessary to build production facilities close to each major market. The manufacturer of abrasives and industrial grinding wheels, for example, must locate factories near each significant market so the cost of transportation does not make prices uncompetitive. Sophisticated products that require a large amount of servicing and repair, also usually require heavy investment in local foreign markets. Service facilities must be made available close to users. As with raw materials, it is important to develop local identification for these foreign facilities in order to reduce local interference with operations.

### Patent Protection

In most important markets, international marketers have access to protection of patents and trade names through a series of international conventions.[3] But it is often more difficult to protect patents than trade names. A number of countries which will offer reciprocal protection on products patented in the United States will cancel such patents if the products covered are not actually marketed in the country within a specified period of time—in some cases, as little as one year. In Europe, registration in one country with the European Patent Office gives a firm a grace period of protection before registration in others. However, after that time the firm may be unprotected. Added to this is the problem of defining newness on the original patent application. The result has been a decline in the number of patents granted in most countries in recent years.

Even where patent protection has been acquired, there is always a temptation for a licensee to decide to set up a new competing business using knowledge gained from a foreign licensor. This is a frequent problem in industrial marketing because so many industrial firms use licensing as a strategy for entering foreign markets. Foreign licensing may be the only feasible way to exploit opportunities in a market with limited demand, but the risks of training a future competitor can be high. The decision as to how much protection is needed really depends on the complexity of the technology or production process, and its predicted life. If the technology in question is highly complex, unique, and involves substantial investment in research and development, the firm should exercise the maximum control over its introduction in foreign markets. On the other hand, if the life cycle of a technology is expected to be short, it is probably best to use quick methods such as licensing, to introduce the product, process, or technology to the widest possible world market at the earliest feasible time.

## DEVELOPING FOREIGN PROSPECTS

Industrial marketers have a more difficult time identifying prospects than do consumer goods marketers, even in the domestic market. Determining what kinds of businesses and organizations are potential users of a product is not always an easy task. Industrial marketers may discover unserved potential users even in markets that have been covered for long periods of time. For the marketer in a strange, new foreign market this identification of industrial prospects is particularly difficult, because the same information sources may not be available as in the home market. In the United States, for example, the Census Bureau has established an orderly procedure for classifying business firms—the Standard Industrial Classification Code (SIC). The marketer can categorize each customer into one of the classes and then seek new prospects from other firms in the same classifi-

---

[3]"Foreign Patent Protection Gets Easier," *The Wall Street Journal*, November 21, 1977, p. 6.

cation. Even though foreign governments may not provide information along the lines of the SIC, use of this or the International Standard Industrial Classification (ISIC) provides a good basic starting point in identifying potential customers in a new market. Unfortunately, the ISIC is not universally available for firms in some nations, and it may not be up to date. The marketer can help new sales representatives by instructing them to call on all foundries, or machine shops, or dentists, or food retailers that may be prospective customers for the product in question.

Even when types of prospective customers are identified, it may not be easy to locate such prospects. In some countries, a useful source of prospects is the classified telephone directory (when available) because it has listings by type of business. Chambers of commerce or similar promotional organizations often provide lists of businesses by types within their communities. Alternatively, trade associations may be willing to provide lists of their members. If the problem of identifying prospects is approached imaginatively and with the help of local experts, it can be solved in almost any market. In Chapter 8, Figure 8–1 listed categories of published sources that can help identify potential buyers. Further details on secondary sources are given in Appendix B. Care must be taken in the use of these sources to focus on potential product *uses,* because these really determine what industries are good candidates.

## INDUSTRIAL PURCHASING BEHAVIOR

Industrial marketers who are unfamiliar with foreign markets are likely to make the mistaken assumption that business people act the same throughout the world. Even though they easily recognize that consumers act differently and are motivated by different factors in different countries, they still assume that all business and institutional buyers are seeking maximum value for money spent and, thus, will act in the same "rational" manner. In actuality, industrial buyers may act quite differently in different countries. They may be more or less willing to do business with strangers; they may have different notions of loyalty to sources of supply; they may have varying feelings about countries of origin; they may prefer alternative sources of remuneration; and, they may use more- or less-sophisticated techniques for evaluating proposals. The industrial marketer must take all these factors into consideration when dealing with foreign buyers.

### Making the Contact

In the most highly developed countries, industrial salespersons are accustomed to approaching new prospects "cold," without an introduction, and rely on advance promotional material and the prospect's desire to get a better deal to open the door. In other nations, particularly in some of the Middle Eastern and Far Eastern countries, business people are reluctant to deal with strangers. In such instances it is necessary for the salesperson to obtain an introduction through the services of an intermediary. For example, in the Arab world it is almost impossible to do business without the help of a local sponsor or partner who has the contacts and experience to make sales.[4] Some countries require by law that a firm sell through local agents or distributors and do not allow foreign firms to contact buyers directly.

Intermediaries or sponsors expect to be paid for their services in bringing seller and buyer together, and marketers accept such payment as a cost of doing business. American marketers have a disadvantage in this respect because the U.S. government may view some such payments as bribery, particularly if the size of the commission is large. The American marketer may find it necessary to make the intermediary a partner or sales representative. If this rep is unwilling, or unable because of the complexity of the product, to do a real selling job, the marketer will still have to provide company sales personnel to make the sale. A permanent relationship is much more costly than a one-time introduction, so it is important to try to enlist the intermediary's continuing help in the actual selling process.

### Building Repurchase Loyalty

Once the industrial buyer has made an initial purchase, the marketer attempts to develop a habitual pattern of repurchase. The industrial buyer prefers to make repeat purchases from the same source, since such transactions are easier and less time consuming. Yet, he or she is seldom as brand loyal as individual consumers who repurchase the same brand in spite of changes in competitive offerings. In industrial situations, if competitive manufacturers offer purchasing agents a more attractive deal, they are very likely to accept.

In some cultures it is a common practice to offer the purchasing agent a commission or kickback on all purchases. In the Far East this practice is called *cumshaw,* and it is an accepted method of business. In other markets, particularly in the highly industrialized ones, such kickbacks are considered unacceptable and even unethical. The National Association of Purchasing Managers in the United States, for example, has a stated policy that the acceptance of kickbacks or gifts is in conflict with the best interests of the employer, since the purchasing decision is influenced by personal interest rather than company interest. Many marketers consider the use of *cumshaw* to be a weak and unethical competitive tactic, even in

---

[4]Ian K. Huntington, "Doing Business in the Arab Middle East," in *Copyright World*, Peat, Marwick, Mitchell & Co., 1981.

those markets where it is accepted practice. More positive marketing efforts need to be used to retain customer loyalty.

Price is one of the most important continuing competitive tools in the industrial market, where buying decisions tend to be made on rational rather than emotional grounds. Price differentials must be justified in terms of the total cost of using the product. Greater durability and lower servicing cost will justify higher prices, but the marketer has the difficult job of convincing the buyer of the importance of these long-term benefits. Exporters often concern themselves only with their own net selling price, giving no consideration to the prices paid by buyers in foreign markets. The result is that they shut themselves out of many markets that could be served profitably.

Since industrial marketers usually try to meet competitors' prices whenever possible, they must gain a competitive advantage through other marketing inputs. Customer service provides a special opportunity for competitive advantage in international marketing. Since supply and communication lines are long, buyers in importing nations may wait longer for deliveries and servicing, and the quality of the servicing provided may be poor. The international marketer who makes the effort to improve these services can obtain an important competitive edge in building repurchase loyalty.

## Influence of Country of Origin

Marketers have long known that consumers sometimes have strong stereotypes, both positive and negative, of the products of certain nations. It used to be assumed that the more rational industrial buyers confined their decision criteria to measurable differences such as price, durability, and performance; but research has demonstrated that professional purchasers are also influenced by country of origin when other variables are held essentially constant.[5] In a study conducted among members of the National Association of Purchasing Managers, when product and service specifications were held constant, the respondents showed a preference for the products of the most highly industrialized nations. There is even some evidence that buyers do not believe that the products of subsidiaries of well-known firms in less-developed countries have the same quality of production as the same products that are produced at headquarters.

It is important for the international marketer to recognize country-of-origin stereotypes when they exist and to incorporate this knowledge into marketing strategy. When the image is a favorable one, the sales personnel should emphasize the country of origin and subtly remind prospective buyers of the quality of that country's products. When the image is negative

---

[5]Phillip D. White and Edward W. Cundiff, "Assessing the Quality of Industrial Products," *Journal of Marketing,* January 1978, pp. 80–86.

or neutral, the sales personnel should emphasize product quality and servicing, giving evidence to support such contentions and playing down country of origin.

### Countertrading

Countertrades are used in instances where the buyer does not have access to a hard currency easily exchanged in international money markets.[6] In underdeveloped and developing countries, the supply of hard currency is often very limited and local governments are likely to restrict the use of this currency to high priority imports that fit in with governmental development goals. The marketers whose products are not included in government priorities can only sell in such markets if they are willing to accept goods in exchange for products produced there, or some combination of goods for goods and cash. Local marketers find it difficult to sell their own products in foreign markets to get foreign exchange, so they offer these products in exchange for the goods they wish to import. The USSR has even bought grain with vodka when currency wasn't available.

Countertrading takes several forms. Barter is as old as trade itself, and involves the exchange of a specified amount of one product for a specified amount of another. The buyer often offers a local raw material or commodity in exchange for a manufactured product. Thus, a Malaysian buyer might offer raw rubber or tin in exchange for a manufactured import; or a Nigerian buyer might offer crude oil. If the product offered in exchange is a widely traded commodity, it is easy for the foreign marketer to determine its value and to resell it on the open market. If the product is a manufactured good, the foreign marketer can only estimate its value and must adjust price to provide a cushion. It may also be necessary to obtain the services of a third party to find a market for the goods. Purely barter transactions impose limits on the attractiveness of some sales for industrial firms that may not wish to become involved in seeking buyers for the products they gain in exchange for their goods. Buyers are limited to choosing from suppliers who are willing to barter.

Another form of countertrading is the counterpurchase. In such transactions the foreign marketer sells goods for cash, but agrees, as a condition of the sale, to purchase a specified amount of goods from the customer for cash. Thus, the customer uses purchased machinery to produce goods to sell back to the original supplier. The original marketer buys these goods for the firm's own use or for resale in international markets. Some counterpurchase agreements may not necessarily require the marketer to buy specifically designated goods, but simply to buy an amount of any local goods sufficient to cover the value of the foreign currency exchange. A

---

[6]"U.S. Firms are Pressed to Offer Barter Terms to Overseas Customers," *The Wall Street Journal*, May 18, 1977, p. 1.

more complicated version of counterpurchases are compensation trades, where the seller trades purchasing credits to other buyers.

American firms have been more reluctant to participate in counter-trading than many of their competitors. They are accustomed to selling their goods for cash or its equivalent and are unwilling to adjust to different conditions. Yet, this method of transaction may offer the only access to markets with soft currencies, or to state trading markets. The volume of countertrading has grown significantly in recent years and offers potentially rich marketing opportunities to the firms willing to make the extra effort. The terms of a sale have become as important as the products themselves in currency-poor countries all over the world. Signs are that they will continue to be important in "closing the sale" in international markets, particularly for industrial products.

## SUMMARY

The characteristic that most clearly differentiates industrial goods from consumer goods is universality. Differences in cultural, political, and legal factors among nations have less effect on the perceptions of how industrial goods should perform. Differences in the level of economic development may affect the level of product sophistication required, but not the basic use and function of most products.

Expectations of quality do vary between nations, and the industrial marketer must adjust the real and perceived level of quality of products to each market. International marketers may also face the varying importance of key aspects of performance; speed versus durability, for example, may have different emphasis in different countries. The product should be viewed not just as a physical good, but as a bundle of services and physical characteristics that satisfy the total need of the buyer. Provision of service and replacement parts, for example, are critically important, but different, in different countries.

The industrial marketer must keep up with the trends in the international marketplace that have changed the relative position of major competitors and the relative importance of major markets. He or she must learn how to adjust to differences in industrial buying behavior in different markets, and be willing to adapt traditional ways of doing business to the needs of new markets.

## DISCUSSION QUESTIONS

1. Explain the concept of universality of demand for industrial products.
2. How does the level of economic development affect the size and nature of demand for industrial products in different nations?

3. Describe the differences in the political environments for industrial products in advanced versus less-developed countries.

4. How do perceptions of the quality of industrial products vary in international markets?

5. Describe the relationship between performance expectations and operating conditions for industrial products.

6. Why is the servicing and replacement of parts often adapted to market conditions in foreign markets?

7. What is the role of universal standards in international industrial product strategy?

8. Differentiate between the characteristics of standardized and adapted services in international markets.

9. What are the risks of "following the leader" in international industrial product marketing?

10. Why has the U.S. been losing its dominant position in world industrial markets?

11. Explain why multinational corporations dominate industrial markets worldwide.

12. Why are industrial firms more likely to use foreign production as a foreign-market entry strategy than consumer goods companies?

13. List the major sources you would use in identifying potential buyers for an industrial product in a new foreign market.

14. How does the initial contact with potential buyers differ in different countries?

15. What factors determine buyer repurchase loyalty?

16. Explain countertrades. What is their role in selling industrial products in world markets?

# ELSCINT

In 1980, Elscint management was faced with a number of decisions about directions of adaptations or change in the CAT scanner, a new diagnostic device that provides a much better picture of a patient's insides than the traditional single-shot X-ray. Elscint, a high-technology company based in Haifa, Israel, started as an independent company in 1969—as a spin-off from Elron Electronics Industries. Its first products were research devices for use in nuclear physics, but it now has three divisions: radiology, nuclear medicine, and scientific instrumentation. During its first ten years, the company grew at a dramatic compounded annual rate of 35%, based primarily on tremendous overseas expansion. In 1980, Elscint's sales were in excess of $50 million and 95 percent of this was outside Israel.

The phenomenal success of Elscint derives largely from two factors—excellent in-house R & D and a strong marketing organization. The president, Avraham Suhami, a former professor at Technion-Israel Institute of Technology, has allocated 15 percent of sales to R & D since the company was founded. Elscint management believes that no technological firm can survive without a marketing network to provide a continuous flow of information on markets, clients, technologies, and ideas to R & D. In addition, they believe that it is cheaper for them to sell through their own marketing network than to sell to distributors.

When Elscint was spun-off as an independent company, its management started seeking new ways to capitalize on its expertise in scientific instrumentation, and selected nuclear medicine, using radioactive isotopes in diagnostic tests, as one major target. By 1971, this division had grown to five hundred employees and more than $15 million in sales from a full line of instruments for imaging and data processing. In 1979, Elscint had 10% of the world market in the nuclear medical instrumentation field, accounting for 20 percent of sales in Western Europe and over 10 percent of sales in northeastern U.S.A. Management's long-term strategy for the nuclear medicine division was to develop a new generation of nuclear medical instruments that would enable Elscint to assume technical leadership in the field and secure a 20 percent worldwide market share. Elscint product strategy is based on the assumption that for high-technology products, the market is worldwide, and products need not be adapted and changed in each market in which they may be sold.

Elscint management estimated that by 1982, the world medical imaging market would be likely to reach the $3 billion mark, with the new CAT (Computerized Axial Tomography) scanner as a major sales item. Elscint announced its CAT scanner program in 1976 with a marketing campaign in Europe and the United States. Two machines, one in Israel and one in New

York, were set up and operated in a clinical environment to demonstrate their high-quality images obtained with lower radiation dosages than other CAT scanners. The 1980 model incorporated new features such as zoom scanning and minidose scanning for pediatric use. However, the price of the machine, $600,000, was already so high that only a small number of wealthy major medical institutions and hospitals can afford them. The major engineering and technological challenge facing the industry for the eighties was to broaden the market by cutting the cost of the CAT scanner. A lower price on its scanner would enable Elscint to both enlarge the market and capture a larger share, by selling to smaller hospitals and clinics.

Mr. Suhami, Elscint president, was quoted as saying that another advance in our scanner system would be a perfect way to start our second decade. However, cost reduction and product innovation go hand in hand.

## QUESTIONS

1. Which product strategy makes more sense for Elscint at this time, cost reduction to broaden the market appeal or continued product innovation to maintain leadership?
2. Evaluate management's assumption that product characteristics for high-technology products need not be varied from one country to another.
3. Would the international product life-cycle concept be of importance for the CAT scanner?

# chapter 12

# PRICING DECISIONS FOR INTERNATIONAL MARKETING

In the ethical drug industry in America, we set our own prices without reference to the government, based on the competitive situation and the need to obtain an adequate profit. Not so in Italy, where we first have to submit a price to a government pricing bureau and negotiate an acceptable price. Some kind of price control, not necessarily as stringent as in Italy, exists in most of the countries with social security systems. The price has to be approved as well as the product. Fortunately, the authorities in these countries who have so much power over us, generally speaking, take an intelligent view of our need to make adequate profits to pay for good research, overhead, and other expenses.

There are many parts of the underdeveloped world where people are so poor that they cannot afford our drugs at any price and where the governments cannot tax the people sufficiently to pay for complete social security schemes. This is a real problem: how to get life-saving drugs to the indigent people who need them around the world.*

## INTRODUCTION

In international marketing there are four pricing inputs that affect marketing strategy, and one or more of these inputs is involved in every price. The first of these inputs is the market, the second is cost, the third is com-

*Richard C. Fenton, "Worldwide Ethical Drug Markets," *Drug Market Industry*, 93: 624, 19, Drug Markets Inc., New York, N.Y.

petition, and the fourth is government. How these inputs affect the final price depends, at least to some extent, on the company's perception of price in its overall marketing strategy. Some managements perceive price as the least effective of the elements of marketing strategy because of the ease and speed with which competition can duplicate pricing changes. In such instances the marketer may not include price as a part of competitive strategy—a situation described as nonprice competition. Prices would be changed only in reaction to actions of competitors or changes in the market and/or costs. With a great many companies, however, price is a more significant element in total strategy. This is especially true in international marketing strategy.

Several factors in recent years have led to an increase in emphasis on international pricing. Increasing fluctuation in exchange rates makes the reassessment of prices a continual necessity. The appreciation or depreciation in the value of the international marketer's currencies requires a re-evaluation of the competitiveness of prices. Accelerating inflation worldwide and differences in inflation rates between countries require almost constant adjustment of prices. Increasing competition in many world markets means prices must be more carefully evaluated.

In this chapter we review the major factors that impinge on pricing decisions in international markets. Most of these are the same as those that affect prices at home—demand, costs, competition, and government regulations. Our discussion is focused on the unique and variable influences of these factors in international pricing decisions. In addition we review the special case of intracompany pricing decisions for firms that market products in multiple foreign markets.

## MARKET PRICING FACTORS

Market demand is the most important input to a pricing decision when the product is essentially undifferentiated. Cost has little influence on the price of grain, copper, or oil because the buyer is not really convinced that the product of one producer is better than that of another. But even with these products, government actions or price agreements among competitors can radically change prices, as was the case with oil in 1972, when OPEC was first effective in controlling world prices for petroleum products. Even for differentiated products, the market's perception of price in relation to quality and product uniqueness makes price an important element of image.

### Demand

The elasticity of demand is always an important element in pricing decisions. If demand is inelastic, there is little reason to lower price; it may even be wise to raise it. But if demand is elastic, a price change may be the most important factor in increasing the size of the market. In the United States in 1983, the demand for microcomputers for the home was very small but growing very rapidly, and initial price reductions indicated a high degree of demand elasticity. It seemed likely that a quantum reduction in price would result in a quantum increase in demand, just as had happened in the introductory years for television.

The price-quality relationship has an opposite effect on demand from price elasticity. Whereas elasticity may suggest that a price decrease will increase demand, the discovery of a price-quality relationship will militate against price decreases; it may even dictate price increases. One of the reasons a consumer may be willing to buy an imported product is that it is perceived as better. A part of this quality image may be its "foreignness," and for this reason foreign products can often compete at prices higher than local products. As an importer increases volume in a market, marketing activities can be performed more efficiently and it becomes possible to meet local prices. The marketer must then decide what the effect of a price reduction will be on the product's unique image of quality. The decision may still be to reduce price if the quality market is much smaller than the mass market, or if there is potential competition.

In Communist countries, the demand for products, from the viewpoint of the seller, is monolithic. The government and its bureaucracies represent the only buyer of foreign goods, so demand is determined by the perception of a bureaucrat who decides how foreign exchange will be allocated among products to be imported. This perception may be totally unrelated to the potential demand in the market; it may be based instead on economic and developmental goals for the nation.

## Competition's Effect on Demand

Since price is the starting point for comparison between products, the nature and extent of competition has an important effect on market demand. If at first there is no direct competition in foreign markets, the price can be set as it would be by a monopolist, to maximize long- or short-term profit. However in most markets, this situation is temporary; competitors will quickly appear. In other markets, competition will be there ahead of you. Existing competition in new markets may be unaggressive and unwilling to use price as a competitive weapon. They may also be small, high-cost operators so that your product can be sold profitably at lower prices. In this case, a lower price will provide the new product with a wedge for entering the market against established products.

Often, though, a marketer may enter a foreign market where local competition is agressive and efficient. In this case, the importer's landed cost may be higher than the cost of local products because of freight and handling and tariffs. To compete effectively in this market, the firm may have to reduce margins by absorbing all or part of the freight costs. Alternatively, it should consider another market entry strategy, such as a joint venture or local production.

### Dumping

Sometimes a firm with excess capacity or excess inventories on hand will sell this excess in foreign markets at low prices which only cover direct costs. This is called dumping. If demand in the local market is inelastic, a lower price for the imported product will not affect demand significantly and the firm may still be stuck with excess inventories. Even if demand is inelastic, the firm may not want to disturb the market—perhaps starting a price war—just to dispose of a temporary excess. Therefore, dumping in foreign markets makes sense only if the firm has short-term objectives and demand is sufficiently elastic there.

Dumping is viewed with mixed feelings in the market where it takes place. Product buyers welcome a chance to buy at a lower-than-normal price, but competitors are openly hostile to this threat to their markets. They are likely to bring pressure on the government to prohibit dumping. As a consequence, a number of nations have adopted antidumping regulations—the United States among them.

## COST PRICING FACTORS

Cost is always one element in the pricing decision because it provides a long-run minimum below which the price cannot fall. A firm may knowingly sell below cost for given periods of time for reasons such as a goal of market penetration or reaction to competitors' actions. But in the long run, a firm cannot stay in business unless its prices cover all manufacturing, shipping, marketing, and overhead costs. In some instances, each product or each production unit may not be expected to carry an equal share of overhead as long as total overhead is met. Thus, a marketer might make use of excess capacity by selling at a lower price (without fully allocating a share of overhead) in foreign markets.

When a firm enters foreign markets, additional costs are usually incurred which are not present in the domestic market. These include tariffs and special taxes, where applicable; additional transportation and handling costs; special packaging; insurance; and losses from currency fluctuation. These costs may appreciably increase the final cost of the product to the customer. It is for this reason that Volkswagen finally acquired production facilities in the United States, after exporting from the German factory to the American market for many years. Because of the high additional costs of landing their cars in American ports, the German firm found itself consistently priced above comparable domestic cars and other imports.

## Taxes and Tariffs

Tariffs and other special import taxes are applied to goods at the port of entry in the foreign market. Some of these assessments are seen as sources of income to the nation levying them, but many are designed to provide some price protection for local industry by increasing the landed costs of imported goods. Whatever the intent of the assessments, they increase the prices at which imports can be sold and thereby reduce the ability of such imports to compete on a price basis. During the past thirty years, great strides have been taken at an international level to reduce tariffs and other barriers to trade throughout the world, but in individual cases such restrictions still exist and impact to varying degrees on imports. In such instances the duties increase the minimum profitable price at which the exporter can sell in a market.[1]

The international marketing manager must consider the impact of tariffs and taxes on the price that buyers will have to pay in foreign markets. Not only do these assessments increase the costs of local middlemen, but they may make the firm's products not affordable to its primary markets there. This in turn will affect the firm's own cost structure if forecast sales volume is not attainable. If the firm cannot reduce its costs in production and transportation, it may have to license production elsewhere at a lower cost, or abandon the market in the long run.

## Middleman Costs

The costs of moving a product through the marketing channel exist in every market and are a necessary part of the final cost of any product. However, these costs are not necessarily the same in every country. IBM, for example, sells its computers at higher prices in Europe than in the United States, and they blame a part of this cost differential on higher distribution costs.[2] These higher costs result from at least two differences among markets. First, marketing channels vary in length in different markets. In the United States and other highly sophisticated markets, the channels tend to be shorter than in other markets. Since each middleman is entitled to a markup to cover costs of operation and services performed, additional middlemen result in higher distribution costs.

In some foreign markets, the traditional channels are firmly established and are almost impossible to circumvent. Japan is a good example; the middlemen there are organized into strong industry associations that control both distribution and price.[3] The newcomer and outsider is likely

[1] J. H. Chan-Lee, "Intercountry Cost and Price Comparisons," *International Monetary Fund Staff Papers*, July 1971, pp. 153–59.

[2] "I.B.M. Cheaper in America," *The Economist*, June 24, 1978, vol. 267, p. 93.

[3] "Pricing Japanese Success," *Management Today*, May 1980, pp. 84–89.

to find it difficult even to get access to the channel, and has practically no control over final costs and prices.

In highly developed markets, middleman markups tend to be standardized. In the United States, for example, margins for different middlemen in various trade or product categories are matters of common knowledge in the trade. However, in other countries these markups may not be standardized at all and are subject to negotiation. The newcomer to the market may have to try to achieve some uniformity if a standard price for the product is sought in different channels.

## Financing and Risk Costs

International marketers find that the cost of capital varies enormously among countries. Normally the more highly developed the nation, the lower are its interest rates. As an example, the interest rates charged by banks in El Paso, Texas are consistently lower—often as much as 50 percent less—than those charged by Mexican banks across the border. If the international firm must make use of local credit to finance marketing or production costs, the higher interest rates in less-developed countries make it necessary to pass on these costs to buyers, in the form of higher prices.

Risks of loss are frequently greater in foreign markets than in domestic ones. Transportation by water involves greater risks of damage and pilferage than transportation by truck or rail. Warehousing may involve greater risk if there is inadequate fire or theft protection. The risk of credit loss is often higher, particularly if the firm has poor access to credit information. Whether these risks are covered by insurance or by the establishment of reserves for loss, they must ultimately be passed on in the form of higher prices than might be charged in the domestic market.

## Effect of Inflation and/or Recession

Inflation has been present to some degree in most countries since World War II. The rate of inflation varies over time in particular nations. For many years the United States' inflation rate was 2 percent or less per year, but in 1981 it reached levels of 11 percent and 12 percent. Some nations, however, experience much higher levels of inflation. For many years, several Latin American countries, including Brazil and Argentina, experienced annual inflation rates in excess of 100 percent. Israel experienced 60 percent rates of inflation during the early 1980s. Differential rates of inflation among markets require that prices be set and adjusted separately in each market. And in markets with very high inflation rates, a completely different procedure may be required to administer prices with pricing reviews as frequently as weekly, or even daily. This also requires the continuous and immediate conversion of sales-generated cash into other goods or into more stable currencies.

The business cycle may also vary from country to country. Although it is true that major worldwide recessions such as occurred in the early 1980s will affect the economies of most nations, the level of effect may vary widely between nations—one country may be experiencing a very sharp recession, while another experiences only a mild slowdown, depending upon how much each is affected by international influences. The international marketer often has to adjust prices to reflect the differences in these markets. It may be wise to reduce margins and/or prices in the more depressed economies so as to maintain a high enough level of sales to support distribution and promotional programs.

### Exchange Rate Fluctuations

Many countries allow their currencies to float freely against each other. Other countries peg the value of their currencies to some other currency for long periods of time. When currencies are allowed to float, the rate of exchange may vary a few percentage points during a period of a few weeks or months; however, when important financial developments take place in one of the countries, changes may be more dramatic. But at any time the spot (or current) rate can be expected to be somewhat different from the ninety-day forward rate. For example, in December 1982 the spot rate for French francs in U.S. dollars was 7.18, but the ninety-day forward rate was 8.35. This means that speculators expected the dollar to increase in value relative to the franc during the ninety-day period. Marketers who do not want to have profits wiped out because of deflation in the value of a foreign currency before the profits can be repatriated, can hedge by trading simultaneously in the forward market. (See example in Chapter 2.)

Responses to a changing rate of exchange may depend on the product involved. If the product is somewhat unique and cannot be easily duplicated, the seller has more bargaining room. The same would be true even with commodities, if they are in short supply. In such cases, the marketer may be able to renegotiate price somewhat to compensate for a loss resulting from exchange-rate fluctuations.[4] The ability to pass on to the buyer losses from currency fluctuation will depend on who the buyer is. If the buyer is a middleman, he may be able to pass on a higher price to customers; but if the buyer is an end-user, such as a government, it may be more difficult to obtain price concessions.[5]

A particular problem for the international marketer is the impact of a major currency devaluation on both profits and demand. When the Mexican government in 1982 drastically devalued the peso to 40 percent of its

---

[4]Llewellyn Clague and Rena Grossfield, "Export Pricing in a Floating Rate World," *Columbia Journal of World Business*, Winter 1974, p. 18.

[5]"How Exchange Rates and Prices Really Link Up," *Citibank Monthly Economic Letter*, November 1976, pp. 6–10.

former value in dollars, it effectively priced most American products out of the Mexican market. Most Mexicans could not afford imported products at the now drastically inflated prices. At the same time, Mexican exports became very attractive in world markets. Many exporters to Mexico were faced with the alternatives of abandoning the market or of producing their products within the country so as to get prices down to a competitive level.

## Price Escalation

When products are manufactured in one nation and exported to another nation, two factors will cause the end price to increase. First, there are additional costs, such as extra transportation, extra insurance, stronger packing, tariffs, and port costs. Second, there are usually more middlemen involved in international marketing channels. Since these two factors interact, the result may be that prices in the country of destination increase geometrically.

Figure 12–1 illustrates how price escalation works. Since the additional costs of landing the product in the foreign market are included by each successive middleman when computing markups, the necessary additional layers of middlemen increase the ultimate price out of proportion to domestic prices. In the illustration in Figure 12–1, the additional costs of landing the product in the foreign market are $6.80, or 68 percent of the

**Figure 12–1**  International Price Escalation.

|  | *DOMESTIC CHANNEL* | *FOREIGN CHANNELS* | | |
|---|---|---|---|---|
|  | *(a)* | *(b)* | *(c)* | *(d)* |
| Manufacturer's net price | $10.00 | $10.00 | $10.00 | $10.00 |
| Insurance & shipping costs |  | 4.00 | 4.00 | 4.00 |
| Landed cost |  | 14.00 | 14.00 | 14.00 |
| Tariff (20% on landed cost) |  | 2.80 | 2.80 | 2.80 |
| Importer's cost |  |  | 16.80 | 16.80 |
| Importer's margin (25% on cost) |  |  | 4.20 | 4.20 |
| Wholesaler's cost | 10.00 | 16.80 | 21.00 | 21.00 |
| Wholesaler's margin (33-⅓% on cost) | 3.33 | 5.60 | 7.00 | 7.00 |
| Local foreign jobber cost |  |  |  | 28.00 |
| Jobber's margin (33-⅓% on cost) |  |  |  | 9.33 |
| Retailer's cost | 13.33 | 22.40 | 28.00 | 37.33 |
| Retailer's margin (50% on cost) | 6.67 | 11.20 | 14.00 | 18.67 |
| Retail price | 20.00 | 33.60 | 42.00 | 56.00 |
| % Price escalation |  | 68% | 110% | 180% |

(a) Manufacturer to wholesaler to retailer.

(b) Manufacturer to foreign wholesaler to retailer.

(c) Manufacturer to foreign importer to wholesaler to retailer.

(d) Manufacturer to foreign importer to wholesaler to jobber to retailer.

manufacturer's selling price. When the product is sold through the same channel in the foreign market (from producer to wholesaler to retailer), the foreign retail price is also 68 percent higher. However, when another middleman (an importer) is added, the retail price is escalated to 110 percent above the domestic price. When a second additional middleman (a jobber) is added to the foreign channel, the price rises to 180 percent of the domestic retail price. Let us assume the product is an electronic calculator. At a price of $20 in the domestic market, it is within the affordable price range of almost every potential user. If the foreign market is equally affluent, the minimum possible price of $33.60 (assuming the same channel is used abroad) might be enough higher to eliminate 25 percent of potential buyers. But, if it is necessary to use two more layers of middlemen to reach this market, the resulting price of $56 might eliminate 75 percent of the potential users, who simply cannot afford to invest $56 in a calculator. If the foreign market is a less affluent one, price escalation may have even more serious effects on potential market size. Perhaps only 25 percent of the market can afford the calculator at the same price it is sold domestically, and practically no one can afford it if offered through two additional middlemen.

If a product is to succeed in a foreign market, prices must be attractive to the end customer, yet they must yield margins adequate enough to motivate channel members, to cover costs, and to provide the manufacturer an acceptable return for risk. A logical way of approaching this foreign pricing dilemma is to start with what is deemed to be an accepted foreign retail price and work backwards to determine middlemen and manufacturer's selling prices. This is called demand-backward pricing. If the resulting manufacturer's selling price is lower than desired, several alternatives are available. First, the seller might settle for a smaller margin; if foreign sales are considered incremental, bearing no share of overhead, they can provide additional net income. Second, the firm may be able to persuade middlemen to accept somewhat lower-than-normal margins; however, this will reduce the appeal of the product to the middlemen and reduce their willingness to support it. Third, the manufacturer might reduce costs by reducing the number of layers of foreign middlemen. And fourth, the manufacturer might reduce the cost of the product by adapting and simplifying it, by exporting parts for assembly abroad, or by manufacturing it abroad.

## GOVERNMENT PRICING ACTIONS

Governments involve themselves in pricing decisions in many ways. Government officials see themselves as protectors of various groups and institutions within a society, and frequently use control over pricing decisions as a means of reaching such goals. In the United States, for example, the government has had a long-term commitment to the protection of free enterprise and small business. The resulting antimonopoly laws prohibit price fixing between competitors. This particular kind of governmental control is not common in other countries, so in many nations the international marketer is not barred from reaching price agreements with competitors. Of course, the most common method used by governments to protect local business against foreign imports is the establishment of tariffs that increase the price of imported goods in the local markets. Another way of protecting local small businesses from more aggressive, large businesses—whether local or foreign—is through the use of government-dictated minimum margins or markups. This prevents what is viewed to be ruinous price competition. Finally, some governments provide protection for local industry through outright subsidies. For example, the United States subsidizes the American transportation industry by restricting all interstate transportation (surface, water, and air) to American-owned carriers. Subsidies may also take the form of financial aid, such as tax remission or discounts. In such cases, the foreign marketer finds it difficult to compete on a price basis. When evaluating prospective new foreign markets, the international marketer should identify and avoid those markets where government subsidies make price competition impossible.

Government also interferes in pricing decisions through concern for the consumer. In less-developed nations where a large share of the population is at or near subsistence level, governments may feel the need to exercise control over the price of living essentials, particularly of basic foodstuffs. This control may be through the establishment of price ceilings or even the setting of specific prices for some of the most important elements in the diet, such as rice, bread, or cornmeal. An even broader type of government restriction is price control, because it may be applied to all goods sold in the market. Price controls are established where creeping inflation threatens to dilute consumer buying power. In Great Britain, for example, price controls were installed during World War II, and for many years after that all price changes required approval of the Price Control Board. When inflation rates get very high, it becomes impossible to control prices. Governments have occasionally decided that the best way to protect prices of consumer goods is to enter the market as a direct competitor. Thus, the Mexican government has established a government-owned-and-operated chain of food stores that sells a basic line of staple foods in low income areas of cities, small towns, and rural areas.

Governments also influence prices as buyers. The government is frequently a major buyer, sometimes the only buyer, in a market for particular products. This is the case in most communist countries. Depending upon the amount of the government's involvement, it can have considerable impact on price through its bargaining strength alone. In the communist countries where the government is usually the only buyer, this monopsonistic power provides great price bargaining strength.

Another way governments can influence pricing decisions is through their control of buyers' access to foreign exchange. Governments can limit the price that foreign buyers actually can pay for imported goods by granting, or not granting, the buyers a license to buy foreign currency to pay for the goods. The license may be granted for purchases of industrial equipment, but not for luxury or discretionary items; alternatively, the government may even enter negotiations directly with the seller for a reduced price or for some form of barter or countertrade arrangement that does not use up scarce or unavailable foreign currency reserves.

Barter schemes have become very important in international trade for several reasons. One is that international debts of many governments have rapidly increased in the last decade as a result of expensive development projects and escalating energy costs, and foreign exchange reserves are being depleted to pay for these needed goods. Also, as trade with Soviet bloc countries and the People's Republic of China has expanded, international firms have found it necessary to negotiate some barter arrangements in order to have access to those markets. Payment in kind is preferable to payment in a nonconvertible currency.

A barter arrangement can involve the direct exchange of goods (barter); partial payment in goods and partial payment in cash (compensation deal); payment in cash contingent on a contract to purchase from the buyer in the future (counterpurchase); or payment through products produced by the equipment the buyer is purchasing (product buy-back). Counterpurchases and product buy-back agreements are especially popular with governments in the Eastern European nations. The major difficulty in barter deals is in determining the market value of the products to be traded, especially when the trade is not immediate or when the products have not yet been produced. For this reason, many international firms have avoided bartering with foreign governments; their loss is usually some other firm's gain in the competition for expanding world markets.

## COMPETITIVE PRICING ACTIONS

Pricing decisions must always be made with an eye to competitors' actions and reactions. If an industry is truly price competitive, the marketer can anticipate that any pricing action will be immediately evaluated and counteracted by the competition. Since the United States government mandates free price competition within the American market, American businesses are accustomed to avoiding collusive action, including all kinds of price discussion or agreements with competitors.

In many nations, however, price agreements are not illegal, and collusion may take a number of forms. The most comprehensive is the cartel, an organization of producers of a product who band together to establish minimum selling prices for their product in all markets. To be effective, cartel members must jointly control a major portion of the output of the product in their markets. OPEC is a classic example of a cartel. Its effective control over the supply of petroleum in world markets enabled it to increase the price of oil tenfold for a number of years. Eventually, however, the enormous increase in price sharply reduced international demand for oil. This decrease in demand brought pressure on individual members to reduce prices, and eventually, by 1983, the OPEC negotiators were unable to reach an agreement on a common price.

A stronger version of the cartel is the combine. The combine operates in the same manner as a cartel except that it has the authority to levy fines against its members for noncompliance with price agreements. Such an agreement among OPEC members would have prevented individual members from selling below agreed-upon prices.

Trade associations provide another, less-formal medium for price fixing between competitors. The primary purpose for such associations is to provide a medium for exchange of market information of value to all members. For example, through the use of jointly gathered statistics, the trade association can tell each member what its precise market share is—a statistic that can only be roughly estimated by individual firms. Although they are specifically prohibited from price collusion in the United States, trade associations in many countries do negotiate price agreements.

Another vehicle for collusive action on prices is the patent licensing agreement. When the owner of a patent licenses its use in a new market, the licensor may retain control over minimum prices for the product in the market. In effect, the owner of the patent is able to control price competition from licensees.

American antimonopoly laws not only prohibit price collusion among firms in the American market; they also prohibit price collusion by American firms in world markets. Thus, an American exporter cannot participate in international cartels or participate in trade associations that fix prices. They may or may not decide to sell at the same prices that these organizations establish, but they may not participate in negotiations to establish such prices.

## INTRACOMPANY PRICING STRATEGY

The development of the pricing strategy within a company involves three steps. First, the strategist must become familiar with the external constraints over price control described in the preceding sections. Second, pricing strategists must define company pricing objectives. And third, the pricing strategy must be integrated with the overall marketing mix.

A firm's pricing objectives may vary widely for different products or for different markets. In one instance, management may use price to secure quick market penetration, setting prices as low as possible to obtain wide coverage of the market in a minimum amount of time. In another instance, a high price may be set in order to skim off the high profits from sales to affluent early adopters before competition enters the market and forces down prices. In another instance, management may wish to keep prices high in order to establish a prestige image. When buyers are unable to judge product quality by objective criteria, too low a price will lower the perceived prestige of the product.

In international markets, price objectives must be related to the firm's overall market goals in each market, to the price's effects on the firm's cost structure and profit goals, and to the product's pricing in other markets. If a firm has limited objectives within a foreign market (such as a one-time outlet for excess inventories), then its own costs and profit goals will be preeminent in the pricing decision. On the other hand, if penetration of a foreign market is critical to the firm's growth objectives, then that country's market and competitive factors must be considered in addition to costs. Furthermore, the extent of sales in one market can affect production and marketing costs for the entire firm, and it must decide price in terms of the optimal use of its resources in multiple markets. If price has a strong relationship to product image, then pricing decisions in one market must not have a negative effect on product image in other markets. Last, multinational firms must consider multicountry prices simultaneously, because a low or high price in a neighboring market can undercut sales in another. Now we will address some of the important issues in administering and setting prices in international firms.

### Transfer Pricing

The transfer price is the price at which a company sells its products to its own foreign units. The options for the transfer price range from the cost of manufacture to the market price in the country involved. Even cost may vary; it can range from the cost at the company's most efficient plant to cost at the plant from which the merchandise is being shipped. In each instance, the actual transfer price may be negotiated at some level between the two extremes. Often this final price may be an "arms-length price"— that is, a price that other, independently owned parties would have reached in the same transaction.

The transfer price in a decentralized international firm can have a dramatic effect on net income because of several factors. Tax minimization goals may make it desirable to show as much profit as possible in one of two countries involved. Import duties and taxes may make it necessary to keep the transfer price low. Inflation and currency rationing may affect the transfer price, and restrictions against repatriation of profits would suggest a high transfer price in order to take the profit as the product enters other nations. Unstable governments may also lead the price setter to retain profits in the home country. On the other hand, high transfer prices may reduce competitive advantage in a local market. They may also mitigate against the interests of foreign partners and against public relations in the foreign market.

Transfer prices between units of multinational firms have become a controversial topic. If the transfer price is set at any point other than the point at which marginal revenue equals marginal cost for the producing unit, the firm's own profits will not be maximized. If all transfer prices in a corporate system are set in relation to the variable costs of production and distribution for each unit, systemwide profits will be maximized. Variations from these policies interfere with the view that each subsidiary is a profit center—a concept widely used in the internal management and control of multinational enterprises. Also, the use of transfer prices to repatriate profits or to minimize taxes is being looked at more closely by governments throughout the world. Transfer pricing is no longer an effective or simple way of meeting company goals other than profit maximization.

### Multicountry Pricing

When a product is sold in more than one market, management must choose between establishing one price worldwide or adjusting prices in each market. The use of a single world price is described as ethnocentric pricing. If a truly common final price is sought, the seller must absorb freight duties and other costs in the price. When costs vary too much between national markets, ethnocentric prices are not practical. Similarly, if demand or market plans vary greatly between markets, prices should be allowed to vary.

The opposite extreme of ethnocentric pricing is polycentric pricing, which provides for the establishment of separate and unrelated prices in each national market. This pricing strategy allows the marketer to tailor the price to the level of demand and financial resources available in each market. Equally important is the ability of the marketer to react quickly to changes in market conditions with appropriate price changes. A disadvantage of this method of pricing is that pricing decisions are often delegated to a low managerial level where there is little expertise in such things as the effects of price on perception of quality and preference between brands. Also, the company will not present a common image to the world market. This is no problem if most customers in each market are locals, as is the case with many consumer goods. But, if some customers are multinational firms, as is often the case with industrial goods, these buyers may expect, or hope, to be charged the same price in all markets. Polycentric pricing can also encourage dealers to undercut dealers in other markets. A Belgian retailer may find it cheaper to buy from your German wholesaler than your Belgian wholesaler.

Geocentric pricing provides a compromise between ethnocentric and polycentric pricing, because it provides prices that lie between absolute uniformity and total variability. It uses a base starting price for all markets, with a formula for adjusting this base upwards or downwards in accordance with present guidelines. These guidelines should take into consideration market, cost, government, and competitive conditions in each market. It has the advantage of retaining home-office control over prices, but allows the flexibility of adjusting prices to different markets.

### Controlling Resale Prices

It is a very common practice for international marketers to focus their pricing decisions on the amount to be charged the first middleman in the foreign market, and to leave to that person the final price the ultimate buyer will pay. Such a policy assumes that the ultimate retail price will provide an adequate margin to each level of middlemen and will be attractive to final buyers too. However, if competitive pressures from similar products have brought retail prices to a low level, the margin to middlemen will be unattractive, and they may be unwilling to carry the product. This will be particularly true if middlemen are being asked to take on the product as a new line. In such cases, the marketer may find it advisable to suggest and maintain minimum resale prices in the market so that dealer margins are protected. Another benefit from this resale price approach is that the marketer is forced to start the price-setting process with a realistic assessment of what price will be competitive and attractive at the retail level. The manager can then adjust prices backward up the channel so that the manufacturer's price is market driven rather than cost driven.

### Price Quotations and Credit

The method of quoting prices reflects the degree of commitment by the exporting firm in the foreign market. When a firm views its exports as a means of disposing of excess capacity, and has little long-term interest in the development of the foreign market, prices are likely to be quoted at the factory or point of origin—F.O.B. prices—and they are likely to be quoted in the exporter's currency. In such cases, export middlemen cover the costs of insurance and freight to the destination, covering these costs in their markups. When a firm wants to build a long-term position in a foreign market, it is more likely to deal directly with middlemen in the foreign market and to quote prices that include costs of insurance and freight to the port of destination—C.I.F. quotations (a price that includes selling costs, insurance, and freight) common in international trade. The refusal to quote prices in the buyer's currency or to accept foreign currency payments is a sure way to reduce both risk and competitiveness. It makes sense for the intermittent exporter to minimize risk because there is no long-term commitment to developing foreign market potential. However, if the firm wants to be truly competitive in world markets, it may have to be willing to quote prices in foreign currencies and to quote prices C.I.F. Methods of reducing currency risk were discussed in Chapter 2. For examples of documents related to an export shipment, see Appendix C. Note that the invoice price is C.I.F.

Credit is another tool that can improve the firm's ability to penetrate foreign markets. If there is little commitment to international markets, the firm may be understandably reluctant to use credit as a competitive tool. On the other hand, providing middlemen and other buyers with credit helps to establish long-term relationships, and even loyalty. The use of a letter of credit (also shown in Appendix C) is a technique that international sellers use to ensure the credit-worthiness of buyers. When a firm has established a relationship with foreign buyers, it may be willing to provide longer-term credit to them as a means of improving its competitive position.

## SUMMARY

The pricing decision in foreign markets should always be approached as an integral part of total marketing strategy. If an optimal price is to be chosen, it must reflect unique characteristics of the product, the method of distribution to be used, and the planned level of promotion. Within this framework, pricing decisions will be affected by four factors: cost, demand, government influences, and competition. Cost always provides a price floor and some target profit. Demand sets a ceiling price which relates to perceived value and demand elasticity in the market. Government policies may restrict price changes or margins. Governments can also affect a firm's prices through direct competition and through their bargaining strengths. Competition establishes a narrow range around which the price may be allowed to vary. Each firm must consider these factors as well as its own internal pricing objectives when setting international prices. Special pricing problems faced by the international marketing manager are transfer prices, multicountry price setting, and control of resale prices.

## DISCUSSION QUESTIONS

1. What environmental factors have led to an increased importance for international pricing decisions?

2. Differentiate between the effects of elasticity and perceived product quality on demand.
3. How does competition affect demand in international markets?
4. What is dumping?
5. What are the additional costs faced by international marketers in exporting to foreign markets?
6. How do foreign middlemen affect international prices?
7. Explain how multicountry prices are influenced by differential rates of inflation.
8. How do floating exchange rates increase international product prices?
9. Define the causes and effects of price escalation.
10. What is demand-backward pricing?
11. How can a firm minimize price escalation in foreign markets?
12. Describe government roles as buyers, competitors, protectors, and regulators as they affect foreign market prices.
13. Explain how competitors' joint actions can influence international pricing decisions.
14. What is unique about price objectives for foreign markets?
15. Define transfer price. What factors influence the setting of transfer prices in multinational firms?
16. Describe ethnocentric, polycentric, and geocentric approaches to multicountry pricing decisions.
17. Why is it difficult for a firm to control resale prices in foreign markets?
18. Explain how price quotations and credit affect international competitiveness.

**PROGRESSIVE FOODS CORPORATION***

Tom McGuire, marketing manager for the Household Cleaning Products Division of Progressive Foods Corporation, is currently pondering his "greatest" international project established three years ago in Mexico. Upon appointment to his position four years ago, Tom had sought a prime foreign market in order to continue the company's commitment to international expansion. The new venture into the Mexican market had seemed fitting because it was so close to the North American market. However, product sales in Mexico had not acquired sufficient levels to generate the minimum desired 20% return-on-equity. Furthermore, the product line appeared to have very low demand. Hence, Tom's "greatest" project required a thorough analysis of pertinent factors which were contributing to the market's ambivalence.

Progressive Foods Corporation is a multi-product company based in Chicago, Illinois. Since its founding in 1950, the product mix has expanded from canned goods alone to include such diverse products as personal hygiene and personal care products. The company has been regarded by the industry as a formidable competitor in the introduction of successful products. The corporate annual growth rate has averaged 23% since 1963 and it has experienced a 40% average increase in its licensing and joint venture programs since 1973. Mr. William Scheffield Jr., president and chief executive officer asserts: "We will capitalize on our product success record in pursuing a market development strategy. Our products will have no difficulties establishing themselves within new markets."

Historical Review of the Joint
Venture

On March 16, 1980, the Household Cleaning Products Division, under the direction of Tom McGuire, formed a joint venture with Rectos Comerciantes Mexicanos S.A., an established (privately owned) manufacturer of toiletries and sundries products in Monterrey. Rectos Comerciantes was an attractive partner for various reasons: (1) the local manufacturer had an established distribution system in major Mexican cities; (2) Rectos Comerciantes was operating at 65% capacity and had been seeking to expand its product mix; and, (3) during its 20 years of operation, Rectos Comerciantes had established a stable network of local suppliers.

The bilateral agreement ensured that Rectos Comerciantes would begin manufacturing and distributing the All-Purpose Cleanser line consisting

*This case was prepared by Carol G. Spindola.

of liquid sprays and liquid concentrates. However, the manufacturing of the Detergent and Dishwashing line would not commence until 1986. Progressive Foods Corporation would provide 49% equity financing for new manufacturing and packaging machinery investments. In addition, the Household Cleaning Products Division of Progressive Foods would assume full responsibility in the selection and implementation of marketing strategies.

The liquid spray is a general cleanser which is positioned in the United States as a quick, wipe on/off (no scrubbing) multiple-use product. It does not contain ammonium but contains a disinfecting ingredient, is orange-red in color and comes in three forms: aerosol, spray pump and spray foam. The liquid concentrate is basically a floor cleanser positioned in the U.S. as a heavy duty cleaner and disinfectant. It contains both ammonium and a disinfectant, is blue-green in color and comes in two scents: pine and fresh. Both products come in two sizes: regular and economy, and both have a low price per standard unit of measurement.

### Progressive Foods' Marketing Strategy in Mexico

Only minor product alterations had been used for the Mexican market—namely, labeling. Eighty percent of the product line was distributed through chain supermarkets while the remaining 20% was distributed through private/local stores. Prices for each product line had been set at 8% above the local competing brands. This policy was established to compensate for local advertising costs. The media chosen for promotion of each product line were television (80% of the advertising budget) and radio (20% of the advertising budget). Advertising messages were essentially "mexicanized" versions of effective advertisements running in the United States. References to the origin of the products were usually included in an attempt to capitalize on the status bestowed upon American brands by the Mexican market. A historical review of product performance (sales) in Mexico for 1980–1983 is depicted in Exhibit 1.

**EXHIBIT 1**    Product line sales for 1980–1983 (in U.S. dollars).

|  | 1980 | % of Mkt | 1981 | % of Mkt | 1982 | % of Mkt | 1983 | % of Mkt |
|---|---|---|---|---|---|---|---|---|
| A. Liquid Spray (totals) | $51,000 | 33 | 55,000 | 36 | 41,000 | 29 | 27,000 | 22 |
| aerosol | 17,000 | 11 | 19,000 | 12 | 14,000 | 10 | 9,000 | 07 |
| spray pump | 22,000 | 14 | 24,000 | 16 | 18,000 | 13 | 13,000 | 11 |
| spray foam | 12,000 | 08 | 12,000 | 08 | 9,000 | 06 | 5,000 | 04 |
| B. Liquid concentrate (totals) | $102,000 | 21 | 115,000 | 24 | 98,000 | 21 | 80,000 | 18 |
| regular, pine | 27,000 | 05 | 30,000 | 06 | 25,000 | 05 | 21,000 | 05 |
| regular, fresh | 13,000 | 03 | 15,000 | 03 | 13,000 | 03 | 10,000 | 02 |
| economy, pine | 43,000 | 09 | 48,000 | 10 | 42,000 | 09 | 35,000 | 08 |
| economy, fresh | 19,000 | 04 | 22,000 | 05 | 18,000 | 04 | 14,000 | 03 |

**EXHIBIT 2**    Peso–dollar exchange values.

| YEAR | EXCHANGE RATE |
|------|---------------|
| 1976–1979 | 22.5–1 |
| 1980 | 25 –1 |
| 1981 | 25/27–1 |
| 1980—July | 49 –1 |
| Sept. | 70 –1 |
| Dec. | 150 –1 |
| 1983 | floating |

Tom McGuire had blamed the unexpected peso devaluations as the major factor contributing to reduced product sales. While targeting the product lines to the middle-to-upper class segments of the market, the government's decision to nationalize the banking industry and to convert all dollar accounts to peso accounts in 1982 further affected purchasing patterns. Rectos Comerciantes had reported an apathetic attitude among consumers toward product testimonials. A depressed economy and an inflated currency had introduced a market predisposition to "generic" brands—with more emphasis being given to price versus quality or image. A historical summary of peso devaluations for 1980–1983 is presented in Exhibit 2.

Tom realizes that his foreign venture needs to improve sales performance in order to generate desired return-on-equity. He is confident about the success potential of the All Purpose Cleanser line in the Mexican market. It is imperative that the company find a proper combination for the product mix, advertising, and pricing.

Tom is currently wondering whether to reposition the product lines or reduce the retail prices to match the local brands. Additionally, he is questioning the market strategy employed in Mexico; should distribution be modified or should the target market be re-defined? To complicate things further, Tom must decide on the feasibility of marketing the additional detergent and dishwashing line in 1986. Tom feels he must also review the joint venture contract with Rectos Comerciantes—specifically, if the partnership remains in the best interest of the corporation.

*Demographic:*    The total population figure, according to the 1980 census, is approximately 69,902,000 inhabitants. The population growth rate has decreased from 3.6% in 1975 to 2.9% in 1980—the result of a governmental plan encouraging family planning. Yet, the government is striving to attain a 1% population growth rate by the year 2000.

Exhibits 3 and 4 provide an overview of Mexico's demographic profile. The country is increasingly urban. In 1960, 49.3% of the population

**EXHIBIT 3**   Total population breakdown by sex for 1970, 1980, and 1990 (estimated).

| YEAR | MALE | FEMALE | TOTAL |
|---|---|---|---|
| 1970 | 25,584,800 | 25,109,800 | 50,694,600 |
| 1980 | 35,260,700 | 34,641,300 | 69,902,000 |
| 1990 | 44,107,800 | 43,380,900 | 87,488,700 |

*Source:* Mexico Demografico, Consejo Nacional de Poblacion, Mexico, Circular de Morelia
No. 8, Mexico 7, D.F., pp. 9–69.

were rural and 50.7% were urbanites. In 1970, 41.3% lived in rural areas
and 58.7% were urbanites. The 1980 census estimated a 34.3% rural to
65.7% urban proportion.

It was estimated that by 1977, more than 18 million inhabitants (approximately 27% of the population) were concentrated in three metropolitan
areas: Mexico City with 14 million inhabitants; Guadalajara with 2.5 million;
and Monterrey with 2.1 million inhabitants. The life expectancy rate in 1979
was 66 years for women and 62 years for men.

*Social:*   The official language is Spanish, although there exist at least
seven indigenous dialects spoken in rural Mexico. The average per capita
income for 1979 (latest figure) was $1,640 US. The social income structure
is approximately proportioned as shown in Exhibit 5.

Primary education (up to sixth grade) is obligatory and free. Historically, the illiteracy rate in urban Mexico has decreased from 20.2% in 1960
to 15.2% in 1970. The illiteracy rate in rural Mexico has also decreased but
at a slower rate from 47.5% in 1960 to 36.5% in 1970. Consequently, the
latest census showed that illiterate women had an average of 7.3 children
versus 3.2 children borne by women with some scholastic education.

**EXHIBIT 4**   1979 population breakdown by age and sex (millions).

| AGE | MALE | FEMALE | TOTAL |
|---|---|---|---|
| 4 yrs–9 yrs | 11,113 | 10,754 | 21,867 |
| 10–19 | 8,302 | 7,997 | 16,299 |
| 20–29 | 5,634 | 5,449 | 11,083 |
| 30–39 | 3,643 | 3,602 | 7,245 |
| 40–49 | 2,460 | 2,494 | 4,954 |
| 50–59 | 1,558 | 1,635 | 3,193 |
| 60–69 | 867 | 941 | 1,808 |
| 70 and over | 679 | 775 | 1,454 |
| | 34,256 | 33,647 | 67,903 |

*Source:* México Demográfico, Consejo Nacional de Población, México, Circular de Morelia
No. 8, México 7, D.F., pp. 9-69.

**EXHIBIT 5**   1978 income distribution.

| PERCENTAGE OF POPULATION | PERCENTAGE OF TOTAL INCOME |
|---|---|
| Top 10% | 27% |
| Top Middle 20% | 43.5% |
| Lower Middle 20% | 14% |
| Lowest 50% | 15.5% |

While women had traditionally been discouraged from entering male-dominated professions, today women compete with men in all endeavors.

***Economic:***   The official Mexican currency is the peso, which has been floating on the free market since 1976 producing a series of monetary devaluations. However, Mexico's strong commitment to industrial growth continues to attract foreign investment. Furthermore, the Mexican government maintains a favorable disposition to foreign investors.

Mexico's economy depends on agricultural production, mineral extractions, industrial production (including petroleum) and the communication and transportation industries. The country's main source of revenues is the state-owned petroleum industry which has a status of fourth largest oil producer in the world. In 1982, the petroleum industry supplied approximately $15 billion in export revenues, making the industry the country's most delicate and protected economic resource.

***Political:***   Mexico is a federal republic whose democratic government is similar in structure to that of the United States. Mexico has 31 states and a federal district (Mexico City) where the capital is located. The president of Mexico is elected directly by popular vote for a six-year term with no opportunity for re-election. The legislative branch consists of a House of Representatives (one per 200,000 inhabitants) and a Senate (32 members). The judicial system is comprised of a Supreme Court as well as federal and local courts.

There exist many political parties, however the two dominant ones are the PRI (Institutional Revolutionary Party) and the PAN (National Revolutionary Party). In any event, every candidate for the presidency has been nominated by the incumbent president of the Republic and approved by the ruling PRI. Hence, as the dominant coalition for the past 53 years, the PRI has remained undefeated—a contribution to governmental stability.

***Cultural:***   The Mexican culture is rich in heritage and boasts renowned patriots, artists, humanists, intellectuals, scientists and technicians. It is therefore not surprising to encounter strong nationalistic and patriotic attitudes among Mexicans.

Essentially, the culture is very traditional due in part to the fact that 94% of the population are of strong Catholic faith. This culture strongly attributes that which cannot be explained by fate as acts of God. They, in effect, believe themselves to have only limited control over the course of their individual lives.

Although changing somewhat, the household is predominantly male-dominated. The female still plays the traditional mother/housewife role while the male is the sole provider of income; this limits expenditures to "essentials."

Daily visits to the neighborhood "mercado" and "tienda" are still predominant although upper and middle class families are more likely to patronize chain supermarkets (which are not always centrally located).

Daily household duties include: sweeping and mopping; general cleaning; clothes washing and dish washing (both mostly done by hand). Great pride is taken in performing household duties. It is considered an enjoyable task and is regarded as a reflection of personal and familial hygiene.

## QUESTIONS

1. Evaluate each of the following:
   a. Progressive Food's foreign market entry strategy.
   b. Rectos Comerciantes' distribution system with respect to the Mexican target market.
   c. Advertising messages used in Mexico.
   d. Pricing strategy 1980–83.
2. Assume you are Tom McGuire. What course of action would you take? Support your strategy.

A Supplement on the Mexican
Market

# chapter 13

# PROMOTION DECISIONS FOR INTERNATIONAL MARKETING

You cannot know the subtleties of consumers' preferred media from a 24-hour visit to an overseas market. Neither can your agency unless it has been in—and has worked in—each country over a period of time.

You've got to work with your local marketing or salespeople to really know the local media peculiarities that exist. (Quirks to American, but "obvious" to a local marketing man/woman.) Some markets are strong on TV—yet available time is incredibly tight.

You give them the commercial; they tell you that, "When it appears, it will appear." It can be at 2:00 A.M., mixed in with six or 10 other TV commercials run back-to-back. That is the government's TV ad policy. (In some countries, all of your advertising—theme, copy, and visuals—must be approved by government agencies.)

Other countries (often those with lower literacy rates) may be called "poster" media countries. But there are no hard-and-fast rules. You've got to know your territory, and you can't know your target country from examining the local media catalogue pages while sitting in your office in New York, Chicago, or Los Angeles.*

· · ·

The advertising manager faced with launching a campaign in Europe is immediately struck by the enormous fragmentation of the media.

He quickly recognizes the major points: their structures vary from country to country. Readership and circulation data, when available, come from a variety of unrelated sources. Circulations from large markets, like

*Richard Manville, "33 Caveats for the Prospective Overseas Marketer," *Marketing News,* March 10, 1978, p. 7. Published by the American Marketing Association.

Germany and France, often overlap into smaller markets, like Belgium and Austria.

The only way to handle these and other problems is through systems that capitalize on similarities, where they exist, without neglecting national and regional variation. It has helped immeasurably in assuring our clients the greatest reach for their advertising budgets.**

## INTRODUCTION

Promotion is the communication function of marketing. By providing information about a product or service to potential users, it focuses demand upon a particular item or brand and thus stimulates buyer action. In the case of new users it helps arouse latent demand for an untried or unfamiliar product. This communication activity is a necessary part of the distribution of products from producers to users in all societies. The socialist central planner finds it just as necessary as does the capitalist entrepreneur, to inform potential users of the existence and availability of his or her product.

A wide variety of promotion tools are available to the marketing planner. These include advertising in its various forms and media; personal selling via direct contact between buyers and sellers; displays for examining products at a point of purchase or in other convenient places; packaging that provides product identification and convenience of handling; direct mail; and special promotions of various types. These numerous promotion tools are not equally available or effective in all cultures and societies, so the international marketer often finds it necessary to adapt the promotional mix to each market served. Thus, a marketer may find television to be a very useful advertising medium in one country, but totally unavailable in a second country where television programming is controlled by the government. In a third country, commercial television may be available, but the audience the marketer wishes to reach may not have access to television.

In this chapter we will look at each of the promotion tools just mentioned. Since promotion is communication, we first center on the communication process and identify areas of possible failure in international communication. Next, we look at the role of advertising as a promotion tool in different countries, and the difficulties in developing advertising messages. Media and their variations in foreign markets are the next topics, followed by issues that affect the choice of advertising agencies for international markets. Next we discuss the unique problems associated with managing and motivating sales personnel in foreign markets. Last, we review some

**Jo Lhoest, "A Systematized Approach to Media Selection in European Markets," *Industrial Marketing*, October 1975, p. 77.

of the special promotion tools, such as trade fairs, that are effective in specific markets abroad.

## THE COMMUNICATION PROCESS

The communication process is usually described as a sequence of activities that takes place in a common environment. The simplest explanation of this process involves only three inputs: source, message, and receiver.[1] In the first stage, the source originates or composes the message; in the second stage, the source transmits the message so that it moves within the reception range of the receiver; and in the third stage, the receiver picks up the message. More sophisticated explanations of the communications process acknowledge an encoding step before and a decoding step after message transmission to ensure that the message sent is the same as the message received. These explanations also identify a channel or medium as the means of transmission, and they recognize the existence of noise or interference in the communication process. Noise may preclude receipt of a message, or may result in receipt of a garbled message. It includes other demands on the attention of the receiver and conflicting information or claims by producers of competitive products. Today we also recognize the importance of feedback to the communications process—when the receiver seeks additional information about a message or clarifies its meaning.

When this communication process takes place in more than one environment, it becomes much more complex. First of all, the message itself may have to be changed because the foreign buyer may not be motivated to buy the marketer's products for the same reasons as the domestic buyer. Figure 13–1 illustrates a situation in which communication does not take place between source and receiver because of a breakdown at some point in the processes of encoding, transmission, and decoding. In the encoding process the sender may be unable to express a thought precisely because of a lack of familiarity with language and/or culture. A classic example of a translating error was the General Motors slogan "Body by Fisher": in Flemish, the phrase became "Corpse by Fisher" when decoded by recipients. Similarly, the interpretation of a message by receivers may be af-

**FIGURE 13–1**  Communication failure in different environments.

[1]See E. Crane, *Marketing Communications* (New York: John Wiley, 1965), p. 11.

fected by their reaction to the method of transmission. Newspapers, which may be considered reliable sources of information in one nation, may be considered an unrealiable source in another nation. There must be some overlap between the source and the receivers' experiences and communication patterns before communication can take place. The circles in Figure 13–1 are separate, indicating no overlaps between source and receiver.

In order for communication to take place between different environments, the marketer must provide a bridge between them. Figure 13–2 illustrates an intercultural communication process. A bridge can be created when there is proper encoding, transmission, and decoding of a message as well as a channel for feedback. The key to bridge building is the ability of the source to understand the cultural frame of reference of potential receivers. The source must be able to span the two environments in which the communication process takes place. Unfortunately, many international marketers do not recognize the need for such bicultural expertise and the result is communication failure. The biggest danger for the international marketer is not the complete failure of communication as illustrated in Figure 13–1, but inaccurate communication; a garbled message may do more harm than no message at all.

Language is the most common way that we use to encode messages. It is possible to convey a message on a purely visual basis without the use of language symbols, but in most cases language must be a part of the total communication, even when the message is predominantly visual. In addition to being a communication tool, language shapes people's thought patterns. People think somewhat differently about the same topic in different languages.[2] It should be apparent that translating an idea into a foreign language risks the possibility that a totally different message will be "heard" by receivers. Although it is only one of the hazards of developing effective international communication strategies, message development is perhaps the most critical element. Any one of the components of communication shown in Figure 13–2 can be a source of misunderstanding. You can see some other examples of classic international communication failures in Figure 13–3.

**FIGURE 13–2** Effective communication in different environments.

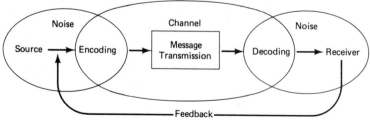

[2]Adon Almoneez, "Intercultural Communication and the MNC Executive," *Columbia Journal of World Business,* Winter 1974, p. 23.

**FIGURE 13–3**  Examples of international communication failure.

| MESSAGE SENT | MESSAGE RECEIVED (LANGUAGE OR COUNTRY IN PARENTHESES) |
|---|---|
| "Body by Fisher" | "Corpse by Fisher" (Flemish) |
| "Come Alive with Pepsi" | "Come Alive out of the Grave" (German) |
| "Schweppes' tonic water" | "Schweppes' Bathroom Water" (Italian) |
| "Put a Tiger in your Tank" | "Put a weakling in your tank" (Man is always superior to animals in Thailand) |
| "Rendezvous lounges" (for U.S. airline) | "Rooms for lovemaking" (Brazil) |
| Cue toothpaste | . . . pornographic word in French |
| "Cleans the really dirty parts of the wash" | "Cleans your private parts" (French Canada) |
| Boy and girl shown discussing how Listerine cures bad breath | Public portrayal of boy-girl relationships is objectionable (Thailand) |
| Green used on packages of water recreation products | Green is symbol of the jungle with its dangers and diseases (Malaysia) |
| "Don't go wild—just enough is all you need of BiNoca talc"—shown with apparently nude woman | considered indecent and publicly distasteful (India) |
| Coin giveaway marked "$1 billion" | considered symbol of pompous U.S. superiority of firm (Germans use DM to denote their money) |

*Source:* David Ricks, Marilyn Y. C. Fu, and Jeffrey S. Arpan, *International Business Blunders,* rev. ed. (Columbus, Ohio: Grid, Inc., 1982).

## ADVERTISING IN INTERNATIONAL MARKETING

Advertising is a major communication tool for the marketer. Although it often plays a minor role in marketing industrial goods, it is an important part of the promotional mix in the marketing of many consumer goods. Even so, attitudes toward advertising are not always favorable. Even in the United States, the leading user of advertising in the world, some consumers suspect that advertisers are manipulating them; and classical economists and other groups view advertising as unproductive and hence a wasteful addition to the cost of goods. In many other nations, these negative views of advertising are more strongly held and by broader and more influential segments of the population. For example, the World Health Organization of the United Nations has issued directives covering the distribution and marketing of pharmaceuticals, in the belief that advertising has contributed to overconsumption.[3] They have also investigated the promotional practices of baby-formula manufacturers, prompted by publicity that

[3] "Anti-Advertising Movement Worldwide, I.A.A. Head Says," *Advertising Age,* 43 (September 25, 1972), 68.

accused Nestlé of contributing to infant deaths in less-developed nations. The International Association of Advertisers has found it necessary to promote industry self-regulation as a defense against attacks from legislators and consumerists throughout the world. Smaller nations also view advertising as a tool for imperialistic economic penetration by large economic powers. Reflecting this fear, three Latin American nations—Venezuela, Chile, and Peru—have mandated 80 percent local ownership for all advertising agencies.[4] The marketer from a highly developed nation, who is accustomed to acceptance of advertising so long as the message is responsibly presented, must carefully reevaluate the role of advertising as a part of the promotional mix in other nations, especially when advertising plays a different role in the economy.

### Advertising and Levels of Economic Development

The more highly developed nations are clearly the heaviest users of advertising.[5] As you can see in Figure 13–4, the nations where advertising spending is highest tend to be industrial, highly developed economies. United States advertisers by far outspend those in other countries. With the exceptions of Brazil, Australia, and Japan, the countries with the highest per-capita expenditures are European or North American.

The importance of all promotional activities, and of advertising in particular, tends to increase as the complexity of a society and the size of its population increase.[6] As the physical and social distance between producers and their prospective customers widen, producers find it necessary to formalize communication efforts. Advertising is less important in simple societies because less-sophisticated methods of communication, such as word-of-mouth, are effective in reaching the total market. In addition, in less-developed countries the range of available advertising media is limited. Print media may reach only a portion of the population, as a result of widespread illiteracy. Television may be publicly owned and not available as an advertising medium; or if available, it may reach only the small portion of the population that can afford to buy a television receiver.

In light of the varying perceptions and acceptance of advertising in different nations, as well as the variations in advertising effectiveness at different stages of economic development, the marketer must carefully review the role of advertising in the promotion mix for each new market. If international firms follow guidelines established in highly developed coun-

---

[4]Ibid.

[5]Noorami Hafetz, "Third World View of Ad Spending," *Advertising Age,* April 9, 1979, p. 50.

[6]"Ad Growth Mirrors Rise in World Living Standards," *Advertising Age,* April 21, 1980, pp. 136–39.

**FIGURE 13–4**   Leading advertising nations of the world, 1977.

| COUNTRIES | TOTAL MEASURED MEDIA ADVERTISING[a] | RANK |
|---|---|---|
| Argentina | 382.2 | 15 |
| Australia | 1,186.4 | 8 |
| Austria | 306.9 | 18 |
| Belgium | 295.4 | 20 |
| Brazil | 1,610.9 | 7 |
| Canada | 1,699.8 | 6 |
| Denmark | 444.6 | 14 |
| Finland | 380.7 | 16 |
| France | 1,720.0 | 5 |
| Italy | 648.7 | 10 |
| Japan | 4,779.0 | 2 |
| Mexico | 298.3 | 19 |
| Netherlands | 1,031.0 | 9 |
| Norway | 376.3 | 17 |
| Spain | 551.3 | 11 |
| Sweden | 532.8 | 13 |
| Switzerland | 550.4 | 12 |
| United Kingdom | 2,568.3 | 4 |
| United States | 25,209.0 | 1 |
| West Germany | 3,148.9 | 3 |

[a]In millions of U.S. dollars.

*Source:* "1977 Ad Expenditures in 50 Countries," *Advertising Age,* March 24, 1980, p. 39.

tries, they might find in less-developed countries that they are overadvertising—spending far too much money to reach a very small portion of the market. Or, discouraged by the inability to adapt domestic advertising programs to new markets, international marketers may ignore different advertising opportunities and advertise at less-than-optimal levels.[7]

### The Advertising Message

When a firm launches its first advertising campaign in a foreign market, the natural inclination is to choose themes and messages which have been most successful in the domestic market and to apply them directly, with language translation as required, to the new markets. However, this policy of adaptation offers many potential pitfalls. For a number of reasons, successful campaigns may not travel well to new environments.

*Translation problems.*   The most successful advertising messages frequently rely on the turn of a particular word or two—a precise meaning

---

[7]For an interesting discussion of this problem, see Nathaniel H. Leff and John U. Farley, "Advertising Expenditures in the Developing World," *Journal of International Business Studies,* Fall 1980, pp. 64–73.

that allows an attention-getting play on words. Such messages may not be directly translatable at all, or if translatable they lose the impact of the unique play on words. The following examples illustrate this point.

"The Difference Will Floor You."—Perk floor wax.

"Be a Good Egg."—illustration of a present in an Easter basket.

"Isle to Aisle, from Island Hopping to Weekend Shopping"—Foley's Department Store.

"Sweet Nothings by Maidenform"—illustrating brief lingerie.

People react to messages in terms of their cultural background. The Virginia Slims campaign based on the phrase "You've Come a Long Way, Baby" has been successful in the American market because it identifies with changes in women's roles and the feminist movement. In societies where feminism has made little or no headway, or in societies where women have historically had greater rights, this particular campaign would be perceived as meaningless at best, or even as threatening to traditional cultural values. Many other cultural factors can affect perceptions of advertising messages in foreign markets: conformity versus individualism, conservatism versus a desire for change, social stability versus social mobility, credibility versus suspicion. For example, Australians value individuality more than do Americans; the British respond to products with a "heritage" more than ones that are "new and improved"; and the average German is suspicious of all advertising because of a fear of being cheated.

*Consumer education.* In any environment, advertising plays both persuasive and informational roles as part of a firm's promotion mix. In international marketing, the informational role takes precedence because the firm is introducing a new product concept, not just a new brand, to the foreign market. This is especially true in less-developed countries. When Coca-Cola International was establishing bottling plants in India during the 1940s and 1950s, it not only had to introduce Coke to Indians, but few people at that time knew how to drink out of bottles. Their advertising had the dual function of educating consumers and creating brand preference. Even in more sophisticated markets, consumer education through ad messages can be the critical element in overall marketing success. Campbell's neglected to explain to British consumers why its smaller soup cans cost more than the larger ones of competitors; the firm did not realize until too late that Britons were unfamiliar with condensed canned soups.

*Individual versus multinational approaches.* In spite of differences in language, culture, and consumer product knowledge that would seem to require the tailoring of advertising messages to each market, some marketers have successfully used a standard message in a wide variety of foreign markets. Both Coca-Cola and Pepsi Cola have almost literally translated messages designed for the American market and used these ads, otherwise unchanged, in many foreign markets. Coke has even taken successful foreign slogans ("La chispa de la vida") and adapted them for use in the U.S. ("Coke Adds Life"). Exxon's "Put a Tiger in Your Tank" advertisement was used very successfully in many different nations, although it was not as effective in Thailand where the tiger is a symbol of fear and jungle dangers rather than of power. Scottish manufacturers of scotch whiskey have used identical ads, except for language translation, in a number of foreign markets. Producers of other liquors and vermouth have also been successful using a multinational approach to their advertising.

The important question is, when will a multinational approach work and when are individually tailored messages necessary? First, the message itself must be very simple in order to be easily translatable into different languages and environments. Heavy reliance is often placed on visual messages. In fact, some successful multinational ads are essentially nonverbal, using only the trade name and essential information such as price and retail location. In addition, the multinational advertisement must deal with consumption patterns that are basically similar across cultures. Thus, although the number of consumers of soft drinks and liquors may vary considerably from nation to nation, the basic motivation and reasons for brand selection are pretty similar among users everywhere. And again, although the number of automobile owners varies widely in different countries, the motives of these owners in buying gasoline are similar.

However, the motives for buying the automobile itself are widely different in different countries, and automobile advertising must be tailored to appeal to the needs of each market. Therefore, when a product satisfies the same needs, is used in similar ways, but has the same buyer motivation, and when the message is simple and translatable, one message can be used effectively in all markets. When multinational ads are used, they provide savings in the production and design of advertising messages as well as a stronger international identity. However, for advertising to be effective, in the majority of cases it must be designed or adapted to meet the unique needs of each new market. Most multinational corporations first try to explore the possibilities of using an ad internationally, before developing unique messages for each market.

## INTERNATIONAL MEDIA DECISIONS

The larger and more complex the society is, the wider is the choice of advertising media available to the marketer. In the simplest, least-developed societies, the choice of usable media may be limited to radio or newspapers. Although most nations have some type of newspapers, if the level of illiteracy is very high, their readership may be restricted to a small economic elite. To reach the masses through advertising, the only media historically available have often been handbills, sidewalk posters, and billboards—and these could only be used with visual, nonlinguistic messages. In recent years, with the development of the very inexpensive transistor radio, the radio medium has changed from a channel for reaching only the economic elite to a mass medium in even the most underdeveloped countries. Today it is estimated that over 90 percent of the world's population has access to at least one radio.

## Print Media

The importance of printed media depends directly on the level of literacy of a population and the target market in each country. In general, the more developed nations are the heavy users of printed media advertising. Figure 13–5 shows the ten leading advertising nations in the world in terms of three media: print, television, and radio. Eight of the ten leading advertisers in terms of total expenditures shown in Figure 13–4, are also among the ten leading users of print media. The large, highly developed nations also have the highest levels of literacy and the greatest availability of print media. Except for Latin America where television advertising is heavy, the print media account for the largest share of ad expenditures in most countries of the world. Nevertheless, the reach that can be obtained varies from country to country.

Newspapers provide access to different groups of the population in different countries. Some nations, such as Britain and Japan, have one or more newspapers with truly national circulation; other nations, such as the United States, have mostly newspapers with local or regional appeal. Local newspapers serve primarily as a medium for local advertisers, because the job of reaching the national market through a number of local papers is a complex and expensive one.

**FIGURE 13–5**   Heaviest advertisers by media, in 1977.

| Rank | *ADVERTISING EXPENDITURES[a] IN 1977* | | | | | |
|---|---|---|---|---|---|---|
| | *Print* | | *Television* | | *Radio* | |
| 1 | U.S.A. | 14,605 | U.S.A. | 7,612 | U.S.A. | 2,734 |
| 2 | W. Germany | 2,485 | Japan | 2,218 | Brazil | 338 |
| 3 | Japan | 2,256 | U.K. | 702 | Japan | 305 |
| 4 | U.K. | 1,710 | Brazil | 697 | Canada | 253 |
| 5 | France | 972 | W. Germany | 386 | France | 185 |
| 6 | Canada | 936 | Canada | 353 | Australia | 111 |
| 7 | Netherlands | 860 | Australia | 340 | W. Germany | 109 |
| 8 | Australia | 594 | France | 280 | Italy | 57 |
| 9 | Sweden | 495 | Mexico | 202 | Spain | 53 |
| 10 | Brazil | 483 | Spain | 158 | Argentina | 51 |

[a]In millions of dollars.

*Source:* "1977 Ad Expenditures in 50 Countries," *Advertising Age*, March 2, 1980, p. 39.

In places like Mexico City, where there are over fifteen local dailies, it can be difficult to reach a large portion of the local market without incurring high costs per thousand (CPM). As a result advertising costs often vary from country to country for equivalent market coverages. Unfortunately, readership data are not always monitored by independent agencies, as in the U.S., and reader demographics are nonexistent. All these factors combine to make advertisers dependent on good sources who really know the local environment and market. Nevertheless, nationally circulated newspapers in general provide a good medium for reaching a broad national market. In those nations where such newspapers are not available, advertisers must turn to other nationally circulated printed media, mainly magazines.

Magazines do not have nearly as broad a readership as newspapers. They often attract different segments of the population according to their subject matter and emphasis. Even though magazines provide a less-expensive way of reaching specific segments of the market than do newspapers, these segments may not correspond to the firm's target market in that country. For example, magazines such as *Time* and *Cosmopolitan* have international editions and are often translated into the major language of different national markets. As such, they would appear to be good ways to reach multiple markets through one vehicle, but the problem with this approach is that their appeal is often geared toward international travellers or the local elite—people more interested in international events and trends than in local ones. These groups usually do not comprise a large sement of local consumers. The data on magazine circulation and demographics in international markets are perhaps more difficult to acquire than for newspapers. In general it could be said that magazines are an effective mass-market medium in only the most highly developed and literate countries of the world.

### Television

Television is best available as a medium in the wealthier countries, because the cost of a receiver to the individual consumer is too high to allow broad coverage in less-developed countries. Television viewing in less-developed countries is likely to be a group activity, if available at all. Group viewing, of course, improves TV's reach, but it still has a smaller audience than in advanced countries. Even in wealthier countries, the use of this medium may vary considerably from other media because of variations in the availability of commercial television. Some nations severely curtail the amount of television time available to advertisers, and other countries prohibit commercially sponsored programming altogether. Due to low market coverage and government prohibitions, TV ad expenditures rank below those for print media in most countries. Satellites have increased the amount of truly international television programming in recent years. In the future perhaps more governments will seek commercial sponsorship of programming as their costs increase and they are pressed to offer more variety and access to international programs.

### Radio

The leading radio advertisers in the world were also shown in Figure 13–5, and it is interesting to note that the major advertisers are pretty much the same no matter which of the major media are compared. Italy moved into the top ten of radio advertisers, just as Mexico and Argentina moved into the top ten in television advertising. Yet, these, too, are nations that would be classified as relatively advanced.

Radio is a limited medium in that it appeals only to the auditory senses. The old maxim that a picture is worth a thousand words is often true, and the radio advertiser is frequently frustrated in the inability to get a message across completely in this limited medium. A soft-drink advertiser may get ten times the impact from a picture of a frosty drink than from an oral reminder that the listener may be thirsty. For this reason, in those nations where a large enough audience of television viewers is available to justify the high costs of the medium, television has supplanted radio in the advertising of many products. Still, radio has the advantage of broad coverage. If the economic situation of a firm's target market is limited, or if it is marketing a product in a low per-capita-income country, radio, even with its message limitations, may still be the best medium to reach the market.

### Posters and Billboards

Posters and billboards are an important medium in metropolitan areas where they can have an impact on large numbers of prospective customers. Although the cost of space in central-city locations may be high, the visual impact and the numbers of viewers reached may also be high. In nations with a high proportion of automobile ownership, highway billboards are an effective medium. In many cities around the world, posters represent a useful outdoor medium when placed at eye level on buildings and other structures in areas of heavy pedestrian traffic. All of the outdoor advertising media heavily emphasize illustrations and pictures with a minimum use of language, and for this reason are equally useful in developed and less-developed countries.

An important medium in some urban areas is "car cards," which are ads placed in mass transportation vehicles and at stations in urban areas, where the passengers represent a captive audience. Examination and readership of these ads is perhaps higher than for any other medium because the readers have little else to do with their time while travelling or waiting to travel. In areas where mass transportation is used heavily, this is an important mass medium.

### Cinema Advertising

A medium many U.S. firms overlook in foreign markets is cinema ads. Movies are a popular form of entertainment in most countries of the world, and in some countries it is standard practice to subsidize the costs of showing movies by accepting advertising that is shown before or after the main feature. A real advantage of cinema ads is that the message is not subject to the time limits of television or radio, or to the space limits of the print media. In addition, the audience usually is less distracted than when exposed to other media. India has the highest per-capita movie attendance of any country in the world, and consequently, cinema ads in India give broad exposure to market segments that are almost inaccessible through other media. Although cinema advertising is new in the U.S. and is not yet popular with advertisers, it can be an important medium in other countries.

There are other specialized media available in various nations, and each has been designed to serve some unique advertiser and market need. The marketer must be familiar with the unique media available and design a media package that will give best access to the target market in each country.

## CHOOSING AN INTERNATIONAL AGENCY

Choosing an advertising agency to prepare messages and to select media is an important part of the firm's promotion mix in international marketing. For communication to be effective, the message must be meaningful within the context of the local culture. In addition, the agency must be familiar with the media available in foreign markets and with the methods of purchasing space in the selected media. Therefore careful consideration must be given to the choice of an agency in preparing a foreign market advertising plan. In the following section, we will discuss briefly the three alternative choices that a firm has and the strengths and weaknesses of each option.

The easiest, most comfortable alternative for the firm is to invite its local agency to design the advertising message and to contact media in the new market. In general, the local agency is already familiar with the firm's products, the overall image it is trying to project, and the firm's preferences in messages and media. However, lack of experience in the foreign market or culture can have disastrous results. The danger is not just that the agency's efforts will be ineffective; they could also establish a negative image for the product in the new market. While all the communication failures listed in Figure 13–3 cannot be blamed on choosing inexperienced advertising agencies, they do highlight the problems inherent in wholesale adaptation of domestic messages for foreign markets.

A second alternative is to select a large international agency that maintains offices in the major markets around the world.[8] Several of the large American agencies have had large international operations and foreign offices for many years. J. Walter Thompson, Young & Rubicam, Dentsu, McCann-Erickson, and Ted Bates & Co. rank among the largest advertising agencies in the world, with offices in most major capitals. Use of these international agencies provides the firm with continuity across more than one market, and makes it easier for the advertiser to project one common image in all markets. It is also easier to deal with one agency than with several, and thus to coordinate efforts across markets. The good international agencies try to provide a top level of local expertise in the markets they serve by using local nationals as copywriters and media experts. However, critics of these organizations say that their approach to advertising tends to reflect the advertising philosophy of the home office rather than the nations in which they are located. Consequently, there is not enough adaptation to local conditions. The trend in recent years has been for multinational agencies to acquire top-flight local firms whose talents and expertise are compatible with the domestic clients and with the orientation of the headquarters office. This has been the approach of Benton & Bowles, for example, who chose to follow their main clients abroad (Procter & Gamble, General Foods), rather than precede them in the risky world of foreign markets. Local talent plus international coordination may be best offered by these types of international agencies.

The third alternative is to work with local advertising agencies in each foreign market served, using the home country agency as a coordinator. This alternative, while more difficult to administer (because the advertising executives are required to work with account executives in each agency), has the advantage that the local agencies will recognize when to adapt message and media strategy to their own country with its unique mentality. When carefully chosen, these agencies can help to ensure that an optimal campaign will be launched in each market.[9] The number of foreign agencies is large and growing; local ad agencies in sixty-eight countries reported gross income on billings of $2.6 billion in 1978.[10]

Whatever agency structure is used in foreign markets, the firm must remain aware of its own responsibility to become familiar enough with each foreign market so that its managers will be able to make and approve final decisions. In such instances, the temptation is strong to allow foreign experts to make the final decisions about messages and media strategy; but

[8] "International Agency Veterans Welcome New Rivals," *Advertising Age,* vol. 41 (June 8, 1970), 1.

[9] "EMAD Unit Head Says International Advertising Done Best by Nationals," *Advertising Age,* vol. 40 (October 27, 1969).

[10] Craig Endicott, "Foreign Ad Expenditures Check U.S. Domination," *Advertising Age,* vol. 50, sec. 2 (April 9, 1979), p. 3–6.

in the final analysis, only the marketing and advertising executives in the home office know what is best for their overall marketing policy.

## PERSONAL SELLING
## IN INTERNATIONAL MARKETING

Personal selling is the most important promotional input for many international marketers. Advertising and some of the other promotional tools are particularly useful in the promotion of branded, packaged consumer goods. Yet, many of the consumer goods sold in less-developed countries are unbranded and must be sold to consumers by salespeople. In addition, a great many of the products sold internationally are industrial rather than consumer goods. Industrial buyers pay much less attention to advertising; they rely almost solely on information received from salespeople when making buying decisions. The extent of involvement with, and use of sales forces in foreign markets is, of course, dependent on the firm's foreign-market entry strategy, market objectives, and channels of distribution.

### Selecting Sales Personnel

Personal selling is carried out by people—the sales personnel who make the sales contacts and who close sales, the office backup personnel, the service and maintenance persons, and sales managers. When a marketer moves into a new national market, it may be necessary to hire and train each of these types of personnel, and they may have to be recruited from different sources. All sales and sales-connected personnel must be capable of performing their communication functions effectively. This means that the sales personnel must be completely conversant with the local language and purchasing customs, familiar with company product lines and policies, and how to sell effectively. Sales managers must understand the local culture and be able to communicate both with sales personnel and with the home office in their appropriate languages.

There are several sources of sales department personnel in new foreign markets. A logical source is local citizens, preferably people with sales experience. They would also need an understanding of the home office language in order to be able to understand company directives and correspondence and to communicate with top management. Since the supply of experienced sales personnel with facility in two specific foreign languages is likely to be very limited, the hiring company may have to provide training in one or both of these areas. The person's linguistic ability should have the higher priority, since it is easier to teach people to sell than to teach them a foreign language; but in some instances it may be necessary to provide instructions in both. A real advantage of tapping local sources of personnel is their built-in knowledge of local business customs, government-business relationships, and their possible contact with potential customers. In some countries, such as Mexico, there may be laws that limit hiring foreigners anyway, and a local salesforce lowers the firm's "foreign" profile in the country. For this reason, many firms seek out persons who have studied or lived abroad but who know the nuances of the local market and will help the firm to "fit in" there.

Another source of personnel is expatriates of the home office country who are permanent residents of the new market. These people would appear to understand both cultures and both languages, and should only have to learn the job skills and company policies. However, expatriates are likely to be very limited in numbers, and are not often trained in sales techniques. As a result, the firm's investment in training may be as high or higher than for other sources of personnel. A similar source is the cosmopolite from some other part of the world who is fluent in both required languages and has a facility for understanding different peoples and cultures. However, these individuals are also in limited supply, and may not have good potential as sales personnel.[11]

The remaining source of personnel is residents of the home office nation who are willing to work and live abroad, and who ideally have language skills and an understanding of the particular culture involved. If qualified people cannot be found with the language skills and understanding of the culture, they must be taught these things. Since few Americans are linguists, American firms are very likely to have to provide such instruction when using their own nationals. Language learning is time consuming and frustrating, and unless a high level of proficiency is achieved, the selling process will be badly handicapped. Firms may find this source most useful for filling sales management positions in the foreign country, because familiarity with home office procedures and the home country culture are essential at the managerial level. Use of home country personnel has one additional major limitation—it fortifies an image of foreignness in the new market. Many countries and their nationals resent foreign penetration or domination of their markets and show preference for local competitors, even to the extent of legislating against foreign firms. In such circumstances, the foreign firm that is run mostly by local nationals is perceived as less foreign and thus more acceptable.

## Management of Personal Selling

In order to develop an effective sales organization in a foreign country, the employer must understand the normal employer-employee roles and the expectations of employees in that country. Such relationships vary

[11]For criteria to use in selecting salespersons, see a basic source such as Richard R. Still, Edward W. Cundiff, and Norman A.P. Govoni, *Sales Management: Decisions, Strategies, and Cases*, 4th ed. (Englewood Cliffs, N.J.: Prentice-Hall, 1981).

considerably from country to country. The American model, which emphasizes the individual's ostensible control over his or her own destiny, is
completely alien in some societies. The American employee expects to be
rewarded according to performance and merit. He or she expects pay
based on merit, and promotion in accordance with performance relative to
other employees. In other societies, such as Japan, the employer-employee
relationship may be much like a family relationship—the employee expects
job security, seniority, and reward for loyalty. These issues were discussed
in Chapter 4. To be effective in a new culture, the employer must adapt
compensation and rewards to the expectations of employees in that
culture.

*Recruiting sales and management personnel.*    To the extent that a firm
uses its own nationals in foreign markets, it may be able to use the same
recruiting sources that would be used for domestic employees, except that
prospective employees with international marketing interests would be
sought. During this recruiting process, particular attention should be paid
to identifying any nationals from the foreign market who are studying in
the home country. These students, with an understanding of both nations
and both languages, are a uniquely valuable source of sales employees.

The majority of employees, however, must be recruited in the host
country's job market, and sources used by local employers should be
tapped. Depending upon the level of the job to be filled, these sources
might include recruiting of university or secondary-school graduates, use
of employment agencies or government bureaus, advertising in newspapers
and appropriate periodicals, and seeking the help of customers or
suppliers.

The criteria for selecting personnel may vary somewhat from one
country to another. In a country where job turnover is very low and employees tend to stay with one employer throughout their careers, recruiting
efforts will concentrate on young people first entering the job market. For
management-level jobs, particularly in foreign environments where diplo-
matic skills may be important, maturity may be an important selection criterion. Personal history information can be equally useful in different countries, although the factors most useful for predicting job performance may
vary. Some employers use psychological tests as one selection citerion,
but such tests are frequently not available in different languages, and in
any case, they may be culturally biased. The employer in a foreign market
will probably have to rely heavily on recommendations from people who
know the applicant and from former employers, if they are willing to discuss the prospect.

*Training sales and management personnel.*    The nature of the training
program will depend on the type of personnel hired. Home-country em-

ployees who will be sent abroad will need concentrated training in language and culture, and this training should probably be contracted to outside experts. All personnel will need training in salesmanship (unless they have prior selling experience), in company policies and procedures, in the product line and its operation and performance characteristics, and in local market conditions with respect to competition and potential customers. This training should be provided by company personnel. The length of the training program will depend on the situation. For example, a company selling a highly complex, technical product like computers will allocate more time to product training than a company selling packaged consumer goods.

*Compensating sales and administrative personnel.* Compensation is a particular problem for companies that use home-country personnel in foreign sales operations. If it is necessary to offer premium pay, special allowances, or hardship pay to persuade employees to move to a foreign assignment, it is also difficult to repatriate them because of the necessity of readjusting their pay downward. Repatriation can also be difficult for the employee and his or her family; this is especially true for the employee who has often had broad responsibilities in the overseas assignment and feels "unused" and unchallenged back at home. If a country uses both local and imported personnel, the premium pay necessary to attract the expatriate makes it necessary to offer widely varying pay for equal work, or to overpay the locals in relation to local competition.

Among employees hired in the local market, the primary goal of the compensation plan should be to attract and hold top people. Compensation levels should be at or slightly above the market level. Differential rewards should be provided for differential effort as in any good compensation plan. In addition, selling expenses should be considered in setting the compensation level, if they are not separately reimbursed.

*Motivating sales and management personnel.* Money is often a useful motivational device for sales personnel, especially in the United States. By providing special incentives or bonuses, an American employer may be able to persuade employees to concentrate their efforts in desired directions and to stimulate an above average level of performance. In contrast, Japanese and Middle Eastern sales reps have not been accustomed to the commission form of sales compensation. Nonmonetary factors (such as training programs, increased responsibilities, or job security) appear more effective in motivating their sales performance. Even in a purely domestic sales force, it is a mistake to rely solely on money as a means of motivation. In a foreign sales force it can be an even bigger mistake because of the impact of cultural factors. Foreign nationals may be strongly motivated by the opportunity to advance their position in the eyes of their peers, by increasing their sphere of influence within their own society, or by acquiring new information that expands their own concept of self-worth. The possibility of earning more money may have little effect on performance. The plan for motivating sales personnel must be very carefully adapted to the local culture if it is to succeed.

*Other management factors.*    Each society presents unique managerial challenges for the sales executive. Population mobility is one example. American employers are accustomed to moving employees to new locations—frequently at considerable distances from home—to achieve optimal market coverage for the firm. Such moves are an intrinsic part of promoting deserving individuals to greater responsibility and reward. Americans have become accustomed to accepting such moves as a necessary price of career progress. In many other nations, however, tradition and strong family ties make employees unwilling to move, and sometimes even hostile to the idea of moving. In such instances, the employer will have to learn to adjust to local mores and to achieve the firm's goals without transferring employees.

Job roles and sex roles also vary greatly among countries, and the foreign marketer must understand these differences. Twenty years ago, most American sales executives firmly believed they could not use women in outside selling jobs because customers would refuse to accept them. With the change in the role of women in the United States today, a number of women are operating successfully as outside sales executives. However, in many countries these roles are deemed highly inappropriate for women, and any attempt to use women for outside selling could be disastrous for the employer. No matter what an employer's opinions might be about the rights of women, such an employer cannot afford to promote social goals in a foreign nation that considers such goals unacceptable. The sales force is usually by far the most important promotional tool of the marketer abroad. It is also the most difficult tool to use because it requires a greater adaptation to the local environment than most other elements of the promotional mix.

## OTHER PROMOTION TOOLS

In terms of total effort and money, other promotional efforts are not nearly as important as advertising and personal selling; but for particular products and in specific situations, some other promotional inputs are critical to marketing success. The use of these inputs and their relative impacts vary widely among countries. Among the more important of these are branding, packaging, trade shows, point-of-purchase displays, and direct mail.

## Branding

Movement into foreign markets makes it necessary for the marketer to carefully reevaluate the brand name or names being used for the firm's products. Names that are highly satisfactory in the domestic market may turn out to be inappropriate in other markets, either because they are difficult to pronounce and remember, or because they take on undesirable new meanings in a different language. For example, the name *Cardiff* has an entirely different sound in French where it is pronounced Cardy. The Italian name *Ghirardelli* is difficult for English-speaking people to pronounce or remember. The same is true of many German, Japanese, and Indian names, which can prove to be tongue twisters in other languages. It can be even more difficult if a brand name is discovered to have a different or inappropriate meaning in another language. One of the most dramatic examples of such "second meanings" was the name *ENCO,* selected by Standard Oil Company of New Jersey to replace the brand name *ESSO,* which for legal reasons could not be used in all markets. ENCO, a mnemonic for Energy Company, was chosen with care to be easy to remember and pronounce in almost any language. After its introduction was well underway in the United States as a replacement for existing brand names, it was discovered that *ENCO* described a sewage disposal truck in Japan. The company had to start all over and eventually produced the name *EXXON* that now is used worldwide. Another example was Chevrolet's model Nova; the model name was initially used in Latin American markets until the company realized that it can mean *won't go* in Spanish.

The major brand decision to be made when a company enters foreign markets is whether to use a common international brand name, or to use a different name in each market. The common brand name provides a carry-over of the prestige and brand image already developed for a product in existing markets. This carry-over can be particularly important with major industrial products where the typical buyer may be well informed about products around the world. If a company like Texas Instruments should decide to enter a new foreign market, they would probably find that knowledgeable buyers of electronic circuitry in that nation were already familiar with their name. In such a case, use of the Texas Instrument name in the new market would be a definite advantage. The same would be true of highly technical and expensive consumer goods such as cameras. Buyers of expensive cameras would probably recognize the names of leading foreign manufacturers, and it would be an advantage to reach them under the existing name. Firms that market products such as personal-care items and film to highly mobile consumers could also benefit from use of a common brand name in all markets. However, with many routinely purchased consumer goods, the typical customer is not familiar with foreign brand names and could just as easily be attracted with a new name selected specifically for that country.

Using different brand names in each market allows the marketer to select names that are appropriate to each language and culture. Instead of being, at best, neutral in the new market, the individually chosen name can have positive connotations. In addition, if a firm decides to use a common international brand name, it may, like EXXON, still face the expensive and difficult task of changing its brand name in existing markets because the current name is inappropriate in the new markets. The firm must also not neglect the process of registering brands and trademarks in all markets where it intends to use them, as discussed in Chapter 7.

### Packaging

Packaging is an important promotional device for many routinely purchased, branded consumer goods. It provides recognition and tie-in with advertising, and in self-service outlets it can call attention to the product. Packaging also has the traditional functions of product protection, economizing in the handling and transportation of products, and as a provider of information to intermediaries and consumers. These functions may vary in importance from one national market to the next. There are varying preferences in packaging from one country to another, and the marketer must be aware of these when entering new markets. In a classic study, for example, it was pointed out that European homemakers have clearly different preferences in packaging[12]—they want to have more information about what is inside the package, more specifics on ingredients and instructions on use. Europeans want their packages to appear more durable, and they like packages that have secondary uses. They are accustomed to a greater emphasis on aesthetics in packaging. In other parts of the world, preferences may be quite different; consumers may prefer cheap, nondurable packaging because they do not want to pay for longer-lasting, more informative packages.

### Trade Fairs

Trade fairs provide a very important promotional medium for industrial and consumer goods in many parts of the world. Some of these fairs have been in operation for many decades, some are relatively new, but they all provide a unique opportunity for marketers to communicate with prospective customers about their products. Industrial-goods manufacturers do not normally have retail outlets available to display their goods. Their products are usually sold by sales representatives who call directly on prospective customers. But when the products are large and bulky, the salespeople cannot carry samples; they can only carry illustrations and written descriptions. Regularly scheduled industrial trade fairs provide the

[12]Ernest Dichter, "What's Inside? Tell the European Housewife What She Really Wants to Know," *Business Abroad,* June 1970, p. 27.

opportunity for manufacturers to display their products and for prospective buyers to examine products and compare them directly to competing ones. Although trade fairs are not held in every country in the world, they are held in most of the major industrial countries, and prospective buyers from smaller countries travel to these fairs in their regions. Marketers of industrial and consumer goods who plan to enter foreign markets should identify the nearest trade fairs and make certain that their products are represented. Though relatively less important for consumer goods, trade fairs can be an important way that consumers gather information about durable goods for later purchase decisions. For example, The Home Fair exhibition of home furnishings and appliances in Lima, Peru in August 1980 drew over one million visitors in a city of six million.

### Point-of-Purchase Displays

Retail displays and promotions can be a very important method of attracting the prospective buyer's attention to a product. They are particularly important in self-service stores, where the provision of extra shelf facing or a special counter display can have an enormous impact on sales volume. In every market, the firm has the task of persuading retailers to increase display efforts for its products by showing how such efforts will be profitable for both parties. The manufacturer's own sales force usually has this promotional responsibility. The firm should not assume that the only benefit it has to offer retailers is increased sales volume; in fact this may not even be of primary concern to small retailers with limited business or income goals. Point-of-purchase displays are often valued for the color and excitement they lend to a store. The manufacturer may also subsidize the store owner's costs for signs and pricing. Coca-Cola gets retailer support by providing coolers, tables and chairs, display stands, and other "freebies" that also happen to have the company's name on them. Especially in underdeveloped countries, the marketer has the challenging task of educating retail outlets in the effective use of displays and the potential benefits accruing therefrom.

The point-of-purchase display is a useful promotional device for consumer goods because it calls the attention of the prospective customer to the product through posters or mass displays. However, in retailing establishments where the opportunity for and the likelihood of pilferage is high, management is reluctant to put goods within easy reach of customers. Also, in those societies where the consumer expects to have the help of a sales clerk in making buying decisions, a display would be viewed as an unacceptable substitute for the clerk's recommendations. Furthermore, many sales promotions are legally restricted in different national markets. Radio Shack violated German law by giving away free flashlights as a premium; "freebies" are illegal in Germany.

### Direct Mail

Direct mail is another important promotional tool for industrial goods. It performs many of the same communication tasks in the industrial market that advertising performs in the consumer market. Well-designed letters to prospective customers inform them of new products or product improvements; they also describe special product features, and serve as a reminder of the company and its representatives between sales calls. This promotional input is available to marketers in every foreign market, since all nations provide some sort of mail service. Because reliability and cost of the mail service may vary, these factors must be taken into consideration when planning a direct-mail campaign. One of the major problems facing the direct-mail promoter in a new foreign market is the development of mailing lists. In a few countries, companies are available that will provide mailing lists by industry or type of business operation, for a fee; but in most countries the marketer will have to develop his or her own mailing list from such sources as chamber of commerce lists, classified directories, and lists of trade-fair registrants.

## SUMMARY

In every country, promotional inputs are necessary to communicate information about the firm and its products to prospective buyers. The same promotional inputs are potentially usable in any country, but variations in the local environment and peoples require adaptation of communication to local needs. Advertising is a potentially important promotional tool in every market, but variation in media and media access, and differences in cultural mores, require that advertising programs be evaluated with respect to the need for adaptation or revision. The agency for international advertising can be chosen from domestic, local, or international firms.

Personal selling is the most important promotional input in most markets, but the task of developing and managing a sales force varies enormously, and these factors, in turn, affect the end product—the sales message. Each of the other promotional inputs may vary according to the market in which they are applied—brand names may have to be changed; packaging may be expected to serve different functions; point-of-purchase displays may be more difficult to achieve. The important point for the international marketer to keep in mind is that, although promotional efforts must be adjusted to each market to achieve maximum impact, every effort should be made to coordinate and keep them as similar across markets as conditions permit.

## DISCUSSION QUESTIONS

1. Define the elements of a complete model of communication and describe how each affects the communication process.
2. Explain the causes of communication failure in international markets.
3. How does the role of advertising vary in different nations?
4. What are the arguments for and against the use of standardized advertising messages in world markets?
5. Name five countries where you would, and five where you would not, use print media to promote a product. Explain your choices.
6. Why is television most effective in advanced countries?
7. Describe the advantages and disadvantages of radio in foreign markets.
8. Why are billboards and cinema ads effective media in underdeveloped countries?
9. Compare the benefits and disadvantages of international versus local advertising agencies.
10. Why is the sales force more often adapted to local variations than is advertising in foreign markets?
11. Contrast home- and host-country persons as sales force personnel.
12. Describe how the sales training program must be adapted for foreign markets.
13. Discuss the differences in compensating and motivating Japanese and American sales personnel.
14. What factors affect branding and packaging decisions in international marketing?
15. Why are trade fairs used more frequently in foreign markets for both industrial and consumer goods?
16. What problems do international marketers face in the use of displays as promotion tools?

# CASE 14 THOMPSON RESPIRATION, INCORPORATED*

Thompson Respiration, Inc. has been in business for approximately twenty years. The corporation was formed to produce breathing aids and associated accessories to people rendered incapable of breathing for themselves by the polio epidemic of the early 1950's. Ralph Thompson is presently producing a positive pressure respirator called the "Mini-Lung". The distinctive characteristic of the Mini-Lung as opposed to an Iron-Lung, is that it is a positive pressure respirator as opposed to a negative pressure respirator. Thompson respirators are designed primarily for people needing permanent respiratory aid. The target market segments Thompson has specified for its products are polio patients and persons rendered incapable of breathing due to spinal injuries. Both of these segments could require breathing aid for the rest of their lives and Thompson sees its product as being capable of meeting this need. Since the 1950's, the incidence of polio has been on the decline around the world. Modern medicine, the Salk vaccine and surgery techniques have all but eliminated the crippling effects of this disease. Because of this, there did not seem to be any long term market potential for this segment and consequently Thompson was beginning to look elsewhere for potential sales. Spinal injuries, however, seem to be on the increase. While data on debilitating spinal injuries that result in respiratory collapse are scanty, the feeling on the part of Thompson was that these patients are the ones in the greatest need of the Thompson products. Thompson's present market is primarily domestic. No marketing program has been instituted to promote units, and as a result sales are made primarily in response to inquiries, referrals, word-of-mouth and doctor prescriptions. Some international sales have occurred but they are not the result of marketing effort; rather they were in response to inquiries received from abroad. Thompson's response to such inquiries is to send literature to the inquirer, no more, no less. Sales are consummated through aggressive efforts on the part of the person wishing to buy the respirator. Thus, at present, Thompson is not actively marketing its product anywhere in the world. In spite of this nonmarketing orientation, the firm has been relatively successful. The Mini-Lung sells for $8,000 to $10,000 and being the only mobile positive pressure respirator on the market that is capable of being carried on a wheelchair, patients seem quite willing to pay this price. Part of the problem with the Mini-Lung is that while the user is the ultimate consumer, the person making the purchasing decision is frequently a physician

*This case was prepared by Dr. Robert J. Hoover, Associate Professor of Marketing, Corpus Christi State University.

or inhalation therapist. Another problem that Ralph Thompson saw in expanding to the international market had to do with the lack of knowledge about spinal injuries outside the United States. Lastly, there was another problem concerning international expansion of Thompson. Most spinal injuries occur as a result of accidents such as falls or automobile related accidents. In cases where the patient has a need for a Mini-Lung, the accident site must be accessed quickly by emergency medical services. A person suffering respiratory arrest as a result of a spinal injury can only be expected to survive 7 to 8 minutes. Therefore competent and fast emergency rescue must be available in a country for patients to survive this critical period. Given these problems, Ralph wondered if expansion into the international market was viable.

## QUESTIONS

1. What sort of data sources would Ralph Thompson want to access prior to building an integrated marketing plan for his firm?
2. Develop a promotion plan for the Mini-Lung in Europe.
3. How should Thompson distribute his products in foreign markets?

# chapter 14

# DISTRIBUTION DECISIONS FOR INTERNATIONAL MARKETING

Nobuyoshi Tomizawa, fortyish and balding, owns a small grocery store near a park in the world's largest city.

Described by his customers as "kind" and "honest," Mr. Tomizawa certainly doesn't look like a bogeyman. Yet he, and millions of Japanese like him, have become the favorite whipping boys for overseas critics of the Japanese distribution system.

In general, the Japanese system encompasses a wide range of wholesalers, other middlemen and retailers that differ more in number than in function from their American counterparts. Here, however, such people abound. There is a myriad of tiny retail shops, and supplying goods to them is an even greater number of wholesalers, piled layer on layer, more than most Westerners would think necessary.

Under the Japanese system, soap, for example, may move through three wholesalers and a sales company after it leaves the manufacturer and before it reaches the retail outlet. A cotton dress made overseas travels from the foreign textile factory through a Japanese trading company, which usually has its own distributors or other middlemen, and thence to the shop. A steak is hauled from the livestock raiser to the consumer back and forth along a route that resembles moves in a Chinese-checkers game and often involves a dozen middlemen.

It's this complexity that frustrates foreigners. Says Charles Wilson, chairman of the small businessman's committee of the American Chamber of Commerce in Japan, "The system is so complicated that nobody can understand it unless they have a Japanese partner."*

## INTRODUCTION

Distribution from the marketer's viewpoint centers on two kinds of tasks: transfers of ownership and physical movement through time and space. Transfers of ownership or title are described under the heading *marketing channels* or *channels of distribution;* the second task is described under the heading of *physical distribution* or *logistics.* Each presents unique problems in the area of international marketing. The marketing channel traces the movement of ownership of or title to a product from the producer to the user or ultimate consumer, and it concerns all parties who actually take title to the goods as well as those who help to achieve the transfer of title. All of the parties engaged in this title transfer between the producer and the consumer are loosely described as middlemen. The other major area of distribution—physical distribution—is concerned with the physical and temporal movement of the goods, and includes transportation, handling, storage, and inventory control.

Clearly, the job of transportation alone is more complex at the international level due to the great physical distances that often separate producers and buyers. The cultural, legal, political, and business practice differences that are inherent in the environment of international marketing also complicate the process of developing a smooth transfer of goods from producer to ultimate buyer. This chapter focuses on the important issues that face a firm in its attempt to build a coherent plan for moving products and their ownership across international boundaries.

## MARKETING MIDDLEMEN

Middlemen are the marketing institutions that comprise the building blocks of the marketing channel. They include all institutions that take title to the goods as they pass through the channel. The ones that take title are called merchant middlemen. But the term *middlemen* also includes all institutions that aid in the transfer of title, even though they themselves may not take title; these are called agent middlemen.

*Kanabayashi, Masayoshi, "Marketing in a Maze: Japan's Complex Distribution System Hinders Foreign Companies' Efforts to Sell Goods There," *The Wall Street Journal,* May 3, 1978, p. 40. Reprinted by permission of Wall Street Journal, © Dow Jones & Company, Inc. All Rights Reserved.

## Wholesalers

Wholesalers are middlemen who sell to other middlemen or to industrial users, but not to consumers. They may buy from the producer or from other middlemen. In the complex channels necessary for the distribution of goods between nations, there are often several layers of middlemen (between the producer and the consumer or user) who sell to each other. These middlemen can be merchants, who take title; or agents, who do not take title.

*Merchant middlemen.*   These middlemen are called by several names; the most commonly used is wholesaler, but they may also be called jobbers, distributors, or trading companies. In fact, one of the peculiarities of international marketing is that middlemen using the same name, such as jobber or full-service wholesalers, may not perform the same marketing functions in different countries, or even in different regions of the same country. While the term *wholesaler* loosely describes a variety of merchant middlemen, there is considerable crossover in usage of the term. In the simpler marketing channels, the producer may sell through only one level of wholesaler, who, in turn, sells to retailers or direct to industrial users. The wholesalers who sell to retailers, particularly the small ones, are frequently called jobbers. Wholesalers who sell to industrial users are usually called industrial distributors. In longer, more complex channels, another layer of wholesaler—responsible for large regions or even nations—buys from the producer and sells to other small wholesalers. These wholesalers are sometimes called distributors.

At the international level, some very large wholesalers have an enormous impact on trade. These international wholesalers are usually described as trading companies. As early as the sixteenth and seventeenth centuries, the British East India Company operated with a monopoly of trade between India and certain other parts of the Far East and Great Britain. Subsequently, in the nineteenth century, the Hudson Bay Company developed trade between Canada and Great Britain. The most important trading companies in the modern market are the Japanese Sogo Shoshas. In 1975, the ten largest of these huge trading companies accounted for $155 billion in total revenue, or 56 percent of all Japanese exports and imports, and 30 percent of the country's gross national product.[1] Wholesalers of this size are frequently larger than many of the producers they represent, and in some lines they have even acquired production facilities of their own. A producer trying to enter a market dominated by such a wholesaler would find it almost impossible to penetrate the market without the wholesaler's cooperation. Likewise, retailers cannot ignore the power these trading

---

[1] "Ten Sogo Shosas: Trade Monarchs," *Marketing in Japan,* 1978 supplement to *Industrial Marketing.*

companies have, especially in Japan, in providing them access to the variety of products that they want to offer their buyers.

*Agent middlemen.*   Some middlemen are critically important in securing the transfer of title to goods, even though they do not themselves take title. They range from brokers, who may bring a buyer and seller together for a single transaction, to selling agents, who have long-term relationships with producers and essentially serve as the producer's sales force. The most important agent middleman in international markets is the manufacturer's representative (rep) or manufacturer's agent. Each rep may be given an exclusive territory, which might be a region or an entire nation, in which he or she sells the manufacturer's products on a commission basis. The agent usually agrees not to sell competing products and to provide the manufacturer with strong promotional effort in the foreign market. The use of such reps allows a manufacturer access to local expertise and local sales personnel without the managerial problems and expenses of setting up a local sales organization. A manufacturer hoping to enter a foreign market may count itself very fortunate if it is able to establish a relationship with an experienced local rep. Other agents unique to international marketing are discussed later in this chapter.

### Retailers

Retailers provide the last link in the marketing channel for consumer goods. Although a growing number of consumer goods are sold direct to the consumer by the producer through direct mail or door-to-door, most consumer goods are sold through retail establishments. Despite the enormous geographic, cultural, and economic differences among nations, retail establishments around the world have evolved in a surprisingly similar manner.

*Retailing in underdeveloped nations.*   In the least developed countries much of the retailing in each community takes place in an open area where sellers and buyers assemble on selected days. Producers set up stalls in these markets where they sell what they have made, on a cash or barter basis. In addition to producers, there are middlemen who bring in goods from other communities, set up stalls, and sell their wares. Some of these middlemen find that there is enough demand for their products on nonmarket days, and develop more permanent establishments at the edge of the market. Thus, a group of permanent retail establishments, usually small shops, develops near the market. The typical retail establishment is a small, family-owned business that specializes in a narrow line of products. Even though a number of permanent retailers may develop, the weekly market continues to be an important source of goods (especially food) to residents of underdeveloped countries.

*Retailing in developing countries.*   As a nation develops economically, a growing proportion of its population moves to towns and cities, which support a wider variety of retailers. Although many towns may continue to have public market days, these markets tend to specialize almost entirely in farm produce and handicraft items. All other products are generally sold through permanent retail outlets. The larger the city, the more highly specialized are some of the retailers. Different retailers develop to serve different market needs and price ranges. Chain stores also appear, with standardized stocks of merchandise and physical layouts. Another development in the major cities is the department store, with a huge physical plant and a wide range and assortment of merchandise. Smaller general merchandise retailers also supplant some of the specialty stores. For example, grocery stores are introduced to sell all the products formerly sold by dry grocers, green grocers, bakers, dairy product stores, and butchers, to name a few.

In evaluating the retailing structure of a nation, it is important to differentiate between the methods of operation and merchandise selection of each institution, rather than to rely solely on names. For example, many developing countries have stores called supermarkets, but a quick observation would show that they are totally unlike the supermarkets in some highly developed countries. In countries like the U.S., a supermarket is a self-service outlet with a high stock turnover (twenty times per year). It requires a high amount of capital investment for equipment and inventory, provides a minimum of service, and serves a large trading area (over seven hundred families). In contrast, "supermarkets" in developing countries may be the same as the old specialty grocery stores, stocking a minimum number of different products but using self-service. They also serve much smaller trading areas, are more labor-intensive, and typically will provide credit, deliveries, or other services. In Latin America, supermarkets are preferred by the middle and upper classes because they have the financial ability to plan their purchases in advance and they like the modern shopping atmosphere. The working classes, however, still patronize the open markets and specialty stores. A marketer who sells products successfully through supermarkets in the home market may find that the very different "supermarkets" in developing countries are not good outlets at all to get equivalent market coverage or exposure.

*Retailing in affluent countries.*   The next evolutionary step in retailing is mass retailing. Although mass retailing is found to some extent in developing countries, it only becomes a major channel of distribution in the more affluent nations. It is based on a managerial philosophy that seeks to attract patronage by low prices, resulting from low markups. In order to be able to offer low markups, these merchants require rapid turnover of merchandise.[2] Although the profit per unit is lower, the massive volume of

---

[2]Edward W. Cundiff, "Concepts in Comparative Retailing," *Journal of Marketing,* January 1965, p. 59.

sales yields a large total profit. The mass displays give the impression that the selection of merchandise is extra large, but these merchants often carry a smaller variety or selection than smaller retailers because only those items that will yield a large turnover are stocked. These mass merchants generally take the form of food supermarkets, discount houses, or hyper-markets (combined supermarkets and discount houses found particularly in Europe)[3]—but this same mass retailing method of operation is sometimes applied in other merchandise areas such as carpeting, clothing and furniture.

Another form of retailing that is found mostly in affluent nations is automated retailing, where merchandise is dispensed by coin-operated machines. This retailing service, since it does not depend on retail sales help, can be available twenty-four hours a day. It provides convenience of access for commonly consumed items, both in terms of time and place.

Because of these variations in the development of types of retail outlets, marketers sometimes have to adjust their marketing channels drastically when they move into foreign markets. For example, a soft-drink manufacturer who relies heavily on coin-operated vending machines to sell products in the American market, may have to find different ways of reaching prospective customers in less-developed countries. In these countries a large portion of the product may be sold by street-corner vendors. The channel required to reach these vendors may be quite different from the one used to stock vending machines. Other products sold heavily in vending machines, such as cigarettes and candy, will require the same adjustments in marketing channels. In the same manner the marketer whose products are sold by mass merchants in the more affluent countries may have to rely on small, independent retailers in less-developed markets. The marketing channel required to reach these small businesses is a longer and more complex one.

### International Middlemen

Special middlemen have evolved to serve international markets. Middlemen of this type have operated in international markets as long as there has been trade between nations. These export and import middlemen look beyond domestic markets for potential business that may have been ignored by domestically oriented producers.

*Export middlemen.* Export middlemen find markets in other parts of the world for products produced in their own countries. There are two kinds of exporters, export merchants and export agents. Export merchants frequently operate entirely independently of the producers whose products they sell. They identify a need for some product in a foreign market, buy

---

[3]"European Supermarkets Offer Creative Direction to U.S. Grocery Retailers," *Supermarket Business*, 34 (November 1979), 24.

such products from their home-country markets, and export and sell them abroad. Producers who seek to broaden the market for their products may take the initiative in calling their product to the attention of large export merchants, and they may even offer them price concessions to compensate for promotion support they provide in foreign markets.

Manufacturers seeking new markets abroad often find the service of export agents (often called export management companies) most useful. Since these agents do not have to invest their own capital in the goods, but merely sell them on commission, they may be more willing to take on new lines than the merchant, who must buy products for resale. For the producer who has little knowledge about foreign markets and foreign marketing, the export agent provides contacts and expertise that may be invaluable. For the firm interested in foreign markets only as a way to meet short-term goals (for example, as an outlet for excess inventories, newly obsolete products, or as a test of foreign demand for products prior to an international marketing commitment), export agents provide useful services by locating foreign buyers at little additional expense to the producer. The manufacturer who plans a major penetration of a foreign market may prefer to deal directly with middlemen in the desired foreign market; but in the short term a firm may still find the services of the export agent useful.

*Import middlemen.*    As their name implies, import middlemen bring products manufactured in other countries into their own market for sale. Their role is to identify unmet local needs and search out products in world markets that can serve these needs. As with export merchants, import merchants buy and sell in their own names and are more likely to operate independently of the manufacturers of the products they sell—using their own marketing strategies and choosing their own target markets.

Import agents often have a continuing relationship with the producers of products they sell. Any producer who seeks distribution in a new foreign market may contact such agents, either directly or through export agents in their own markets, and arrange for them to get products into the hands of wholesalers and retailers throughout a foreign market on a commission basis. Though the manufacturer loses marketing control, import agents may provide the only access to desired markets.

## INTERNATIONAL MARKETING CHANNEL ALTERNATIVES

Although the marketing institutions (retailers, wholesalers, and so forth) vary somewhat from nation to nation, the options for basic channel structures are pretty much the same at local levels. It is in the movement of goods between nations that the channel alternatives are different. Specialized export and import middlemen provide these unique options for building distribution channels in international marketing.

### International Consumer Goods Channels

Most of the channel alternatives available in the distribution of consumer goods are illustrated in Figure 14–1. The first set of five alternatives in the figure involves the use of export merchants. In these instances, producers may not be actively involved at all in the marketing of their products in the foreign market. This is called indirect exporting, as discussed in Chapter 2. The export merchant sees the foreign opportunity and takes the initiative to penetrate the new market. The second set of five channel alternatives involves the use of export agents. In this case, the initiative to export has probably been taken by a producer, who has sought out an agent to locate viable foreign markets. In the third set of alternatives, producers choose not to use export middlemen and to establish their own direct contacts in the foreign market. This is direct exporting.

After deciding the most appropriate method of getting products to a

**FIGURE 14–1**    Channel alternatives in international marketing of consumer goods.

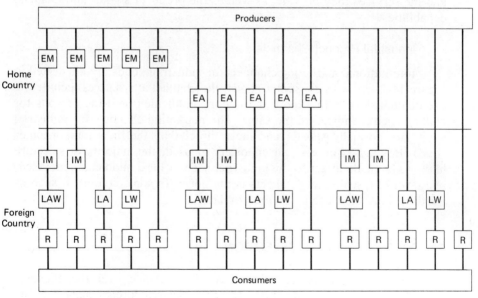

EM  –  Export Merchant
EA  –  Export Agent
IM  –  Import Middleman
LA  –  Local Agent
LW  –  Local Wholesaler
LAW  –  Local agent wholesaler
R  –  Retailer

foreign market, the next decision in export channels is whether or not to use import middlemen in the chosen market. The export middlemen and the direct exporting producer are all faced with this choice, and the best choice depends largely on the level of sophistication of the proposed marketing campaign and the desired depth of penetration in the foreign market. The shorter the channel, the more control the marketer is able to exercise over the total marketing program with respect to pricing, promotion, target markets, and so forth. The marketer must balance the time and cost of developing a marketing organization in a foreign market—with the attendant problems from cultural and economic differences—against the gain in precision of execution of the marketing plan. As one expert said, "If you let a broker handle all of your foreign distributions, and rely on agents, you get to the point where they control the situation, not you."[4]

Whether the product moves through import middlemen or not, the channel alternatives beyond that point are pretty much the same in all markets. The principles upon which a marketing manager should choose among channel institutions are best left to more detailed discussions in a distribution management textbook. However, as a point of reminder, the ideal channel length depends on such factors as market size and concentration, consumer purchasing patterns, the nature of the middlemen available and the services they provide, as well as the producer's goals and financial capabilities.

### Industrial Product Channels

International marketing channels for industrial goods are illustrated in Figure 14–2. As with consumer goods, the channel alternatives include the use or nonuse of both export and import middlemen; and the reasons for making such a choice are the same. The marketing channels for industrial goods are normally shorter and more direct than the ones for consumer goods. Beyond exporters and importers, if used, the majority of sales are likely to be made direct to the industrial user. If local middlemen are used, one level of distributors or agents is the norm. In some countries, such as Saudi Arabia, their use is required by law.

## FACTORS IN CHANNEL SELECTION _____

International marketers frequently have little choice over the channels through which their goods travel to reach desired foreign markets. The available alternatives may be few, and the middlemen willing to add a new product to their current line may be even fewer. To the extent that there is a choice available, the marketer must take several factors into consid-

---

[4]"Shrank on International Distributions," *Distribution*, September 1980, p. 44.

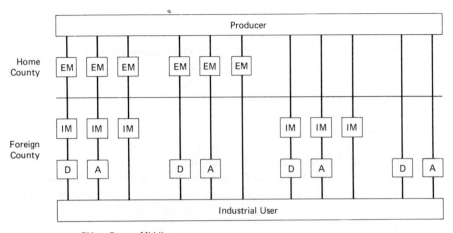

EM  -  Export Middleman
IM  -  Import Middleman
D  -  Industrial Distributor
A  -  Agent Middleman

**FIGURE 14–2**   Channel alternatives in international marketing of industrial goods.

eration: the nature of the product, the characteristics of the consumer or user, the types of middlemen available and their operating methods, and the extent of local participation in the marketing venture.

### Nature of the Product

Some products require a short channel of distribution no matter where they are sold. If a product is perishable, for example, it is necessary to move it through as few middlemen as possible to ensure that it gets to the consumer before it spoils. The need for a high degree of technical expertise in selling, installing, or maintenance makes a short marketing channel essential. The marketer of a complex piece of machinery, whether it is a computer or an electric generator, is unwilling to turn over to middlemen the job of determining which model best serves the needs of a prospective customer and how it should be installed for optimum performance. At the other extreme, products purchased frequently and routinely on a convenience basis must be available to the consumer wherever he or she might normally seek it. Such products are normally distributed through a great many retail outlets, and a long marketing channel may be required to reach all of these outlets, particularly in underdeveloped and developing countries.

### Nature of the Consumer or User

The same product may require different marketing channels in different countries because of differences in consumption patterns. For example, in the United States the home is an important place of consumption for beer and soft drinks, and the marketing channel must include retailers such as food stores and liquor stores. In other countries, because of lack of refrigeration or simply differences in consumption patterns, these products are often consumed only in public places, and the marketer must seek more intensive distribution in taverns, cafes, food stores, and even with street-corner vendors. In some countries magazines and newspapers are to a large extent delivered to the home on a subscription basis; in other countries they are sold almost entirely via newsstands.

The way a product user perceives the source of supply is also important. Industrial buyers may prefer dealing with a local distributor with whom they are familiar and have done business in the past. In this situation, the salespersons of a manufacturer who are strangers and/or foreigners, may be at a disadvantage even though their product knowledge may be superior.

## Nature and Role of Middlemen

In new foreign markets it is often necessary to have the help of local agents to get access to industrial or government buyers or to persuade retailers to consider purchase of a product. In the Middle East, for example, business is still conducted on a very personal basis.[5] In this booming oil-rich market, the local representative's ties to important customers may provide the only access to the market. These representatives require careful training and occasional supervisory visits. It may also be necessary to provide technical support for local reps, either from the home office or from regional offices specializing in an area—such as a Middle Eastern office. Local reps often expect to have a personal relationship with their client-supplier that goes beyond formal business dealings. Their loyalty may even be based upon such personal feelings.

## Legal Role of Agents and Middlemen

In some countries the use of local agents or middlemen is essential to meet legal requirements for local participation in foreign ventures. If an exporter is required in a particular market to have at least 50 percent local participation, at least a part of the distributive structure in that market must include local nationals.

The ownership rights of an agent or distributor in a territory vary from country to country. In the United States, for example, a marketer has the right to replace a distributor who is deemed to be doing an unsatisfactory job; but in some countries, where the distributor gains an ownership right in an assigned territory, the marketer can only eliminate these repre-

[5]Dan T. Dunn, Jr., "Agents or Distributors in the Middle East," *Business Horizons,* October 1979, pp. 69–78.

sentatives by buying them out. It is important, then, to know the local ownership rights of agents and distributors and to adjust the process of selection accordingly. Agents and middlemen should always be chosen with care, because a poor representative, even when legally replaceable, may be worse than no representative at all. Each representative should be chosen as if he or she were permanent, using the criteria of flexibility to adapt to changing market conditions, ability to control the marketing program, and having the minimal economic and financial requirements to perform needed marketing services.

The joint venture provides one potentially useful solution to finding good local reps.[6] If local partners can be found, their loyalty will be higher than that of paid representatives, and they will share a part of the cost of developing the market. Having a local partner, if a good one can be found, is an efficient way of operating abroad. Host governments usually prefer such arrangements, and having someone there who is thoroughly familiar with local customs helps greatly in market penetration.

The success rate in selecting foreign representatives has not been very good. One expert estimates that only three out of every ten foreign licensing arrangements has come up to expectations.[7] Most of these failures are not from heavy competition in the new market, but from failures on the part of the exporting company in selecting local partners. The following are nine reasons for failure of a local distributive organization, in order of frequency.

1. Inadequate market analysis by licensor.
2. Product defects not known or understood by licensing executives.
3. Higher start-up costs than licensee anticipated.
4. Insufficient attention, interest, and support from licensee's top management, marketing, and engineering executives.
5. Poor timing.
6. Competition (not just local but from third countries).
7. Insufficient marketing effort on the local scene (by licensor and/or licensee).
8. Inadequate licensee after-sales effort.
9. Weakness in licensee's market research and competitive intelligence.

The companies that are most successful in joint venture and foreign licensing arrangements do a better job of research and screening before making commitments and have improved communications between the home-country office and local representatives.

[6]"The Secret of Successful Selling Overseas in the Joint Venture," *Business Abroad,* February 1971, p. 15.

[7]Thomas P. Collier, "Do's and Don'ts of Foreign Licensing Arrangements," *Business Abroad,* February 1971, p. 17.

### Developing Long-Term Relationships

A successful long-term relationship between exporter and foreign representatives is based on more than mere mutual profits to be gained. Although profit is absolutely essential to motivate agents and to maximize their sales efforts, long-term success is also dependent on the development of a feeling of identification and loyalty.[8] There must be a mutual understanding of relationship responsibilities and expectations. The agent should respect the business expertise and judgment of the principal, but the principal should also consult with and follow the agency's instructions and knowledge of local conditions whenever possible. Communication is an important tool; the principal should anticipate information needs of the agents. The manufacturer should provide necessary promotional tools, but should seek the agents' input on what media and market support are most appropriate.

### Division of Marketing Responsibilities

In any marketing channel there are certain marketing responsibilities that are best handled by the product manufacturer, and others that are most effectively performed by middlemen. In foreign markets it is particularly important to define the role and tasks of each party in the total marketing program.

The exporting company is often in the best position to carry out marketing research and forecasting, but these are most effective with input from the local distributor. The development of detailed marketing programs and the planning and coordination needed to carry out these programs are best planned by the exporting marketer. When technical questions are raised about the product the producer-exporter is the natural source of information. This is also true for the design of formal sales presentations when the complexity of the product makes such presentations desirable. Finally, the exporter should establish general pricing policies.

The local agent or distributor is in a much better position to carry out other marketing responsibilities. For example, local knowledge of the market allows the rep to spot sales opportunities given changing market and competitive conditions, and to pinpoint the purchase influences most significant to potential buyers. Personal connections should make it easier to make contact with the customer. Finally, the local rep is in the best position to handle the details of importing, problems of physical distribution, and after-sale service.[9]

---

[8]C. S. Hickle and C. A. Mahn, "Getting the Agent to Sell for You: Building Sales Loyalty Abroad," *Business Abroad,* July 1971, pp. 23–24.

[9]Dunn, Jr., "Agents or Distributors," p. 78.

## PHYSICAL DISTRIBUTION
## IN INTERNATIONAL MARKETS _____

Physical distribution or logistics involves the movement of goods through time and space from the point of production to the point of consumption. It includes transportation, storage, packaging, materials handling, and inventory control. The management of physical distribution is more complex in international marketing because of the vast distances that goods must be transported. Distribution is now estimated to represent somewhere between 10 percent and 25 percent of the total landed cost of international shipments.[10] In addition, fewer and fewer international buyers will accept prices quoted F.O.B. factory. Instead, they demand the international marketer assume the responsibility for delivering merchandise directly to their loading docks. Under these circumstances, the role of the distribution department in the success of international marketing becomes very important.

International marketers who do not themselves have the expertise to handle international shipments and other aspects of physical distribution, often make use of the freight forwarder—a special agent available to exporters and importers.[11] The exporter only has to move the goods to a port area and arrange for a letter of credit. The rest of the details—licenses and declarations, packing lists, bills of lading, and other documentation—are the responsibility of the forwarder. The forwarder may even do any required export packing and may contact the foreign customer to learn of possible special requirements for the shipment. In a recent survey by *Distribution,* 94.6 percent of the respondents who were active ocean shippers used freight forwarders.[12] For examples of the documents mentioned here that are essential to physical distribution of exports and imports, see Appendix C. The glossary in Appendix D explains the purpose of these documents.

### Transporting Goods Between Nations

In most countries, domestic movement of goods is handled to a large degree by rail or truck. These methods of transportation are relatively fast and inexpensive. Since physical distribution decisions often involve a trade-off between transportation costs and inventory and storage costs, these surface methods of transportation often minimize total costs. In international transportation these methods are frequently not available as a viable alternative. Rail and highway facilities are good throughout most of Europe and North America, so that fast and efficient rail and truck surface

[10]"The Export Decision: Distribution's Vital Role," *Distribution,* October 1980, pp. 14–15.
[11]"Freight Forwarders: The Export Experts," *Distribution,* March 1980, pp. 39–40.
[12]Ibid., p. 38.

transportation is available within these respective areas. But in much of Latin America, Africa, and Asia, highway and rail connections between countries are spotty. If the distances are great, water transportation may not only be cheaper, but faster.

Between continents, sea and air transportation are the only alternatives, and when the distance between points on the same continent are great, they are still frequently the best transportation options. Sea transportation has traditionally been the most significant method of transport in international trade. It is a very inexpensive method of transportation, but it is also very slow, and loss through damage and pilferage is higher than for other methods of transport. New developments in ocean transportation have helped to reduce these disadvantages somewhat. Containerized ships can be loaded more quickly (reducing travel time), and they reduce damage and pilferage.

Ocean transportation is by far the most important method of moving goods between international markets, but air transport is growing in importance. The cost per mile travelled of sending goods by air is far higher than by water; however, when total physical distribution costs are analyzed, air transport is winning out in more and more cases.

The majority of international shipments involve some combination of land (truck or rail) and sea transportation. Intermodal shipping has been developed to provide optimal shipping costs in these situations. Intermodal shipping provides "through rates" over several forms of transportation, with the transportation companies sharing the tariffs on a prearranged basis.[13] Intermodal shipping is more effective if the merchandise is shipped in standard containers that can be rehandled with a minimum of effort. Under this system the ocean carrier can often quote door-to-door rates to shippers, using either rail, truck, or a combination of both. Depending on the conditions of the shipment and the carriers used, these intermodal shipments may be described as minibridge, microbridge, or motorbridge.

Intermodal shipping is not restricted to international shipments. In the United States, for example, Union Pacific conducts a sizable part of its intermodal business in international freight.[14] The result of intermodal shipping is that the most efficient method of shipment, in terms both of time and cost, can be used. A shipment from London to Alaska, for example, could include ocean shipment to New York, rail shipment to Seattle, and ocean shipment from Seattle to the Alaskan port.

### Storage in International Marketing

The main role of storage in international marketing is to provide reserve stock at the point of sale so that customers and suppliers are rarely faced with stockoutages. Within a domestic market, where distances are

[13]Denis Davis, "Exporting: An International Game," *Distribution*, March 1981, p. 44.
[14]"Intermodal Business on the Union Pacific," *Distribution*, April 1980, p. 12.

not great and transportation may be fast and dependable, it may not be necessary to provide large reserve stocks at the points of consumption. In fact, many domestic firms maintain reserve stocks only at the point of manufacture. However, when the distances between nations are great and transportation is slow and undependable, it is necessary to retain large backup stocks in important markets. Under such circumstances the investment in finished goods inventory and parts can become sizeable.

The exporter may find that available storage facilities are inadequate in many markets. Public warehouses may not be available, or they may not provide adequate protection from the elements. Special climatic conditions, such as high humidity in the tropics, may require special storage facilities to protect goods from deterioration. In such instances, exporters are faced with the additional cost of building or leasing their own storage facilities.

### Inventory Control in International Markets

Inventory control decisions are concerned with keeping investment in inventories as low as possible without doing too much damage to customer service. The investment in finished goods inventories can become a large cost, but any attempt to reduce this investment could result in situations where products are not immediately available to meet customer demand. The inventory control problem is particularly important in international marketing because the greater distances and slow travel time result in higher inventories than in domestic markets.

Foreign trade zones, or free trade zones, can sometimes be used to reduce inventories in local markets. Foreign trade zones are areas set up in international ports where goods can be stored, processed, and/or transshipped without going through local customs. Without the use of foreign trade zones, a marketer serving Singapore, Indonesia, the Philippines, and Thailand would probably find it necessary to maintain a reserve stock in each of these markets. It would not be possible to establish a single regional reserve inventory in any one these countries, such as Singapore, because import duties would be charged on all the goods moved in, even though some were eventually transshipped to the other markets. But, by establishing a single reserve inventory in the foreign trade zone in Singapore, the marketer can ship to any of these markets as needed and only pay Singapore duty on the goods that are sold in Singapore. Storage in foreign trade zones can be useful even when the goods are destined for sale in the country where the foreign trade zone is located, because it allows the marketer to delay paying duty on the goods until they are sold.[15]

---

[15]Tom Dulaney, "Foreign Trade Zones: What's in it for the Shipper," *Distribution,* March 1980, pp. 44–48.

## Materials Handling and Packaging

The recent development of greater sophistication in materials handling has helped to reduce total physical distribution costs. Proper packaging often makes it possible to replace human handling of goods entirely with machines, thereby reducing both cost and damage to materials. Palletization into wholesale shipping units at the factory often makes it possible to ship goods all the way to the final destination without their ever being handled by individuals. Mechanization is particularly important in ocean shipping, where the shape of storage spaces and the location of hatches once made it necessary to load almost entirely by hand. Palletization has decreased the manpower requirements in loading ships, but an even more promising development is the construction of special container ships which can be loaded very quickly and efficiently with large preloaded containers. Extra dividends of this method of materials handling are the reduction of damage to goods by reducing the amount of handling, and the reduction of pilferage (always an enormous problem in ocean shipping) by encasing the merchandise in presealed containers.

Shipment to foreign countries sometimes requires the adaptation of packages to meet local preferences and prejudices.[16] Numbers, colors, and shapes have different meanings and impacts in different countries. A certain number, color, shape, or phrase used in packaging a product may be harmless or perhaps even helpful in one country, but will reduce sales or even close out a market in another country. As an example, a leading U.S. manufacturer of golf balls targeted Japan as an important new market because of the expanding popularity of golf in that nation. Although golf balls were packaged in units of six or twelve for the domestic market, a special package of four golf balls was developed for the export market where it was presumed that the golfer would prefer to buy fewer at a time. The company found its sales way below its expected volume. Research eventually targeted the reason for the poor performance: packaging in units of four led to lagging sales because four is the number of death in Japan. Colors and shapes and designs can be as important as numbers in particular cultures. The international marketer must identify potentially negative factors in each particular market and adapt packaging to facilitate both materials handling and market acceptance.

## Optimizing Physical Distribution Costs

Physical distribution costs can be optimized only by considering the various inputs simultaneously. Minimizing individual inputs, such as transportation, can lead to higher total costs and poorer service to the customer. For example, a Japanese truck manufacturer needs a replacement

[16]"Adapting Export Packing to Cultural Differences," *Business America: 1979*, 2 (December 3, 1979), pp. 3–7.

axle for one of its dealers in Sao Paulo, Brazil. If the method of transporting this axle was based on a suboptimizing cost decision, it would be shipped by ocean freight as a part of a general order of replacement parts for Brazil. However, in order to take advantage of this low transportation cost, it would be necessary to maintain an inventory of axles in Sao Paulo. Otherwise, the customer might wait six weeks or more (shipment time) to get the truck back into operation. Since axles need replacement only infrequently, the storage and inventory costs of maintaining replacement axles always on hand in Brazil might be higher than the cost of shipping an axle from Japan by air freight when needed. The manufacturer could still provide almost immediate availability of this part on the occasions when it is needed. Of course, the firm would continue to maintain an inventory of frequently used parts in Sao Paulo because the fast turnover would justify storage and inventory costs. For these products, ocean transportation would probably be the optimal method of transport since it would minimize total physical distribution costs while still providing a satisfactory level of customer service.

## SUMMARY

The marketer entering a new foreign market may have only very limited choices about how to distribute products in that market. The selection of available middlemen in the market may be limited by availability or willingness of existing middlemen to take on a new foreign line. If the exporter's foreign experience is limited or if the export business is small, consideration may be given to the use of specialized export or import middlemen to help establish an international marketing channel. Differences in local consumption patterns and differences in the local role of middlemen may require the use of different channel structures in different markets. Physical distribution decisions are also complicated by the increased distances between marketer and customer, and by unique inventory control problems. Storage and transportation decisions must be made in light of local conditions and potential market size, as well as their impact on total physical distribution costs and level of customer service.

## DISCUSSION QUESTIONS

1. Differentiate between merchant and agent middlemen in international markets.
2. How do retailers differ in underdeveloped, developing, and affluent countries?
3. Describe the services performed by export middlemen.

4. What is the major role of import middlemen in international channels of distribution?

5. How do consumer and industrial product channels differ in foreign markets?

6. How do buyer characteristics affect international channels of distribution?

7. Identify the types of channels and distribution below:

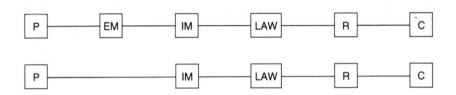

8. Explain how legal ownership rights in different countries affect international channel decisions.

9. Why are there problems in selecting foreign representatives or partners for intermediary roles in international markets?

10. Which marketing tasks should be handled by the exporter and which ones by its intermediaries in foreign markets?

11. Why is physical distribution important to the success of international marketing?

12. What services are performed by a freight forwarder?

13. Discuss the relative advantages and disadvantages of sea and air transportation between continents.

14. What is intermodal shipping?

15. Explain how storage and inventory decisions are related to transportation decisions in international markets.

16. What is a foreign trade zone?

17. How can physical distribution costs be optimized in international markets?

# CANAC DISTRIBUTION, LTD.
## SEA-WING SERVICE*

Sea-Wing is an intermodal container service operated by CANAC Distribution Ltd. of Montreal, offering a shipping service from Europe to destinations in North America. The first Sea-Wing container was shipped from Southampton to Los Angeles in October 1975, involving sea transportation to the port of Halifax, truck to Halifax International Airport, and air freight to Los Angeles via Montreal. Early experience suggested to the CANAC management that a broadening of the service would result in revenue and profit growth. Accordingly, new departure points were established at Rotterdam in Holland, and at Genoa in Italy. On the North American side, the network was expanded to include the following destination points: Miami, Detroit, Chicago, Denver, and Dallas/Fort Worth.

The rationale for the establishment of the Sea-Wing Service was the feeling by CANAC's Vice-President of Marketing, Mr. MacLaren, that there were shippers who found all-surface transportation too slow for their needs, but who were unable to bear the costs of an all-air mode of transport. Sea-Wing was established in response to this perceived need, positioned between all-air and all-surface modes in terms of speed and cost.

### Future Development

After eight months of operations, Mr. MacLaren concluded that the westbound Sea-Wing operation was a viable concept which fulfilled a proven need. Encouraged by this, he felt compelled to divert some of his energy from administration of the westbound operation to the prospect of creating a similar service, but in the opposite direction—that is, eastbound from North America to Europe. He was convinced that what had worked westward could work again eastward. He felt, however, that decisions were required in a number of areas before plans to set up the service could progress. One of his major concerns was the question of agent organization and management. Mr. MacLaren felt that his recently recruited assistant, Raymond LeBlanc, could provide some help on these matters. Raymond was a recent MBA graduate with a good background in marketing. As a prelude to making recommendations on the eastbound service, Raymond collected information on the existing Sea-Wing Service, drawing material from dis-

*This case was written by Professor Philip Rosson and Janet Forrest, Dalhousie Univ., © 1977 by Philip Rosson. Reproduced by permission.

cussions with executives involved in its establishment, and from company files and documents. The information assembled is detailed below.

### The Sea-Wing Service: Westbound Operations

Sea-Wing has three types of agents involved in its westbound operations. These are origin agents, transfer agents, and destination agents. Their responsibilities are as follows:

**ORIGIN AGENT**

Marketing, promotion, and selling of Sea-Wing service

Exercising supervision and control over the acceptance, storage, groupage, and movement of traffic to ocean carriers' premises

Preparation of all necessary documents relative to Sea-Wing traffic, invoicing and collection of tariff charges to Sea-Wing customers

Disbursing from Sea-Wing revenues, invoices in payment of services purchased from others with respect to the handling and movement of Sea-Wing traffic

Submission of necessary reports and remittances of funds to CANAC

Negotiations, under the supervision of CANAC, of financial and other arrangements with common carriers and depot operators

Communication of data and information relative to Sea-Wing traffic to CANAC and its agents at transfer points and destinations

Processing of loss and damage claims

**TRANSFER AGENT**

Planning for the acceptance and movement of traffic from port of entry to airport cargo terminal, or from airport of entry to container terminal

Exercising supervision and control over such traffic

Negotiations, under the supervision of CANAC, of financial and other arrangements with local truckers

Preparation of all necessary documents to ensure efficient movement of Sea-Wing traffic through transfer system, including customs

Advising CANAC of any loss or damage to Sea-Wing traffic identified at transfer point

When required, arrange for the stuffing or destuffing of the air or ocean containers

**DESTINATION AGENT**

Marketing, promotion, and selling of Sea-Wing service and communicating trade information concerning shippers and consignees to origin agent and CANAC

Arranging for the transfer of traffic from airport terminal (container terminal) to consignee and customs clearance when requested by consignee

Monitoring the receipt of traffic at destination airport terminal (container terminal) based on information provided by origin and transfer agents

Initiating tracing procedures as requested

Processing loss and damage claims

### Agent Recruitment and Experiences to Date

The task of recruiting agents was tackled as follows. The most straightforward appointment was that of the Halifax *transfer agent*. The responsibilities of the transfer agent are well defined, requiring timely and coordinated action to efficiently transship containers from the ocean terminal to the airport. The local Scotian Transfer Company was soon found, and proved to be very satisfactory. Decisions concerning the origin and destination agents were more difficult to make. After some deliberation CANAC decided that they should look for ocean-oriented origin agents, and air-oriented destination agents. This seemed a logical decision given the nature of the responsibilities of each type of agent.

The first *origin agent* to be recruited was Williams Shipping Ltd., a long established company based in London, England. This company was highly recommended to CANAC and when they agreed to operate as Sea-Wing agents, CANAC management was very pleased. In return for marketing the Sea-Wing Service and handling the resulting freight, Williams Shipping was offered a contract which included the following basic conditions:

A one-year term, subject to termination on 90-days written notice by either party

Exclusive representation of Sea-Wing in the U.K. unless otherwise agreed in writing between the parties

A 40% share of the annual net profits resulting from traffic originating in the U.K., (as an advance on the distribution of net profits, a commission of 4% of revenues earned is payable monthly)

Williams Shipping Ltd. has proved to be excellent freight handlers for Sea-Wing, but some misgivings exist concerning its abilities to market the service. A feeling exists among CANAC management that Williams is not an aggressive promoter of the service.

In continental Europe, Sea-Wing operations are more recent, so that it is perhaps too early to judge appointed agents. However, there is some good reason to believe that both the Dutch and Italian agents are doing a reasonable job of handling freight and selling the Sea-Wing concept to shippers. These agents enjoy the same contract terms as Williams Shipping

Ltd., with the Dutch agent responsible for business in Benelux, Germany, and France (north of Paris). The Italian agent is responsible for Italy and Switzerland.

Budgeting restrictions had precluded CANAC from hiring full-time air cargo personnel as their *destination agents* except in the important Los Angeles market. Instead CANAC management hit upon the idea of recruiting recently retired airline cargo employees. CANAC approached the United Airlines Employees Association and obtained names of relevant persons. Those selected receive a $500 fee payable monthly in return for two to three days work per week. Here a 30-day termination clause is in operation. The terms of employment are thought to be attractive to the retired person, offering the right level of inducement, and an interesting yet not exacting task. Furthermore, the working conditions permit the agent a certain work flexibility. Destination agents receive a fee rather than a salary and are contracted as agents rather than employees. These subtle points mean that the U.S. Internal Revenue can lay no claim to this earned income, thus making the $500 fee a more attractive amount.

Agent Marketing Strategies and
Problems

The full-time agent CANAC hired in Los Angeles has been relatively successful in soliciting business for Sea-Wing. Initially, Carol Klein faced some problems in generating sales since shippers were not familiar with their sales transactions. By examining U.S. government documents, she learned that the U.S. Bureau of the Census published computer runs of exports by commodity type, district of customs, and name of importer. These printouts appeared in the Journal of Commerce, a commercial paper, to which Klein quickly subscribed. After detailed examination of the computer runs, Klein noted that in many cases imports were consigned to an agent and not to the ultimate buyer. This prevented her from identifying specific importers. She also recognized that many imports arrived in consolidated shipments, making it impossible to isolate particular commodities. In spite of these difficulties, Klein has found these statistics helpful and some business has resulted.

Klein also contacted the British Trade Commission for possible leads. The Commission suggested she join the California-U.K. Importers Association and, as a result of contacts developed there, she generated business with an importer of British-made "Albatross" sailboat motors. Experience with the "Albatross" importer provided useful insight for both Sea-Wing management and the agent. Carol Klein was able to sell the importer on the idea of Sea-Wing since he was the person who paid for the transportation bill and decided on the routing of the shipment. This followed from the terms of sale agreed between the engine supplier and the California importer, namely F.O.B. at the British plant. No marketing effort was required in Britain in this case, because the sales transaction took place with the California importer. However, had the terms of sale been C.I.F. Los Angeles, then the supplier would have been responsible for transportation. In this case, the Sea-Wing personnel began to realize that the major marketing responsibilities could lie either at origin or destination points, depending upon the prevailing terms of sale. This realization was important for CANAC.

In other cities, a different approach was employed to identify buyers and potential users of the Sea-Wing service. CANAC hired ex-air cargo employees to conduct marketing surveys among local companies in Denver, Chicago, Dallas–Fort Worth, Miami, and Detroit (some of these persons were subsequently appointed agents in these locations). The problem of which companies to approach was partially solved by CANAC management's providing leads based on the type of traffic most frequently transported to Los Angeles by Sea-Wing. Sample questionnaires completed in the marketing survey were included. The survey, as well as providing basic information on shipping practices for CANAC management, developed some business from the contacts made.

Sea-Wing agents have had difficulties promoting Sea-Wing to potential customers because many importing companies do not possess accounting systems where total distribution costs are made explicit. This means that the extra freight costs of a faster mode of transportation are all too clear to the shipper, whereas the potential savings—e.g. lower inventory costs, reduced insurance, and lower packaging costs—are difficult to quantify.

In spite of certain problems, the westbound Sea-Wing service has been sufficiently successful to handle forty-three containers in the first eight months' operations. These shipments have amounted to about 850,000 lbs. of various commodities, and have been transported to a number of North American destinations.

### Future Eastbound Transfer Agent

Although CANAC is as yet uncertain about the agent organization that will deal with eastbound traffic, an additional transfer agent will be necessary if CANAC proceeds with an eastbound service. An eastbound Sea-Wing service will have to operate out of Montreal. This is necessary because Halifax has no direct shipping services to Europe. All container ships calling at Halifax proceed down the eastern seaboard of the United States before leaving for Europe. Montreal is the only major eastern Canadian port with direct shipping services, and as such will be the eastbound transfer point. A new transfer agent will have to be found to transfer Sea-Wing containers from Mirabel Airport to one of the Montreal container piers. The agent will have the same responsibilities as the Halifax agent.

## Recommendations for an Eastbound Service

With this information before him, Raymond LeBlanc was expected to make some recommendations to Mr. MacLaren for an eastbound service. LeBlanc knew that the following questions were foremost in the vice president's mind:

## QUESTIONS

1. Should the same agents be responsible for eastbound and westbound traffic?
2. What kinds of tasks should agents be allocated, and how might they be motivated to achieve Sea-Wing goals?
3. What steps should CANAC take to ensure that the Sea-Wing service is efficiently promoted and sold to shippers?

# PART V

# PLANNING AND CONTROL FOR INTERNATIONAL MARKETING

OVERVIEW

This last section of the text is designed to focus the international marketing effort in two complementary directions. The first of these, discussed in Chapter 15, is the task of coordinating international marketing strategies. The need to integrate international planning with overall company goals and control procedures is a growing concern of companies and managers involved in international markets. In Chapter 15 we review the tools that are helpful in coordinating and controlling international marketing strategy. Chapter 16 summarizes current and predicted trends which will affect future international marketing strategies. It is as important to plan for and anticipate the future environment of international marketing as it is to coordinate and control current efforts. We leave you with an optimistic view of the career potential in the field of international marketing management.

# chapter 15

# COORDINATING AND CONTROLLING INTERNATIONAL MARKETING STRATEGY

Much is made of "Japan, Inc."—in fact, overmuch. However, government planning is very much in evidence in the economy, as is the influence on government of various trade associations and business councils. One of the most noticeable features of government planning is its designation of sunrise and sunset industries. Japan sees itself as a high-technology, knowledge-based economy. Labor-intensive manufacturing is being removed to lower labor cost countries.

Japan exploits the learning curve, the concept through which unit costs are driven down by consecutive doubling of output volume. First, Japanese companies invest in employees, sending them all over the world to learn the latest technologies. Then, new technologies are tried out in a relatively sheltered, very large (population one-half that of the U.S.), relatively wealthy domestic market. As competition rises, mergers are enforced, and markets are expanded internationally. Lower prices (and lower profits) are accepted in order to have higher sales and move more quickly down the learning curve.*

## INTRODUCTION

International firms have a uniquely difficult problem in coordinating and controlling the activities of their foreign branches, intermediaries, and sub-

*Ellen Cook, "Japan's Challenge," University of San Diego School of Business Newsletter, Spring 1980, p. 1.

sidiaries. Exporters may not even know in which countries their products are sold. Coordination and control are difficult enough (even in a purely domestic firm) when branches are widely dispersed geographically, but when sales, marketing offices, and even production facilities, are located thousands of miles away across continents or oceans, it is particularly difficult to maintain strong central planning and control of activities. In such circumstances, decentralization on some decisions is inevitable, yet management prefers, as much as possible, to develop a single marketing strategy for all parts of its operations, and to place the planning and coordination responsibilities with the highest levels of management.

In this chapter we review the issues that affect the ability to coordinate and control international marketing decisions. The first issue is the desired extent of centralization in marketing decision making. This was discussed briefly in Chapter 8, but here the topic is viewed in the context of control and coordination, rather than allocation of decision responsibility. Next we highlight the variables that provide strategic focus to the firm's foreign expansion efforts. We review the relative merits of market diversification and market concentration as expansion strategies, and then show you how to use product-market analysis in selecting an appropriate strategy. The next topic concerns planning in multinational corporations. This is followed by a survey of competitive factors, such as international product life cycles and cost-volume relationships, that affect international marketing strategies. Last, we discuss the processes of developing and optimizing strategy for international markets. We provide a checklist for strategic decision areas, which is complemented by the detailed outline for developing a marketing plan found in Appendix A.

## CENTRALIZATION VERSUS DECENTRALIZATION

The degree of centralization of marketing authority and planning ranges from the highly centralized, where marketing power resides at a headquarters that prescribes the marketing approach for subsidiaries to follow, to the highly decentralized, where local managers make all the decisions. The supporters of centralization argue that consumer needs around the world are basically the same and that the company will obtain maximum benefit from a common strategy. The opponents of centralization point out the obvious dissimilarities of market conditions, especially for consumer goods, in different national markets. It is clear that neither extreme is acceptable. Extreme decentralization could result in a number of separate businesses under a common ownership, without the benefits of exchange of ideas and experience, or the benefits of economies of scale. Extreme centralization will result in rigidity and an inability to adapt to local conditions.

## Degree of Centralization

The decision of the international marketer is not whether to have centralized management, but rather how much to centralize managerial decisions. The obvious trade-offs are (1) obtaining maximum leverage from the company's worldwide experience and marketing strength through centralized decision making; or (2) having fast and effective response to local market conditions by allowing maximum freedom to local managers. Determination of the degree of centralization is influenced by the amount of cultural and economic diversity among the markets of each particular company. For certain types of goods, such as industrial products, buyers and markets are more similar across national boundaries than for other products.

Centralization is a widely used integrative device in multinational firms. In a survey of one hundred multinational marketing managers,[1] one study found a strongly held belief that many marketing activities should not be delegated. Half the firms surveyed reported a "high" degree of centralization, and an additional one-third reported a "medium" degree of centralization. The interviews indicated a trend toward increasing centralization because of a growing awareness of the need and opportunities for global or regional planning, instead of country-by-country planning. This trend was particularly noticeable in Europe with its reduced trade barriers and growing mobility of consumers.

## Strategy Inputs and Centralization

Centralization is not equally strong with all types of marketing decisions. The greatest degree of headquarters' control is often exercised over product policy decisions. Home-office marketers are particularly interested in the consistency of the physical characteristics of products, brand names, and packaging. Companies in the field of consumer packaged goods consider the establishment of international brand names as an essential source of competitive strength. Most companies also require that new product ideas from subsidiaries first obtain headquarters' approval. In a survey of eighty-four Western European affiliates of U.S.-based firms, 55 percent of product design decisions were imposed on local management by home offices (see Figure 15–1). Only 30 percent of such decisions rested with local management. While centralization of product policy decisions was generally high, it differed by industry groups. Cosmetics and soft-drinks companies exercised extremely tight control over product decisions, whereas food firms allowed more input from the management of foreign subsidiaries.

Other marketing decisions are viewed by management more as local

---

[1]The field research involved 27 multinational firms in 4 major industries (food, soft drinks, soap/detergent/toiletries, and cosmetics). See Ulrich Wiechmann, "Integrating Multinational Marketing Tasks," *Columbia Journal of World Business,* Winter 1974, p. 26.

decision areas. As shown in Figure 15–1, local management is given primary authority for decisions on advertising, price, and distribution in the majority of cases. Advertising is the most decentralized decision area, with 86 percent of the firms allocating primary control to local management. Decisions on retail price are delegated to local management in 74 percent of the companies, and selection of distribution outlets was delegated locally in 61 percent of the companies. Policy objectives are often still set at a centralized corporate level, but the actual strategies and tactics in these areas are decided locally.

The data presented in Figure 15–1 represent a good generalization about the centralization of marketing decisions, but in some special cases policies may differ. The generalizations apply to firms with large commitments to international marketing. Firms with a small share of volume in international sales are less likely to decentralize their marketing decisions. The same study[2] showed that firms with less than 15 percent of sales at the international level handled all advertising, selection of dealers, and pricing decisions centrally. As the proportion of sales to international volume increases, the number of firms delegating pricing, distribution, and advertising authority to subsidiaries increases.

**FIGURE 15–1**   Degree of local management autonomy classified according to type of marketing decision.[a]

| | **LOCAL MARKETING DECISION** | | | |
| --- | --- | --- | --- | --- |
| *Degree of Local Management Autonomy* | *Product Design* | *Advertising Approach* | *Retail Price* | *Distribution Outlets/1000 Population* |
| **Primary authority rested with local management** | 30% | 86% | 74% | 61% |
| **Local management shared authority with other levels in organization** | 15% | 8% | 20% | 38% |
| **Decision primarily imposed upon local management** | 55% | 6% | 6% | 1% |
| | 100% | 100% | 100% | 100% |
| **N (Marketing programs observed)** | N = 86 | N = 84[b] | N = 84[b] | N = 86 |

[a]For Western European affiliates of 9 U.S.-based manufacturers.

[b]Classification information not available in two cases.

*Source:* R. J. Aylmer, "Who Makes Marketing Decisions in the Multinational Firm?" *Journal of Marketing,* October 1970, p. 26. Published by the American Marketing Association.

[2]R. J. Aylmer, "Who Makes Marketing Decisions in the Multinational Firm?" *Journal of Marketing,* October, 1970, pp. 25–30.

The degree of centralization of marketing authority also varies with the products involved. The marketing programs for soft drinks and cosmetics, for example, seem to require less modification from country to country than for food products, which generally seem to be more culture bound. The variations in the perceptions of and consumption of coffee provide a good example: café au lait is popular in France and Switzerland; strong expresso is preferred in Italy; coffee is a milk modifier in England and Australia; and in Germany and Scandinavia, coffee is smooth, rich, and acidic. When products are climate or culture bound, they require more tailoring of marketing programs to the local situation, and management of local subsidiaries plays a more dominant role in marketing decision making. Industrial and high-technology products may require a high degree of centralization in control and coordination because of significant development costs, international buyer awareness of products, and the advantages of worldwide economies of scale.

### Integrating Marketing Strategy Under Decentralization

In those markets where it is considered necessary to decentralize marketing decisions to a large degree, it is important to achieve an integration of decisions made at the subsidiary level with central management's marketing philosophy. Otherwise the advantages of a common marketing stance are lost. Home-office management tries to achieve this philosophical integration in several ways.

The first way is called corporate acculturation. It attempts to establish in subsidiary managers, the attitudes, behavior patterns, and state of mind that will conform to headquarters' intentions. To achieve corporate acculturation, a firm must select subsidiary managers carefully, and then train them to be strongly aware of corporate objectives and philosophy. Such acculturation requires a long managerial training program and promotion from within.

Another way of achieving integration is through systemwide transfers. Even decentralized multinationals can make use of a uniform framework for marketing planning and budgeting in all parts of the enterprise. The use of common systems helps to standardize the processes of thinking, analyzing, and decision making. Finally, firms can achieve integration through the transfer of personnel. Multinationals maintain a maximum amount of contact across borders among headquarters and subsidiary personnel. Headquarters personnel visit the subsidiaries during planning and budget-preparation periods, and subsidiary personnel are brought to headquarters periodically for conferences. Regular contact among the far-flung personnel helps to weld the subunits into the overall enterprise.

## MARKET EXPANSION STRATEGIES

Companies that plan to expand into foreign countries must establish strategic options among markets and products, and the optimization of resources. Three necessary steps are involved. First, potential markets must be identified and orders of priority set for entering these markets. Second, a determination must be made of the amount of resources to be allocated for foreign expansion. And third, management must decide the rate of expansion in each market.

### The Importance of Critical Mass and Selectivity

If a company wants to develop and maintain a profitable position in a foreign market, it must reach a minimum level of size and effectiveness—a critical mass. Once critical mass is reached with respect to investment of resources, the company can meet the competitive demands of the marketplace and profits will go up. Critical mass includes all of the major marketing strategy inputs. Thus, product characteristics must meet competitive levels; distribution coverage must be in line with that of competitors; direct sales coverage, and advertising and promotion inputs, must be competitive; and so forth.

No company can succeed in an unlimited number of foreign markets, because both manpower and financial resources set limits on effectiveness; therefore, selectivity must be a governing principle for foreign marketing strategy. Although the idea of selectivity is widely accepted, management frequently finds it difficult to turn down opportunities for profit in new markets. The need for critical mass helps reinforce the principle of selectivity.

To make selectivity work, management must have a means for selecting the most promising group of markets to develop. If there are resources left over after developing these markets, the company can then decide where and when to pursue more opportune business. Most companies have no systematic way of selecting among foreign market investment opportunities. The nine-box grid in Figure 15–2 presents a useful way of systematizing such decisions. The horizontal axis measures the attractiveness of individual markets in terms of market potential. This information could be obtained through marketing research, country visits, or consultation with local subsidiaries or agents. The vertical axis describes the company's position in each market with respect to critical mass. In each instance the firm should evaluate the requirements for competing in each individual market and judge the difficulty of reaching such competitive levels.

Using a selectivity system, the firm can concentrate efforts on the richest and most promising markets in terms of profits. Occasionally, however, the firm will be presented with a promising opportunity to move into

**FIGURE 15–2**    A grid for evaluating foreign markets.

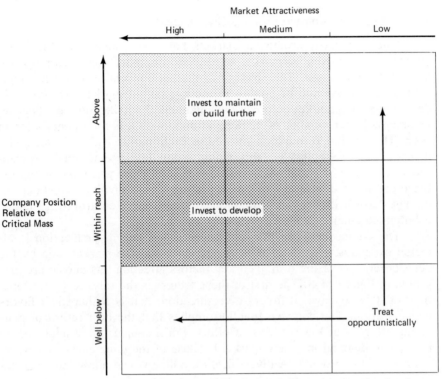

This framework helps to determine the appropriate allocation of resources for foreign market development.

In the lightly shaded areas at the upper left-hand corner of the grid are found attractive markets where the company already has a strong position. In these markets the appropriate strategy is usually to maintain that position or build it further.

The heavily shaded areas indicate attractive markets where the company is within reach of critical mass. Here the company can greatly improve results by investing the necessary time and resources to gain the step-function benefits of crossing the critical mass threshold.

The lightest areas of the grid indicate those markets with low attractiveness, or markets where it is unlikely that the company can reach critical mass. Here, a strategy of careful opportunistic response and limited or reduced investment is probably called for.

*Source:*    Robert S. Attiyeh and David L. Wenner, "Critical Mass: Key to Export Profits," *Business Horizons,* December 1979, p. 32.

a new market with only limited demands on resources. It can be rewarding to pursue a limited number of such opportunities as long as all hidden costs are taken into consideration.

## Market Concentration Versus Diversification

Once the most promising markets have been identified, the major strategic alternatives in market expansion are market concentration or market diversification. The strategy of market concentration is characterized by a gradual rate of growth in the number of markets served, fully developing each market before adding another. Diversification involves developing a larger number of markets at once with less total penetration in each. The level of resources allocated to each market will be lower under diversification. Specifically, this would mean less promotional expenditures, more use of commission middlemen, and more price skimming. On the other hand, a strategy of concentration would involve investment in market share, with heavier promotional outlays, more control over the distribution channel, and lower prices.

The choice between market concentration and diversification is affected by characteristics of both the product and the market, and by the decision criteria of the firm. Ten key factors affecting this choice are presented in Figure 15–3. The first of these factors is the sales response function—if it is concave, it favors diversification; if it is S-shaped, it favors concentration. The concave function implies that the best return of marketing effort is at lower levels of effort. For example, there might be an immediate demand in a new market because of the uniqueness or innovativeness of the product. A diversification policy would allow the marketer to skim the cream from each market. However, if the sales function is S-shaped, a concentrated marketing effort is necessary before reaching

**FIGURE 15–3**  Product-market factors affecting choice between diversification and concentration strategies.

| PRODUCT-MARKET FACTOR | Prefer Diversification if: | Prefer Concentration if: |
| --- | --- | --- |
| 1. Sales response function | Concave | S-Curve |
| 2. Growth rate of each market | Low | High |
| 3. Sales stability in each market | Low | High |
| 4. Competitive lead time | Short | Long |
| 5. Spillover effects | High | Low |
| 6. Need for product adaptation | Low | High |
| 7. Need for communication adaptation | Low | High |
| 8. Economies of scale in distribution | Low | High |
| 9. Program control requirements | Low | High |
| 10. Extent of constraints | Low | High |

*Source:* Igal Ayal and Jehiel Zif, "Market Expansion Strategy in Multinational Marketing," *Journal of Marketing,* Spring 1979, p. 89. Published by the American Marketing Association.

maximum market potential—that is, sales increase geometrically as the cumulative impact of marketing effort is felt. In this instance, market concentration would be the better policy.

The other factors affecting the diversification-concentration decision are fairly clear. If the growth rate of the market is more rapid in some countries, the firm may prefer to concentrate efforts there. If the demand in a number of foreign markets is unstable, the international firm can diversify risk by selling in a large number of markets. If competitive lead time is short, and the manager perceives an advantage in being first in a new market, diversification may be the better choice. Spillover effects from one market to another are another factor that would favor diversification. If the product and/or the communication program require little adaptation from market to market, diversification is achieved easily. But, if product or promotional programs must be changed considerably in each new market, concentration is the more efficient and profitable alternative. This would be particularly true if management sees the opportunity for economies of scale. When distribution costs are high, economies of scale in distribution will also favor a policy of concentration. When products are highly sophisticated or innovative, management often needs to maintain close control over marketing effort and customer relations, and in such instances, diversification may make excessive demands on managerial time. Finally, the extent of local constraints such as tariffs and currency restrictions on marketing efforts will determine whether it is better to enter many markets or only a few.

### Product-Market Analysis

The basic task of marketing, whether on a domestic or an international scale, is to match products with markets so as to profitably serve the markets' needs with the products the firm is able to offer. However, the international strategic planner too often tends to make separate evaluations of the competitive strengths of products and the comparative attractiveness of individual markets. That is, a certain product may be considered highly competitive in Country X; or Country X may be considered a stronger potential market than Country Y; but simultaneous consideration is not given to the competitive strength of the product in relation to Markets A, B, and C. The strategic planner finds it easy enough to evaluate products or markets individually, but since it is more difficult to compare them simultaneously, these comparisons are seldom made. This process of comparison can be made understandable by presentation in a graphic form such as a matrix.[3] This matrix is presented in Figure 15–4.

The key-country matrix shown in Figure 15–4, was designed for use

    [3]Gilbert D. Harrell and Richard O. Kiefer, "Multinational Strategic Market Portfolios," *MSU Business Topics*, Winter 1981, pp. 5–15.

**FIGURE 15–4**   Key-country matrix.

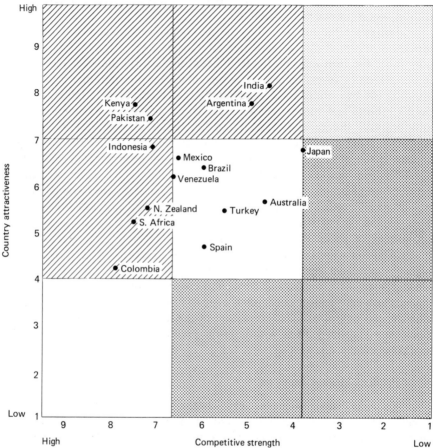

*Source:* Gilbert D. Harrell and Richard O. Kiefer, "Multinational Strategic Market Portfolios," *MSU Business Topics,* Winter 1981, p. 13.

by Ford Tractor in its international operations. The horizontal axis rates the competitive strength of the company's product to be evaluated. It includes an assessment of market share; the product fit with key products sold locally; company profit per unit; dealer profit percentage; company, distributor, and dealer representation; and promotional and other required market support. These factors can be weighted and ranked on a scale of one to nine, but information may be difficult to obtain in some foreign markets. The vertical axis is for rating the attractiveness of current and prospective foreign markets. Relevant factors can also be ranked on a scale of one to nine on the vertical axis. The factors used to rank country attractiveness will vary considerably according to the product to be sold. Thus, in the case of Ford Tractors, measures of agricultural production, size of farms, and economic strength of farms would be included in the index. For other firms it might be important to include political or legal limits on entry strategies, or cultural impact on product standardization.

## MARKETING PLANNING
## IN MULTINATIONAL CORPORATIONS

Marketing planning in multinational companies takes place both in the home office and in subsidiaries. The extent to which planning is centralized or decentralized varies from company to company, but in all cases some coordination is necessary—coordinated plans and strategies are the hallmarks of a truly multinational company. In a survey of eighty subsidiaries of multinational firms in Brazil, the planning processes used were usually patterned after the procedures in the home office.[4] Plans originated at the subsidiaries are often sent to the home office for final review and approval before implementation.

A major problem in multinational planning is the coordination of information flows within the company. Planning can be harmed by failure to get relevant information from the home office to subsidiaries. For example, a subsidiary may be given a new product to introduce without the relevant information on how it fared when introduced in other markets. In many international companies, more attention must be paid to planning the flow of intracompany information.

Another frequent problem is the lack of personnel who have training in planning. Local management may not have previous experience in planning; and in some cultures, there may even be an antipathy toward planning (see Chapter 4). Subsidiary management may feel threatened by the desire of home-office management to use the plan as a control device—a common practice among American firms that use a plan as a contract for performance evaluations. European and Japanese firms are more likely to treat plans as a means of achieving coordination and integration, and to put less emphasis on meeting standards than do American firms. Overemphasis on using the plan as an end in itself, rather than as a means of setting objectives, may result in underestimation by subsidiary planners.

The only way the home office can obtain appropriate and feasible plans from subsidiaries is to work in cooperation with them. Participative planning is necessary. Home-office staff must have an understanding of

[4]James M. Hulbert, William K. Brandt, and Raimar Richers, "Marketing Planning in the Multinational Subsidiary: Practices and Problems," *Journal of Marketing,* Summer 1980, pp. 7–15.

problems in planning abroad. Ideally, home-office personnel should include a core of managers with experience in the relevant overseas countries. Home-office personnel should also encourage as much local initiative in planning as possible. Where opportunities for marketing economies of scale and cross-country synergism exist, planning should be centralized; but each such situation must be decided according to the particular circumstances.

## COMPETITIVE FACTORS AFFECTING INTERNATIONAL MARKETING STRATEGY _____

In order for managers to develop an integrated approach to their international marketing strategy, they must develop a conceptual framework for analyzing and predicting patterns of international competition. Such a framework for competitive analysis includes international product life cycles, competitive conditions in each market, product-market segmentation, cost-volume relationships, and innovators versus followers.[5]

### International Product Life Cycles and Competition

International product life cycles were described in Chapters 3 and 10. It was pointed out that different countries are often at different stages in the adoption and usage of products, depending on the country's level of economic development. The international marketer can gain competitive advantage by expanding into markets where products are at an early stage in the product life cycle—where profits are high and the opportunity for gaining a large market share is best. Market-entry strategies (such as exporting, joint ventures, and foreign production) are also affected by international product life cycles. For low-cost production—so important in the maturity stage of a product's international life cycle—the international firm must continually assess whether its entry strategy is appropriate for each national market. Of course, this is true for all stages of the life cycle.

Comparative advantage for a particular product or industry may allow a marketer to compete effectively in certain countries and not in others. A decline in an industry's ability to produce and to market competitively, will restrict the foreign markets in which it can successfully sell. This can eventually affect the ability to sell in the domestic market. Such has been the experience of the American steel and auto industries in relationship to Japan. When a firm experiences a reduction in comparative ad-

[5]William V. Rapp, "Strategy Formulation and International Competition," *Columbia Journal of World Business*, Summer 1973, pp. 98–112.

vantage, management must either take steps to modernize and to increase the advantage, or it must move on to new products or markets where there will be an advantage.

### Product-Market Segmentation

Successful domestic marketers are aware of the importance of identifying product-market segments. A television manufacturer may have to offer a dozen different models, with varying size and performance characteristics, in order to serve a total market successfully. The same is true of foreign markets. European and Japanese automakers recognized in the American market a growing demand for smaller cars that was not being served by local manufacturers, and successfully penetrated the American auto market with compacts and subcompacts. In some instances they were able to penetrate this rich, new market with only minor adaptation of existing products; in other instances they designed completely new products for the U.S. market. American firms ultimately designed new compact cars for the same market, but they were often at an economic disadvantage because their new compacts represented entirely new products rather than slight modifications of existing products. Thus, a marketer is at the greatest competitive advantage in foreign markets when an existing product can be introduced into new markets with minimal change.

### Cost-Volume Relationships

Consultants and researchers have demonstrated with a variety of products that total costs per unit, in constant dollars, will decline by a characteristic amount (usually 20 percent to 30 percent) with every doubling of the total amount produced. This same performance has been demonstrated in many countries, including the United States, Europe, and Japan. It is used as a standard method of cost projection in the aircraft and semiconductor industries. This cost-volume relationship seems to result from a combination of learning by doing, management experience, cost-reduction investments, and economies of scale. Since a marketer's ability to lower costs depends on volume produced, the successful international marketer must think in terms of world market share in order to increase potential volume and to lower per-unit costs.

Due to the experience curve and cost relationships just described, the innovator firm will achieve the most efficient cost levels, often before follower firms can get into the market. If all other cost factors between innovator and follower firms are equal, the innovator will maintain an unassailable cost advantage. However, if any of the following factors exist over time, the followers may soon equal the cost structure of the innovators. These factors are lower start-up and initial production costs, a steeper experience-curve slope, lower inflation rates or less exposure to risks of currency devaluation, and faster rates of growth in sales volume.[6] In such instances, the innovator firm finds it necessary to continue to introduce new or improved products in order to retain its competitive advantages over the follower firms.

## OPTIMIZING AN INTERNATIONAL MARKETING STRATEGY

Ultimately, the whole field of international marketing revolves around the answer to one question—how to adapt marketing strategy to prevailing local conditions. Despite the potential benefits of standardization, the great majority of experts still operate on the premise that each national market is different and must, therefore, be provided with a distinctive marketing program. Obviously, the costs of differentiating strategies among markets are high and have a negative impact on profits.

Complete standardization would involve selling identical products, through identical distribution systems, at identical prices, and with identical promotional programs in more than one country. At the opposite extreme is the complete tailoring of products and marketing programs to each national market. The international marketer can undoubtedly maximize sale volume by customizing marketing strategy, but costs will inevitably be higher. Ultimately, the governing factor is profit. If standardization reduces costs more than it does potential sales, it should be carried on to that extent.

The economies of large-scale production have been demonstrated in many industries throughout the world. It has also been recognized that different market segments want different variations in a basic product. But, similar segments may exist in different markets. The Italian appliance industry demonstrated this fact in the European market in the 1950s. The market in each country was dominated by local firms selling products designed to serve local needs. The Italian manufacturers found that a relatively simple, standardized product could be sold successfully throughout Europe. By 1965, Italian-made refrigerators accounted for 32 percent of the French market, 40 percent to 50 percent of the Benelux market, and 12 percent of the German market.[7]

The economies of standardization are not only applicable to product costs. Package costs are an important part of total costs in some industries. For example, the manufacturer of Knorr soups sells prepared soups in different packages and package sizes in eleven European countries. Standard-

---

[6]William V. Rapp, "Strategy Formulation," p. 103.

[7]Robert D. Buzzell, "Can You Standardize Multinational Marketing?" *Harvard Business Review,* November-December 1968, pp. 102–13.

ization of the package could produce a sizeable savings in cost and at the same time reduce customer confusion.

Advertising costs can also be reduced through standardization. Although language differences limit the amount of standardization, the production of artwork can be standardized and thus save millions of dollars for large multinational marketers. Pepsi Cola, which sells in 110 countries, has found it possible to produce advertising material that, if planned carefully, can be used in most markets.

But costs and profit are not the only reasons for standardizing marketing strategy abroad. Standardization also provides consistency in dealing with customers. Managers in some international companies believe that consistency in product style, in sales and service, and in brand names and packages, projects a general image to customers that is a powerful competitive tool. Products can develop international images that have positive value in establishing consumer perceptions of the product. In addition, in many parts of the world, economic and social trends are working in favor of greater standardization. Tourism and improved international communication have the effect of making consumers mobile and their demands more and more similar. In summary, the extent of marketing standardization in strategy today is limited only by long-term profit factors.

Marketing strategy for the international marketer is the sum or total of the individual strategies developed in each of the major marketing decision areas. As shown in Figure 15–5, it includes decisions on the marketing organization structure, the strategy vis-à-vis competition, product and price decisions, distribution channels, promotion tools, physical distribution, and customer service. If an optimal strategy is to be developed, these individual marketing decisions cannot be made in isolation; decisions about each area affect decisions on others. For example, a decision to spend heavily on advertising and sales promotion may make it possible and necessary to charge a higher price, or vice versa. The close relationship between the various marketing inputs should result in a synergistic effect, so that the results far exceed the cost of the inputs.

Strategy decisions in international marketing are particularly complex because in addition to the problem of reaching an optimal balance between individual inputs, it is necessary to reach an optimal combination of strategies between foreign markets. Will the total marketing input invested in Market A yield as high a return as an equal or smaller investment in Markets B or C? The optimization process is further complicated by a differential in growth rates and competition. Although the South African market might offer a greater potential profit in the current year, it may be that, due to differentials in the rate of growth of the economies or in the nature of competition, Australia might offer greater potential growth and profit in the next five to ten years. Such strategy decisions between markets must frequently be made on the basis of incomplete or inadequate data—but that is an inherent weakness in multinational marketing planning.

**FIGURE 15–5**    A checklist for international marketing strategy.

I.    Organizational Strategy
 A.    Allocation of personnel between headquarters and overseas
 B.    Identification of areas of local autonomy and headquarters control
 C.    Provisions for upward and downward communication and regular reporting

II.    Overall Strategy
 A.    Definition of market niche
  1.    Deluxe versus mass image
  2.    Low profile versus high attention
 B.    Explicit justification for differentiation from domestic strategy
 C.    Single versus segmented market approach at local level
 D.    Foreign market entry strategy

III.    Marketing Mix Strategy
 A.    Product
  1.    Competitive options available in the market
  2.    Models to be marketed
  3.    Modifications for local market
  4.    Product simplification, if any
 B.    Price
  1.    Policies on intracompany transfer pricing
  2.    Skimming versus penetration; other company price objectives
  3.    Price relative to competition (present and potential)
  4.    Price relative to policies in other markets—effects if considerably higher or lower
 C.    Promotion
  1.    Promotional budget
  2.    Theme—standard, adapted, or combination
  3.    Media plan—adapted to what is available locally
  4.    Timing of promotional program
  5.    Measurement of promotional effectiveness
 D.    Distribution channels
  1.    Choice of intermediaries to use
  2.    Functions to be performed by channel members
  3.    Margins at each level in the channel
  4.    Short- versus long-term commitments
 E.    Physical distribution
  1.    Method, or combination of methods, of transportation to be used
  2.    Location of finished-goods inventories
  3.    Inventory levels and storage costs
  4.    Materials handling
 F.    Customer service
  1.    Service and warranty systems
  2.    Spare parts—where stored and where manufactured
  3.    Handling of customer complaints

*Source:*    Adapted from Helmut Becker and Hans B. Thorelli, eds., "Strategic Planning in International Marketing," *International Marketing Strategy.* rev. ed. (New York: Pergamon Press, 1980), pp. 367–78.

## SUMMARY

The central issue in control and coordination of international marketing strategy is the extent of centralization in decision making. The need for global and regional planning tends to increase in proportion to a firm's increased commitment to international markets. On the other extreme, environmental differences demand different approaches for effective and competitive market strategies in different national markets. While the advantages of centralized decision making vary by market and product type, the best strategy is a compromise where the firm uses centralized planning of policy, objectives, and control and performance systems, with decentralized implementation and strategy development. International training and acculturation are also effective measures in balancing local market responsiveness with intracompany coordination.

Effective international marketing requires another balance—between economies of scale and selectivity. Market effectiveness is related to scale of effort; below a certain point, called a critical mass, marketing efforts are suboptimal. Limits on resources, however, impose constraints on the ability to pursue market opportunities. Therefore, firms must choose between strategies of market concentration and diversification based on market and competitive factors. A tool for choosing the most appropriate strategy is product-market analysis.

Competitive conditions are also important to worldwide market strategy development. The stage of a product's life cycle, and the firm's comparative production or marketing advantages, affect entry strategies for foreign markets as well as the choice of markets to pursue. Foreign market experience and efficient cost-volume relationships can be key competitive tools.

To optimize international strategies in the multinational firm, there must be a capability within the corporate system to adjust strategy to different market conditions, but this must be within an integrated planning framework. Not only must marketing decisions be integrated geographically, they must also be synergistic in terms of short- versus long-term goals and the effects of overall strategy inputs on each other.

## DISCUSSION QUESTIONS

1. Explain the arguments for and against the centralization of marketing decisions and planning for the international firm.
2. Why does centralization vary in practice for different types of products and different marketing inputs?
3. Describe the ideal conditions for centralized market planning in the multinational firm.

4. How can decentralized marketing be coordinated for the international firm?

5. What is critical mass in relation to international marketing?

6. Describe how selectivity is a factor in choosing between strategies of market concentration and diversification.

7. What competitive factors affect the choice of concentration versus diversification?

8. Describe product-market analysis.

9. What are the problems of planning in multinational firms?

10. What relationship do international product life cycles have with competitive strategy in worldwide marketing?

11. How do competitors affect product and market choices of international firms?

12. Explain the correlation between competitive effectiveness and innovator firms in foreign markets.

13. How can international marketing strategy be optimized?

# SOURCE PERRIER

In 1976, Bruce Nevin was appointed as the new American marketing manager for Source Perrier, and he was assigned the task of developing an overall marketing strategy to enter the American soft-drink market. At the end of 1979, he was ready to evaluate the first three years of sales. Source Perrier, a bottler of natural mineral water, had been a familiar brand name in higher-class European restaurants and specialty shops since the nineteenth century. The water flows in a naturally carbonated condition from a spring near Nimes in Provence in southern France. This water was highly prized locally for its sparkling taste and its healthful properties for centuries, but it was first bottled commercially in 1863. By mid–twentieth century it was being sold in the familiar green bottle throughout France and much of Western Europe. Historically, it had been promoted for its "medicinal" qualities, such as helping prevent heart disease and easing the discomfort of hangovers. By the 1970s the European market for Perrier and other mineral waters had become much broader than the health-cultist market. It was being used as a source of safe drinking water in places where the local water might be unsafe. But more important, Perrier management found that many users preferred their water primarily because of its fresh and pleasant taste.

The American market had never appeared promising for Perrier. Americans had never developed the habit of drinking mineral water for health purposes, and it was impossible to develop such a market since the FDA forbids the use of unsupported medical claims. The major market for bottled water in the United States was in the West in locations where sulfur or other mineral content made the local water unpleasant to the taste. The largest producer in this market was Sparkletts, a California firm. Its water was sold in five-gallon bottles and was served in the home or office through cooler dispensers as regular drinking water. Perrier could not hope to compete in this market. The cost of transportation from France made it too expensive for drinking water.

In 1976, Perrier management made the decision to launch Perrier in the American soft-drink market, the largest and richest soft-drink market in the world. Although Perrier had been imported into the United States in very small quantities for use as a soft drink and mixer for a number of years before then, it had only served a very limited group of wealthy Perrier enthusiasts who were willing to pay a dollar or more for a 23-ounce bottle. Perrier set up a United States marketing organization as a New York subsidiary, called Great Waters of France. Bruce Nevin, a vice-president of Levi-Strauss, was hired to manage the American venture. The goal was to position Perrier as a soft-drink or liquor substitute, a fashionable drink for the nondrinker, and for the health, physical fitness, and diet-conscious American.

Through exporting mass quantities, Perrier planned to reduce landed cost in the United States by 20 percent to 30 percent to a level where it could compete as an expensive soft drink. Sixty-nine cents per 23-ounce bottle was considered low enough to appeal to the middle-income market but high enough to retain the snob appeal it had attained in the American market.

Perrier sales were less than $1 million in the United States in 1976. Distribution was limited to several major urban markets. Deliveries were made directly to the retail accounts. Nevin proposed to replace this direct distribution to distribution by soft-drink bottlers and/or beer wholesalers to achieve more frequent contact with the retail accounts.

Advertising and promotion began in 1977 with a $2 million program concentrated on the New York City and Los Angeles markets. By 1979 this budget had been increased to $11 million, divided between television and print media. Commentator for the television ads was Orson Welles, who explained to American viewers about naturally carbonated Perrier and its source. Print ads were concentrated in diet and health-oriented magazines and stressed the lack of calories and artificial additives. As a part of the health market Perrier also sponsored marathons and other foot races.

Perrier sales rose rapidly after the introduction of the new marketing program. From less than $1 million in 1976, sales rose to $30 million in 1978, and were expected to reach $120 million for 1979. Management was faced with the decision whether to continue the so-far successful strategy or to adjust it to broaden the market appeal.

## QUESTIONS

1. Describe the market you think Perrier should be seeking.
2. Evaluate the current pricing policy. Are there more promising alternatives?
3. Would you recommend changes in the distribution policy?
4. How might the advertising and promotion campaign be adapted, in terms of audience to be reached, media, and appeals?

# chapter 16

# PLANNING FOR THE FUTURE

The wristwatch industry is a perfect illustration of a major trend in international marketing—the development of "world companies" that sell "world products" to increasingly brand-conscious consumers.

Intense competition in the watch business is carried out on a worldwide basis. Production is specialized by country, according to costs of specific processes, components, and subassemblies.

Industry sales are dominated by a few leading companies in a few leading countries that have established their brand names throughout the world. Unfortunately, U.S.-based firms show signs of falling behind in the worldwide competitive struggle, although they may be able to rebound.

The corporate combat over shares of the gigantic American watch market, and the weakening position of U.S. companies in the battle seems to be similar to trends in other industries such as automobiles (Ford calling its new Escort a "world car"), consumer electronics, and telecommunications. Greater success in these competitive struggles will depend in part on improved marketing management by American firms.

So this 300-year-old, $3.5 billion-a-year industry provides an excellent example of how new technology, falling trade barriers, and changing cost relationships can affect the competitive patterns of companies and countries.*

*"International Marketing's Competitive Arena Now Features Battle of World Firms, World Brands," *Marketing News,* October 17, 1980, p. 10. Published by the American Marketing Association.

## INTRODUCTION

The period since the Second World War has seen a continuing growth in economic interdependence among the nations of the world. During the 1950s the United States was the dominant world trader. It had a comparative advantage in many products needed in world trade, so there was an increase in U.S. exports and in foreign direct investment by U.S. corporations. During the 1960s and 1970s the composition of world trade gradually changed. As the countries in the European Community and Japan improved both technology and marketing ability, their share of world trade increased. The less-developed countries have also become concerned about their place in world trade and the widening gap in standards of living between developed and less-developed countries. This has resulted in growing animosity toward foreign investment that takes unfair advantage of the LDC's cheap labor force and raw materials.

In this chapter we review four aspects of the future of international marketing. First, we discuss the relative intensity of activity in international markets that we expect for the next few years. Next we provide an overview of anticipated changes in the external environment for international business. We then focus on the changes that are likely to come in international marketing strategies and organization of international marketing activities. Last we point out your potential in a career in international marketing.

## EXPECTATIONS OF ACTIVITY
## IN INTERNATIONAL BUSINESS

For the rest of the twentieth century, economic growth worldwide will be at lower levels than it was in the years following World War II. The energy crisis of the 1970s was an important factor in halting the rapid economic growth characteristic of those earlier times. Many countries experienced high unemployment, food shortages, and wide fluctuations in exchange rates in the early 1980s. Despite such interruptions and setbacks, certain trends seem to be identifiable for the foreseeable future.

### Growing Emphasis on International Markets

Marketers will continue to broaden their perspective beyond national boundaries. As local markets become saturated or overly competitive, aggressive marketers will seek new customers abroad. For firms in small markets, or stable industries in larger markets, foreign customers provide the only opportunity for continued growth and expansion. The result should be a continuing increase in interdependence among markets and a continuing growth in total market share by the large companies with strong international orientation. This increasing interdependence makes international marketing essential to nations wishing to maintain their current standard of living. In 1979, for example, one of every seven U.S. manufacturing jobs, and one out of every four acres under cultivation, depended on exports for continued existence.[1]

### Differential Growth Rates in Less-Developed Nations

One of the major influences on world trade in the 1980s will be increasing competition from less-developed countries with rapidly rising levels of industrial exports. Exports of manufactured goods from less-developed countries are projected to increase 11 percent to 13 percent annually, while those from advanced countries will increase by only 7 percent to 8 percent. By the year 2000, less-developed countries should account for 27 percent of the world's gross international product, an increase from 17 percent in 1976.[2] The advanced nations will have to deal with this competition without reducing living standards in their own countries. To try to inhibit less-developed countries' world trade would cause world economic instability; exporting is the only way these countries can pay back their huge debts to the advanced nations.

A group of LDCs that has grown most rapidly might be classified as advanced developing countries (ADCs).[3] These are countries which no longer depend on agricultural products and raw materials for export earnings, but instead export manufactured goods. Their internal domestic markets are also faster-growing than those in other countries. The ADCs include South Korea, Taiwan, Singapore, Mexico, Brazil, and Hong Kong. These ADCs have already been able to gain a comparative advantage in textiles, electronic components, and small appliances due to high productivity and low labor costs. And, the number of ADCs is likely to increase. Other countries, such as India, Malaysia, Sri Lanka, Turkey, Chile, Kenya, and the Philippines, are at a take-off stage. Industries that are likely to shift to this growing number of ADCs are steel, shipbuilding, and large standardized appliances like refrigerators. As the developed countries have become increasingly concerned with pollution and the environment, they have at least to some extent welcomed the departure of the more polluting industries.

---

[1]Harvey Kapnick, "New Isolationism Threatens America's Future," *American Import/Export Bulletin,* March 1979, p. 140.

[2]Howard G. Sloane, "New Realities of World Trade," *American Import/Export Bulletin,* May 1978, p. 260.

[3]Gerald R. Rosen, "Looming Threat from the ADC's," *Dun's Review,* March 1979, p. 88.

### Shifting Market Position
### of the Developed Countries

As the developing countries export more and more manufactured goods, the developed and affluent countries, with their higher labor costs, will find it necessary to reassess their market positions and shift to products in which they still have comparative advantage. The United States, for example, still maintains a comparative advantage in such industries as satellite communications, deep-sea mining, electrical generating systems, aircraft, banking, insurance, and agricultural products. If nations such as the U.S. are to avoid foreign trade deficits, they must identify more areas of comparative advantage and do a better job of international marketing in these areas. Also, their governments must stop protecting the industries that operate at a comparative disadvantage and encourage the movement of resources into the more efficient areas.

Since the developed countries are not self-sufficient in many raw materials, they must rely on exports to pay for the importation of this necessity. It is important, therefore, for the governments involved to provide a program of aid and support for exporters. The United States, for example, has not had a consistent program of support for international marketers. Some government activities have been of help to exporters; others have specifically handicapped them. Government assistance will be necessary to make exporting and foreign investment more financially attractive to U.S. companies. An example of such assistance would be the provision of a deferred tax on income earned abroad until the money is repatriated.

### Types of Investment in Foreign
### Markets

For many international marketers exporting will continue to be the best way of serving new foreign markets. It allows centralization and maximum control over production and minimizes the capital investment in risky new markets. However, in order to enter some of the more strongly nationalistic markets at all, marketers will find it necessary to seek local financial participation. The result will be an increased use of joint ventures, or even licensing, in such markets. Also, manufacturers who see a decline in comparative advantage in their home countries will find it necessary to diversify production into foreign markets where they can take advantage of labor and capital opportunities or lose their ability to compete worldwide.

## EXPECTED CHANGES IN THE ENVIRONMENT _____

Probably the greatest change in the environment for international marketing in the future will be a reduction in the differences and dissimilarities between nations. With the continuing advances in communications and transportation, increasing the movement of people and ideas, nations will become more alike in superficial ways, and in some cases in basic matters. Even so, the differences will still be great, and will continue to be of major concern to international marketers.

Not only will nations grow somewhat more alike in future years, they will also continue to experience a number of evolutionary developments and changes common to all nations. Generalizations about many of these environmental changes are presented in the following pages.

### The Economic Environment

After twenty-five years of a fairly consistent worldwide trend in the direction of lower tariffs, there has been some resumption of pressures toward protectionism. This attitude gains popularity during periods of world economic recession, and the 1980s have not been an exception to this rule. Protectionism reflects the attitude that problems in the home-country economy can be solved by stamping out foreign competition. The rapid rise in energy costs during the 1970s as a result of OPEC's price increases has lead to inflation, currency devaluation, and, ultimately, to widespread unemployment in a great many energy-importing nations. By the early 1980s the pressures were strong for protection against foreign competition. One of the clauses in the Tokyo round of talks of the 1979 General Agreement on Tariffs and Trade made it easier to protect local competitors by allowing members to use informal controls to restrict imports which cause or threaten to cause injury to domestic industry. Protectionism via nontariff trade barriers will be an important aspect of trade in the future.

The International Monetary Fund will continue to develop a more active role in international monetary matters. The recession of the early 1980s revealed that the overly optimistic development programs of many developing nations, encouraged by excessive credit extension on the part of a number of international banks, had brought the international financial structure to a dangerous position of instability. With additional funding from its members, the International Monetary Fund was able to provide additional financing in several crisis situations.

The growing level of trade between the communist nations of Eastern Europe and the Western capitalistic countries should continue to increase. Western marketers have discovered huge potential markets in the communist nations, and will continue to find ways, such as countertrading, to tap these markets.

The market potential in less-developed countries will continue to grow because of differential population growth and continuing industrialization. In some instances, however, population growth will continue to equal or outpace industrialization; these countries will offer little economic potential as markets. Credit and financing will provide a greater challenge to the marketer as international banks retrench from their overly optimistic lending policies of the 1970s.

Pressures will continue to be brought on nations which, through their currency, licensing, visa, and other restrictions, have successfully limited foreign competition. More standardization, at an international level, of customs regulations, labeling, and other operating procedures will help to reduce these barriers.

### The Political-Legal Environment

Smaller nations will continue to feel frightened of, and threatened by, the sheer size and economic power of the large multinational corporations whose annual sales exceed the GNP of many less-developed nations. The result of such concerns will be the imposition of more controls on multinational activities. These controls may take the form of regulations with respect to transfer pricing, ownership of production and marketing facilities, movement of international personnel, and the like.

As a counterfoil to their negative image, the multinationals will engage in more imaginative roles in host countries. Actions to foster economic development and create new jobs will be launched to build a stronger positive image for these multinationals.

Since separate legal structures are inherent in nationalism, little can be done toward development of international business codes. However, international marketers will continue to refine the forms of their contracts in order to anticipate problems of cross-national jurisdiction and provide for international arbitration in a larger number of situations. As industrialization continues to progress in the less-developed countries, pressures to control environmental pollution will grow in these nations. Exploitation of natural resources and the environment will be much more difficult to achieve than previously, even in the LDCs. As more countries become industrialized and develop a bigger stake in protecting patented products and processes, international protection of patents and copyrights should become stronger and more consistent via regional licensing and registration.

### The Social-Cultural Environment

The mass communication media—television, movies, and radio—will continue to reduce the magnitude of cultural differences in various nations throughout the world. The resulting greater familiarity with foreign customs will reduce resistance to foreigners, foreign ideas, and change. The middle class will become more internationalized in most nations.

Less-developed countries, with their strongly traditional societies, will be most resistant and slowest to change. Religion will also affect the rate of change and/or internationalization. The strong sense of cultural identity of the Arabs makes them less willing to adopt foreign ways. The

Iranian government is now engaged in an attempt to reverse the process of internationalization and return to traditional ways. It remains to be seen whether such a reversal can be accomplished in the long run. The family will become less important as a transmitter and preserver of the culture; and nonpersonal socialization agents, such as schools, will become more important, as they already have in most developed countries. With the movement away from traditional societies, social mobility will increase.

### The Business Environment

All nations, as they develop economically, will move away from small family-owned businesses to corporations. The size of individual businesses will continue to grow, even in the LDCs. In marketing, the move will be toward more mass merchandising to reduce the costs of distribution and, hence, the prices to consumers. As business education modernizes in individual countries, more similarities in managerial values and decision making will evolve. Business decisions will be less personal and more objective. There will be increasing similarity in standards of ethical conduct; concepts such as bribery and consumer rights will come to have more common meanings.

As countries develop economically they tend to become more nationalistic. Thus, as the LDCs develop, they will show more favoritism to local firms and will feel less incentive to encourage foreign-based firms with special treatment. Businesses that will experience the greatest difficulty in adjusting to foreign business environments will be those that become most deeply involved in those environments by establishing local manufacturing facilities or joint ventures.

## CHANGES IN MARKETING STRATEGY

Chapter 10 through Chapter 14 dealt in detail with the adjustments in domestic marketing strategies necessary to develop a successful international marketing strategy. In coming years some of the current differences will become less important; others will remain unchanged.

### Product Strategy

Product attributes of importance to buyers will still have to be adapted to the individual market because of differing financial capabilities (buyers in less-developed countries will want simpler, less-expensive models), and because of regional and cultural preferences as to style, size, maintenance, and so forth. Nevertheless, mass communication with its homogenizing effect will make it possible to apply more standardized product strategies than heretofore. This increase in product standardization will result in strong pressures for adoption of universal standards. Countries such as the United States, which is still clinging to the English standard of weights and measures, will find it more and more necessary to change to the metric system, as individual American firms have already done. An added incentive for greater coordination of worldwide product models will be the continuing escalation in production, research and development, and inventory costs.

In the past, international marketers have benefited from the fact that the product life cycle for a particular product was at a different stage in different countries. A marketer could extend the life of a product currently at a mature stage in the home market, by exporting it to other markets where it would be perceived as an innovation. With greater coordination of worldwide products, the variations in stage in the life cycle will be reduced. For some products the life cycle will develop simultaneously in major world markets. The after-market will be restricted to only the most marginal country markets.

Country-of-origin stereotypes will also change. Stereotypically, the products of the most advanced nations have been generally perceived to be of higher quality and style, and technically superior. Conversely, the products of the less-developed countries were perceived as inferior. Thus, men's shirts made in France or the United States were sold in specialty stores at high prices, whereas shirts made in Taiwan or Korea were sold in discount stores at half or less than half the price. The stereotype of products from less-developed countries may continue to remain low, but the advanced developing countries are experiencing more success in upgrading the images of their products. With better communication and product diversification, this trend should continue, or even accelerate.

As less-developed world markets become more sophisticated, the demand for industrial products in general, and high-technology products in particular, will increase during coming decades. These products will still have to be adapted for the needs of the less-sophisticated markets, made easier to maintain and repair, and simplified so as to reduce the price. The large multinational corporations will continue to be dominant in the market for industrial goods, but they will be more likely to face multinational competitors from ADCs.

## Pricing Strategy

Many international marketers have historically treated pricing as an independent managerial decision in each foreign market, with no attempt to offer the same product at the same price throughout world markets. There will continue to be a rationale for varying prices among markets. Variations in transportation and distribution costs make such price differentials mandatory. It will cost more to transport a product from the United States to Australia than from the United States to Canada. Similarly, a product that can only be sold through small independent retailers in Indonesia, because no other outlets are available, will cost consumers more than in Singapore where discount retailers are available. The only way a marketer can establish a standard world price is by averaging marketing costs and charging more in the low-cost markets and less in the high-cost markets. However, such an alternative gives competitors the opportunity to undercut such prices in the low-cost markets. So, even though cost differentials may make it difficult to establish one price throughout the world, international marketers will increasingly coordinate pricing strategy with the goal of achieving uniformity.

Several other developments in pricing appear likely. As buyers in less-developed countries become more informed and sophisticated, supplier loyalty will become less important and price will become a more important factor in choosing among competitive products. Credit will become a much more important competitive tool. The marketer who demands cash on delivery for foreign exports will find that competitors willing to offer the same credit terms to foreign buyers as to domestic buyers will be taking away their business. More marketers seeking entry into markets with inadequate foreign exchange and tough currency restrictions will turn to countertrading and other methods of barter. Finally, as foreign governments become increasingly sophisticated in dealing with international business, there will be more and more restrictions against transfer pricing designed to circumvent the intent of local tax laws.

## Promotion Strategy

Continuing improvements in communications will change the promotional options available to international marketers. The growth in international and internationally-oriented magazines and newspapers will continue. The international dissemination of radio and television programs through tape recordings will continue to grow, and increased use of satellite transmission will provide more live broadcasts worldwide. The live transmission of the 1982 world soccer finals reached an enormous world audience—an exciting advertising medium for an international marketer.

The development of international media will hasten the development of international brands which can be recognized in all markets around the world. It will also encourage the development of uniform slogans, logos, and images, with the continuing recognition that cultural differences may still demand uniquely tailored appeals in certain markets. The same will be true of product positioning. To the extent that market differences permit, products will be positioned in the same manner in all markets. This increasingly worldwide approach to advertising will encourage the expansion of internationally-oriented advertising agencies.

If current trends continue, there will be an increase in advertising expenditures per capita in most world markets. Expenditures in Europe, where advertising has not been as strongly emphasized, will more nearly approach current U.S. per-capita levels. Expenditures will also continue to increase markedly in the less-developed countries. This will increase the competition for prime media time, but more media will be available as governments allow for increasing amounts of commercial time to pay the rising costs of the broadcast media.

As business education is made available to increasing numbers of young people in countries throughout the world, the pool of competent, well-trained potential salespersons will increase. Multinational companies will increasingly apply international standards in their recruitment and selection of sales personnel in order to provide uniform exposure in all markets. In addition, international sales training programs to ensure uniform sales presentations will become more common.

### Distribution Strategy

There will be more growth in mass merchandising in the less-developed countries, although the traditional retailers will continue to fill a much more important role than in developed countries. With the increase in mass merchandising, the basic types of retailers will look more alike from country to country, so that a supermarket in Ecuador will more closely resemble a supermarket in Spain or the United States than heretofore. One of the factors contributing to increases in similarity in institutions between nations will be the growth of international chains such as Sears and Safeway. These chains will provide more coordination in operating practices among nations and will hasten the introduction of innovations in the less-developed countries. The specialized middlemen for importing and exporting will be more sophisticated in information handling and marketing research, and they will do a better job of finding sources of merchandise—local and foreign.

More international marketers will take control of their foreign marketing channels. As a result they will develop closer and more long-term relationships with middlemen. With this closer relationship marketers will be better equipped and more willing to grant credit locally. The provision of credit will cement even further the relationship between foreign marketer and local representatives and, as a result, the international marketer will be able to obtain more local support in the use of displays and other promotion.

Continuing improvements in transportation and materials handling should result in a significant reduction in transportation costs. At the same time, the high cost of money will increase inventory costs, thus providing an incentive to use faster methods of transportation so as to reduce inventories in local markets. As a result, air transportation will grow at the expense of sea transportation, and sea transportation will be speeded up through mechanization, containerization, and other improved handling methods.

## Organization and Coordination of International Marketing

In the coming years there will be better coordination of marketing strategy among foreign markets via centralized decision making, and international planning activities will become part of central corporate planning. This movement will be away from the use of "export departments" or strongly decentralized foreign subsidiaries. To achieve this better coordination it will be necessary to have more movement of personnel among the various markets, but most of this movement will be for short periods of time. This centralization will provide better financial control systems and stronger marketing research sources. At the same time, care must be taken not to lose necessary individuality in each market. This will require more precise market segmentation to identify markets that can be treated similarly and those that must be approached with different strategy inputs.

## YOUR FUTURE IN INTERNATIONAL MARKETING

Firms seeking long-term growth and development must ultimately turn to international markets for new sales. Those firms that concentrate their efforts solely on domestic markets run out of growth opportunities eventually, even in a market as large as the United States. As an increasing share of management attention in the larger companies is focused on foreign markets, a larger share of total management time will be spent on international marketing. Those members of the management team who have an understanding of foreign markets and foreign marketing will be particularly in demand. Opportunities for employment in international marketing will grow at the entry level as prospective employers become more heavily involved in foreign markets. But in addition, management at all levels, in large firms, can expect to spend a greater share of time on international rather than domestic marketing problems.

Until recently small and medium-sized firms were not a good prospect for people wanting to build careers in international marketing. As competition for domestic markets increases and the markets themselves show low growth, more small and medium-sized businesses will become active in international marketing. Therefore, career opportunities in international marketing will become more diverse in terms of sizes of firms and types of products.

What kinds of training and experiences can you pursue to help build an international marketing career? First, we recommend a solid grounding in management and marketing principles, because these tend to be universal. This can come from experience and/or study. Second, we recommend that you take coursework in international content areas, such as the course you have likely just completed in international marketing. Other options might be language study, comparative politics, cross-cultural research methods, or other courses in international business. Third, we emphasize the need to build personal experience in foreign environments. Nothing else can really substitute for building an understanding of differences and similarities among people of the world. You can acquire this knowledge through study or travel or work abroad.

## SUMMARY

This chapter emphasizes changes that will affect international marketing in the future. Involvement in international markets is predicted to increase overall, but particularly for firms looking for continued high rates of growth, for new competitors from developing countries, and for producers of industrial and high-technology products. Markets will grow fastest in developing countries. All forms of foreign market-entry strategies will continue to be viable, but licensing and joint ventures are likely to increase the most due to intense competition—and nationalistic policies.

In the external environment, the general trend is toward fewer differences among the various nations. Economically speaking, international marketers will probably face more protectionism, a stronger role for the International Monetary Fund, more trade with communist and less-developed countries, and increases in nontariff barriers. Multinationals will continue to face conflict with national interests and will be forced to develop better political-business interfaces. The legal environment will remain stable with more emphasis on contracts, arbitration, regional licensing of industrial property rights, and regional regulation of environmental pollution. In the social and cultural environments there will be less resistance to change as social mobility increases and as educational systems become more significant in traditional societies as transmitters of culture. Business size will increase in scale, especially in developing countries, and local firms will be given more preference in investment incentives and regulation.

In marketing strategy we expect more standardization in all policy areas as international marketing managers seek ways to improve their cost structures and international images. This will be made easier by the internationalization of product standards, product images based on country of origin, media and programming, mass merchandising, and chain retailing. As a student you are in a good position to begin a career in an expanding, exciting field . . . international marketing management!

## DISCUSSION QUESTIONS

1. How will international patterns of business change in the near future?
2. Why are less-developed nations experiencing more growth in international business than are the advanced countries?
3. How are market-entry strategies going to change in the future?
4. What are the significant aspects of the future economic environment for international marketing?
5. Why do you believe our legal environment for international marketing will remain stable in the future?
6. How will social and cultural environments change in developing countries? What will be the impact on marketing strategy?
7. Explain how nationalism is expected to affect the business environment.
8. What countries do you feel will improve their stereotypical images in international markets?
9. Differentiate between consumer and industrial products in terms of future product strategies.
10. How will international price setting differ from current policies in the future?
11. How will promotion strategy be affected by changes in media structure and programming?
12. What changes are on the horizon for international distribution planning?
13. How can you prepare yourself for a career in international marketing?

# appendix A

# OUTLINE
# FOR
# INTERNATIONAL
# MARKETING PLAN

This appendix is designed to help students develop marketing plans for international marketing projects. It suggests the types of information needed to execute a marketing plan for foreign markets—but it cannot answer these questions or even tell you where to find the answers because the guidelines must be general enough to apply to industrial products, consumer goods, and/or services. Furthermore, the issues suggested in the outline may need extensive study and detailed research in some countries, while in others they may be unimportant to successful marketing. Only you can judge the importance of these issues for your project.

Before beginning the project it would be helpful to review Chapter 2. This chapter focuses on the steps a firm goes through in becoming "international," as well as the different goals and entry strategies it might choose for international markets. You will also find Appendix B helpful since it lists possible sources to use in researching foreign markets and their environments.

Welcome to the practice of international marketing management!

### Step 1: Assessment of Your Firm's
### International Goals and Capabilities

A. *Situation of the Firm*
   1. What are our present domestic marketing and corporate goals?
   2. What are our competitive advantages and disadvantages in current products and organizational resources?
   3. What are our present capital and personnel resources? What effect will they have on any foreign marketing activities?

4. What do we hope to achieve in foreign markets? What is our overall international marketing goal?
5. What are our foreign sales objectives in relation to domestic sales goals?
6. What amount of control and market penetration do we want abroad? Are we interested in one or multiple foreign markets?
7. What are significant economic, legal, regulatory, demographic, technological, social, cultural, and/or competitive trends affecting our firm and our industry? How will these affect our abilities to develop foreign market opportunities?

B. *Analysis of the Firm's Products*
1. What needs do my products satisfy? Are these needs culturally determined?
2. Who are my current markets? Will these groups be similar demographically, attitudinally, or in behavior to foreign markets?
3. What are the sales trends for my products and my industry domestically and internationally?
4. What are my competitors' strengths and weaknesses in similar products here and abroad?
5. What marketing mix elements are important to the sale of my product? (For example: transportation methods, intensity of distribution, types of intermediaries and services provided, communications media, type of messages to target markets, market information, caliber of sales force, packaging, new product or feature development, product quality and price relationships, branding, price tactics, sales promotion to the trade and to consumers.)

DECISION POINT 1.

You must summarize what are your goals, resources, strengths, and weaknesses for international marketing. These provide the basis on which you should develop criteria for judging foreign market opportunities. You should screen out countries that cannot possibly meet your goals, or that do not match the resources you might have in marketing, managing, or financing an investment in developing foreign opportunities.

Now, select a few target national markets and proceed with your analysis. If the market appears to meet your criteria and provides an attractive general environment, you should deepen your level of information-seeking in Step 2. If a national market does not have a necessary, supportive political or other environment after initial investigation, abandon it and begin researching another more promising country.

## Step II: Analysis of Foreign Market Environments

A. *Economic and Demographic Environment*
1. What are the country's gross national product, per-capita income, and income distribution like? Will these affect demand for my product?

2.  What are the trends in the country's major economic indices? (For example: rates of inflation, interest, industrial growth, purchasing power.)
3.  What is my target market's economic position with respect to the rest of society?
4.  Will demand for my product be subject to fluctuating economic conditions? (For example: essential vs. luxury items, different plans for economic development.)
5.  What measures of economic development are relevant for determining size and growth of this potential market? (For example: kilowatt-hours generated per capita, miles of road per capita, mortality or birth rates, hospital beds per capita, literacy rates.)
6.  What are the general levels of exports and imports within the country?
7.  What is the country's balance-of-payments position? Is its currency stable? If not, what is the major cause of instability or nonconvertibility of its currency?

B.  *Political and Regulatory Environment*
1.  What form of government does the country have? Is it politically stable? How long has the current government been in power and how did they achieve power?
2.  What is the government's attitude toward imports and foreign investment?
3.  What controls or restrictions, if any, are placed on foreign investors in my industry?
4.  Will my products or investment be politically vulnerable? (See Chapter 7.)
5.  What are the major political parties (or opposition forces) in the country and what are their attitudes about foreign investment and imports?
6.  What policies exist to favor local producers?
7.  What is the general regulatory environment for my products and industry? (For example: capital sources; labor laws; product, quality, or design controls; restrictions on resource inputs.)
8.  Are my firm or its products likely to be affected by forces such as nationalism, regional antagonism, strikes, or other political disruptions?

C.  *Technological and Competitive Environment*
1.  How do my competitors transfer their marketing, production, or management expertise to the local foreign market?
2.  How difficult will it be to transfer the technologies associated with my product to the foreign market?
3.  What role does the local government assume when foreign technology is involved?
4.  How can we protect our industrial property rights, such as patents and trademarks, abroad?
5.  What are the quality-control requirements for production of this product? Can they be met in this foreign market?
6.  What stage of the life cycle will my products be in, in the foreign market?
7.  What will be my products' perceived relative advantage, divisibility, communicability, complexity, and compatibility in the foreign market?

What type of innovation is my product—if it will be viewed by the foreign market as an innovation?

8. Who will be my major competitors in the foreign market? What are their strengths and weaknesses in such things as products, production capabilities, management?

9. What are the bases of competitive strategies in the foreign market? (For example: prices and product quality.)

D. *Social and Cultural Environment*

1. Is language, religion, education, art, or aesthetics likely to affect interest in or demand for my products? If so, how?

2. What is the social structure of the foreign market? Are there distinct subgroups (nationalities, cultural or subcultural minorities)? What are the relationships of the various groups to each other?

3. What is the basis for social or economic mobility in this society? Is there mobility?

4. What is my target market's social status in relation to the rest of their society?

5. What are the important cultural values that will affect demand for my product, or preferences for different types of marketing strategies?

6. What are the societal and target-market attitudes toward change in this society?

7. How will adoption of my products affect life styles or business practices of my target market?

8. Does economic or cultural dualism exist in the market (traditional and modern ways of life existing side by side)?

9. How will the "silent language" (see Chapter 4) affect business interaction in the foreign market?

10. What are general attitudes in the foreign market about foreign products and foreign companies?

DECISION POINT 2.

You must now decide if each country you have reviewed presents a supporting environment for an international marketing investment of *some* kind. (You have not yet determined an entry strategy.) If a country seems to have an attractive environment in your Step-2 analysis, you need to investigate the actual market and market structure there. This constitutes Step 3.

## Step III: Analysis of Market Characteristics and Structure

A. *Market Characteristics*

1. What are the demographic characteristics (age, sex, income, education, occupation, geographic location, stage in family life cycle, social class position) of my potential market?

2. What attitudes will this target group have initially toward my products?

Will product adoption require a change in attitudes about positive benefits of product use or possession?

3. What product attributes will be important in determining this target group's patronage of my products?

4. What person(s) or groups will influence this target group's evaluation and purchase of my products?

5. Will product adoption require the target market to change its purchasing behavior or use of other products? If so, how important are these to their overall life styles and/or value systems?

6. How often and where is the target group most likely to purchase similar products (products in current use that meet the same needs)?

7. Who will be the most likely actual buyers of my products? Who will be the most likely users of my product?

8. What will be the relative importance of factors such as preselling through mass media, price, convenience, product durability, service after the sale, word-of-mouth information sources, packaging, and branding to the likely target market?

9. What is the target group's opinion of and attitude toward foreign products and foreign companies? How will such attitudes affect demand for my products?

B. *Market Structure*

1. What types of intermediaries are available for products similar to mine? What services do they perform?

2. How broad is the market coverage of the different types of intermediaries among different types of buyers, if such segments exist within the market?

3. What are the financial and technical capabilities of current intermediaries to perform necessary distribution services for my products?

4. Who has the power within current distribution channels? What is their basis of power? How do they exercise power?

5. How are intermediaries motivated to cooperate with each other and with manufacturers for products similar to mine?

6. What amount and type of communication is needed to keep distribution tasks running smoothly for similar products?

7. Are there standard "margins" or pricing techniques for resellers of products similar to mine? If so, are they sufficient to motivate my desired level of distribution service?

8. What is the average time for products to move from producers to consumers in this market? How will that affect product design and distribution of my products?

9. What are the major means used for transporting similar products in this market?

10. Are there any geographic or climatic conditions that will affect transportation or storage of my products?

DECISION POINT 3.

You are now in a good position to select a target market for each national market where you wish to compete. It may also be appropriate to go back through Step 2 and gather more details about the external environment in each country, given your particular target market. You should now also be able to identify the broad parameters in each market that will constrain your choice of marketing strategies. As in any design project, parameters are helpful because they suggest what direction to take in choosing strategy options. This should make it "easier" for you to select your marketing mix.

You should now set out marketing objectives for each national market you have decided to explore. Your statement of objectives should include identification of your target market, and your sales and market share goals for one year and longer term, maybe five or ten years.

The next step will be to decide the best method for entering your target foreign market, given the environment there and your specific market objectives. You will also take these objectives and knowledge of the target market and external environment as a basis for developing your marketing strategy.

### Step IV: Development of Market Entry and Marketing Mix Strategies

A. *Market Entry Decisions*
1. What are my short- and long-term marketing goals for this national market?
2. What form of market entry is used by other foreign companies in my industry in this market?
3. What legal requirements must be met for each market entry option (exporting, licensing, franchising, joint ventures, foreign production)? How will these affect the cost of my investment and competitiveness of my products?
4. Behind the legal structure, what are attitudes of political and other leaders in this market toward companies operating there using different market entry strategies?
5. How much control over my target market and market strategy can I actually have with each entry option?
6. What adjustments should I make in my marketing strategy for different methods of market entry?
7. If sales are less than expected, what ability will I have to change our strategy in this market?
8. Are there desirable import agents, distributors, franchisees, or joint venture partners in this market? If so, who are they likely to be? What will be their strengths and weaknesses as compared to mine?
9. Which market entry method is most likely to deliver a reasonable level of market penetration, given the external environment, competition, and my marketing strategy?
10. What will be the pay-back period and break-even points for each method of market entry and investment?

11. Two, five, or ten years from now, will I be content with my choice of market entry? If not, will I be able to change it?

B. *Marketing Strategy Decisions*

1. What is my objective for product positioning in this market?
2. What product(s) will I introduce in this market?
3. What stage of the product life cycle will each be seen in, by the target market?
4. What design or other changes in the physical product are needed before successful entry into this market?
5. Are there any foreign regulations that will affect product design or packaging, branding, servicing of the product?
6. What role(s) will packaging have (protection, promotion, economy in storage/transport, information) in my overall marketing strategy?
7. What cultural or aesthetic preferences will affect package, brand name, and product designs?
8. What is the best branding policy in this market? Why?
9. What intensity of market exposure do I want?
10. What are the channels of distribution and types of retailers used by my likely competitors?
11. What types of intermediaries and how many do I want in order to get adequate market coverage, given my sales and market share goals?
12. What forms of support can I expect from my intermediaries? How will I supplement their support?
13. What factors will motivate intermediaries to buy and support my products?
14. What margins will be expected by intermediaries and will these be sufficient to compensate them for services I expect them to perform? How will these margins affect my competitiveness in this market?
15. What will be my overall pricing goals?
16. What are my costs, and what are competitor's prices for similar products?
17. What will be the perceived relationship between my prices and product quality?
18. Are there any legal restrictions on my pricing policies?
19. What control will I have, and do I want, over final prices that consumers pay?
20. What ability will I have to react to competitors' price changes?
21. How will tariffs affect product or supply-parts prices?
22. What media are available for commercial advertising? Who are their respective audiences? How do they match with my target market?
23. What is the relative importance of promotional tools (advertising, personal selling, sales promotion, public relations) in my competitors' promotion strategies?
24. What legal restrictions, if any, will affect my choice or use of media, advertising messages, or sales force?
25. What is the needed size for our sales force? Where will we recruit salespersons? How will they be trained, compensated, and motivated?
26. What will be the responsibilities of the sales force in addition to product selling?

27. What will be our mass communication media and messages?
28. How does our target market perceive products that are promoted through these media?
29. What media are available and important in this market that I do not use at home?
30. How will I allocate the promotion budget?
31. What is my plan for publicity and public relations in this market?
32. How will I schedule my media plan? What are my frequency and reach goals?
33. Who will be responsible for overseeing our marketing plan at headquarters? In this country?
34. Who will implement each part of the above marketing plan?
35. How will we measure effectiveness in reaching our goals?
36. What flexibility and controls are there for adjusting our marketing plan during the year?

# A COMPENDIUM
# OF SECONDARY SOURCES
# OF INFORMATION
# ON INTERNATIONAL
# MARKETING

I. Government Sources
  A. United States Government
    The United States government is anxious to encourage the exportation of goods by American industry. In order to keep business informed of export opportunities, the government has generated a large and varied amount of information of use to marketing analysts. The most important single source of such information is the U.S. Department of Commerce, but other government agencies also provide useful data. These data take three forms: regular publications, statistical studies, and special information services.

    1. Regular U.S. Government Publications
      a. *A Basic Guide to Exporting*. U.S. Department of Commerce. Designed to help firms that have decided to get into exporting to begin the process. Included is a summary of Commerce Department services available to exporters and a bibliography of export publications.
      b. *Business America,* weekly. This is the principal publication of the U.S. Department of Commerce. It provides news on domestic and international business. It also lists requests from foreign governments who may want to purchase from U.S. firms, and tenders for payment as well as overseas sales, representation, and licensing opportunities.
      c. *Foreign Trade Report,* FT 410. Provides a monthly statistical record of shipment of all merchandise from the United States to foreign countries by commodity and by country, including both quantity and dollar value of these exports. It contains cumulative export statistics from the first of the calendar year on more than 150 countries and 3,000 U.S. products.
      d. *International Economic Indicators*. Quarterly reports provide basic data on the economy of the United States and seven

other principal industrial countries, including gross national product, industrial production, trade, prices, finance, and labor. It measures changes in key competitive indicators and highlights economic prospects and recent trends in the eight countries.

  e. *Market Share Reports,* annual. Shows U.S. participation in foreign markets, for manufactured products, during the previous five years. The 88 reports in a country's series represent import values for the U.S. and eight other leading suppliers, and the U.S. percentage share for about 900 manufactured products.

  f. *Labor Developments Abroad,* U.S. Department of Labor. Compares foreign countries with the U.S. in regard to labor conditions and outlook.

  g. *International Marketing Information Series.* Publications that focus on foreign market opportunities for U.S. suppliers.

   (1) *Global Market Surveys.* Findings from extensive foreign-market research on target industries and target business opportunities are developed into global market surveys. Each survey condenses foreign market research conducted in fifteen or more nations into market summaries of individual countries.

   (2) *Country Market Sectoral Surveys.* In-depth coverage of the most promising U.S. export opportunities in a single foreign country, on leading industrial sectors. Surveys are currently available on Brazil, Nigeria, Venezuela, Indonesia, and Japan.

   (3) *Overseas Business Reports.* Provide basic background data for business people who are evaluating various export markets or are considering entering new areas. Reports include both developing and industrialized countries.

   (4) *Foreign Economic Trends and Their Implications in the United States.* Gives in-depth reviews of current business conditions, current and near-term prospects, and the latest available data on the gross national product, foreign trade, wage-and-price indices, unemployment rates, and construction starts.

  h. *Overseas Trade Promotions Calendar.* Provides a 12-month schedule of U.S. Trade Center exhibitions and international trade fairs in which U.S. companies are planning to participate.

  i. *Commercial News U.S.A.* A publication distributed to U.S. Foreign Service posts, where personnel extract relevant information, translate it, and publish it in their commercial newsletters. Includes photos and descriptions of new U.S. products.

 2. U.S. International Information Services

  a. *Foreign Traders Index,* U.S. Department of Commerce. A

computerized file on over a hundred thousand foreign importers, agents, distributors, manufacturers, service organizations, retailers, and other potential users of American exports. Information is available in the following forms:

    (1) *Trade List Service.* Contains names and addresses of distributors, agents, and other firms classified by the products they handle and the services they offer. Available in two forms: business lists that provide commercial data, and lists of state-controlled trading companies.

    (2) *Export Mailing List Service.* Lists of foreign organizations classified by geographic and commodity groups. Available on mailing labels, computer printout, or magnetic tape, the lists include—to the extent available—the name and address of the firm, name and address of the executive officer, type of organization, year established, relative size, number of employees, and product or service codes by SIC number.

b. *Tailored Export Marketing Plan Service.* Limited to one or two products and covering a maximum of eight overseas markets, it identifies the best markets and provides a step-by-step marketing plan for firms new to exporting.

c. *Agent-Distributor Service.* Designed to help U.S. firms find agents or distributors in most countries. Overseas Commerce Staffers identify up to six distribution representatives in a country and send their names and addresses to the U.S. exporting company.

d. *World Traders Data Reports.* Profiles of individual foreign firms, including financial information and description of the nature of operations (sales area, number of employees, products handled). Reports also include other sources of supply to the firm, and its suitability as a trade contact for the U.S. firm.

e. *Trade Opportunities Program* (TOP). A computerized mail service gathered by the U.S. Foreign Service matching U.S. firms with trade opportunities. Subscribers receive weekly trade bulletins on trade opportunities and promotional activity in their product areas.

3. U.S. Government Statistics and Special Studies

    a. U.S. Department of Commerce

        (1) *Consumer Goods Research.* Reports covering the best foreign sales opportunities for a single U.S. consumer industry or group of industries.

        (2) *Export Information for U.S. Business Firms.* Describes a wide range of services to help export businesses.

        (3) *Foreign Business Practices.* Basic information on laws and practices governing exporting, licensing, and investment abroad.

        (4) *Foreign Economic Trends and Their Implications for*

*the United States.* A series of commercial reports issued annually or semi-annually by Foreign Service posts abroad, describing current business and economic developments in practically every country that offers a present or potential market for U.S. goods.

(5)  *Foreign Market Reports.* Lists unclassified economic and industry reports prepared by U.S. commercial officers abroad.

(6)  *Global Market Surveys.* In-depth reports on twenty or thirty of the best markets for a selected U.S. industry or group of industries, such as computers, food processing, or packaging equipment.

(7)  *International Economic Indicators and Competitive Trends.* Provides exporters with an overview of international trends which can be used as a basis for making more detailed analyses of particular countries.

(8)  *International Marketing Newsmemo.* Includes information bulletins prepared by the U.S. Foreign Service and reports of American business people, covering a wide variety of industries, products, and countries.

(9)  *Market Share Reports.* A basis for evaluating overall market size trends, comparing the competitive position with foreign exporters, and selecting foreign distributors. Each report gives five-year statistical data on over 1,100 commodities by 88 countries.

(10)  *Overseas Business Reports.* Provides background information, such as basic economic data, information on foreign trade regulations and market considerations, on specific countries.

(11)  *Producer Goods Research.* Provides reports covering the best foreign sales opportunities for a single U.S. producer-goods industry or group of industries.

(12)  *A Summary of U.S. Export Administration Regulations.* Provides a brief description of current export controls, for use by the occasional trader.

(13)  *Worldwide Trade List.* Contains data on foreign credit reporting services that are willing to respond to requests for credit information by U.S. companies.

b.  Department of State. *Background notes.* These are reports on individual countries which deal with the history, economy, government and political conditions, and foreign relations.

c.  Other government departments. Information on international trade is also provided by other government departments and agencies. These include the Federal Trade Commission, the Agency for International Development, the Department of Agriculture, and the International Trade Commission.

4.  U.S. Government Publications. All such publications can be obtained by writing to the Superintendent of Documents, U.S. Gov-

ernment Printing Office, Washington, D.C. 20402.

5. Other U.S. Government Services

   a. *Country Marketing Managers.* Country marketing managers in the Department of Commerce, who can be reached by telephoning the U.S. Department of Commerce, can furnish commercial and economic information on the following countries:

   France and Benelux countries
   Germany and Austria
   Italy, Greece, and Turkey
   Nordic countries
   Spain, Portugal, Switzerland, and Yugoslavia
   United Kingdom and Canada
   Australia and New Zealand
   East Asia and Pacific
   Japan
   Southeast Asia
   Brazil, Argentina, Paraguay, and Uruguay
   Mexico, Central America, and Panama
   Remainder of South America and the Caribbean countries
   North Africa
   Near East
   Iran, Israel, and Egypt
   Eastern Europe
   USSR,
   People's Republic of China

   b. Export-Import Bank. The bank offers a special service involving information for small exporters on discount loans, and foreign bank credits. It also sponsors several programs of financing to exporters.

   c. Overseas Private Investment Corporation. A U.S. government agency which will share the cost of market feasibility studies with firms interested in selling in developing countries. It also provides insurance protection on currency inconvertibility; expropriation; and loss or damage caused by war, revolution, or insurrection.

   d. Small Business Administration. This agency provides aid to small or minority exporters through programs of information and education and through funds for the purchase of equipment and materials necessary to manufacture for export.

B. Port Authority of New York and New Jersey

   This authority provides two information services.

   1. *Interfile.* Abstracts of magazine and journal articles that include foreign market data—Source, World Trade Center, New York, N.Y.

   2. *Marketmatch.* A computerized information system that provides American sellers and buyers with information about prospective sellers and buyers of their products in other countries. A fee is

charged for each sale made.

C. Other Governments

Although no government provides as extensive information about foreign markets as the U.S. government, foreign governments are often an inexpensive and valuable source of foreign market information. This information is often available through the country embassies or consulates in the United States.

Many foreign governments publish booklets providing general business information about their countries. Most are prepared for circulation outside the country and are made available through embassies.

II. International Organizations

A. *United Nations*

The U.N. provides the widest range of data.

1. *Standard International Trade Classification,* 2nd rev., 1975, United Nations, Sales Section, New York. This is a guide to the Standard International Trade Classification System (SITC), used by 80 percent of UN member countries.

2. *Commodity Trade Statistics,* Series D. United Nations, Sales Section, New York. Includes export and import figures by country for many UN member countries.

3. Economic Statistics. Information on population, income, industrial ownership, and other factors that should be considered in drawing up a market profile. Among the sources of economic statistics are the following United Nations publications:

a. *Statistical Yearbook of the United Nations,* annual. Presents data on social and economic conditions in over 250 countries. A monthly statistical supplement to the Yearbook is also available.

b. *Demographic Yearbook.* Includes tables giving population breakdowns for individual countries.

B. Organization for Economic Cooperation and Development

1. *Statistics of Foreign Trade,* Series C. Organization for Economic Cooperation & Development (OECD), Paris. An exporter can get an excellent quick overview of exports and imports of OECD member countries from this publication. Breakdowns are by product and are indexed under the Standard International Trade Classification System.

2. *General Statistics,* bimonthly. Organization for Economic Cooperation and Development, Paris. Includes data on industrial production, population, wholesale and retail indices, and salaries and wages for OECD countries. Annual subscription includes monthly supplement giving seasonal adjustments for the main economic indicators.

C. European Communities

1. *Foreign Trade, Analytical Tables* (NIMEXE series). European Community, Washington, D.C. Market data on European Community member countries, and on selected nonmember countries. Classifications are under the Brussels Tariff Nomenclature System.

2. *General Statistical Bulletin,* published eleven times a year. European Community, Washington, D.C. Provides population and economic data on member countries.

3. *Nomenclature for the Classification of Goods in Customs Tariffs,* 1970. Brussels Customs Cooperative Council. This directory covers the Brussel Tariff Nomenclature System (TRN), used largely for tariff purposes. The system also serves as a reference tool for locating market information on certain developing and Western European countries.

4. Statistical Data. Council of Europe, Strasbourg, France. Provides data on industrial production, transport, trade, finance, and population for member countries.

III. Nongovernment Published Sources
   A. U.S. Magazines Published for Circulation Abroad
      1. *The American Exporter,* Johnson International Publications, New York.
      2. *Modern Government/National Development,* International Publications, Westport, Conn.
      3. *Worldwide Projects,* International Publications, Westport, Conn.
   B. Reference Services
   The following is a selection of commercial reference services which provide concise reports, drawn from a number of sources, on economic conditions in specific countries. Available on a fee or subscription basis, they are not inexpensive. Many large banks have subscriptions to these services; frequently they make reports available to clients requesting them.
      1. *Indicators of Market Size for 140 Countries,* annual. Business International Corp., New York. Publishes worldwide statistical charts of market indicators (population, national income, gross national product, average hourly earnings) for individual countries.
      2. *Quarterly Economics Review.* The Economist Intelligence Unit, Ltd., London, England. Provides reports on economic and commercial conditions in individual countries.
      3. *Investing, Licensing, and Trading Conditions Abroad.* Business International Corp., New York. Deals with conditions for doing business in 56 major world markets.
      4. *Marketing in Europe Series,* monthly. The Economist Intelligence Unit, Ltd., London, England. Publishes reports on distribution of consumer products in European countries.
      5. *World Trade Annual and Supplement.* Walker and Co., New York. The Annual provides data on exports and imports of most developed countries. Classifies data by product and by country. The Supplement includes trade statistics on countries not in the Annual. The statistics appearing in the Supplement are not contributed by the respective countries themselves, but are compiled on the basis of data provided by other countries.
   C. Directories
      1. *ABC Europe Production,* annual. Export Edition GmbH, Darm-

stadt, West Germany. Lists 500,000 names and addresses of manufacturers in 29 countries.

2. *Bottin International Directory.* Bottin International, Paris. Lists over 300,000 firms in 110 countries under 1,000 product classifications.

3. *International Reference Handbook.* Simon & Schuster, Inc., New York. Statistics and information on 120 countries.

4. *Kelly's Manufacturers and Merchants Directory.* Kelly's Directories, Ltd., New York. Lists firms in the U.S. and other countries that do a large amount of exporting.

5. *Kompass.* Kompass Register, Ltd., Surrey, England. Includes lists of manufacturers and resellers by product line, country, and amount of imports or exports.

6. *Made in Europe.* Marketing Organization GmbH & Co., KG, Frankfurt/Main, Unterlindaue, West Germany. Directory series lists European manufacturers looking for product outlets: a *Technical Equipment Catalog, Furniture and Interior Catalog,* and *Consumer Goods Catalog.*

7. *Marconi's International Register,* 1978. Telegraphics Cable & Radio Registrations, Inc., Mamaroneck, N.Y. Lists 40,000 international trading, shipping, and manufacturing firms.

8. *Trade Directories of the World.* Croner Publications, Queens Village, N.Y. Guide to trade and business directories published in foreign countries.

D. Handbooks

1. *Editor & Publisher Yearbook.* Encyclopedia of the newspaper industry. Presents useful information for companies considering advertising in newspapers abroad.

2. *Exporters' Encyclopedia.* Dun & Bradstreet, Inc., New York. Describes import regulations and procedures, and other matters bearing on trade, by country.

3. *Exporters Financial and Marketing Handbook,* 1973. Noyes Data Corp., Park Ridge, N.J.

4. *International Handbook of Advertising.* McGraw-Hill Book Co., New York. Deals with many facets of advertising.

5. *Handbook of International Marketing: How to Export, Import and Invest Overseas.* McGraw-Hill Book Co., New York. Provides management advice and reminders for exporters.

6. *Modern Packaging Encyclopedia,* annual. McGraw-Hill Book Co., New York. Provides information on all aspects of packing and packaging.

7. *Ulrich's International Periodicals Directory.* R.R. Bowker Co., New York. A worldwide listing of magazines and periodicals by country and subject heading.

E. Monographs

1. *Financing International Operations.* American Management Association, Inc., New York. This monograph covers sources and methods of financing international business operations.

2. *Improving Worldwide Distributor Service.* Business International Corp., New York. This service makes recommendations for selection of distributors; evaluates and sets standards for their performance.
3. *International Code of Advertising Practices.* International Chamber of Commerce, U.S. Council, New York. Information on advertising practices and ethics throughout the world.
4. *Researching Foreign Markets.* Conference Board, Inc., New York. A guide to overseas market research.

F.   Articles

1. "Designing Products for Export," *Forum,* International Trade Center, Geneva, Switzerland (July–Sept. 1975).
2. Dunn, S. Watson, "The Changing Legal Climate for Marketing and Advertising in Europe," *Columbia Journal of World Business* (Summer 1974).
3. Michael J. Etzel and Bruce J. Walker, "Advertising Strategy for Foreign Products," *Journal of Advertising Research* (June 1974).
4. Hodgson, S. C., "Exporting on a Small Budget," *Forum,* International Trade Center, Geneva, Switzerland (Jan.–March 1977).
5. N. T. Joyner and S. Lurie, "Picking the Right Agent," *Forum,* International Trade Center, Geneva, Switzerland (Oct.–Dec. 1977).
6. Kacker, M. P., "Export Oriented Product Adaptation," *Management International Review,* Wiesbaden, West Germany, 15, no. 6 (1975).
7. A. H. Kizilbash and A. A. Mail, "Export Marketing in a Changing Environment," *Journal of Business,* Seton Hall University, South Orange, N.J. (December 1976).
8. Meidan, Arthur, "The Export Marketing Matrix," *Management International Review,* Wiesbaden, West Germany, 15, no. 6 (1975).
9. Montgomery, H. B. G., "Export Marketing,"*Forum,* International Trade Center, Geneva, Switzerland (July–Sept. 1975).
10. Picard, J., "How European Companies Control Marketing Decisions Abroad," *Columbia Journal of World Business* (Summer 1977).
11. "Product Brochures: Your Silent Representative," *Forum,* International Trade Center, Geneva, Switzerland.
12. "Reluctant Exporters," *Business Week* (April 10, 1978).
13. David A. Ricks, Jeffrey S. Apran, and Marilyn Y. Fu. "Pitfalls in Advertising Overseas," *Journal of Advertising Research* (December 1974).
14. Schmoll, F. A., "Make a Marketing Plan," *Forum,* International Trade Center, Geneva, Switzerland (Jan.–March 1971).
15. Susman, C. L., "The Changing Nature of Export Management," *Atlanta Economic Review* (Sept.–Oct. 1975).

G.  Publications of Auditing Firms and Banks

Sources of current information about developments of importance to business people in particular countries.

1. *Country Reports.* Barclays International Bank, 200 Park Ave., New York, N.Y. 10005. One-page reports covering the economic outlook for particular countries (African, Caribbean, West Indian, etc.). Among the topics are employment, inflation, and political conditions.

2. *East-West Market,* biweekly. Chase Manhattan Bank. Covers new developments in trade with Communist bloc countries. By subscription.

3. Ernst & Ernst International Quarterly, 1977. Ernst & Ernst International Operations, Citicorp, 153 E. 53 St., New York, N.Y. 10022. Covers new tax developments in foreign countries where the bank has offices.

4. *Information Guides.* Price Waterhouse & Co., International Tax Department, 1251 Ave. of the Americas, New York, N.Y. 10020. A series of booklets on requirements for doing business in specific countries. Each booklet is on a different topic such as taxes, international exchange rates.

5. *International Finance.* Manhattan Bank. This covers broad economic issues—such as balance of trade—and their importance to U.S. companies doing business in particular countries. Provided free of charge to clients.

6. *Mideast Markets,* biweekly. Chase World Information Corp., One World Trade Center, New York, N.Y. 10048.

7. *World Financial Markets.* Morgan Guaranty Trust Co. In-depth focuses on international economic developments—OPEC. Available at no charge to bank clients.

IV. Other Sources of Information

A. Chambers of Commerce
Many foreign countries maintain chamber-of-commerce offices in the United States which function as a type of permanent trade mission. These chambers of commerce generally have research libraries available and are knowledgeable regarding further sources of information on specific products or marketing problems. The United Chamber of Commerce publication, *Foreign Commerce Handbook: Basic Information and a Guide to Sources,* is an excellent reference source for foreign trade information.

B. Business and Trade Associations
The industry trade association will often provide information to its members. The International Advertising Association, for instance, makes an annual survey of international advertising and acts as a clearinghouse for the interchange of experience in the field. Both users and practitioners can benefit from this specialized expertise.
*The National Foreign Trade Council* is the principal association of American companies doing business abroad. Also, on a local level, there are over fifty foreign trade associations of world trade clubs in major cities around the United States. They are extremely valuable for the personal exchange of information and experience among members.

C.  Service Organizations
    Many companies selling services to firms in international trade must
    keep up with international developments to do their own job effec-
    tively. The information they gain is usually available free to their
    clients. Included are:
    1.  The major American banks
    2.  Major transportation companies, principally the international air-
        lines and the steamship companies
    3.  Advertising agencies with offices in foreign countries
    4.  International consultants.

# Appendix C

# "DIARY" OF AN EXPORT SHIPMENT

Buyer:   Ex-Im Industries
             San Antonio, Texas

Seller:   Kingtex International Corporation
             Taipai, Taiwan

Goods:   Brief Cases
             Jogging shoes
             Bill Folders

# KINGTEX INTERNATIONAL CORPORATION

April 1, 1982

ATTN:  Sr. Rudy Sandoval
       Sr. Ish Casanova


EXIM Industries Corporation
109 Lexington, Suite 217
San Antonio, Texas  78205
U.S.A.

Estimados Rudy & Ish:

We are pleased to inform you that your orders #82001, #82005, and #82006 have been shipped via S.S. "NEPTUNE GARNET V-9WA", from Keelung to Houston on March 24, 1982.


Enclosed please find the shipping documents for your detailed reference.  You will find that the total amount of Invoice # 82001 has been increased  US$ 2,071.20.  This is due to an increase in the costs charged by Sea Freight by 25% as of March of this year.  You should note that the FOB value of the order has been kept the same. If you have any questions about this, we will explain more clearly on your next trip.  O.K.?


Please be advised that your letter of credit currently has a balance of  US$ 8,037.81.


Thank you again for your valued orders.  Hoping to hear from you always, we remain:

                              Sinceramente,

                              John Lee

                              KINGTEX INTERNATIONAL CORPORATION

JL/margarita
Anexos:  Shipping Documents


**EXHIBIT A:**  Letter confirming receipt of order and informing buyer that goods have been shipped

# KINGTEX INTERNATIONAL CORPORATION

## INSPECTION CERTIFICATE

Date: March 24, 1982

ACCOUNT:     L/C   NO.   C-3452

DEPT. NO.:

YOUR ORDER NO.:   82006 & 82005 & 82001

MERCHANDISE:     Jogging shoes & Brief Cases & Bill Folders

QUANTITY:        1750 prs.   &   1900 pcs.

A random check was made of the merchandise listed above on   March 15, 1982

by our representative. A random sampling of   10%   dozen were inspected

and the goods fully comply with the quality and standard of execution required

by the order and/or samples shown.

This certificate in no way exonerates the manufacturer from his responsibility

to guarantee that all the merchandise he ships is found to be of good quality

when it arrives at its destination. The manufacturer is wholly liable for any

claim resulting from shipments made of poor quality or badly executed goods.


**KINGTEX  INTERNATIONAL  CORPORATION**

_____

GENERAL  MANAGER

Copy of inspection certificate issued by seller before packing.

# KINGTEX INTERNATIONAL CORPORATION

## I N V O I C E  P(1)

| MESSRS. EXIM INDUSTRIES CORP.<br>109 Lexington #217<br>San Antonio, Texas 78205<br>U.S.A. | INVOICE NO. KI-82320 | DATE Mar 24, 1982 |
| | YOUR ORDER NO. | |
| | TERMS OF PAYMENT by L/C | |

| NAME OF VESSEL Neptune Garnet V-9WA | DATE OF SHIPMENT March 24, 1982 | |
| PORT OF SHIPMENT Keelung | PORT OF DESTINATION Houston | |

| MARK & NOS. | DESCRIPTION OF GOODS | QUANTITY | UNIT PRICE | AMOUNT |
|---|---|---|---|---|
| | | | CIF Houston | |
| | Brief Cases, Contrl. #82005 | | | |
| Houston, Texas<br>U.S.A.<br>IN BOND<br>Control #<br>82005<br>C/NO. 1-325<br>Made in Taiwan<br>R. O. C. | Style # CW-229C<br>  # CW-2701<br>  # TK-502 | 500 pcs.<br>"<br>" | @ US$20.17<br>@ US$ 9.90<br>@ US$13.63 | US$10,085.00<br>US$ 4,950.00<br>US$ 6,815.00 |
| | Jogging Shoes, Contrl. #82006 | | | |
| --DITTO--<br>Control #<br>82006<br>C/NO. 1-73 | Style # A-5350<br>  # A-5503<br>  # A-5474<br>  # A-5472<br>  # A-5504<br>  # A-5420<br>  # A-5478 | 250 prs.<br>"<br>"<br>"<br>"<br>"<br>" | @ US$ 5.63<br>@ US$ 3.99<br>@ US$ 5.43<br>@ US$ 4.84<br>@ US$ 4.47<br>@ US$ 5.43<br>@ US$ 4.84 | US$ 1,407.50<br>US$ 997.50<br>US$ 1,357.50<br>US$ 1,210.00<br>US$ 1,117.50<br>US$ 1,357.50<br>US$ 1,210.00 |
| | Bill Folders, Contrl. #82001 | | | |
| --DITTO--<br>Control #<br>82001<br>C/NO. 1-3 | Style # 744306<br>  # 754007<br>  # PW006<br>  # 484006TW<br>  # 484006 | 80 pcs.<br>"<br>"<br>"<br>" | @ US$11.20<br>@ US$11.33<br>@ US$11.63<br>@ US$ 9.11<br>@ US$ 9.20 | US$ 896.00<br>US$ 906.40<br>US$ 930.40<br>US$ 728.80<br>US$ 736.00 |
| Packed in 401<br>Cartons | | 1900 pcs.<br>1750 prs. | | US$34,705.10 |

SAY TOTAL US DOLLARS THIRTY FOUR THOUSAND SEVEN HUNDRED FIVE AND
TEN CENTS ONLY

DRAWN UNDER NATIONAL BANK OF COMMERCE OF TEXAS   L/C # C-3452
Dated:  Feb. 10, 1982

WE HEREBY CERTIFY THAT MERCHANDISE ARE OF TAIWANESE ORIGIN

------ TO BE CONTINUED ------

**EXHIBIT B:** Commercial invoice of shipment of goods.

430

# KINGTEX INTERNATIONAL CORPORATION

## INVOICE P(2)

| MESSRS. | | INVOICE NO. | DATE |
|---|---|---|---|
| EXIM INDUSTRIES CORP.<br>109 Lexington #217<br>San Antonio, Texas  78205<br>U.S.A. | | KI-82320 | Mar 24, 1982 |

**YOUR ORDER NO.**

**TERMS OF PAYMENT**
by L/C

| NAME OF VESSEL | DATE OF SHIPMENT |
|---|---|
| S.S. Neptune Garnet  V-9WA | March 24, 1982 |

| PORT OF SHIPMENT | PORT OF DESTINATION |
|---|---|
| Keelung | Houston |

| MARK & NOS. | DESCRIPTION OF GOODS | QUANTITY | UNIT PRICE | AMOUNT |
|---|---|---|---|---|
| | Breakdown: | | | |
| | Brief Cases, Contrl. #82005 | | | |
| | Style # CW-229C | | @ US$19.16 | US$ 9,580.00 |
| | # CW-2701 | | @ US$ 9.40 | US$ 4,700.00 |
| | # TK-502 | | @ US$12.95 | US$ 6,475.00 |
| | Jogging Shoes, Contrl. #82006 | | | |
| | Style # A-5350 | | @ US$ 4.95 | US$ 1,237.50 |
| | # A-5503 | | @ US$ 3.40 | US$ 850.00 |
| | # A-5474 | | @ US$ 4.75 | US$ 1,187.50 |
| | # A-5472 | | @ US$ 4.20 | US$ 1,050.00 |
| | # A-5504 | | @ US$ 3.85 | US$ 962.50 |
| | # A-5420 | | @ US$ 4.75 | US$ 1,187.50 |
| | # A-5478 | | @ US$ 4.20 | US$ 1,050.00 |
| | Bill Folders, Contrl. #82001 | | | |
| | Style # 744306 | | @ US$ 5.83 | US$ 466.40 |
| | # 754007 | | @ US$ 5.90 | US$ 472.00 |
| | # PW006 | | @ US$ 6.18 | US$ 494.40 |
| | # 484006TW | | @ US$ 3.78 | US$ 302.40 |
| | # 484006 | | @ US$ 3.78 | US$ 302.40 |
| | FOB VALUE . . . . . . . | . . . . . . | . . . . | US$30,317.60 |
| | FREIGHT  . . . . . . . | . . . . . | . . . . | US$ 3,333.41 |
| | INSURANCE . . . . . . . | . . . . . | . . . . | US$ 144.11 |
| | COMMISSION  . . . . . . | . . . . . | . . . . | US$ 909.98 |
| | CIF  HOUSTON  . . . . . . . . . . . . . . . . . . | | | US$34,705.10 |

KINGTEX INTERNATIONAL CORPORATION:

| SHIPPER | B/L NO. |
|---|---|

KINGTEX INTERNATIONAL CORPORATION

**"K" LINE**

**CONSIGNEE**

To the Order of EXIM INDUSTRIES, INC.

## BILL OF LADING

NOTIFY PARTY   Soto's Air Freight and
Customs Broker, San Antonio In/tl. Airport
PH: 826-3247  or  EXIM INDUSTRIES, INC.
109 Lexington, San Antonio, TX PH:220-1021
or Soto's P.O.BOX 5344 Houston, TX
PH:256-1928

ALL TERMS,  CONDITIONS
AND  EXCEPTIONS AS PER
ORIGINAL BILL OF LADING

PRE-CARRIAGE  BY        PLACE OF RECEIPT

Taipei

OCEAN VESSEL      VOY. NO.     PORT OF LADING

S.S. Neptune Garnet   v-9WA       Keelung

PORT OF DISCHARGE          PLACE OF DELIVERY

Houston                  Houston

| CONTAINER NO. | SEAL NO. | NO. OF CONTAINERS | DESCRIPTION   GR. WT |
|---|---|---|---|
| PT-SU200079 | (247793) | 01 | Brief Cases,     4.54 CBM |
|  |  |  | Jogging Shoes, |
|  |  | 401 CTNS. (Packed in | Bill Folders |
|  |  | 1 Container) |  |

PARTICULARS FURNISHED BY SHIPPER

EXIM

HOUSTON, TEXAS U.S.A.
IN BOND
CONTROL. NO. 82005
C/NO.  1-325
MADE IN TAIWAN
R.O.C.

EXIM

HOUSTON, TEXAS U.S.A.
IN BOND
CONTROL. NO 82001
C/NO. 1-3
MADE IN TAIWAN
R.O.C.

EXIM

HOUSTON, TEXAS U.S.A.
IN BOND
CONTROL. NO. 82006
C/NO.  1-73
MADE IN TAIWAN
R.O.C.

"FREIGHT PREPAID"

NO. OF CONTAINERS OR PACKAGES ( IN WORDS )
Say  Four Hundred and One Cartons Only

| FREIGHT AND CHARGES | REVENUE TONS | RATE | PER | PREPAID | COLLECT |
|---|---|---|---|---|---|
| O/F | (37.45) | $61.00/CBM |  | US$2,284.45 |  |
|  | (7.09) | $60/CBM |  | 425.40 |  |
| BAF |  | $14.00/F/T |  | 623.56 |  |
| CFS | NT$126/F/T |  |  | US$3,333.41 |  |
|  |  |  |  | NT$5,612.04 |  |

| EX. RATE | PREPAID AT | PAYABLE AT |  | PLACE / DATE |  |
|---|---|---|---|---|---|
| Mar 24, 1982 | Taipei | (XX) |  | (ZZ)      Taipei |  |

LADEN  ON  BOARD VESSEL

**EXHIBIT C**   Bill of Lading

432

CONSIGNEE :

EXIM Industries Corp.

BILL OF LADING NO.
K992-08615

NOTIFY :

Soto's Air-Freight & Customs
Broker; San Antonio Int'l.
Airport

--- FOR INQUIRIES / PAYMENTS CONTACT ---

K-Line Kerr Corporation
American General Tower
2727 Allen FRWY Suite 1500
Houston, Texas 77019

NOTIFY :

EXIM Industries Corp.
109 Lexington #217
San Antonio, Texas 78205

SHIPPER :

Kingtex International Corp.

CARGO AVAILABLE AT :

| VESSEL<br>Neptune Garnet | VOYAGE NO.<br>V-9WA | ARRIVE<br>04/24/82 | PIER NO.<br>234 L0 | PORT OF LOADING / DISCHARGE<br>Keelung/Houston | | |
|---|---|---|---|---|---|---|
| DATE OF DELIVERY<br>4-30-82 | | FINAL DESTINATION<br>Houston | | FLAG<br>Japan | | |
| CONTAINER NOS. | NO. PCKGS. | DESCRIPTION | FREIGHT | | PREPAID | COLLECT |
| | | | WEIGHT | MEASURE | | |
| EXIM<br>HOUSTON, TEXAS<br>U.S.A.<br>IN BOND<br>CONTR. #82005<br>C/NO. 1-325<br>MADE IN TAIWAN<br>R.O.C.<br><br>--DITTO--<br>CONTR. #82006<br>C/NO. 1-73<br><br>--DITTO--<br>CONTR. #82001<br>C/NO. 1-3 | (401) | CTNS. S/NO. 247793 | | | | |
| | 401 | CTNS: Brief Cases,<br>Jogging Shoes, Bill<br>Folders | | | | |
| Total this B/L | 401 | | 13844 LBS. 1573 CFT<br>6.189 KT 44.540 CM | | | |
| (S.S. Neptune Garnet V-9WA) | | Keelung | | | | |
| | | TOTAL FREIGHT AND CHARGES | | | US$ 3,489.30 | |

Lorem ipsum dolor sit amet, consectetur adipiscing elit, sed diam nonnumy eiusmo
metpor incidunt ut labore et dolore magna aliquam erat volupat. Ut enim ad minir
veniam, quis nostrund exercitation ullamcorpor suscrit laboris nisi ut aliquip ex ea
commodo consequat. Duis autem vel eum irrure dolor in reprehenderit in volupta
esse molestiae consequat, vel illum dolore eu fugiat nulla pariatur. At vero eos et ac
et iusto odio dignissim qui blandit praesent luptatum delenit aigue duos dolor et mc
exceptur sint occaecat cupiditat non provident, simil tempor sunt in culpa qui
deserunt mollit anim id est laborum et dolor fuga. Et harumd dereud facilis est er c
distinct. Nam liber tempor cum soluta nobis eligend optio congue nihil impedit dor
quod maxim placeat facer possim omnis voluptas assumenda est, omnis dolor
Temporibud autem quinsud et aur office debit aut tum rerum necessit atib saepe eve
er repudiand sint et molestia non recusand. Itaque earud rerum hic tentury sapient

PLEASE PAY THIS AMOUNT

# THE FIRST INSURANCE CO. LTD.

MARINE CARGO POLICY NO.
1000M82050024370

CLAIM, IF ANY, PAYABLE IN   US  CURRENCY

AT     Houston

ASSURED       Kingtex International Corporation

INSURED VALUE

(US$38,175.61) US Dollars Thirty Eight
Thousand One Hundred Seventy Five and
Cents Sixty One only.

DECLARED TO BE UPON

Jogging Shoes, Bill Folders, Brief Cases
Total: 1750 prs.  & 1900 pcs.
Packed in 401 Cartons
L/C #   C-3452

EXIM

HOUSTON, TEXAS U.S.A.
IN BOND
CONTRL. NO. 82006
C/NO. 1-73
MADE IN TAIWAN
R.O.C.

--DITTO--
CONTRL. NO. 82001
C/NO. 1-3

--DITTO--
CONTRL. NO. 82005
C/NO. 1-325

Per: S.S. Neptune Garnet V-9WA
At and From: Keelung to Houston
Sailing on or about: March 22, 1982

COVERAGE: ALL RISKS

SIGNED IN: Taipei     ON: 21, March 1982

Issued in Duplicate

For The First Insurance Co., Ltd.:

Lorem ipsum dolor sit amet, consectetur adipiscing elit, sed diam
tempor incidunt ut labore et dolore magna aliquam erat volupat. I
veniam, quis nostrund exercitation ullamcorpor suscrit laboris nis
commodo consequat. Duis autem vel eum irrure dolor in reprehe
esse molestiae consequat, vel illum dolore eu fugiat nulla pariatur.
et iusto odio dignissim qui blandit praesent luptatum delenit aigue
exceptur sint occaecat cupiditat non provident, simil tempor su
deserunt mollit anim id est laborum et dolor fuga. Et harumd dere
distinct. Nam liber tempor cum soluta nobis eligend optio congue
quod maxim placeat facer possim omnis voluptas assumenda e
Temporibud autem quinsud et aur office debit aut tum rerum nece:
err epudiand sint et molestia non recusand. Itaque earud rerum hic
delectus au aut prefer endis dolorib asperiore repellat. Hanc ego
quid est cur verear ne ad eam non possing accommodare nost ros
memorite tum etia ergat. Nos amice et nebevol, olestias access
cum conscient to factor tum poen legum odioque civiuda. Et ta
pecun modut est neque nonor imper ned libiding gen epular re
nulla praid om undant. Improb pary minuit, potius inflammad ut
dodecendesse videanteur. Inviat igitur vera ratio bene sanos ad iu:
fidem. Neque hominy infant aut inuiste fact est cond qui neg fa
conetud notiner si effecerit, et opes vel fortang vel ingen liberalita
but tuntung benevolent sib conciliant et, aptissim est ad quiet. E
cum omning null sit caus peccand quaert en imigent cupidat a nate
explent sine julla inura autend inanc sunt is parend non est nihil e:
Concupis plusque in ipsinuria detriment est quam in his rebus en
Itaque ne iustitia dem rect quis dixer per se ipsad optabil, sed quir
Nam dilig et carum esse iucund est propter and tutior vitam et lu;
non ob ea solu incommod quae egenium improb fugiendad im
mult etiam mag quod cuis. Guae ad erat amicos pertineren gare
expetend quam nostras expetere quo loco videtur quibusing sta
tuent tamet eum locum seque facil, ut mihi detur expedium. It enir
dictum est, sic amicitiand neg posse a luptate discedere. Nam cu
amicis insidar et metus plena sit, ratiodispa monet amicitian comp
confirmatur animuset a spe pariender luptam seriua non poest. A
despication adversantur luptabit, sic amicitiao non modo fautrices
Lorem ipsum dolor sit amet, consectetur adipiscing elit, sed diam
tempor incidunt ut labore et dolore magna aliquam erat volupat. I
veniam, quis nostrund exercitation ullamcorpor suscrit laboris nis
commodo consequat. Duis autem vel eum irrure dolor in reprehe:
esse molestiae consequat, vel illum dolore eu fugiat nulla pariatur.
et iusto odio dignissim qui blandit praesent luptatum delenit aigue
exceptur sint occaecat cupiditat non provident, simil tempor su
deserunt mollit anim id est laborum et dolor fuga. Et harumd dere
distinct. Nam liber tempor cum soluta nobis eligend optio congue
quod maxim placeat facer possim omnis voluptas assumenda e:
Temporibud autem quinsud et aur office debit aut tum rerum nece:
er epudiand sint et molestia non recusand. Itaque earud rerum hic
delectus au aut prefer endis dolorib asperiore repellat. Hanc ego
quid est cur verear ne ad eam non possing accommodare nost ros
memorite tum etia ergat. Nos amice et nebevol, olestias access
cum conscient to factor tum poen legum odioque civiuda. Et ta
pecun modut est neque nonor imper ned libiding gen epular re
nulla praid om undant. Improb pary minuit, potius inflammad ut
dodecendesse videanteur. Invia tigitur vera ratio bene sanos ad iu:

Marine Insurance

# KINGTEX INTERNATIONAL CORPORATION

# PACKING LIST

| MESSRS. EXIM INDUSTRIES CORP.<br>109 Lexington, #217<br>San Antonio, Texas  78205<br>U.S.A. | INVOICE NO.  DATE:<br>KI-82320  March 24, 1982<br>YOUR ORDER NO.<br>PACKING |
|---|---|

| NAME OF VESSEL  DATE OF SHIPMENT<br>S.S. Neptune Garnet V-9WA  March 24, 1982 | 401  Cartons |
|---|---|

PORT OF SHIPMENT       PORT OF DESTINATION
Keelung                Houston

| MARK & NOS. | DESCRIPTION OF GOODS | QUANTITY | WEIGHT NET | GROSS | MEASURMENT |
|---|---|---|---|---|---|
| EXIM<br><br>Houston, Texas<br>U.S.A.<br>IN BOND<br>CONTRL. NO. 82005<br>C/NO. 1-325<br>MADE IN TAIWAN<br>R.O.C. | Brief Cases, Contrl. #82005<br><br>Style # CW-2701<br>C/# 1-100<br><br>Style # TK-502<br>C/# 101-200<br><br>Style # CW-229C<br>C/# 201-325 | @ 5 pcs.<br>500  "<br><br>@ 5 pcs.<br>500  "<br><br>@ 4 pcs.<br>500  " | 10.5 kgs 13 kgs<br>1050  "  1300 "<br><br>11.5 kgs 14.5 kgs<br>1150  "  1450  "<br><br>16  kgs 19  kgs<br>2000  "  2375  " | | |
| --DITTO--<br>CONTRL. NO. 82006<br>C/NO. 1-73 | Jogging Shoes, Contrl. #82006<br><br>Contrl. # 82006<br>C/# 1-72<br><br>C/# 73 | 824 prs.<br>1728 "<br><br>22  prs. | 12.8 kgs 14.2 kgs<br>921.6 "  1022.4 "<br><br>11.7 kgs 13.0 kgs | | |
| --DITTO--<br>CONTRL. NO. 82001<br>C/NO. 1-3 | Bill Folders, Contrl. #82001<br><br>Style # 484006TW,484006<br>C/# 1<br><br>Style # PW006,754007<br>C/# 2<br><br>Style # 744306,754007,<br>PW006<br>C/# 3 | 160 pcs.<br><br>125 pcs.<br><br>115 pcs. | 7.76 kgs 9.3 kgs<br><br>8.50 kgs 10.1 kgs<br><br>7.90 kgs 9.5 kgs | | |
| | SAY TOTAL FOUR HUNDRED ONE<br>(401) CTNS. ONLY | 1900 pcs.<br>1750 prs. | 5157.46 kgs 6189.3 kgs | | |

Packing List

# SPECIAL CUSTOMS INVOICE

| 1. SELLER<br><br>Kingtex International Corp.<br>P.O.Box 67-80 Taipei    Taiwan | 2. DOCUMENT NR. | 3. INVOICE NR. / DATE<br>KI-82320    Mar. 24, 1982 |
|---|---|---|
| | 4. REFERENCES | |

| 5. CONSIGNEE<br><br>TO ORDER OF :  Exim Industries Corp. | 6. BUYER<br>Exim Industries Corp.<br>109 Lexington # 217;  San Antonio, TX  78205 |
|---|---|
| | 7. ORIGIN OF GOODS<br>Made in Taiwan |

| 8. NOTIFY PARTY 1) Soto's Air-Freight & Customs Broker PH: 826-3247  2) EXIM Industries PH: 220-1021  3) Soto's Air-Freight & Customs Broker PH: 236-1928 (Houston) | 9. TERMS OF SALE, PAYMENT, & DISCOUNT<br><br>Terms of Sale:  CIF Houston<br><br>Payment:  By L/C |
|---|---|
| 10. ADDITIONAL TRANSPORTATION INFO.<br><br>PER    S.S. Neptune Garnet V-9WA<br><br>FROM: Keelung    TO: Houston | |
| | 11. CURRENCY   12. EXCH. RATE  13. DATE<br>US |

| 14. MARKS / NOS. | 15. NO. PCKG. | 16. DESCRIPTION | 17. QUAN. | 18. PRICE | 19.   TOTAL |
|---|---|---|---|---|---|
| EXIM<br>HOUSTON, TEXAS<br>U.S.A.<br>IN BOND<br>CONTR. #82005<br>C/NO. 1-325<br>MADE IN TAIWAN<br>R.O.C. | 401 CTNS. | Brief Cases, #82005<br><br>Style # C-229C<br>C-2701<br>TK-502 | <br><br>500 pcs.<br>"<br>" | PER UNIT<br><br>US$20.17<br>US$ 9.90<br>US$13.63 | <br><br>US$10,085.00<br>US$ 4,950.00<br>US$ 6,815.00 |
| --DITTO--<br>CONTR. # 82006<br>C/NO. 1-73 | | Jogging Shoes, #82006<br><br>Style # A-5350<br>A-5503<br>A-5474<br>A-5472<br>A-5504<br>A-5420<br>A-5478 | <br><br>250 prs.<br>"<br>"<br>"<br>"<br>"<br>" | <br><br>US$ 5.63<br>US$ 3.99<br>US$ 5.43<br>US$ 4.84<br>US$ 4.47<br>US$ 5.43<br>US$ 4.84 | <br><br>US$ 1,407.50<br>US$ 997.50<br>US$ 1,357.50<br>US$ 1,210.00<br>US$ 1,117.50<br>US$ 1,357.50<br>US$ 1,210.00 |
| --DITTO--<br>CONTR. # 82001<br>C/NO. 1-3 | | Bill Folders, #82001<br><br>Style # 744306<br>754007<br>PW006<br>484006TW<br>484006 | <br><br>80 pcs.<br>"<br>"<br>"<br>" | <br><br>US$11.20<br>US$11.33<br>US$11.63<br>US$ 9.11<br>US$ 9.20 | <br><br>US$ 896.00<br>US$ 906.40<br>US$ 930.40<br>US$ 728.80<br>US$ 736.00 |

fidem. Neque hominy infant aut inuiste fact est cond qui neg fácile efficerd possit duo conetud notiner si effecerit, et opes vel fortang vel ingen liberalitat magis conveniunt, da but tuntung benevolent sib conciliant et, aptissim est ad quiet. Endium caritat praesert cum omning null sit caus peccand quaert en imigent cupidat a natura proficis facile turnet explent sine julla inura autend inanc sunt is parend non est nihil enim desiderable interno Concupis plusque in ipsinuria detriment est quam in his rebus emolument oariunt iniuri Itaque ne iustitial dem rect quis dixer per se ipsad optabil, sed quiran cunditat vel plurifyi Nam dilig et carum esse iucund est propter and tutior vitam et luptat pleniore efficit. Tia non ob ea solu incommod quae egenium improb fugiendad improbitate putamuy sed mult etiam mag quod cuis. Guae ad erat amicos pertineren garent esse per se sas tam expetend quam nostras expetere quo loco videtur quibusing stabilit amicitiae acillard utent tamet eum locum seque facil, ut mihi detur expedium. It enim virtues, de squib ante

| 20. PACKING COSTS<br>US$ 3,031.00 | US$34,705.10 |
|---|---|
| 21. FREIGHT CHARGE<br>(INTERNATIONAL)<br>US$ 3,333.41 | BY<br>L/C C-3452<br>N. Bank of Commerce<br>of Texas |
| 22. FREIGHT CHARGE<br>(DOMESTIC)  US$450.00 | |
| 23. INS. COSTS<br>US$ 144.11 | |
| 24. OTHER COSTS<br>US$ 400.00 | |

**EXHIBIT D:**  United States Customs Document.

THE DEPT OF THE TREASURY
BUREAU OF CUSTOMS     NOTICE OF DAMAGE, SHORTAGE OR SAMPLES RETAINED

| ITEMS (QUANTITY, DESCRIPTION, ITEM NO., ETC. | ENTRY NO. | DATE |
|---|---|---|
| 6   Shoes | 82111780 | 5-13-82 |

| | PORT OF |
|---|---|
| | San Antonio |

| | INVOICE NO. |
|---|---|
| | |

| | MARKS AND CASE NO. |
|---|---|
| | |

NAME AND ADDRESS OF IMPORTER

EXIM Industries Corporation
109 Lexington #217
San Antonio, Texas   78205

THIS PACKAGE HAS BEEN OPENED BY OFFICERS OF THE U.S. CUSTOMS SERVICE.

ITEMS LISTED ABOVE WERE:

☐ NOT FOUND

☐ FOUND TO BE DAMAGED

☒ RETAINED AS SAMPLES FOR OFFICIAL PURPOSES AND ARE (NOT) TO BE RETURNED

☐ SEE REVERSE

CUSTOMS FORM
JAN 67   6423

SIGNATURE AND TITLE OF SAMPLING OFFICER

U. S. CUSTOMS SERVICE                                          C-12

# INVOICE DETAILS FOR FOOTWEAR

| (1) IMPORTER'S NO. | 82006 | | | |
|---|---|---|---|---|
| (2) MANUFACTURER'S NO. | STYLE # A5350,A5503,A5474,A5472,A5504,A5420,A5478 | | | |
| (3) DETAILED DESCRIPTION | JOGGING SHOES | | | |
| (4) CATEGORY | CEMENT | | | |
| (5) MATERIALS OF SOLE | RUBBER EVA | | | |
| (6) MATERIAL CHIEF VALUE OF SOLE | RUBBER | | | |
| (7) MATERIALS OF UPPER | LEATHER NYLON PVC | | | |
| (8) MATERIAL CHIEF VALUE OF UPPER | LEATHER | | | |
| (9) MATERIAL CHIEF VALUE OF ENTIRE SHOE | LEATHER | | | |
| (10) PERCENT BY WEIGHT OF ENTIRE SHOE — FIBRE | 15% | | | |
| RUBBER | 40% | | | |
| PLASTICS  LEATHER | 20% 25% | | | |
| (11) PERCENT BY AREA OF MATERIAL OF EXTERIOR SURFACE OF UPPER | LEATHER 51% | | | |
| (12) GENDER | MEN'S | | | |
| (13) TYPE | JOGGING | | | |
| (14) HEIGHT | OTHER | | | |
| (15) NUMBER OF PAIRS | 250 prs., 250 prs., 250 prs., 250 prs., 250 prs., 250 prs., 250 prs. | | | |
| (16) VALUE PER PAIR  @ US$ | 5.63    3.99    5.43    4.84    4.47    5.43    4.84 | | | |
| (17) TOTAL VALUE  @ US$ | 1407.50    997.50    1357.50    1210.00    1117.50    1357.50    1210.00 | | | |
| (18) IF SUCH OR SIMILAR FOOTWEAR IS SOLD FOR HOME CONSUMPTION STATE PRICE | | | | |

CUSTOMS FORM  5523  ( 2 - 4 - 74 )

SIGNATURE OF SELLER, SHIPPER OR AGENT

KINGTEX INTERNATIONAL CORPORATION

*[signature: John Lee]*

KINGTEX INTERNATIONAL CORPORATION

C E R T I F I C A T E
*************************

TO WHOM IT MAY CONCERN:

RE: JOGGING SHOES, CONTRL. # 82006

    Name of Manufacturer: Cosmic Industrial Corporation

RE: BILL FOLDERS, CONTRL. # 82001

    Name of Manufacturer: Yine Chung Co. Ltd.

RE: BRIEF CASES, CONTRL. # 82005

    Name of Manufacturer: George Enterprise Co. Ltd.


Q'TY: 1900 pcs., 1750 prs.  (401 CTNS.)

PER: S.S. NEPTUNE GARNET V-9WA

FROM: Keelung to Houston


DRAWN UNDER NATIONAL BANK OF COMMERCE OF TEXAS

L/C NO. C-3452          DATED:   FEB. 10, 1982

ADVISING BANK: BANK OF AMERICA, SAN FRANCISCO, CALIF. 94137

ADVISING NO. 904102

*********************************************************************************

WE HEREBY CERTIFY THAT MERCHANDISE IS OF TAIWANESE ORIGIN AND MANUFACTURER'S NAME


KINGTEX INTERNATIONAL CORPORATION: _____


**EXHIBIT E:** Certificates of Origin.

KINGTEX INTERNATIONAL CORPORATION

DATE:    March 24, 1982

CERTIFICATE OF ORIGIN

TO WHOM IT MAY CONCERN:

THIS IS TO CERTIFY THAT UNDERMENTIONED GOODS ARE THE PRODUCTS OF

TAIWAN  R. O. C. ORIGIN.

SHIPPER:   KINGTEX INTERNATIONAL CORPORATION

BUYER:  EXIM INDUSTRIES CORPORATION, 109 LEXINGTON, NO. 217;

SAN ANTONIO, TEXAS  78205     U. S. A.

COMMODITY:   Brief Cases, Jogging Shoes, Bill Folders.

QUANTITY:    1900 PCS.,  1750 PRS.   (401 CTNS.)

SHIPPED PER S.S. NETPUNE GARNET   V-9WA

FROM:   KEELUNG    TO    HOUSTON

SHIPPING MARK:              EXIM
                    HOUSTON, TEXAS U.S.A.
                    IN BOND
                    CONTR NO. 82005
                    C/NO.  1-325
                    MADE IN TAIWAN
                    R.O.C.

                    --DITTO--
                    CONTR NO.  82006
                    C/NO.  1-73

                    --DITTO--
                    CONTR NO.  82001
                    C/NO.  1-3

440

# APPLICATION AND AGREEMENT FOR IRREVOCABLE COMMERCIAL LETTER OF CREDIT

TO: NATIONAL BANK OF COMMERCE OF TEXAS
430 Soledad, San Antonio, Texas 78291

DATE: __February 9, 1982__

DEAR SIRS:

SUBSTANTIALLY IN ACCORDANCE WITH THE FOLLOWING TERMS AND CONDITIONS. PLEASE ISSUE YOUR IRREVOCABLE LETTER OF CREDIT AND TRANSMIT BY THE METHOD INDICATED BY " X."

TRANMISSION BY:  ☒ CABLE

☐ SHORT CABLE

☐ AIR MAIL

☒ THROUGH THE ADVISING BANK

☐ DIRECTLY TO BENEFICIARY

| ADVISING BANK | FOR ACCOUNT OF |
|---|---|
| Bank of America<br>43 Kuan Chien Rd. P.O. BOX 127<br>Taipei 100  Taiwan<br>Republic of China    THRU<br>Bank of America--San Francisco | Exim Industries, Corp.<br>109 Lexington, # 217<br>San Antonio, Texas 78205 |

| IN FAVOR OF | AMOUNT |
|---|---|
| NAME: Kingtex Int'l. Corp.<br>P.O. BOX 67-80<br>Taipei, Taiwan   ROC | $60,000.00  US Dlrs.  (Sixty Thousand<br>Dollars and  00/100) |

TO BE AVAILABLE BY THE BENEFICIARY'S DRAFT (S)

DRAWN AT ☒ SIGHT  ☐ _____ DAYS DATE   ☐ _____

DRAWN ON __Bank of America, Taipei   Taiwan__ FOR _100%_ % INVOICE COST

ACCOMPANIED BY THE FOLLOWING DOCUMENTS

☒ COMMERCIAL INVOICE - ORIGINAL AND _5_ COPIES

☒ CERTIFICATE OF WEIGHT  / PACKING LIST

☒ CERTIFICATE OF ORIGIN

☒ INSPECTION CERTIFICATE

☒ CUSTOMS INVOICE - ORIGINAL AND ___3___ COPIES

☒ OTHER __Invoice details for Footwear; US Dept. of Treasury, Form # 5523__

☒ NEGOTIABLE MARINE / AIR INSURANCE POLICY AND / OR CERTIF. (110% VALUE)

☒ INSURANCE TO INCLUDE: x WAR RISKS  x (OTHER RISKS)   ALL

☒ ON BOARD ORIGINAL OCEAN BILL OF LADING

☐ AIR WAYBILL

(See Attachment)

CONSIGNED TO THE ORDER OF 1. Soto's Air-Freight and Customs Broker, San Antonio Int'l. Airport PH: 826-3247 2. Exim Industries Corp. 109 Lexington #217, San Antonio PH: 220-1021  3.  Soto's Air-Freight and Customs Broker, P.O. BOX 53447, Houston, Tx  PH:  256-1928

COVERING:

| | | |
|---|---|---|
| 1. Baseball caps | 4. Bill folders | 7. Soccer balls |
| 2. Jogging shoes | 5. Basketballs | 8. Baseball gloves |
| 3. Brief cases | 6. Volleyballs | |

SHIPMENT FROM:      Taiwan, Republic of China

TO:  Houston, Texas  U.S.A.

SPECIAL CONDITIONS: Partial Shipments-Permitted;  Transshipments-Prohibited;

See Attachment

AGREED TO

**EXHIBIT F:** Documents Establishing Letter of Credit and Showing Transferral of Funds to Seller.

# National Bank of Commerce of Texas
## NBC

Attachment to EXIM Industries Corp. Application and Agreement for Irrevocable Commercial Letter of Credit, dated February 9, 1982.

OTHER DOCUMENTS:

1. Beneficiary's certified statement indicating one complete set of non-negotiable documents has been mailed to Soto's Air-Freight and Custom Broker, P. O. Box 7F, San Antonio, Texas 78217.

2. Beneficiary's certified statement indicating: the brief cases contain tags which describe in descending order, their generic content; the manufacturer's name; and, their country of origin.

SPECIAL CONDITIONS:

1. Commercial invoices should reflect separate value of cost of goods per unit, freight, insurance, and Kingtex International Corp. commission.

2. Commercial invoices should make reference to contract number and description of goods.

3. All goods should have a country of origin identification.

4. This Letter of Credit is transferable.

**BA**

DATE: 12 Mar. 1982

| | OUR REF. NO.<br>957363Y/E327712 | LOCAL AMNT. |
|---|---|---|
| WE HAVE HONORED THE FOLLOWING DRAWING(S) ON YOUR BEHALF. | | |

| | YOUR L/C. NO. | CONV. RATE |
|---|---|---|
| TO.<br>Nat'l. Bank of Commerce of Texas<br>San Antonio, Texas<br>U.S.A. | C-3452 | C.C. CODE<br>102 |

| PRESENTED BY | TENOR | AMNT. OF DRAWING |
|---|---|---|
| Hua Nan Com'l Bank<br>Yuan Shan Br.<br>YSB-201811 | | US$ 15,848.75 |
| THEIR NO. _____ | _____ DAYS SIGHT | |

| DRAWN BY | REMARKS: |
|---|---|
| Kingtex International Corp. | |

COVERING SHIPMENT OF

Jogging Shoes

FROM ___Keelung___            TO ___Houston___

VIA _____ B/L DATE ___Mar. 06   1982___

PER S.S. ___Neptune Garnet  V-9WA___

AGAINST DOCUMENTS SPECIFIED IN THE CREDIT; EXCEPTIONS, IF ANY, LIST BELOW.
XX ALL DOCUMENTS ENCLOSED
    ORIGINAL DOCUMENTS ENCLOSED AND DUPLICATE DOCUMENTS TO FOLLOW

REMARKS
We've sent Draft and copy of Invoice to our San Francisco HQ.

NATIONAL BANK OF COMMERCE OF TEXAS

CHARGE   EXIM INDUSTRIES CORPORATION,        ACCNT⌡ # 083-1247
         San Antonio, Texas

                                              DATE  |March 26, 1982

WE CHARGE YOUR ACCOUNT FOR THE ITEMS DESCRIBED BELOW

| | AMOUNT |
|---|---|
| We debit your account today representing drawing due under L/C C-3452 F/O Kingtex International Corp., Taipei, Taiwan ROC and for your account to expire 4-12-82. Bank of America, San Francisco, Calif. Ref. # 904102.  Drawing Amt. $15,848.75  Nego. Fee 40.00  $15,888.75 | $15,888.75 |

99 — 3

MSM

# National Bank of Commerce of Texas
## NBC

Simon Castillo,
International Banking Officer


March 30, 1982


RE:    Letter of Credit  No.  C-3452


EXIM Industries, Inc.
109 Lexington, Suite # 217
San Antonio, Texas  78205

ATTN:  Dr. Rudolpho Sandoval

Dear Rudy:

We are enclosing original documents negotiated under the above
referred letter of credit.  All terms and conditions have been
met.

Your savings account was charged for the amount of the negotiation (plus Bank of America fees) on March 26, 1982.

Should you have any questions regarding the enclosed, please
feel free to contact us.

Yours truly,

Sam Cannon

International Banking Officer

SC/msm

ENCLOSURE

**BANK of AMERICA BA**

WORLD BANKING DIVISION
SERVICE CENTER NO. 712
SAN FRANICISCO, CALIFORNIA

| WSC | | RAP | | AOC | |
|-----|--|-----|--|-----|--|
| SER | | PAR | | | |

DESTINATION CODE    DSNC

CTRL  A

ADM.
DATE    04/12/82

KEY    34750

ROUTE

ADDRESS
National Bank of Commerce of Texas
430 Soledad Street
San Antonio, Texas  78205

ATTENTION      L/C  SECTION

MESSAGE.

REUR ELCEE  C-3452    OUR REFERENCE  904102

WE ARE DEBITING YOUR ACCOUNT VALUE  04/12/82

FOR US DLRS  34,750.10 REPRESENT DRAWING AMOUNT

US DLRS 34,705.10 PLUS CHARGES US DLRS  45.00

STOP    DOCUMENTS NEGOTIATED BY BANKAMERICA

TAIPEI  BANK    STOP


REGARDS    LC EXPORT SECTION

F.C. REYES  LC EXPORT SECTION

**BILLING INFORMATION**

| DEBIT | |
|-------|--|
| BILL | |
| WAIVE | |

INDICATE COMPLETE NAME
ADDRESS  & OUR AND
THEIR REPRESENTATIVE

| AUTHORIZED  SIGNATURE | AUTHORIZED  SIGNATURE | PREPARED  BY |
|-----------------------|-----------------------|--------------|
| | | hg/13 |

446

# HERDER TRUCK LINES

### 812773

P.O. BOX 875 WEIMER, TX. 78962

| CONSIGNEE: | STREET ADDRESS | POINT OF ORIGIN |
|---|---|---|
| Dir. of Customs<br>% Soto's Air-Freight | P.O. BOX 53447 | Houston, Texas to San Antonio, Texas |

WAYBILL DATES, NO. & POINTS OF TRANSFER OF ALL PREVIOUS CARRIERS

REF #S1 1646

| SHIPPER | STREET ADDRESS | POINT OF ORIGIN |
|---|---|---|
| Soto's Air-Freight | (above) | |

| NO. OF PACKAGES, ARTICLES / MARKS | WT. | RATE | FREIGHT | |
|---|---|---|---|---|
| 1 40 FT CONT STC 401 CTNS OF<br>  BRIEF CASES, JOGGING SHOES,<br>  BILL FOLDS<br>  CONT #   ITSU  200079      AS<br>  SEAL #  15429             IBC<br>  INBOND IT # 77869554 4-4-82<br>  INBOND      INBOND<br><br><br>  INTERSTATE SHIPMENT | 13644<br><br>40000 | FLAT | 51200<br>6818<br>58018 | COLL |

*expeting ea in motuon sit et parvos ad se alliciate et staidy non i
doler, non solud in indutial genelation. What gitur convente at
Ectamen nedue enim haec movere potest appetit anim ned ullam'.
eronylar at ille pellit sensar luptae epicur semper hoc ut pro
expeting ea in motuon sit et parvos ad se alliciate et staidy non i
doler, non solud in indutial genelation. What gitur convente at*

RECEIVED PAYMENT FOR THE COMPANY

5-17-82    19 _____

AGENT

**EXHIBIT G:** Copies of Shipping Documents from Port of Entry to Final Destination.

# appendix D

# GLOSSARY

**Ad valorem tariffs:** Tariffs levied according to the value of imported or exported goods.

**Advanced developing countries (ADC):** A level of development describing the countries falling between the less-developed and the highly developed countries.

**Agency for International Development (AID):** A U.S. government agency which administers U.S. government economic and defense aid programs with foreign countries by providing these countries with low-cost capital.

**Agent middleman:** Person or organization bringing a buyer and a seller together for a transaction without personally taking title to the product.

**Arbitration agreement:** Agreement in a contract by which parties agree that they will take disputes to an arbitrator before they pursue other legal recourses.

**Back translation:** Way of making sure a translation is correct, using four steps:
1) Preparation of the message in the mother language by a first person,
2) Translation by second person,
3) Translation back into the original language by a third person,
4) The three persons get together to compromise on the differences.

**Balance of international payments:** A summary accounting statement showing all financial transactions between one nation and all other nations of the world.

**Balance of payments:** Indicator of the economic health of a country, showing the net inflow or outflow of goods, services, and money.

**Balance on current account:** Indicates the "net" of all flows of current-account items.

**Bilateral agreement:** Agreement involving only two countries and usually concerning specific product exchanges.

**Cartel:** An agreement among international marketers to control the market for their common products through agreements on pricing and distribution.

**Caveat emptor:** A warning principle in trading that it is the buyer's responsibility to be alert and see that he or she gets the quantity and quality paid for.

**Code-law countries:** Countries that have as their legal foundation codes of conduct that are inclusive of all foreseeable applications of law.

**Combine:** The combine operates in the same manner as a cartel except that it has authority to levy fines against its members for noncompliance with price agreements.

COMECON: **Council for Mutual Economic Assistance:** An international trade agreement between the Soviet Union and its satellite countries in Eastern Europe.

**Commodity Credit Corporation (CCC):** A government agency which finances U.S. commodity exports through purchases of the exporter's accounts receivable.

**Common-law countries:** Countries that have been under British influence. These countries decide legal cases upon the bases of tradition and common practice, as well as by interpretation of statutes.

**Common market:** Group of countries organized together to reduce internal trade barriers, establish a common external tariff, and provide a free flow of capital and labor among member countries.

**Comparative advantage:** An economic law stating that each country should specialize in producing products in which it is most efficient, trading these products for goods it cannot make as efficiently; then the whole world would have a higher standard of living.

**Comparative marketing:** Framework for comparing relationships between marketing and its environment in two or more countries, to allow the development of appropriate marketing strategies for each country.

**Confiscation:** A government takes over ownership of the assets of a foreign firm in its country without compensating the firm for its loss.

**Corporate acculturation:** Process used to train foreign subsidiary managers and make them strongly aware of corporate objectives and philosophy.

**Counterpurchase:** Transaction in which the buyer agrees, as a condition of the sale, to purchase a specified amount of goods from the customer for cash.

**Countertrade:** Transactions in which the buyer (frequently a foreign government) pays in goods instead of cash.

**Direct investment theory:** Theory explaining capital flows from one country to another according to the marginal productivity of capital.

**Distributor:** A wholesaler, who might sell to industrial users or retailers. International distributors may be responsible for large regions or even nations.

**Domestication:** Process of transferring ownership and/or control of a foreign-owned firm to local citizens.

**Dumping:** Selling excess inventories in foreign markets at a low price which only covers direct costs.

**Early adopters:** The second group (13.5%) of consumers in a market to purchase a specific new product (after innovators and before early majority). They are usually opinion leaders.

**Early majority:** The third group (34%) of consumers in a market to purchase a new product (after innovators and early adopters).

**Economic dualism:** Feature of a developing economy consisting of an unequal rate of development in its different industrial sectors.

**Economic union:** Group of countries agreeing to all the requirements of forming a common market, but in addition making efforts to coordinate their internal monetary and fiscal policies.

**Economies of scale:** Savings realized when applying a production or marketing technique to (respectively) a larger number of products or markets.

**Edge Act bankers:** Bankers able to offer to the international marketer a broader array of services and financing.

**European Patent Office:** An agency providing that a firm's patent be automatically registered in 16 European countries.

**Export agent:**   Agent who tries to find new markets for products manufactured in its own country. Does not take title to the goods.

**Export-import Bank:**   Makes direct loans and financial guarantees, and provides credit insurance to exporting U.S. firms.

**Expropriation:**   Seizure of the local assets of a multinational firm by a foreign government with some level of compensation set by the confiscating government.

**Extraterritoriality concept:**   Situations in which nations apply their laws to activities of their citizens or corporations which are outside their borders.

**F.O.B. pricing:**   Free-on-board pricing. The importer has to pay for the shipping costs and insurance from the point of shipment.

**Foreign Credit Insurance Association (FCIA):**   A group of American private insurance companies that underwrite commercial credit risks.

**Foreign trade zones:**   Areas set up in major international ports where goods can be stored, processed, and transshipped without officially entering the country, and hence without going through local customs.

**Franchising:**   Agreement under which the franchisor grants the franchisees the right to sell under its trade name and with its technical aid and advice. In return, the franchisees buy certain equipment and supplies through the franchisor and pay franchising fees and a percentage of revenue.

**Freight forwarder:**   Agent taking care of the transportation details (declarations, packing lists, bills of lading, and other documents) necessary to move goods and arrange for transfer of ownership.

**General Agreement on Tariffs and Trade (GATT):**   A group of more than 100 countries committed to nondiscrimination in import duties.

**Gross national product:**   Total "gross value" of all goods and services produced in the economy in one year.

**Hedging:**   Technique used by MNCs to buy or sell goods for a specific amount of currency, to be delivered at a future date. In this case, the firm buys money on the forward market (rate of exchange for a transaction at a specific time in the future) to insure against losses from currency fluctuations.

**Holistic approach:**   Approach to theory considering that a whole cannot be analyzed simply as the sum of its parts; it may be greater than the total input of its parts.

**Import agent:**   Agent oriented toward a single geographic market, searching for products to import and market in the home country. Does not own goods.

**Indirect exporting:**   When a firm sells to domestic middlemen who in turn locate foreign markets for the firm's products.

**Inner-directed society:**   A society dominated by rugged individualists, where social leaders are also industrial leaders. Individuals tend to be very self-centered and competitive.

**Innovators:**   The first group (2.5%) of consumers in a market to purchase a new product. They usually have the highest social status, education, and income.

**Interest-rate parity theory:**   Theory using differentials in short-term interest rates to predict international investments of short-term capital.

**Intermodal shipping:**   Way of shipping goods using several modes of transportation, but dealing with only one intermediary to arrange it all.

**International Bureau for the Protection of Industrial Property:**   Agency giving a person or firm which has filed for a patent in one country, 12-months priority in applying for that patent in 80 countries.

**International corporation:**   Basic difference from other corporations is that top management, the corporate staff at headquarters, is world oriented.

**International division:**   A separately organized group within a firm reporting directly to the president and carrying responsibilities for all international marketing.

**International licensing:**   License granting the right to manufacture and distribute under the licensor's trade name in other specified countries or markets.

**International Monetary Fund (IMF):**   Group of countries that has agreed to place reserves with the IMF to support the value of their currency relative to that of other members, thus diminishing the variations in exchange rates.

**International specialist:**   An individual within the business organization who has been given responsibility for foreign markets.

**International trade cycle:**   Concept suggesting that many new products go through a cycle in which production is concentrated first in the introducing country, then in less-advanced countries. The introducing country gradually becomes an importer of the product it first exported.

**Jobber:**   A term often applied to a wholesaler who sells to retailers.

**Joint venture:**   Merging of two or more firms, at least one of them being local. The local firm provides expertise in the prospective market and the multinational firm provides management and marketing expertise.

**Key-country matrix:**   Matrix ranking the competitive strength of a company's product to be evaluated on the horizontal axis, and the attractiveness of foreign countries on the vertical axis, thus allowing the user to simultaneously consider the competitive strength of a product and the potential of different markets.

**Key currency:**   Currencies kept as reserve by IMF members in addition to their own currency and gold reserves. Key currencies are less subject to large exchange rate fluctuations.

**Laggards:**   The last group (16%) of consumers in a market to purchase a specific new product.

**Late majority:**   The fourth group (34%) of consumers in a market to purchase a specific new product after innovators, early adopters, and the early majority. They have usually below-average income and social prestige.

**Less-developed countries (LDC):**   Sometimes described as underdeveloped countries, these are countries at lower levels of economic development.

**Letter of credit:**   Letter used to transfer funds from one country to another. This letter is issued by a bank which guarantees that funds are available for transfer.

**Licensing:**   Way of exploiting know-how in foreign countries without the need to invest capital.

**Licensing requirements:**   Trade barriers requiring an import license for all products of significant value shipped into a country.

**Life-style groups:**   A life-style group is one whose members share similar attitudes, interests, and opinions. The people in a group are similar in what they like, want, and do.

**Line personnel:**   The line personnel are the people who make decisions in the organization. They usually receive advice from the staff.

**Management contracts:**   Means for a local economy to acquire advanced technology and management expertise without the permanence of direct foreign investment.

**Market segment:**   Subdivision of a market representing a distinct subset of customers to be reached with a distinct marketing strategy.

**Marketing channel:**   Traces the movement of ownership or title to a product from the producer to the user or ultimate consumer, including all middlemen.

**Marketing costs:**   Cost related to the implementation of the marketing strategy; that is, implementation of the marketing mix.

**Me-too firm:**   Firm entering a market, after the introduction phase, with a product similar to the existing products and thus shifting to competition on a price basis.

**Middlemen:**   Marketing institutions that comprise the building blocks of the marketing channel.

**Multilateral agreements:**   Agreements signed by countries from multiple regions of the world, the overall purpose being the reduction of tariffs and other barriers to world trade.

**Multinational corporation (MNC):**   A corporation that acts and thinks internationally, instead of being oriented to a single national market.

**Nationalization:**   Process whereby a government decides to take over ownership of an industry for its own control.

**New International Economic Order (NIEO):**   Resolution passed by the United Nations to restructure economic power in the world by transferring more resources to the LDCs.

**Oligopoly model:**   Model stating that foreign investment is motivated by a firm's desire to exploit the quasi-monopolistic advantages it has in such areas as technology, capital, and products.

**Ombudsman:**   A government official (first used in Sweden) appointed to investigate complaints made by individuals against abuses or capricious acts of public officials or businesses.

**Operational decision:**   Compared to a strategic decision, it is not tied to broad goals but is part of the tactics or actions a firm uses to implement a strategy.

**Organization of Petroleum Exporting Countries (OPEC):**   A cartel organized to regulate the price of oil in international markets.

**Other-directed society:**   Society where reference groups are important. Individuals tend to identify with an "ideal" group.

**Overseas development bankers:**   Nonbanking institutions that are important sources of investment capital for larger-term international projects.

**Overseas Private Investment Corporation (OPIC):**   Provides insurance programs for political risks and guarantees loans made by private lenders to U.S. firms with investments in high-risk countries.

**Paradox of Third World people:**   Perceived superiority (by the peoples of the Third World) of the products of industrial, developed countries, while those peoples simultaneously decry the imperialism of developed countries.

**Patent licensing agreement:**   Agreement by which the licensor retains control over certain marketing strategy inputs for the licensed product.

**Price escalation:**   Increase in price of exports resulting from additional costs of transportation, packing, tariffs, or increased number of middlemen.

**Primary data:**   Data drawn from the original source (e.g., government documents or consumer surveys).

**Primary message system:**   System of 10 primary messages followed by attitudes depicting cultural rules. The examination of these rules allows for better understanding of the complexities of another culture.

**Product life cycle:**   Cycle representing the different stages of local industry sales and profits for new products introduced into a market. The cycle normally involves an *S*-shaped growth curve followed by decline to ultimate extinction.

**Red tape:**   The mass of documentation required by nations to export or import goods (tariffs and custom declaration forms for example).

**Regional agreements:**   Agreements between countries in geographic proximity aiming to facilitate trade between them.

**Repositioning:**   Changing the marketing mix of a product to reach a different segment of the market.

**Secondary data:** Data already available from an outside service or source.

**Self-reference criterion:** Attitude resulting when interpreting another culture in comparison with one's own culture.

**Social mobility:** A measure of the possibility of moving from one class or income bracket to another.

**Staff personnel:** The staff personnel are usually specialists in charge of advising the line personnel in the decision-making process.

**Staging strategy:** This strategy consists in penetrating international markets by stages. The stages are defined by the extent and cost of product adaptation necessary.

**Standard Industrial Classification (SIC):** Orderly procedure for classifying business firms according to types of products or services produced.

**Strategic decision:** A decision that is tied to the goals of the business and often has a long-term concern and impact.

**Synergistic effect:** Effect coming from the combined action of interacting entities. The result of these actions is greater than the sum of the actions taken separately.

**Trade associations:** Associations of firms in a single industry established primarily to provide a medium for exchange of market information to all members.

**Trading companies:** Very large international wholesalers, frequently larger and more powerful than the manufacturers they represent.

**Traditional society:** A society strongly affected by the past, by primary peer groups, by family, and by religion.

**Transfer price:** Price at which a company sells its products to its own foreign units.

**United Nations Conference on Trade and Development (UNCTAD):** Agency of the United Nations, its main focus being to promote the interests of developing countries in trade.

**Wholesalers:** Middlemen who sell to other middlemen or industrial users but not to consumers and who take title to the goods they sell.

**World Bank:** Agency associated with the United Nations that provides financing for development projects through its affiliate, the International Development Association.

# INDEX